Harvard A to Z

Harvard
A to Z

JOHN T. BETHELL

RICHARD M. HUNT

ROBERT SHENTON

HARVARD UNIVERSITY PRESS

Cambridge, Massachusetts
London, England
2004

Library of Congress Cataloging-in-Publication Data
Bethell, John T.
Harvard A to Z / John T. Bethell, Richard M. Hunt, Robert Shenton.
p. cm.
Includes index.
ISBN 0-674-01288-7
1. Harvard University—Encyclopedias.   I. Hunt, Richard M.
II. Shenton, Robert, d. 2000.   III. Title.
LD2155.B48 2004
378.744'4—dc22
2003067564

Contents

Preface

As its title suggests, *Harvard A to Z* is an alphabetical gathering of short, descriptive essays about the nation's oldest institution of higher learning. Written by three veteran observers of the University, this unofficial guide is meant for browsing and in no way pretends to be comprehensive. It begins with *Aab* and *Affirmative Action* and ends with *X Cage, The Yard,* and *ZephGreek.* In between are more than 150 vignettes that offer glimpses of the character and community of Harvard—in scholarship, needless to say, but also in the performing arts and athletics, in the workings of its many libraries and museums, in public service and community outreach.

Much out of the way information is also in the mix. Where are God's Acre and Harvard Hill, and who inhabits them? Who was the only ten-year-old to matriculate at the College? In what film were rappers Method Man and Redman cast as Harvard freshmen? What goes on in Cambridge's largest underground space? Who was the first woman to receive an honorary degree? What is a tippet, and who is entitled to wear one in the Commencement procession? How many miles of bookshelves are in Widener Library? Where is the "crowbar skull" of Phineas Gage displayed? Who wound and adjusted Harvard's hundreds of valuable clocks for 55 years?

To find the answers, read on. Having found them, you may gain a stronger sense of what makes this curious institution tick.

RICHARD M. HUNT
University Marshal, 1982–2002

Top row: The earliest College arms, in use from 1643
to 1885; a shield introduced about 1913; and the first departure
from a rigid shield, by William Dwiggins. Below: A more
elaborate treatment by Bruce Rogers; Pierre La Rose's shield,
still in use; and Rudolph Ruzicka's oak-leaf arms,
which ornaments the University's diplomas.

Aab

For 80 years—starting with the first edition in 1910—Harvard's alumni directory listings began with the name of Raktaprachit Aab, Lieutenant General Phya Salwidhan-Nidhes '13, A.M. '14, of Bangkok, Thailand. Prominent in the military and civil life of his country, Aab held a professorship at Chulalongkorn University, Bangkok, and served as Grand Marshal of the royal court.

Aab enrolled at the College in 1909. Harvard then had 140 international students; only three American universities had more. They came from 28 countries, including Australia, China, India, Japan, and Russia. Harvard currently has more than 3,400 international students, and the most foreign scholars—almost 2,500—of any U.S. university. All told, they represent some 130 countries. Thailand, home to more than 400 Harvard alumni, sends the University as many as fifty students each year.

Raktaprachit Aab died in 1989, aged 96. In his fiftieth-reunion class report, he had noted that in his student days, his passage from Bangkok to Boston by ship and rail took more than six weeks. Today the 9,500-mile air journey requires fewer than 30 hours.

Related entries: Alumni; International Outreach.

Admissions

Harvard College had entrance requirements from the start. But until late in the nineteenth century, you would not have needed a bachelor's degree to enroll at the schools of law, medicine, or divinity.

Admissions standards have changed. Competition is stiff, and applicant pools continue to grow. All told, the admissions offices of the College and the University's ten graduate and professional schools now sift upwards of 50,000 applications each year, starting in mid-September and winding up at the end of June, when admissions officers take a last look at the College's waiting list.

The earliest entrance requirements appeared in the "Lawes, Liberties and Orders of Harvard College," published in the mid-1640s:

> When any Schollar is able to read Tully [Cicero] or such like
> classical Latine Authour ex tempore, and make and speake
> true Latin in verse and prose . . . and decline perfectly the
> paradigmes of Nounes and verbes in the Greeke toungue,
> then may hee bee admitted into the Colledge, nor shall any
> claime admission before such qualification.

There was no admissions office then: candidates were examined orally by President Dunster and his two teaching fellows. By the 1800s, the Latin and Greek requirements had been supplemented by the stipulation that an applicant had to be "well versed in a compendium of Geography, & in the part of Arithmetic contained under the heads of Notation, simple and compound Addition, Subtraction, Multiplication, and Division, with reduction & the single rule of three."

The College then had fewer than 200 students. Four-fifths of the undergraduates came from Massachusetts, and a majority were Bostonians. Not until the end of the nineteenth century, when the proportion of Bay State residents declined to about 50 percent, did the College begin to assemble its famously diverse student body.

President Charles W. Eliot, who took office in 1869, thought it vital, "for the safety of Harvard College, and for the welfare of the country, that the College draw its material not from Massachusetts or from New York alone, but from the whole country." By then the nation's expanding rail system was linking southwestern and western states with the northeast, and a growing network of regional Harvard clubs had begun to recruit promising students from the hinterlands and raise scholarship money to help pay their way. By 1878 Harvard had by far the best-funded scholarship program in America. To keep the College affordable for students of modest means, Eliot held tuition at $150 a year throughout his 40-year presidency; in 1905 he persuaded his faculty to accept the new College Entrance Examination Board tests as a means of extending the catchment area for high school applicants. In the 1930s, President James Conant created "national scholarships" for students in small towns and rural areas where Harvard was not a byword. By midcentury, Harvard was a truly national institution, deploying alumni recruiters and undergraduates to expand its pool of nontraditional applicants—"boondockers," minority members, students from abroad. By the mid-1960s the College had sufficient scholarship funds to support a policy of need-blind admissions and need-based financial aid.

In 1975, as part of a rapprochement with Radcliffe College, the colleges' admissions offices were unified and women applicants were guaranteed equal access to Harvard. Since then, the College's male-female ratio has gone from 4:1 to near-parity. Women have made up about 48 percent of recent classes.

Today's College classes are notable for their demographic diversity. In the class of 2007, Asian-Americans composed 16 percent of the admitted group; African-Americans, a record 10.2 percent; Hispanic Americans, 3.7 percent; Mexican Americans, 3.6 percent; Puerto Ricans, 1.5 percent; and Native Americans, 1 percent. Nearly 26 percent of those admitted were from the Mid-Atlantic states, 17 percent from New England, 18 percent from the Western and Mountain states, 16 percent from the South, 11 percent from the Midwest, and almost 12 percent from U.S. territories and abroad.

Because the size of each entering class is held to 1,650, steady increases in applications have made the College admissions process ever more selective. At the beginning of the twentieth century there were fewer than 650 applicants per year, and more than 80 percent were accepted. By 1950, the applicant pool had risen to 2,500, of whom 40 percent were admitted. In 2003 there were 20,986 applicants; only 9.8 percent got in. In recent years, about 80 percent of admittees have accepted Harvard's offer of admission. This "yield"—in admissions office parlance—exceeds those of the College's closest competitors.

Harvard is one of the relatively few colleges maintaining a need-blind admissions policy. Admissions decisions are made without reference to an applicant's ability to pay the cost of tuition and fees; the College then meets each accepted student's demonstrated financial need with scholarships, loans, and term-time work. More than 70 percent of Harvard's 6,600 undergraduates receive some form of financial aid. The full cost of tuition, room, board, and fees in 2003–2004 was $40,450; the average financial aid package, including a low-interest loan and a College-related job, was in excess of $24,000.

Harvard is also among the few national institutions offering a non-binding Early Action program. Under the plan, which has been in place since the 1970s, students applying to the College by November 1 can expect a decision by December 15—far ahead of the regular date, April 1—and are free to apply elsewhere during the regular action cycle. They may not, however, apply to another college's early action or early decision plan (the latter, unlike early action, is binding). If passed over for early action, a qualified applicant will be reconsidered in the spring. Harvard received 7,600 early applications in one recent year and accepted 1,100 candidates, leaving 1,000 places to fill in the regular admissions process.

Admission to Harvard's ten graduate and professional schools is also highly selective. Of the three largest, the Business School received more than 8,000 applications for its M.B.A. program in one recent year and admitted 11 percent; the Law School had about 6,000 applicants, accepting 9 percent; the Medical School had more than 5,750 applicants, of whom 3 percent were admitted. Each graduate school has its own admissions system, and procedures vary widely. All schools seek a diverse student body and follow selection processes that focus on qualities predictive of success in a particular field or profession.

Prospective applicants should know that the College no longer requires proficiency in Latin, Greek, or geography for admission. To make Harvard more accessible to public school students, the Greek requirement was dropped in 1886. Latin was required until the late 1930s. Today there are no set requirements, but the admissions office recommends four years of English (with intensive composition), mathematics, science, and a foreign language; and three years of history. In a typical year, the 35-person admissions staff winnows applications from more than 3,000 high school valedictorians—they could fill an entering class almost twice over—and about 500 candidates who scored perfect 800s on both verbal and math SAT exams. Each applicant's folder is read by two or three staff members, and in some cases by two or three more. Readers rank applicants for academic achievement, extracurricular activities, and personal promise. Final admissions decisions are made by the staff and a standing committee of about fifteen faculty members and ten senior administrators.

The "fat envelope," mailed in early April, still signals success in the admissions competition. But anxious applicants need not wait for the postman's ring. Today, all may opt for notification by email. For better or for worse, about 96 percent of College applicants now get the word on their computer screens.

Related entries: Alumni; Athletics; Crimson Key; Diversity; Firsts (Women); Harvard College; Ivy League; Radcliffe; Tuition. *Related Website:* www.harvard.edu/admissions.

Adolphus Busch Hall

This curious exemplar of "Munich Modern" design now houses the Minda de Gunzburg Center for European Studies. Its stucco finish, red tile roof, and enclosed courtyard set it apart from other Harvard structures. Built to house America's first Germanic museum, Adolphus Busch Hall was constructed at just the wrong time: though it was completed in 1917, the building was kept closed until 1921 because of the anti-Teutonic feeling aroused during World War I.

Harvard's creation of a Germanic museum had seemed entirely fitting in the late 1890s, when Kuno Francke, the faculty's ranking professor of German, advanced the idea. Teutonic language and literature had been studied and taught at Harvard since the early nineteenth century, and German universities had opened new worlds of scholarship to young American academics—like future

Harvard presidents Edward Everett and Charles William Eliot—
who visited or studied at institutions like Göttingen. Germany had
returned Harvard's affection: in 1819 Johann Wilhelm von Goethe
had sent a set of his works to the College Library, and in 1902
Prince Henry of Prussia arrived to present, on behalf of Kaiser Wilhelm II, reproductions of sculptures and art objects from medieval
to Renaissance times. Initially housed in Rogers Hall—a former
gymnasium built on the site where the Cambridge fire station now
stands—this gift formed the nucleus of the Germanic Museum's
collections. A donation of $250,000 from the St. Louis brewing
magnate Adolphus Busch, his wife, Lilly, and his son-in-law, Hugo
Reisinger, provided funds for a building resourcefully planned to
exhibit the collections and reflect, in its interior design, the evolution of Teutonic art and culture over the centuries.

German Bestelmayer, a young Dresden art historian/architect,
conceived an interior layout with Romanesque and Renaissance
halls and a Gothic chapel, incorporating large-scale reproductions
of the eleventh-century bronze doors of the Church of St. Michael
in Hildesheim; of the thirteenth-century Golden Portal of the
Church of Our Lady in Freiburg; and of the Rood Screen of
Naumburg Cathedral. The building itself was framed in reinforced
concrete, an innovative construction method for that time, and
was topped by a partially precast clock-tower dome. Construction
began in the summer of 1914, just weeks before the outbreak of war
in Europe.

The museum's walled courtyard enclosed flower gardens, a lily
pond, and a copy of a famous bronze statue, the Brunswick Lion.
The original had been erected outside the castle of Duke Henry
the Lion in 1166. Atop windows overlooking the courtyard were
the sculpted visages of Norse figures celebrated in Wagnerian opera: Wotan, Albrich, Siegfried, Brunhilde. In the 1930s, a set of
murals depicting Albrich driving his subjects and grasping for
Rhine gold—a harsher reflection of Teutonic culture—was added
in an entrance rotunda. The work of Lewis Rubenstein '30, the
murals were later boarded over, and they remained unseen for
years.

During World War II the museum was cleared of its movable art works and used as a military chaplains' school. Some 10,000 chaplains, representing "all sects, races, and creeds," took part in four-week training sessions there. The portable holdings in the museum's collection were moved again in 1991, when a new Busch-Reisinger Museum was completed as an annex to the Fogg Art Museum. The Center for European Studies then moved into Adolphus Busch Hall. No academic department at Harvard enjoys such a luxurious and fitting environment.

An organ made by the Dutch builder D. A. Flentrop was installed in the balcony of the Romanesque Hall in 1958. The tracker-action instrument has often been used for recordings and can be heard in concerts during the academic year. The building is open to the public during concerts and on the first Sunday of every month.

Related entries: Architecture; Art Museums; Statues and Monuments.
Related Website: www.ces.fas.harvard.edu.

Affirmative Action

Increasingly under attack in recent years, affirmative action remains an article of faith at Harvard. In practice, the institution's affirmative action policy has significantly altered its constituency. Since 1970, the University's minority population has doubled. The number of women in senior faculty positions has grown from zero to almost 150; the number of minority members holding senior appointments has risen from two to more than 80. By 1997, three of the University's five vice presidents were women, and by 2000 the historically all-male, all-white Harvard Corporation had elected its second woman member and its first minority member.

The principle of affirmative action grew out of the Civil Rights Act of 1964, which prohibited discrimination on grounds of race, sex, ethnicity, religion, physical handicaps, and age, in educational institutions as well as in the workplace. Under the act, colleges and universities receiving federal funds became subject to nondiscrimination regulations. Such institutions were subsequently required to set targets in order to increase the recruitment and promotion of minorities, women, and handicapped persons. Harvard's affirmative action program was established in 1970.

The constitutionality of affirmative action in higher education was tested in *Regents of the University of California v. Bakke,* heard by the Supreme Court in 1978. Harvard was directly involved in this landmark case. Archibald Cox, Williston Professor of Law, represented the plaintiffs. Defending the University of California's right to use race as a selective factor in admissions decisions, Cox argued that the quest for racial diversity not only enriched higher education; from the standpoint of the larger society, it was also necessary to compensate for the effects of past discrimination and to ensure equal opportunity for all Americans. A statement of Harvard's policy on College admissions was part of an *amicus curiae* brief submitted jointly by Harvard and three other universities (Columbia, Pennsylvania, and Stanford). The policy statement opposed admissions quotas, describing minority status as one of many criteria used to rate qualified candidates.

The court found for Bakke, but in ruling that rigid quotas were unconstitutional, it conceded that institutions could pay "some attention" to race in admissions decisions. Justice Powell, writing for the majority, appended a description of Harvard's admissions policy, affirming that "this kind of program treats each applicant as an individual in the admissions process, [yet] does not insulate the individual from comparison with all other candidates for the available seats."

Twenty-five years later, Harvard also filed an *amicus* brief in the University of Michigan cases heard by the Supreme Court in the spring of 2003. Presented on behalf of Harvard, Brown, the University of Chicago, Dartmouth, Duke, Pennsylvania, Princeton, and Yale, the brief stated the case for continuing to consider race as one factor in individualized admissions systems. The brief argued that the "principle underlying Bakke has become the basis of well-settled reliance," and has been absorbed not only by colleges, but also by secondary schools, students, alumni, and businesses. The Supreme Court, the brief held, should not "trigger wrenching disruption" by overturning its own established precedent. A divided court ultimately affirmed the *Bakke* decision, ruling that while racial quotas as such are unconstitutional, subtler forms of affirmative action could still be used to achieve racial diversity.

Only about 12 percent of Harvard's overall student body would have been classified as "underrepresented minorities" in 1970; the proportion has since risen to more than 17 percent in the College and about 24 percent University-wide. Continuing efforts to diversify the ranks of faculty members and administrators have been guided and monitored by a succession of affirmative action officers and, within some of the faculties, associate deans. Progress at the administrative level has been more rapid than within teaching faculties, where openings are rarer, candidate pools are relatively smaller, and competition for outstanding female and minority prospects is intense. Even so, substantial advances have been recorded since the inception of the University's affirmative action program. In 1970, none of the 444 permanent faculty members of the Faculty of Arts and Sciences was a woman. Thirty years later, women held 144 out of 754 tenured positions. Over the same period, the number of minority members holding permanent faculty appointments grew from two to 85. More recent years have shown continuing gains at all levels.

In 1996, as opponents of affirmative action became increasingly vocal, President Neil Rudenstine used one of his occasional annual reports to trace Harvard's tradition of diversity and to argue the educational value of exposing students to peers who brought differing beliefs, backgrounds, and points of view to the table. Of the gains made in achieving diversity over the previous quarter-century, Rudenstine wrote that "no similar transformation has ever before taken place in the long history of higher education."

Related entries: Admissions; Diversity. *Related Website:* www.oap.harvard.edu/affirmative-action.

Allston

How will Harvard develop its extensive real-estate assets in neighboring Allston, where it now has far more land than in Cambridge? Planners have envisioned a vast new campus on the Boston side of the Charles River, including advanced science facilities; student and faculty housing that would fit in with existing neighborhoods; museums and venues for cultural and artistic activity; and new homes for the Graduate School of Education and the School of Public Health. Though limited building could begin in the near future, the full realization of such a plan could take decades—and billions of dollars—to achieve.

Harvard has had a foothold in Allston since 1870, when Henry Wadsworth Longfellow and his family gave the University a 70-acre tract that later formed part of the Soldiers Field athletics complex. In the 1920s, the Business School campus rose on a nearby tract that had recently been deeded to Harvard. In the late 1980s, pressed for space and essentially landlocked in Cambridge, the University began to make secret acquisitions of land in roughly contiguous parts of Allston. By 1997, when these purchases were made public, it had bought fourteen parcels totaling 52 acres, for an aggregate price of $88 million. Harvard subsequently paid almost $152 million for a 48-acre parcel east of the Business School, formerly owned by the Massachusetts Turnpike Authority, and then bought an adjacent 91-acre parcel for $75 million. These purchases brought the University's total Allston holdings to 341 acres. In Cambridge it has just under 220 acres.

Once the site of stockyards, slaughterhouses, and meatpacking factories, Allston has become a melange of warehouses, railroad yards, thrift shops and discount stores, automotive repair shops, and modest residences. (When Harvard's secret purchases came to light, a state senator representing the area observed to the *Boston Globe* that "they're buying so many auto-body shops, I thought Harvard might want to start a vocational school.") The city's population includes many students and young families.

Harvard's *Drang nach Süden* will dramatically reconfigure the University, but it will also produce profound urban changes affecting thousands of Allston residents. In an open letter released in the fall of 2003, President Lawrence Summers stressed the importance of positive engagement with the community. Harvard's eventual master plan, he wrote, will . . . need to incorporate a variety of features essential to a lively and welcoming residential urban community—places to eat, places to shop, gathering places for special events, open spaces to throw a frisbee or spread a picnic blanket or simply sit and talk . . . Our Allston plan should derive its vitality not only from academic activities central to the University's mission, but also from day-to-day activities central to the life of a vibrant neighborhood within one of our nation's great cities. For Harvard, as for the larger community, it is important to envision our extended campus in Allston not just as a place to work, but as a place to live.

The president's letter set forth five "programmatic planning assumptions" to help guide and advance discussions and analyses aimed at developing a coherent master plan.

• *Science and technology.* "Allston should figure prominently in the future of Harvard science, as home to a robust critical mass of scientific activity . . . To succeed, we will need to invest not only in the more traditional approaches to science, led by single investigators with largely autonomous laboratories and research teams, but also in the more integrative approaches that hold growing promise for the future."

• *Professional schools.* "Both the School of Public Health and the Graduate School of Education could benefit . . . from eventual relocation to Allston, given both the nature of their academic missions and their current physical settings. In addition, Allston should be seen as a future home for wider collaborative efforts among the professional schools, in view of challenges common to the professions they serve."

• *Housing and urban life.* "Especially in light of the difficult housing market, we need to increase opportunities for Harvard's graduate and professional school students to live in University housing. More such housing will improve our students' lives and enhance our overall educational environment . . . Our goal should be a campus that, as in Cambridge, both enlivens and draws life from the neighborhood of which it is a part."

• *Culture and community.* "Artistic and cultural activities contribute greatly to the character of the University, and also provide links to the wider community. We should consider more concretely how the Allston properties might provide improved space for some of these activities, in ways that would both serve our academic purposes and add to the vitality of community life."

• *Undergraduate life.* "Allston might in time serve as a locus for facilities and activities aimed at enhancing aspects of the undergraduate experience, including the possibility of new undergraduate houses close to the Charles River. Such a development could help relieve crowding in the current houses; provide more and better space for student activities; strengthen the bonds between the Cambridge and Allston parts of our extended campus; open up the possibility of someday relocating students from the Radcliffe Quad; and allow for the long-run possibility of welcoming more undergraduates from around the world."

Summers's letter also announced the formation of separate task forces, consisting largely of faculty members, "to focus on the principal programmatic domains," and the appointment of a working group to identify and evaluate consulting firms capable of adding their expertise to the master-planning process.

Portions of the recently acquired tracts—particularly the 91-acre and 48-acre "Allston Landing North" parcels, which include the Massachusetts Turnpike's Allston-Brighton interchange and a large railway freight-transfer facility—are encumbered with long-term leases and easements. The president's letter noted that it will "require much effort and expense—as well as time, measured in decades—[for this land] to become available for University use." Even so, the letter concluded, "the kind of opportunity before us comes along rarely in the life of a modern university. That the opportunity entails hard questions and complex choices should not divert us from recognizing its enormous long-term potential to advance our shared commitment to education, scholarship, and service."

Related entries: Architecture; Athletics; Cambridge/Boston; Charles River; School of Education; Harvard Elsewhere; Houses; School of Public Health; Soldiers Field. *Related Website:* www.president.harvard.edu/speeches/2003/ lhs_allston.html.

Alpha-Iota of Massachusetts

Chartered in 1779, Harvard's "Alpha of Massachusetts" had the longest uninterrupted existence of any chapter of Phi Beta Kappa, America's first and foremost honor society. In 1995 it merged with Radcliffe College's Iota of Massachusetts, creating a unified chapter that is now known as Alpha-Iota of Massachusetts.

At Harvard and almost 300 other member institutions, election to Phi Beta Kappa is an academic plum that is proffered to high-ranking undergraduate scholars. Alpha-Iota of Massachusetts elects about 110 seniors and 48 juniors each year.

Phi Beta Kappa was founded in 1776 at Williamsburg, Virginia, by students at the College of William and Mary. A charter for a Harvard chapter was carried northward by Elisha Parmele, class of 1778, a young minister then teaching in Virginia. Delivered to four Harvard students in 1781, the charter is now preserved in the University Archives, its original ribbons of "pink and sky blue" still intact.

Early chapters of PBK were fraternal organizations, with solemn initiations, oaths of secrecy, and a distinctive handshake. For 40 years, the members of Harvard's chapter met frequently and held regular discussions and debates. Among the topics were "whether Benedict Arnold can be considered as a traitor" (1781), "whether Christianity, if fabulous, ought to be supported" (1796), and "whether Adam had a navel" (1807; the ayes won). The last debate took place in 1820. Thereafter, the Alpha of Massachusetts—like most other chapters—ceased to be a forensic and literary association and became substantially what it is today: an honorary society.

Radcliffe's application for a charter in 1910 caused something of a dust-up. The United Chapters of Phi Beta Kappa ruled that Radcliffe undergraduates were eligible for election to the Harvard chapter, obviating the need for a separate charter. But the officers of Alpha countered that Radcliffe was not an integral part of Harvard, noting also that Harvard's charter stipulated that membership was to consist of "gentlemen." Thus spurned, Radcliffe resubmitted its application, and the Iota of Massachusetts was chartered in 1914.

Harvard's annual Phi Beta Kappa Literary Exercises are the first academic event of Commencement Week. The program includes a commissioned poem and an "oration," as it has since 1782. "The roster of orators and poets reads like an abridged dictionary of American biography," wrote the poet and essayist David McCord '21 (a Phi Beta Kappa poet himself). "Four presidents of the United States shed lustre upon it . . . An acceptable history of American literature could be written, using only the biographies of writers who addressed the Society, though there would be one glaring gap, for the name of Mark Twain is unaccountably absent." Ralph Waldo Emerson and his "American Scholar" oration of 1837 take pride of place, but John Quincy Adams, Edward Everett, Oliver Wendell Holmes, Franklin D. Roosevelt, and Woodrow Wilson were other notable orators of the past. The constellation of Phi Beta Kappa poets includes W. H. Auden, Robert Frost, Henry Wadsworth Longfellow, Robert Lowell, and Wallace Stevens.

Related entry: Commencement. *Related Website:* www.college.harvard.edu/academics/phibetakappa.

Alumni

The University head-counts its alumni at five-year intervals; the most recent *Harvard Alumni Directory* lists the names, addresses, and occupations of 255,764 men and women. (The total is actually larger, since 36,580 names are classified as "lost, being traced," or just "lost.") Each year's graduation exercises add some 6,000 new names to the rolls, while death removes just over 2,000 annually—so within this century's first decade the number of living alumni will approach or exceed 300,000.

Harvardians live in every state and in 184 countries, from Afghanistan to Zimbabwe. The largest proportion are in business—not surprisingly, since Business School graduates make up a quarter of the overall alumni body. Education and law are the second- and third-ranking vocations, followed by health and medical services, financial services, and government.

Like the rest of the population, Harvard and Radcliffe alumni are enjoying extended longevity. In 1910, when the first alumni directory was compiled, the median age was 34. By the year 2000 the median age had risen to 49. One out of seven alumni is retired, and the ranks of retirees may double by the year 2010.

The earliest organized alumni activity dates from 1840, when a handful of Boston graduates, seeking to cultivate the spirit of loyalty generated by the 1836 bicentennial celebration, founded the Harvard Alumni Association. Its first president was a former president of the United States, John Quincy Adams, class of 1787. Membership was by application and was limited to graduates of the College, the Divinity School, and the Law School. Dues were a dollar a year. For the better part of a century, the association's chief functions were to produce an oratorical extravaganza on the afternoon of Commencement Day and to nominate and elect officers. Other alumni activities were launched by loyal volunteers who organized regional Harvard clubs, started alumni publications, founded and underwrote the Harvard Athletic Association, put out class reports, planned reunions, and raised money for class gifts. Eventually, the management of almost all these undertakings—and of the Alumni Association itself—was taken over by Harvard administrators.

All alumni now belong automatically to the Alumni Association. The well-worn joke, repeated at every Commencement Day meeting, is that the HAA is an organization that requires no dues and from which there is no escape. Its operations are overseen by a board of almost a hundred directors, eighteen of them directly elected by the alumni body. The board also includes representatives of graduate and professional school alumni groups. The HAA has an administrative staff of 33 and a budget of about $2.5 million.

The Alumni Association nominates candidates for the Board of Overseers and conducts the annual elections. One of many working groups, familiarly known as the Happy Committee, helps plan what has traditionally been called "the happy observance of Commencement." Other HAA committees help guide an ever-growing program of continuing education, which offers "alumni colleges" and travel-study tours to all parts of the world; they also select recipients of the Harvard Medal, recognizing service to the University through alumni activities, and oversee the Harvard Prize Book awards, presented by local Harvard clubs to promising high school juniors. (A 1928 recipient was a California boy named Richard M. Nixon, who chose to attend Whittier College.) The HAA also provides an email forwarding service and publishes *Harvard Monthly*, an online newsletter that recaps University news and contains listings of alumni activities and Web-based resources.

New Harvard clubs continue to spring up. There are now about 160, in 70 countries and all but two states (Idaho and Wyoming). Through club committees, some 4,000 alumni assist the admissions staff by interviewing and evaluating applicants. Club activities are coordinated and supported by HAA staffers. The association's headquarters is at 124 Mount Auburn Street.

Etymological note: Tracing the derivation to a Latin term for "foster child," the *Shorter Oxford English Dictionary* defines *alumnus* as "the nurseling or pupil of any school, university, etc." Though the HAA and other Harvard offices pointedly say "alumni and alumnae" or "alumni/ae" when both sexes are meant, the Latin plural form *alumni* subsumes both the masculine and feminine forms.

Related entries: Continuing Education; Governance. *Related Website:* www.haa.harvard.edu.

American Repertory Theatre

The American Repertory Theatre—known as the ART (and pronounced *A-R-T*)—has at least three facets. First, it is a resident professional theater company that produces five plays a year on the mainstage of Harvard's Loeb Drama Center, and four or five smaller offerings on stages in Cambridge and the Boston area. Second, it is a group of theater professionals who offer undergraduate courses and provide a non-degree training program for aspiring actors, directors, stage designers, and drama critics. Third, it is a work in progress, building on the vision of its founding artistic director, Robert Brustein.

Author, professor, director, and theater critic of *The New Repub-*

lic, Brustein came to Harvard in 1979, after thirteen years as dean of Yale's school of drama. Though he had fashioned the Yale Repertory Theatre into a first-rate company, Brustein had his detractors—and one was Yale's president, the late A. Bartlett Giamatti, another humanist with a strong interest in arts and theater. After a spate of run-ins over financing, budgets, relations with Yale's undergraduates, and other issues, Giamatti fired Brustein. (The latter told his side of the story in an aptly titled memoir, *Making Scenes.*) To the rescue came Harvard president Derek Bok, who offered Brustein and his company a home in Cambridge.

Fifty-five years earlier, Yale had lured Professor George Pierce Baker and his famous 47 Workshop to New Haven. Now a turn of the tide brought dramatic riches to Harvard. As at Yale, there were nay-sayers. Some faculty members viewed the sponsorship of a resident drama company as academically dubious and financially improvident. They'd heard that the Yale Rep shunned conventional theater and went in for bold, sometimes over-the-top productions and that Brustein hadn't helped much with fundraising. Bok himself conceded that Harvard's theatrical venture was "risky business."

It took only a year to mute most of the critics and make skeptics into subscribers. The ART's credo is to offer plays of three kinds:

- Older ones, largely neglected but worth dusting off for contemporary audiences (examples: Molière's *Sganarelle,* Carlo Gozzi's *The King Stag,* Pirandello's *Right You Are if You Think You Are*).
- Classics (like Shakespeare's *A Midsummer Night's Dream,* Strindberg's *The Father,* and O'Neill's *A Long Day's Journey into Night*), rejuvenated by gifted directors.
- New works that opened fresh possibilities for experimentation (world premières of Jules Feiffer's *Grownups,* Marsha Norman's *'night, Mother,* and David Mamet's *Oleanna,* which brought national attention and awards to the ART).

More than a hundred other productions in past decades have involved such major directors, authors, and composers as JoAnne

Akalaitis, Andrei Belgrader, Don DeLillo, Dario Fo, Philip Glass, Jonathan Miller, Suzan-Lori Parks, Peter Sellers, Andrei Serban, János Szász, Paula Vogel, and Robert Wilson. To operate at that level entails substantial costs. Box office receipts for the Loeb Drama Center's mainstage—which has 550 seats and runs at about 80 percent occupancy—meet roughly half of the company's expenses. The balance is covered by a relatively small Harvard subvention and by grants from the National Endowment for the Arts, the National Endowment for the Humanities, and the Commonwealth of Massachusetts; by foundation and corporate support; and by more than 2,000 individual contributions.

When Brustein stepped down in the summer of 2002, the leadership of the ART was transferred to a troika: Robert Orchard, executive director; Robert Woodruff, artistic director; and Gideon Lester, associate artistic director. Woodruff—a New York director noted for his experimental productions at California's La Jolla Playhouse and other regional houses—had been hand-picked by Brustein, whose vision of the living art of theater in a university setting would doubtless color the ART's future undertakings. In Brustein's words, "The theater must free the audience's imagination. To do this it must unsettle the audience. It must shatter their usual way of looking at the world. I want to create a poetry of the theater that haunts the audience's subsconscious . . . I don't want to affect just what people think during the day. I want to affect their dreams."

Related entries: Arts; Gilbert & Sullivan; Theatre Collection. *Related Website:* www.amrep.org.

Architecture

From its red-brick epicenter, the Old Yard, Harvard's built environment fans out into an architectural crazyquilt—the most visible manifestation of the institution's much-celebrated diversity.

The University's physical plant includes more than 500 academic and residential buildings in Cambridge, Boston, and other locales. Some are listed in the National Register of Historic Places;

some are eyesores. Seven of the oldest date from pre-Revolutionary times; more than 70 new ones have risen since World War II. Charles Bulfinch, class of 1781, Henry Hobson Richardson, class of 1859, and Charles Follen McKim are among the best known of Harvard's past architects. Charles Coolidge, class of 1881, and his firm designed the undergraduate houses that line the Charles River, as well as many other twentieth-century structures. During the "White Period," a midcentury phase, the University commissioned angular, large-scaled modern buildings from such international figures as the German Bauhaus master Walter Gropius, the French modernist Le Corbusier, and his disciples Josep Lluis Sert and John Andrews. The raw concrete exteriors of their structures counterpoint the massing of red brick that remains the "home key" of Harvard architecture.

What may seem a confusing kaleidoscope of architectural styles is best understood in the context of Harvard's evolving sense of itself. The oldest surviving building, Massachusetts Hall (1721), initially formed one side of a small quadrangle like those of English colleges, in which the resident scholars and tutors associated not only at recitations but also in chambers, at meals, and at prayers. Harvard thus sought to perpetuate "the Collegiate way of Living" in the New World. Three later halls—Hollis (1762), Stoughton (1805), and Holworthy (1811)—outlined the northwest corner of a much larger quadrangle, now known as the Old Yard. In keeping with the ethic of plain living espoused by Harvard's Puritan founders, these early buildings were simple brick boxes with minimal ornamentation. The granite walls of Bulfinch's University Hall (1815), quarried at Chelmsford, Massachusetts, were intended to emphasize the building's New England character, but classical pilasters and balustrades suggested a worldlier frame of reference.

By the mid-nineteenth century, Harvard had developed some of the attributes of a university in the European sense. New buildings were needed for laboratories, professional-school classrooms, and the library. Though Germany had become the principal training ground for scholars in newer fields, England continued to furnish the architectural models. King's College Chapel, Cambridge, inspired the Gothic lines of Gore Hall (1841, demolished 1913), built to contain what had become the nation's largest and most valuable library. President Charles William Eliot, taking office four years after the end of the Civil War, pledged "to build here, securely and strongly, a university in the largest sense," and over the 40 years of his presidency, the scaling of new residential halls, museums, research facilities, and classroom buildings reflected rising institutional self-assurance.

The most dazzling expression of this newfound confidence was Memorial Hall, completed in 1878. No Harvard building is more remarkable or absorbing. A monument to 136 alumni and students who died on the Union side in the Civil War, the cathedral-sized High Victorian Gothic building—meticulously detailed, gabled and buttressed within an inch of its life, its soaring tower and parti-colored slate roofs bristling with spiky finials—broke dramatically with the boxy Georgian of Harvard's past.

Memorial Hall heralded a prolonged interval of eclectic architecture. Contemporaneous with it, and close by, was Harvard's most ornamental and picturesque building, Hemenway Gymnasium (1878, demolished 1938), a Queen Anne-style fantasy castle designed by the firm of Peabody and Stearns. Within Harvard Yard, the great H. H. Richardson displayed his Romanesque Revival style in Sever Hall (1880), a fortress-like building with intricate brickwork. The asymmetrical façade of the Law School's Austin Hall (1884) was another Richardson showpiece. Half a century later, a dean of the School of Design would describe Sever as "a turning point in American architecture," but the Harvard architects who followed Richardson turned instead to European models for ponderous buildings in the imperial style. Richard Morris Hunt's limestone Hunt Hall, Harvard's first art museum and later a classroom building (1893, demolished 1973), disrupted the colonial context of other Yard buildings; Emerson Hall (1900), designed by Guy Lowell, class of 1892, and Charles McKim's Robinson Hall (1904) filled out the Yard's northeast corner less intrusively. Both were built of brick.

Working in McKim's imperial style, the firm of Shepley, Rutan, and Coolidge designed five white marble buildings (1906) for the Medical School's new Boston campus, and a limestone one for the

Law School, also finished in 1906 and named Langdell Hall. Built when America was proudly conscious of its heady new role as a global power, these cold, formalistic buildings left no doubt that the schools they housed were instruments of high national purpose.

The proliferation of styles during Eliot's presidency was an architectural analogue of his free elective system, which superseded a rigidly prescribed undergraduate curriculum. A. Lawrence Lowell, who succeeded Eliot in 1909, put a stop to both. He modified the elective system with concentration and distribution requirements and revived the red-brick colonial styling of Harvard's eighteenth-century past. Lowell's crowning achievement was the house system, which became the cornerstone of undergraduate education at Harvard. To plan the new houses, modeled on the autonomous colleges of Oxford and Cambridge, Lowell chose his close friend Charles Coolidge. The protean Coolidge, who had also designed the mission-Romanesque campus of Stanford University, initially wanted to create a Gothic Revival grouping; his partners had to convene a meeting of Boston architects to talk him out of it. Taken as a whole, Coolidge's river houses (1930–1932) are a masterwork of Georgian Revival design—broadly derived from the groundplans and styling of the Oxbridge colleges but incorporating architectural forms and details found in the Yard's older buildings. Each house has its own distinctive character. Along with the Yard itself, this is the part of the University that strikes most beholders as quintessentially Harvardian.

The "cloistering" of the Yard (1924–30), and the Business School's new campus (1928), were other landmark projects of the Lowell years. The construction of seven new buildings, all from Coolidge's drawing board, helped define the periphery of the Yard, screening out traffic noise and easing a chronic housing shortage. The Business School campus, designed by McKim, Mead, & White, rose on land south of the Charles River and formed a Georgian Revival counterpart to the houses. All told, Lowell's 24-year presidency saw the construction of some 60 new buildings—more than Harvard had raised in the 273 years since its founding. Especially notable were the huge Harry Elkins Widener Memorial Library (1915), the Fogg Art Museum (1925), and Memorial Church (1931). Between the library and the church (the Yard's largest structures) was an extensive quadrangle that became known as the Tercentenary Theatre, now the site of the annual Commencement exercises and other outdoor ceremonies.

The next wave of construction began after World War II and crested in the 1970s. Lamont Library (1947) and Walter Gropius's Graduate Center (1949), both examples of "International Style," were Harvard's first modern buildings. The decade of the 1960s spawned high-rise structures—Leverett Towers (1960), Josep Lluis Sert's Peabody Terrace (1963), Minoru Yamasaki's William James Hall (1963), and Mather House (1968)—as well as Sert's Holyoke Center (1962) and Le Corbusier's Carpenter Center for the Visual Arts (1963). An iconoclastic departure and Corbu's only building in the United States, the Carpenter Center fills a cramped Quincy Street site. Two assertively modern structures, John Andrews's Gund Hall (1972) and Sert's sprawling Science Center (1973, now undergoing renovation and expansion), are near neighbors to Memorial Hall; it is an architectural irony that in 1933, when the city of Cambridge sited a fire station facing the venerable building, Harvard insisted that it be built in Georgian Revival style.

The red-brick Kennedy School of Government complex (1974–1977) and the striated orange and blue-gray brickwork of James Stirling's Sackler Art Museum (1984) mark the end of Harvard's White Period. Reverting to eclecticism, the University had gone far afield to find its designers—in contrast to the previous half-century, when most of the blueprints came from the "house architects" of Coolidge's firm or such regulars as the president's cousin Guy Lowell. The egos of internationally known architects sometimes seemed to overweigh the contexts of surrounding buildings, contributing to a sense of uneven growth and direction.

Recognizing that deferred maintenance had led to serious deterioration of its physical plant, Harvard began a series of extensive restoration programs in the 1980s. All the undergraduate houses and Radcliffe residence halls were renovated, at a cost of more than $100 million. Repairs to all sixteen of Harvard Yard's freshman residences ran to $65 million. A $55 million restoration of Memorial

Hall was capped by the replacement of its clock tower, destroyed by fire in 1956. Harvard Stadium, built for $310,000 in 1903, got new steel supports and concrete seating in an $8 million overhaul. In 1999, Widener Library launched a five-year renovation program that included refurbishment of the stacks, public spaces, climate control and lighting, at an overall cost of more than $90 million.

A walking tour of Harvard is an architectural feast. *Not to be missed in the Yard:* Memorial Church; Sever Hall; architect Hugh Stubbins's semi-subterranean Pusey Library; Widener Library; University Hall; Massachusetts Hall and nearby Harvard Hall (1766); and tiny Holden Chapel (1742), Harvard's first place of worship, cradle of its Medical School, and now headquarters for choral groups. *East of the Yard:* Le Corbusier's Carpenter Center for the Visual Arts. *North of the Yard:* Memorial Hall; the Undergraduate Science Center; and Adolphus Busch Hall—a curious specimen of "Munich Modern" that began life as the Germanic Museum (1917). *South of the Yard:* The even curiouser Lampoon Building (1909); across from it, Harvard Hillel's Rosovsky Hall (1992), designed by Moshe Safdie; Lowell House; and across the river at the Business School, the renovated atrium of Morgan Hall and Safdie's circular, partially sunken Class of 1959 Chapel (1992). Across North Harvard Street looms Harvard Stadium, another imperially styled work by Charles Follen McKim. Now used almost exclusively for football games, it was once the scene of Class Day festivities and has also provided a setting for al fresco theatricals—among them a professional, cast-of-thousands production of *Joan of Arc* in 1909, and more recently a 1983 performance of Euripides' *The Bacchae.*

Guided tours, emphasizing Harvard's historic landmarks, leave at regular intervals from the Holyoke Center information office.

Related entries: Adolphus Busch Hall; Art Museums; Carpenter Center; Extinct Harvard; Fogg Art Museum; Gold Coast; GSD; Guardhouse; Harvard Hall; Hillel; Houghton Library; Holden Chapel; Houses; Lampoon; Memorial Church; Memorial Hall; Museums; Quincy Street; Sanders Theatre; Towers; Underground; Vanserg Hall; Wadsworth House; Widener Library; the Yard.

Archives

The principal records and historical memorabilia of Harvard's past are stored in the University Archives, located in the Nathan Marsh Pusey Library in Harvard Yard. This subterranean repository is a goldmine for anyone doing research on Harvard history. More specialized archives exist at the Business School, the Medical Area, and the Radcliffe Institute.

The University Archives' holdings date from Harvard's founding in 1636 to the present day. They include:

- Minutes, correspondence, financial data, printed matter, and other essential records produced in the course of University business. Early financial records, for example, reveal that a student's tuition could be paid in cattle or in bushels of wheat.
- Catalogues and directories; presidents', treasurers', and Overseers' reports; University press releases; and publications of Harvard University Press and student organizations.
- Doctoral dissertations, undergraduate theses (graded *magna cum laude* or higher), and prize papers. Among the senior theses are those of Henry Kissinger '50 ("The Meaning of History") and John F. Kennedy '40 (later published as *While England Slept,* which became a best-seller).
- General reference collections, including published and manuscript materials about academic affairs and student life. These include a rich trove of posters and leaflets related to the antiwar demonstrations of 1969–70.
- Biographical and private papers, including clippings and files concerning faculty, staff, alumni, and other individuals connected to the University. Here are the papers of some of Harvard's renowned professors: philosophers C. S. Peirce and Josiah Royce; historians Archibald Cary Coolidge and Arthur Schlesinger Sr.; scientists Willard Gibbs and Theodore W. Richards.
- Visual collections, mainly photographs, prints, and drawings of Harvard people, places, and events. There is extensive cov-

erage, for instance, of the 1947 Commencement speech of Secretary of State George C. Marshall, proposing a history-making plan for the economic recovery of Europe.

The most precious items are stored in a locked vault: the College's original Charter; early record books of presidents, the Corporation, Overseers, and treasurers; and early "badges of authority"— seals and silver keys. Artifacts include seventeenth-century President Charles Chauncy's cane; President Edward Holyoke's baby undershirt; British musket balls pried from the walls of Harvard Hall; the crimson bandanna, purchased in 1858, that set the standard for Harvard's official color; Professor Coolidge's death mask; and, from the papers of the great Shakespeare scholar George Lyman Kittredge, a recipe for witch's brew.

Related entries: Crimson; Extinct Harvard; Presidents; Underground.

Related Website: hul.harvard.edu/huarc.

Arms

Harvard's *Veritas* motto first appeared in a crude design for the College arms adopted by the Board of Overseers in 1643. Samuel Eliot Morison, whose word was usually law in such matters, wrote in *Three Centuries of Harvard* that to seventeenth-century minds the term "undoubtedly meant (as it did to Dante) the divine truth." A College seal of 1650 bears the device *In Christi Gloriam* (for the Glory of Christ); that was superseded in 1692 by *Christo et Ecclesiæ* (Truth for Christ and the Church). But *Veritas*—brief and not exclusively religious—is now a fixture.

Professor Morison records that President Josiah Quincy, preparing to write his history of Harvard, "was delighted . . . to find in the archives the first rough sketch for a College arms, VERITAS on three books. The announcement was made at the [1836] bicentennial celebration; and in 1843, an ugly version of the design was formally adopted by the Corporation as their seal." Morison adds that President Edward Everett, who followed Quincy, "conceived an intense dislike of everything his predecessor had done" and thus had "'this fantastical and anti-Christian Veritas seal removed to the forgotten corner of the records where it had slept undisturbed for two hundred years.'"

It slept again, writes Morison, "until 1885, when, largely as the result of two vigorous sonnets by [Oliver Wendell Holmes Jr.] read before the Harvard Club of New York, *Veritas* was brought forth once more." President Eliot took up the cause, and the Corporation re-adopted the seal of 1843. Plain shields with *ve ri tas* inscribed on the three books appeared around 1913, when Harvard University Press began using them on title pages. Over the next half-century, noted graphic designers—among them William Dwiggins, Bruce Rogers, Pierre la Rose (class of 1895), and Rudolph Ruzicka—tried their hands at restyling Harvard's arms. La Rose's and Ruzicka's designs are still in frequent use.

In heraldic terms, the arms are formally described as "Gules, three open books Argent, edges, covers, and clasps on the books Or, on the books the letters ve ri tas Sable." In a triptych over the stage of Sanders Theatre, the upper books lie open; the lower one is inverted. The customary interpretation is that the open books symbolize existing knowledge, while the third stands for what remains unknown. In other treatments, the three books are shown face up.

Related entry: Presidents.

Arnold Arboretum

Few institutions, apart from religious ones, have a 2,000-year life expectancy. The Arnold Arboretum, with its 265 acres of parkland in Boston's Jamaica Plain neighborhood, is one that may. Harvard deeded the property to the city in 1882, then leased it back for a thousand years, at a one dollar per year rental rate and with an option to renew the lease for another millennium.

The arboretum—the oldest institution of its kind in the United States—was founded in 1872, when a wealthy New Bedford merchant named James Arnold left a portion of his estate in trust for the promotion of agricultural or horticultural research. The terms of his gift stated that the arboretum "shall contain, as far as is practicable all the trees, shrubs, and herbaceous plants, either indigenous or exotic, which can be raised in the open"—making it a living outdoor museum for research on woody plants. Today the arboretum's open-air collection includes approximately 15,000 individual plants, representing 4,500 species of trees and shrubs from around the world.

Frederick Law Olmsted was the arboretum's landscape architect. He was already developing Boston's Emerald Necklace, a continuous chain of greenery that would wend its way through the city from the Boston Public Garden to Franklin Park, and it was natural that the arboretum should be one of the park system's new "jewels." Collectors around the world, particularly in Japan and China, began to ship seeds to Boston for germination. Ginkgos, dove trees, star magnolias, dogwoods, paperbark maples, Douglas firs, and hundreds of other exotic specimens from Asia and the North Pacific Rim were soon thriving in the harsh New England climate, as were woody plants from Europe, Russia, and the American southeast. Trees and shrubs from the southern hemisphere did not fare well, however. Only a few specimens from North Africa— and none from Australia, the East Indies, or South America—survived.

Under the thousand-year lease, the city of Boston agreed to maintain roads, bridges, paths, fences, and security in the park, while Harvard retained responsibility for the plant life and for all educational and research facilities. In theory, the arrangement was extremely favorable to Harvard, saving the University the costs of housekeeping. In practice, it has had to upgrade the public spaces.

The scholarly work of the Arnold Arboretum focuses principally on botany and horticulture, and within those categories, on woody plants hardy enough to survive a northeastern winter. Together with a large herbarium and library, both now primarily in Cambridge, these living collections provide useful research material.

The arboretum is also an educational resource for the Greater
Boston community, offering programs and publications in horticulture, landscape design, and gardening.

The general public may view the arboretum as a vast pleasure garden or country estate in the middle of a city—a tranquil
place that affords "random delight," as one writer has put it. Yet
Olmsted's pleasing design is anything but random. The plantings
were arranged not just aesthetically but taxonomically, by family
groupings that progress from specimens thought to be more primitive to more complex varieties.

In this Edenic environment, leisure and learning intertwine.
The rich colors of the leaves in the fall, the stark shapes of the
trunks and limbs in winter make the arboretum a garden for all
seasons. But the apogee of delight is a five-week spring interval
when arrays of lilacs burst out in all their glory. "Lilac Sunday"—
the second Sunday in May—is an annual city festival for many
Bostonians.

The arboretum's function within the University has been a
vexed issue. Is it a museum, a research institution, or a park? The
question came to a head in the 1950s, when a group of prominent
alumni filed suit to stop Harvard from transferring books and herbarium specimens from the arboretum to a new botany building in
Cambridge. Resolving the suit took thirteen years; a judicial ruling finally affirmed the University's right to move the research materials.

In the years that followed, the Arboretum's academic mission
slowly receded in importance: its collections seemed less relevant
to research being done in physiology and molecular genetics labs
in Cambridge and elsewhere. But since the 1990s, with the revolution in genetic studies typified by the Human Genome Project,
modern molecular approaches to traditional fields like comparative morphology and development have produced a new perspective on the value of a diverse collection of very mature trees from
around the world. In a single place, for example, researchers can
now study the genetic and biochemical pathways that control the
spring growth and development of leaves in Chinese trees and

their close relatives in America. Through the comparison of any differences—and an understanding of their evolutionary history made precise by molecular research on their genes—botanists gain deeper insight into the ways evolution has shaped the diversity of these giant living organisms. In an ironic reversal of history, Harvard decided in 2003 to relocate its botany greenhouses from Cambridge to the Arboretum, where researchers would be able to do their work in concert with the specimens growing nearby.

Related entries: Science Museums; Virtual Harvard. *Related Website:* www.arboretum.harvard.edu.

Art Museums

The University has three major art museums: the Fogg, the Busch-Reisinger, and the Sackler. All are on Quincy Street, as is the Carpenter Center for the Visual Arts, which regularly exhibits contemporary art and photography and holds regular film showings.

• *The William Hayes Fogg Art Museum.* The oldest of the three, the Fogg is a teaching museum. Its collections and exhibitions cover the history of Western art from the Middle Ages to the present and are organized in ways that allow fine arts teachers and students to make constant use of them. The museum's celebrated Wertheim Collection of European paintings and sculpture contains masterworks by Cezanne, Matisse, Monet, Renoir, Van Gogh, Gauguin, and Picasso; the Fogg also has a noted collection of paintings by the French classicist J. A. D. Ingres, as well as the largest holdings of work by John Singleton Copley. Among its recent acquisitions are more than a hundred drawings from the George and Maida Abrams Collection, one of the most comprehensive private assemblages of seventeenth-century Dutch landscapes and genre drawings, with works by Rembrandt and his circle. Other treasures of the Fogg include the Hutchinson collection of English silver and the Spencer albums of old master prints.

The Fogg opened its doors in 1895, and since 1927 has occupied a traditional-looking red-brick, neo-Georgian building on

Quincy Street. Spacious galleries surround a surprising interior courtyard that replicates the façade of a sixteenth-century building in Montepulciano, Italy. Though its acoustics are not ideal for speechmaking, the courtyard makes an attractive venue for University dinners and receptions. Private functions are also held in the museum's Naumburg Wing, with seventeenth-century paintings and two rooms enriched by paneling and tapestries of the period. Bequeathed to Harvard by Mrs. Nettie G. Naumburg in 1930, the rooms were transported intact from her elegant triplex apartment in Manhattan.

The two-story Warburg Hall is the museum's largest exhibition space. A 400-seat lecture room is in the basement; two more lecture rooms are on upper floors. The Fogg is also the home of a half-dozen curatorial departments: prints, drawings, photographs, paintings, sculpture, and decorative arts. Based there as well are the Straus Center for Conservation, devoted to research on the preservation of all kinds of art, and the Mongan Center, which brings scholars and students together to study prints, drawings, and photographs.

• *Busch-Reisinger Museum.* Located in Werner Otto Hall, a wing attached to the Fogg Museum, "the Busch" is the only American museum devoted to the arts of Central and Northern Europe. Its special strengths include German expressionism, 1920s abstraction, the Austrian Secession, the Bauhaus period, and post-World War II painting. On permanent exhibition are works by Max Beckmann, Joseph Beuys, Lovis Corinth, Lyonel Feininger, Erich Heckel, Wassily Kandinsky, Anselm Kiefer, Paul Klee, Gustav Klimt, Emil Nolde, and Max Pechstein. Beckmann's 1927 "Self-Portrait in Tuxedo," an iconic symbol of cultural life in the Weimar Republic, has been called the most important self-portrait of the century.

The Busch's core collections were formed through alliances that linked scholarship, politics, and business. In the late 1890s Professor Kuno Francke persuaded Emperor William II to donate plaster reproductions of German monuments for a projected Germanic Museum. The St. Louis brewer Adolphus Busch and his son-in-law Hugo Reisinger subsequently donated funds for the museum, which rose on Kirkland Street and was dedicated in 1921. In the 1930s the energetic curator, Charles L. Kuhn, traveled throughout Europe to acquire major works of German art, many disowned and disparaged as degenerate by the Nazi government. When the museum's new premises were built more than half a century later, the donor was Werner Otto, a German businessman and Harvard parent. Opened in 1991, Werner Otto Hall also houses the Fine Arts Library (Harvard's third largest research library) and a gallery for works on paper.

• *Arthur M. Sackler Museum.* Occupying a conspicuous contemporary building at Quincy Street and Broadway, the Sackler exhibits art of the ancient world, Islam, India, and Asia. Prize holdings include Greek and Roman statues, vases, and ancient coins from the Mediterranean world; Korean ceramics; Japanese woodblock prints; Chinese cave temple paintings and bronzes; and archaic Chinese jades.

Completed in 1985, the Sackler's building has drawn much attention. British architect James Stirling's idiosyncratic design was the winning entry in a worldwide competition in which more than 85 architects submitted plans. The son of a marine engineer, Stirling imbued the building with nautical motifs: a prow-like facade, some porthole windows, and a narrow interior stairway rising continuously through three stories. The pale orange glazed-brick surface of one exterior wall is horizontally banded with blue-gray brick—a contextual nod to the polychrome roof of nearby Memorial Hall—and is punctuated with windows of varying widths. Above the entrance facade is a space designed to receive an overpass connecting the Sackler to the Fogg Art Museum across Broadway. Cambridge authorities nixed that part of the building plan; two large cylindrical concrete supports, designed as an integral part of the façade, stand in mute testimony to the vagaries of town-gown politics.

In addition to its exhibit spaces, the building includes an Oriental research library, auditorium, and faculty offices. Construction and endowment funding came from many sources, but the major benefactor was Arthur M. Sackler, a research psychiatrist,

publisher of medical journals, art collector, and founder and patron of art museums in the United States and China.

Related entries: Adolphus Busch Hall; Carpenter Center; Libraries;
Memorial Hall; Quincy Street; Virtual Harvard. *Related Websites:*
www.harvard.edu/museums; www.artmuseums.harvard.edu/fogg;
www.artmuseums.harvard.edu/busch; www.artmuseums.harvard.edu/sackler.

Arts

Over the years, Harvard College has been a training ground for all
kinds of artists—painters, musicians, actors, directors, dancers,
choreographers, photographers, filmmakers—who have distinguished themselves in their chosen worlds of artistic expression.

The arts now figure prominently in the undergraduate curriculum. History of art and architecture, visual and environmental
studies, and music are among the College's 40 fields of concentration. Students can take courses in dramatic arts, or in arts-related
subjects like folklore and mythology, Afro-American studies, and
history and literature. Most take courses in at least two of the Core
Program's three areas of literature and arts, as well as in its foreign
culture area.

In any given year, according to one recent study, more than 60
percent of College students participate in extracurricular activities
involving the creative arts. The expanded role of the arts in undergraduate life had its genesis in the early 1970s, when Derek Bok—a
serious clarinet player in earlier days—assumed the presidency of
Harvard. Students had previously been able to take courses in the
visual arts and to choose from a range of extracurricular opportunities in theater and opera, choral and instrumental music, dance,
and ceramics. Believing that Harvard should do more to integrate
the arts with course work and to enlarge extracurricular options,
Bok appointed a Committee for the Practice of the Arts. Its report
endorsed credit-bearing courses in music, drama, dance, and visual
studies; it also called for fellowships in the arts and a central office
to coordinate arts activities. Myra Mayman, a graduate of Bryn
Mawr, was appointed to head the office.

Mayman had a 28-year run as Harvard's arts impresario, retiring in 2001. She introduced a variety of new arts programs and grants and initiated a "Learning from Performers" series that brought professional artists to Harvard as teachers. The Office for the Arts also sponsored "Arts First," a spring-weekend extravaganza of arts activities that turned Harvard Yard's spaces and buildings into settings for hundreds of performances, exhibitions, and happenings, in virtually every medium and modality of expression. Premièred in 1993, Arts First was the brainchild of actor John Lithgow '67, then a Harvard Overseer. He has returned in subsequent years to help host the event. Each year an Arts Medal is conferred on a distinguished artist who is also a product of Harvard: the late actor Jack Lemmon, author John Updike, composer John Harbison, folk singer Pete Seeger, choral conductor William Christie, and filmmaker Mira Nair have been among recent honorees.

Arts organizations continue to proliferate. By one recent count, the University's musical forces included five orchestras, two jazz bands, the Harvard University Band, the Harvard Glee Club, Harvard-Radcliffe Chorus and Collegium Musicum, Radcliffe Choral Society, eleven a cappella groups, and chamber and madrigal groups. In drama and dance, a typical year sees more than 60 student theatrical and operatic productions and approximately 30 dance productions. The number of ethnic dance groups continues to grow, and the Office of the Arts Dance Program offers noncredit courses in modern dance, ballet, tap, jazz, West African dance, bodywork, Pilates, choreography, and improvisation. Assorted undergraduate literary magazines round out the arts spectrum. In addition to the venerable *Harvard Advocate,* there's the quarterly *Harvard Book Review; The Gamut,* an annual poetry review; *Mosaic,* a semiannual journal keyed to Jewish thought and culture; *Yisei,* a Korean-American annual; and *Zalacain,* exploring Ibero-American themes in various genres. Humor is the province of four other publications: besides the long-established *Lampoon,* they include *Satire V; Swift,* also devoted to satire; and *Demon,* which bills itself as "Harvard's oldest humor magazine named *Demon.*" Not an undergraduate publication, but a vital part of the literary scene, is the *Harvard Review,* published twice a year by the Houghton Library, with support from the Extension School.

Related entries: American Repertory Theatre; Core; Dance; Diversity; Gilbert & Sullivan; Harvard Advocate; Hasty Pudding Show; Lampoon; Music. *Related Websites:* www.fas.harvard.edu/~ofa (Office for the Arts); hcl.harvard.edu/houghton/departments/harvardreview/HRhome.html *(Harvard Review).*

Athletics

The days when Crimson teams dominated intercollegiate sports are long past, but Harvard still maintains the most extensive athletics program of any college. "Athletics for All," a policy dating from the 1920s, is a guiding precept. Each year, almost 1,500 student-athletes compete in intercollegiate sports. Some 3,500 undergraduates—more than half the student body—play on intramural or club teams or engage in recreational sports activities.

Harvard fields 41 varsity and 18 junior varsity teams, the most of any NCAA Division I institution, in 21 men's and 20 women's sports. As a member of the Ivy League group, the College does not grant athletic scholarships, though nonleague contests frequently pit its teams against schools that do. Even so, Crimson squads compete at national levels in such sports as baseball, crew, field hockey, ice hockey, lacrosse, sailing, soccer, squash, swimming, tennis, track and field, water polo, and wrestling. Within the league, Harvard stands second only to Princeton in the number of titles won or shared since 1956, when round-robin play began.

Club teams receive minimal administrative and financial support and must cover their own costs, but they thrive nevertheless. There are more than 30, in such sports as badminton, boxing, cheerleading, curling, cycling, equestrian, martial arts, rugby, shooting, table tennis, and ultimate frisbee. Though the length and rigor of their schedules vary, most of these teams compete against clubs from other colleges.

The Department of Athletics also oversees 28 intramural leagues or tournaments. Its intramural program was organized in 1930, when the first residential houses opened. Hundreds of freshman and house teams now contest throughout the academic year. The department's office of intramurals and recreation tracks inter-house competition and awards the Straus Cup to the house that ranks highest at the end of the year. (The top-ranking freshman dorm wins the Yard Bucket.) In addition, it offers more than a hundred hours of recreational classes each week, in such sports as figure skating, snowboarding, squash, swimming, and tennis, as well as group exercise, aerobics, weight training, and personal fitness.

Harvard's venerable athletic tradition goes back to 1852, when a club crew outrowed two Yale boats in America's first intercolle-giate sports event, a two-mile race on New Hampshire's Lake Winnipesaukee. Rowing was Harvard's only intercollegiate sport until a team of freshman baseball players met and defeated a Brown nine in 1863. The first outside football match, a 3–0 victory over McGill University in May 1874, helped make "Boston foot-ball"—a form of rugby, unlike the soccer-style game played at Yale, Princeton, and Rutgers—the precursor of the modern game. In July 1874, four undergraduates entered the first intercollegiate track meet (staged as part of a rowing regatta in Saratoga, New York), and that fall Harvard formed an organized track team.

Sports and games, wrote President Charles W. Eliot in 1881, were transforming the prototypical Harvard student "from a stooping, weak and sickly youth into one well-formed, robust, and healthy." Teams in five more sports—lacrosse, tennis, fencing, golf, and hockey (then called ice polo)—were formed over the next fifteen years. Basketball and soccer arrived early in the twentieth century, though they did not become major sports until 1937 and 1955, re-spectively. In those salad days of team play, Harvard ruled. Its ath-letes won six of the first seven intercollegiate fencing competitions. From 1898 to 1904, its golf team collected six national titles. By the turn of the century Harvard had the world's largest tennis facility, with more than a hundred courts, and America won the first Davis Cup matches with a team made up entirely of Harvard players—

one of them Dwight Davis '00, the cup's donor. On the eve of
World War I, the 1914 Harvard junior varsity heavyweight crew
rocked the rowing world by taking the Henley Royal Regatta's
Grand Challenge Cup.

Crew races and college baseball drew big crowds, but football
was king. Harvard Stadium, built in 1903, was a monument to
its supremacy. The largest collegiate sports arena of its time, the
stadium sold out for big games and coined money for the Harvard Athletic Association, an alumni-run organization that oversaw
College athletics. But American college football was soon under
fire. For years it had been dogged by eligibility and payoff scandals,
illegal betting, and excessive injuries caused by flimsy equipment,
intentional fouling, and "mass plays" like the flying wedge (a Harvard invention). In his annual reports, President Eliot repeatedly
called for an end to the game. In 1905, a year that saw eighteen
gridiron deaths nationwide, President Theodore Roosevelt, class of
1880, pushed for reforms. Led by Harvard coach William T. Reid
'01, an intercollegiate committee rewrote the rulebook, saving
football from probable abolition and making it a better sport for
both athletes and spectators. New rules made graduate students
and freshmen ineligible for varsity teams, penalized dangerous
scrimmaging, and sanctioned the previously illegal forward pass.
(Members of Reid's committee had wanted to "open up" the game
by widening the field, but because of the fixed width of Harvard
Stadium, passing was adopted instead.)

By the middle of the century, the professionalization of football,
cheating scandals, and "slush fund" payoffs to players were increasingly in the national news. Determined to ensure the respectabil-
ity of their football programs, the presidents of the eight so-called
Ivy League colleges agreed in 1952 to observe uniform policies
governing eligibility, academic requirements, and need-based financial aid. The presidents' formal agreement ruled out athletic
scholarships, spring football practice, and postseason games, and
excluded freshmen from varsity teams. The football policies were
soon extended to all sports, and round-robin competition within
the league began in 1956. In the first two decades of league play,
Crimson teams won 109 championships, putting Harvard well

ahead of its leading rivals, Princeton (62 titles) and Yale (48). In the year 2000, however, Princeton overtook Harvard as the Ivy League college whose teams had earned the most league titles.

Since then, some league rules have been eased to conform to NCAA regulations. Varsity squads, with the exception of crew, are now open to freshmen, limited off-season practices are permitted, and teams in all sports but football may play in postseason tournaments. (In some sports, the Ivy champion receives an automatic bid to an NCAA tourney.) But the league's insistence that its athletes meet prevailing academic standards and its repudiation of athletic scholarships remain firmly established principles.

The relaxation of restraints coincided with the increasing specialization that is now seen at every level of intercollegiate athletics. Three-sport athletes are now extinct in men's sports and are rare in women's. With few exceptions, making a varsity team today requires year-round participation in weight training and conditioning programs, skills sessions, and out-of-season practices. Another vanishing species is the walk-on—the unrecruited athlete who "walks on" in preseason sessions and succeeds in making the team. Almost all of today's intercollegiate athletes have been ardently courted by coaches who do little but recruit once the regular season ends.

The rise of women's teams is a relatively recent development in intercollegiate athletics. Since 1972, when the Higher Education Act mandated increased funding for women's athletics, the number of varsity programs for women undergraduates at Harvard has tripled. Over the past quarter-century, Crimson women's teams have held their own in Ivy League competition, winning more than 80 league championships.

Title IX of the Higher Education Act required gender equity in the sports programs of institutions receiving federal funds. The act took effect at a time when a series of agreements with Radcliffe College opened Harvard's residential house system to women and raised their numbers at the undergraduate level. Crew, track and field, ice hockey, and soccer were soon added to the six intercollegiate sports that Radcliffe had sponsored (basketball, field hockey, lacrosse, sailing, swimming, and tennis), and within a decade the budget for women's sports rose from $60,000 to $700,000. The formation of teams in cross-country, fencing, golf, softball, squash, volleyball, and water polo has since brought the number of women's squads to nineteen, equalling the men's total. (Two intercollegiate teams, in sailing and skiing, are coed.) Harvard administrators note with pride that the expansion of women's programs was achieved without cutting men's programs or eliminating any junior varsity teams—as financial constraints forced many other institutions to do. They also take pride in the fact that Harvard now has more female athletes playing varsity-level sports than any other school in the country. Today more than 40 percent of Harvard athletes are women.

Much of Harvard's athletic plant is concentrated at Soldiers Field, an extensive tract on the south side of the Charles River. Dominated by the century-old Harvard Stadium, the Soldiers Field complex includes football practice fields, soccer, field hockey, lacrosse, rugby, baseball, and softball fields, an outdoor track, tennis courts, and seven major structures: Dillon Field House (1931, renovated in 1978); Lavietes Pavilion, built in 1926 as "Briggs Cage," now the headquarters of varsity basketball teams; Bright Hockey Center (1956, renovated in 1979); Blodgett Pool (1977); Gordon Indoor Track and Tennis Center (1977); the Palmer Dixon Indoor Tennis Courts (1962); and the Murr Center (1998), which houses squash and tennis courts, Athletics Department offices, and the Lee Family Hall of Athletic History.

Two recent additions to the Soldiers Field complex are the Beren Tennis Center (1999) and Jordan Field (1999). The latter has artificial turf and lights, allowing almost year-round use by field hockey and lacrosse teams.

Near Soldiers Field are two venerable boathouses, Newell (1900) and Weld (1907), and the Business School's Shad Gymnasium, a state-of-the-art facility open only to Business School students and faculty members. Nearer to Harvard Square is the Malkin Athletic Center. East of Lowell House, it occupies a full block. Built in 1930 as the Indoor Athletic Building, it was renovated in 1985, may be renovated again soon, and currently provides facilities for basketball, swimming, wrestling, fencing, volleyball, weight training, dance, and aerobics.

To the north, Hemenway Gym (1939), on the grounds of the Law School, houses squash courts. A multipurpose gym known as the QRAC (Quadrangle of Radcliffe Athletic Center, 1979, pronounced Q-RAC) provides basketball, racquetball/handball, squash, tennis, volleyball, and weight training facilities for students from Cabot, Currier, and Pforzheimer Houses.

Back to the riverfront. A couple of miles downstream is Harvard's sailing center (1972). And since 1881, friends of Harvard crew have maintained a bucolic training site at Ledyard, Connecticut, where Crimson rowers prepare to outstroke Yale in the annual Thames River boat races.

Related entries: Crimson; Houses; Ivy League; Soldiers Field; Songs and Marches.

B

One of 18 bells, salvaged from a Moscow monastery,
arriving at Lowell House in the fall of 1930.

Bells

No Harvard tradition is older than the tolling of a College bell. In 1638, when clocks and watches were not yet in general use, a bell of modest size roused the first slumbering scholars and called them to prayers and recitations. Today, a two-and-a-half-ton bell high above Harvard Yard still regulates the daily life of the College, sounding for morning prayers and at hourly intervals thereafter. Cast in Loughborough, England, the great bell has hung in the tower of Memorial Church since 1932. Its inscription, "In Memory of Voices That Are Hushed," was written by President A. Lawrence Lowell, the donor of the bell.

Some older bells met violent ends. One melted when Old Harvard Hall burned in 1764. Another was ruinously vandalized. Its replacement, cast by Paul Revere, cracked after 27 years of use. The next bell fell from its Harvard Hall moorings in 1899. Its successor remained in place until 1928, when the future Memorial Church bell arrived from England and was temporarily mounted in Harvard Hall.

A one-and-a-half-ton bell, the gift of the class of 1876, was installed in the belfry of Memorial Hall in 1897. Loftier and more resonant than the Harvard Hall bell, it was destroyed when the building's tower burned in 1956. Cracked and swollen, the bell was scrapped, though a template was made so that it could be copied. But when the tower was rebuilt in 1999, its bell was not replaced.

Harvard's earliest scholars woke to a rising bell at 5:30 A.M. The hour was advanced to 7:00 in the eighteenth century. In 1933, in his first act as president of Harvard, James B. Conant decreed that the bell should not ring until 8:40, five minutes before morning prayers. The ruling ensured Conant's popularity among denizens of the Yard, and 8:40 is when the bell first peals today.

Finding ways to silence the bell—creating an excuse to miss mandatory prayers and recitations—challenged the ingenuity of many student generations. Stealing the clapper was one obvious method, but wily bell-ringers like Austin Kingsley Jones, the College janitor who had charge of the bell from 1858 to 1908, kept a spare clapper in reserve. Blocking the entrance to the belfry was tried, to no avail; "Old Jones" hacked his way in with an axe. With the onset of cold weather came the opportunity to upend the bell in the night and fill it with water, so that it would freeze and immobilize the clapper. But Harvard's redoubtable ringer overcame every test. When Jones retired, a faculty resolution noted approvingly that

> only once in his fifty years' service the clock had been rung late; that then it was but four minutes late; and that this unexampled tardiness was caused by the need of Mr. Jones's help for putting out a fire in the College Yard. He was a man to set clocks by, uniquely combining an aspect of good-natured ease with the promptest efficiency—never in a hurry and never found wanting.

Time ran out on the Memorial Church bell-ringers in 1956, when an IBM clock and motor, attached by wire cables to the bell, took over their function. But automation did not prevent the occasional mishap. The hundred-pound cast-iron clapper broke loose in 1959, and five years later it tumbled again, impaling the wooden cornice at the base of the steeple.

The bell is still hand-rung on certain occasions, principally Commencement. The hourly signal consists of 44 to 46 strokes; a Sunday church service calls for 120. Before and after memorial services, the bell tolls for departed members of the Harvard community.

The year 1930 was a bell-ringer for the first residents of the newly opened Lowell House. A *zvon,* or chime of Russian bells, arrived there in the fall, to be mounted in the just-completed tower. Originally hung in the Danailov Monastery in Moscow, the bells had been saved from a Soviet melting pot and were presented to Harvard by Charles R. Crane, son of a former United States minister to Russia. President Lowell, expecting a carillon that would peal in the style of the Oxbridge colleges, was sorry to learn that Slavic changes were rung on the oriental six-note scale. But seventeen of the Russian bells, weighing an aggregate 26 tons, now have a firm place in the musical culture of Lowell House and Harvard. They are rung every Sunday afternoon in term time by a house group called the Klappermeisters. (The bells also have their own Website, "the Lowell House Virtual Bell Tower.") An additional bell—the oldest (c. 1790) and handsomest, with delicately embossed cherubs' heads on the shoulder—was found to be too close in tone to one of the *zvon* bells of similar size; it now hangs at the Business School, as does the former Harvard Hall bell.

A tintinnabular extravaganza occurs at the end of each year's Commencement exercises, when all the bells of Harvard and fourteen surrounding churches ring out in unison. A relatively new tradition, begun in 1989, thus builds on a far more ancient one.

Related entries: Fires; Memorial Church; Towers. *Related Website:* lowell.student.harvard.edu/Bells.

Brattle Theatre

Now in its second half-century as Cambridge's counterpart of a European art cinema, the Brattle Theatre showcases film classics ranging from *Casablanca* to *Evil Dead,* and from the time of Chaplin, Cocteau, and Eisenstein to that of Fellini, Truffaut, Godard, and the Coen brothers. Just off Brattle Square, Brattle Hall is one of those talismanic Harvard places with a richly storied past.

The gambrel-roofed edifice was built in 1890 by the Cambridge Social Union, one of many self-improvement groups that were formed after the Civil War. Its architect was A. W. Longfellow Jr., class of 1876, a nephew of the poet and the designer of Phillips Brooks House, the Semitic Museum, and several Radcliffe buildings, including Agassiz House and its elegant little theater. For four decades, its principal tenant was the Cambridge Social Dramatic Club, but the hall was also used for lectures and for formal dances known as "Brattle Halls." Professor George Pierce Baker's famous 47 Workshop and the Harvard Dramatic Club used its 250-seat theater; in the 1930s, a series of professional troupes held the stage. Margaret Webster's production of *Othello,* with Paul Robeson in the title role, had its American première at the Brattle in 1942.

After World War II, several dozen returning veterans organized by Jerome Kilty, class of 1949, formed the Harvard Veterans' Theatre Workshop. There was no lack of talent, but the group did lack a stage of its own. When the Cambridge Social Union put Brattle Hall up for auction, the father of Workshop member David Thayer Hersey bought it for $80,000 and turned it over to the troupe. As the Brattle Theatre Company, it began the first of four illustrious seasons in the summer of 1948. Though it was essentially a repertory company, the BTC also engaged famous figures. The British actress Hermione Gingold made her American debut at the Brattle in *It's About Time.* Hume Cronyn and Jessica Tandy, Sam Jaffe, Zero Mostel, Luise Rainer, and Cyril Ritchard were among other visiting luminaries. Mostel starred in the company's final production, an adaptation of Molière's *The Doctor in Spite of Himself,* in 1952. Though most of the BTC's 64 productions had been critical successes, attendance had waned and the company was losing money. When it dissolved, many members went on to establish careers in the New York theater, among them Kilty, Hersey (under his stage name, Thayer David), actress Nancy Marchand, director Albert Marre, and stage designer Robert O'Hearn.

Another actor, Bryant Haliday '49, had bought the Brattle from Hersey's father when the latter became ill. He and Cyrus Harvey Jr. '47, an early member of the Veterans' Theatre Workshop, now converted it to a European-style art cinema. They tore out old seats, repainted walls, and installed a space-saving rear-screen projection system—used on cruise ships but only rarely in terrestrial movie theaters—in what had been backstage space. The Brattle began its new life with a screening of *The Captain from Kopenick,* a German import, in 1953. A ticket cost 80 cents.

Throughout the 1950s and 1960s, the theater's programming mixed foreign films and American classics. A week-long Humphrey Bogart series revived interest in Bogart's films and became an exam-period tradition for stressed-out students. The Club Casablanca and the Blue Parrot café, housed in a concourse below Brattle Hall, catered to the Bogie cult. Harvey and Haliday formed Janus Films, Inc., which distributed the films of Bergman, Fellini, Godard, Kurosawa, Truffaut, and other *auteurs* to American movie houses for more than a decade. Defying a Massachusetts blue law, Harvey and Haliday screened a film adaptation of Strindberg's *Miss Julie* on a Sunday and went on to win a court judgment that vacated the 1908 law. In 1961, the partners became Cambridge cinemagnates by purchasing Harvard Square's University Theatre.

The theater's ownership has changed hands in recent decades, and on one occasion the Brattle was rescued from bankruptcy. It has been refurbished, and its proprietors have varied its fare with film premières, cabaret performances, readings, "Oscar parties," and forays into live classical theater. True to its heritage, today's Brattle Theatre offers local filmgoers "the best in classic, cutting-edge, and world cinema, with a different double feature almost every day." In a cineplex era, the Brattle's rear-screen projectors whir on.

Related entries: Film Archive; Hollywood's Harvard. *Related Website:* www.brattlefilm.org.

Business School

Though each faculty prizes its independence, the Harvard Business School is by all odds the most autonomous. It has its own attractively landscaped campus on the Boston side of the Charles River, facing the undergraduate houses. It also has a billion-dollar endowment, a prolific and successful publishing arm, and a large, loyal, and prosperous alumni body. In times past, the school's financial solvency, its prideful determination to go its own way, and its distance from Harvard Yard sometimes led to tensions between the faculties of Arts and Sciences and Business. In recent years, a closer and more congenial relationship has blossomed.

Launched in 1908 as a department of the Faculty of Arts and Sciences, the Business School was founded to train young men for what President Charles W. Eliot called the "upper walks" of America's burgeoning corporate enterprises. Business-related curricula existed elsewhere, but only at the undergraduate level; Harvard's was the first business school to require a college degree for admission. After a rocky interval during World War I, it flourished in the boom years of the 1920s and quickly outgrew its quarters in the Yard. A three-way capital campaign, announced in 1924, sought $5 million for chemistry and fine arts and another $5 million to fund a new plant for the Business School.

Bishop William Lawrence, Harvard's chief fundraiser, visited George F. Baker, the super-rich "Sphinx of Wall Street," hoping to come away with a campaign pledge of $1 million. Baker, who was not a Harvard alumnus, told the bishop that he did not wish to give a million, or even half a million. "I have no interest in the Chemistry or the Art," he declared—but as for business, "if by giving $5 million I could have the privilege of building the whole school, I should like to do it."

The new campus, constructed on reclaimed marshland, was designed in neo-Georgian style by the New York firm of McKim, Mead & White. The associates of Frederick Law Olmsted, who had planned Boston's "Emerald Necklace" park system, did the landscaping. Viewed from across the river, the original red-brick buildings are still a handsome sight. The school is very much a university unto itself, with its own classrooms and administrative buildings, ample student housing, dining rooms, library, a faculty club, state-of-the-art athletic facilities, and even a chapel, added in 1992.

The Business School has a student body of some 1,800, a faculty of more than 200, a permanent staff of 800, and an alumni body of about 65,000. Its large and well-appointed library contains more than 600,000 books and periodicals. The school's academic forte is the case method of instruction, originated at the Law School and adopted by the Business School in 1924. Its effectiveness is reflected in the full or partial acceptance of the method by almost every other graduate business school.

The school's cases present real business situations. In an interactive process, students act as managers dealing with complex sets of circumstances and competing interests. Classroom instructors must be thoroughly prepared, quick on their feet, and ready to respond to views that may be different from—and perhaps more perceptive than—their own. No school at Harvard puts as much emphasis on strong teaching or is more active in furthering it.

Though the case method is the primary teaching tool, other approaches—business simulations, term projects, small-group discussions, and even conventional lectures—are also used.

The school's core academic program leads to the degree of Master in Business Administration (M.B.A.). It is a full-time, two-year undertaking. Five doctoral programs prepare students for academic careers; joint and concurrent degree programs are administered in conjunction with the Law School, the Kennedy School of Government, and the Faculty of Arts and Sciences. Executive education, a large and profitable enterprise, is a third element of the school's educational offerings. The Advanced Management Program, the best known of the school's 40-odd executive education offerings, is conducted twice a year; the tuition fee for this two-month immersion is more than $50,000. Centered on the case system, the classroom experience is concentrated and intense.

Research activities account for about 50 percent of faculty time and 25 percent of the school's overall budget. HBS researchers cull data in at least 40 countries, and the school has opened field offices in Hong Kong, Tokyo, Buenos Aires, São Paulo, California's Silicon Valley, and Paris. Faculty members produce books and articles in profusion, while busily gathering material for course development and new case studies. More than 500 new teaching cases were formulated in one recent year.

The school's publishing arm sells more than six million case studies to business schools and other organizations in the United States and abroad. The Harvard Business School Press—a unit of HBS Publishing (HBSP)—puts out 30 or 40 new titles in a typical year. The *Harvard Business Review,* also part of HBSP, has a circulation of more than 200,000 and may be the business world's most prestigious academic journal.

On the other side of the Charles, you'll still find some who disparage HBS as "a school of money-making" or resent its restriction of the Shad physical fitness center to Business School students and faculty. But relationships are improving. Joint appointments with other faculties are on the rise, and HBS faculty members have served as Harvard house masters. They are also active in the interfaculty initiatives instituted by former president Neil Rudenstine—notably ethics, the environment, and health-care management. Though the school had zealously guarded its fundraising sources in former times, it cooperated fully in the five-year, University-wide capital campaign completed in 1999. HBS has even made outright grants to less well-endowed schools, a form of generosity almost unknown at Harvard. At least part of the credit belongs to Kim B. Clark, a graduate of the College with a Harvard Ph.D. in economics, who became dean in 1995.

With its centennial coming up in 2008, the Business School is in itself a case study in effective management methods.

Related entries: Fundraising; Virtual Harvard. *Related Website:* www.hbs.edu.

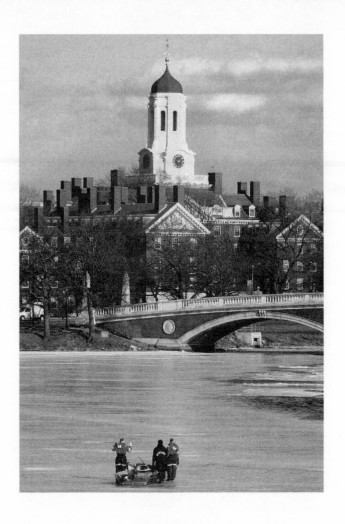

C

A Charles River ice-breaking party—the coaches of the
women's crew—at work in early March. In the background:
the Weeks Bridge and Dunster House.

Cambridge / Boston

One of Cambridge's most notable aspects is its heterogeneity—for it is actually many cities. It's the seat of two world-famous institutions of higher learning: Harvard University and the Massachusetts Institute of Technology. It's home to the corporate headquarters for many companies, such as Akamai Technologies, Biogen Idec, Draper Laboratory, Genzyme, and Millennium Pharmaceuticals. It's the dwelling place of many ethnic groups, including substantial numbers of Irish, Italians, Armenians, Portuguese, Haitians, and African-Americans. The city's demography is reflected in its various squares: Central, Kendall, Inman, Porter, and the best known of them, Harvard. Each has its own neighborhood and distinct character, none more so than Harvard Square.

First-time visitors are apt to experience the Square as a total sensory and intellectual environment. Harvard sculptor Dimitri Hadzi has captured one aspect of its spirit in "Omphalos," a tall, parti-colored marble sculpture that stands next to the Square's landmark newspaper kiosk and subway entrance. Hadzi's obelisk resembles a signpost pointing in many directions: perhaps with a hint of navel-gazing irony, the sculptor conceives the Square as the life-sustaining center of the cosmopolitan world.

Proximity to Boston is among Cambridge's defining attributes. The widening course of the Charles River separates it from the nation's most populous state capital, but Boston's rich cultural resources are a short subway ride away. Boston offers Symphony Hall and the Handel & Haydn Society, the Museum of Fine Arts and the Isabella Stewart Gardner Museum, the Museum of Science, pre-Broadway tryouts and the Huntington Theater, the Boston Ballet and the Boston Lyric Opera, the Freedom Trail, the Red Sox, Bruins, and Celtics—as well as the Boston Marathon, which clocks a good many student and faculty runners each April.

The earliest settlers of what is now Cambridge were drawn there by the river. A curious monument on Memorial Drive, near the Eliot Bridge, marks the supposed site of an eleventh-century outpost left by the Norseman Leif Ericson, but that legend has been exploded. Sixteenth-century European explorers found Indian en-

campments along the river. In 1630 the Puritan fathers designated
the recently founded village of Newtowne as the capital of the Bay
Colony; the seat of government was shifted to Boston in 1638,
and the General Court, creating New England's first college at
Newtowne, ordered that it should "henceforward be called Cambridge" to honor the university where many of the colony's clergymen had been educated.

In 1680 the population of Cambridge stood at 850; a century
later it was still only 1,200. But by then the town was an important
Massachusetts community, distinguished for its support of the
American Revolution. It was in Cambridge, in 1775, that George
Washington took command of the Continental Army. Many patriot leaders—propagandist and firebrand Samuel Adams, class of
1740; Major-General Artemas Ward, class of 1748, whom Washington succeeded in command; Dr. Joseph Warren, class of 1759, a
hero of Bunker Hill, and others—were Harvard graduates.

By act of the legislature, the town became the City of Cambridge in 1846. Its population had now reached 13,000. Harvard
was 210 years old and had held gala bicentennial exercises a decade earlier. MIT was not yet born, and would not move from
Boston to Cambridge until 1916. Cambridge businesses were enjoying boom times. Major products included glass, soap, red brick,
and ice—soon supplanted by machinery, carpentry, furniture,
printing, and pianos. Today the population is 92,000, and the
city's fame rests on its output of high-tech software, educated
minds, and world-class scholars.

The liberal coloration of Cambridge's permanent and transient
population has inevitably invited ridicule, good-natured and otherwise. To the Congressional witch-hunters of the early 1950s,
Harvard was the "Kremlin-on-the-Charles." Boston newspaper
columnists josh about "the People's Republic of Cambridge." And
the city lives up to its reputation. His Harvard Business School ties
notwithstanding, George W. Bush, M.B.A. '75, captured only 13
percent of the Cambridge vote in the presidential election of 2000.

·   Like most urban universities, Harvard has had its share of town-
gown tensions. Until the late 1960s, the University sought to follow a policy of "minimal impact," keeping a low profile in local

public affairs and limiting real estate acquisitions to those deemed essential to its research and instructional needs. But the upheavals that began in 1969 made it clear that the University was widely perceived as an unresponsive and even hostile community presence. Its real estate management and relocation practices were a particular cause of ill will. When President Derek Bok took office in 1971, improving community relations received high priority. A new Office of Governmental and Community Relations was formed and new neighborhood programs were launched.

The results have been beneficial for all parties—though University expansion remains a controversial and sensitive issue. In 1997, the news that Harvard had used front groups to buy up 52 acres of land in Allston set off a firestorm of criticism. In outlining plans for the development of the University's increasing holdings in Allston, President Lawrence Summers would later stress the necessity of taking into account the needs and concerns of existing neighborhoods.

Harvard may still be perceived in many quarters as a 300-pound schoolyard bully, but the record suggests that when a proposed building or development arouses organized opposition, the University finds it best to back off and alter its plans. In 1975, when traffic concerns prompted residents to protest the siting of the John F. Kennedy Library on land formerly occupied by subway yards, the Harvard Corporation finally abandoned the project. A decade later, Cambridge authorities said no to architect James Stirling's design for a Broadway overpass linking the new Sackler Museum with the Fogg Art Museum. More recently, the University and its neighbors parried for nearly six years over a proposed Center for Governmental Studies on Cambridge Street. Harvard repeatedly re-sited and redesigned the plans, reducing the scale of the buildings, and eventually felt obliged to dispense with a provision for a tunnel that would have removed five loading docks from an essentially residential area.

Harvard's property holdings cover only 5.5 percent of Cambridge's land area, 8.5 percent of Allston's, and a much smaller fraction of Boston's. But the University's presence affects its adjacent communities in ways greatly disproportionate to the space it occupies. With a regular payroll of more than 15,000 people—about 6,000 living in Cambridge or Boston—Harvard is one of the state's largest employers. Its outlays for payroll, goods and services, municipal fees and services, taxes and in-lieu-of-tax payments in Cambridge and Boston exceed $750 million a year. The University assists its communities through more than 260 public service programs; supports many neighborhood organizations and events; opens educational and cultural facilities to Greater Boston residents; and provides more than $1 million a year in financial aid to local students enrolled in the College.

Related entries: Allston; Architecture; Charles River; Continuing Education; Elmwood; God's Acre; Harvard Hill; Public Service. *Related Website:* www.ci.cambridge.ma.us.

Cantab

The term *Cantab,* occasionally encountered in sports lingo, is a contraction of *Cantabrigian,* a Latinate word denoting a resident or representative of Cambridge. Etymologists explain that in medieval times, the name *Cantebrig* was applied to a part of what is now Cambridge, England, where a bridge (Middle English *brig*) crossed the river Cam (also called the *Granta*). References to Harvard athletic teams as the Cantabs reflect a paucity of alternatives other than "the Crimson." Yale may be the Eli, the Blue, or the Bulldog, but Harvard has no other counterpart to such collective formations as Bruins, Big Red, Crusaders, the Green, Huskies, Mountain Hawks, Lions, Quakers, and Tigers. "Johns," sometimes used in gauche slogans adopted by followers of opposing teams, is regarded as unacceptable by most Cantabs.

Related entry: Athletics.

Carpenter Center

The Carpenter Center for the Visual Arts occupies one of the University's most unusual buildings. The French modernist Le

Corbusier's only American commission, it is a boldly sculpted work of art and a summation of the architect's genius. The five levels of this reinforced-concrete structure are contained in a massive, curving entrance, suggesting to some the prow of a ship. The walls are perforated by large, deep sun baffles known as *brise soleils,* which admit natural light while blocking the sun's direct rays. As a kind of jeu d'esprit, a graceful, rising ramp winds through the building.

Inevitably, the Carpenter Center has inspired its share of anecdotes and metaphors. One apocryphal story has it that on seeing photographs of the finished building in 1963, the aging Corbu exclaimed, "*Mon dieu,* they've built it upside down." *Architectural Forum* dubbed the Center "the two-guitar house of the arts." The late Professor John Finley, employing a saucier musical-instrument image, found it suggestive of "two pianos copulating." Time has tamed the expression of such analogies. Students using the building tend to like it; architectural critics have praised Le Corbusier's attempt to design a structure for the visual arts that displayed, both outside and inside, "the experience of freedom and unbounded creativity." Most agree, though, that the design is wrong for its site. Sandwiched between Quincy Street's Fogg Art Museum and the Faculty Club, the building needed more elbow room to achieve the effect its architect intended. Corbu's Harvard clients, who approved the design, can be faulted for failing to perceive what now seems obvious. But to students, it's what's inside the building that counts:

- Painting, sculpture and graphic design areas.
- Still and video photography facilities.
- Metalworking and woodworking space.
- Printmaking and publishing, traditional and computer-based.
- Sound recording, mixing, and re-recording.
- Lectures, seminars, exhibitions, installations, performances.
- Works in traditional and experimental media.

Carpenter Center also houses the Harvard Film Archive, custodian for one of the world's larger motion-picture collections—

principally in 35mm, and in prime condition. This priceless cache of more than 9,000 films gives scholars and students an unexampled opportunity to survey American and world filmmaking. Faculty members may draw from the archive for use in courses, and regular screenings are offered to the public.

Le Corbusier died soon after the Carpenter Center was completed, but his vision of a busy art center, inspiring "beneficent relations between the hand and the head," is realized in a building that—no matter how hemmed in—continues to turn heads on Quincy Street.

Related entries: Architecture; Arts; Film Archive; Quincy Street

Characters

"What has become of all the 'college characters'?" asked the Harvard historian Samuel F. Batchelder, writing in the 1920s. In bygone days, he declared, "the Yard was as full of characters as a novel by Dickens." Batchelder opined that "the small and scattered population, the difficulties of intercommunication, the sturdy independence of thought and action, the absence of artificial standards of deportment, and the manifold problems of bare existence—resulting in every sort of irregular substitution and makeshift—produced an amount of diversity in dress, in speech, in habits, and in ideas that must have been really startling."

Batchelder, who graduated in 1893, would have known at first hand the quintessential Harvard character: John Lovett, called by everyone "John the Orangeman." Peddling fruits and vegetables from a cart pulled by his donkey, Annie Radcliffe, this top-hatted, chin-whiskered Irishman was a Harvard Yard fixture for more than half a century. As official mascot of Harvard athletic teams, he even traveled to road games with the football and baseball squads. John's status as a Harvard institution was reflected in his trademark greeting to arriving freshmen: "I knew y'r father, fri'nd."

Many college characters of John the Orangeman's day were also vendors, like "Abe the Cobbler"; Bernard ("Poco") Bennett, old-

clothes dealer and moneylender; the blind newsdealer Daniel
Daniels; and Max Keezer, proprietor of a used-clothing business
that is still extant. Others worked for the College, among them the
indefatigable bell-ringer and janitor Austin Kingsley Jones.

The faculty too had its share of characters, and the classics
department seems to have gathered a disproportionate number.
John Snelling Popkin, an early-nineteenth-century professor of
Greek, kept on his desk a cast of a leg sculpted by Praxiteles. Professor Evangelinus Apostolides Sophocles kept a pet chicken in his
Holworthy Hall rooms. Professor George Martin Lane, a Latinist,
was the author of "One Fishball," a humorous song that was published in 1857 and survived well into the twentieth century.

Charles Townsend Copeland, who taught composition, had students read their themes to him while he lay back, "writhing . . . as
if he were in the throes of acute indigestion, and moaning pro-
fanely" at tortured constructions and inept turns of phrase. Late
in his career, when a former student congratulated him on his ac-
cession to the Boylston Professorship of Rhetoric and Oratory,
"Copey" responded, "Ahhh . . . Gahd! To think that I occupy the
chair that once warmed the cold, forbidding tail of John Quincy
Adams!" Copeland is also credited with falling off a lecture platform and quipping, "Gentlemen, for once in my life I have de-
scended to the level of my audience."

George Lyman Kittredge, the Shakespearean scholar, refused to
wait for the light to change when crossing Harvard Square. He
preferred to wade into traffic, extending an arm to halt oncoming
cars. On one occasion, when a large garbage truck came to a
screeching halt just short of the bearded professor, the driver rolled
down his window and shouted, "What are you doing, Noah—
looking for your ark?" Without missing a beat, "Kitty" replied,
"Yes, and I am missing an ass. Would you volunteer?"

Samuel Eliot Morison, the historian, preferred horses to cars
and sometimes lectured in boots and jodhpurs. Morison made up
his own sartorial rules: he once ordered a pink-shirted student to
leave his classroom. Arthur Darby Nock, an erudite and exceed-
ingly eccentric historian of religion who gained tenure at the age of

twenty-eight, threw elaborate birthday parties for himself and enjoyed reciting parodies of his own obituary. In a genuine obituary—a memorial minute read at a faculty meeting after Nock's
death in 1963—a colleague wrote that "his regular teaching . . . had
the aberrant effectiveness of enormous learning and good humor
mixed with explosive incoherence of speech. Those who could
penetrate the second profited from the first."

Nock kept rooms in Eliot House, from which the United States
Navy tried unsuccessfully to evict him when it appropriated the
House for V-12 trainees at the start of World War II. It is said that
a young naval officer once blundered into Nock's suite and was
startled to find the occupant in meditation, stark naked. "Jesus
Christ!" exclaimed the officer. "Not so," replied the professor. "His
humble servant, Arthur Darby Nock."

Harry Wolfson, a historian of philosophy, lived in an apartment
so crammed with books and documents that he stored some of
them in the refrigerator. He was one of the few scholars possessing
a key to Widener Library, which allowed him to work there on
Sundays.

Wolfson was known for his immense erudition, but his prodi-
gious memory may have been rivaled by that of Adolphus Terry,
Harvard's Human Encyclopedia. An African-American born in
Cambridge, Terry was hired at the turn of the century to do odd
jobs in University Hall. When his mental agility became apparent,
he was assigned to assist George Washington Cram, the University
Recorder. Looking up records took too much time, so Terry would
memorize the names, faces, and course records of every student in
the College. Years later he would greet returning alumni with minute details of their academic careers. It is part of the Terry legend
that he rescued innumerable undergraduates from trouble, bailing
out minor miscreants in the dead of night and even advising
against unwise marriages. An authority on Harvard history, Terry
was always ready to field queries about the year William James died
or when and why the Veterinary College folded.

John Shea, another long-serving staff member, was perhaps the
last of the legendary College characters. A Cambridge-born Irish-

man, he was hired in 1905 as a library coatroom attendant but was
soon assigned to the Widener stacks. There he held forth for 49
years, arriving early and staying late. Shea had an uncanny knack
of locating misplaced books in the cavernous stacks; he was also
memorable for his malapropisms. To find a lost book, he once as-
sured a library user, "I will leave no stone unthrown." Appreciative
scholars collected and exchanged his inspired slips of the tongue.
To a dilatory stack attendant: "You are getting very laxative in your
work." In praise of a colleague: "She has always been a faithful and
conscious employee." To a job applicant: "Do you write an eligible
hand?" In 1953, a year before his retirement, Shea received an honorary Master of Arts degree; the citation read, "He has for many
years helped scholars on their way to knowledge."

   Related entries: Bells; Extinct Harvard.

Charles River

Rivers help etch the character of many major American cities:
think of the Hudson and East Rivers in New York City, the Poto-
mac in Washington, the mighty Mississippi in St. Louis and New
Orleans. The Charles is a more modest and meandering river, nav-
igable only by small craft. Eighty miles in length, it rises in outlying Hopkinton and flows into the Boston Harbor Basin. It defines
the Cambridge-Boston border and divides Harvard's central facilities from the University's new frontier in Allston.

   For those within range of its banks, the Charles is a recreational
paradise—for rowing, canoeing, sailing, sailboarding, power-boat-
ing, skating (with caution), and, on the banks themselves, biking,
rollerblading, hiking, running, painting, sauntering, or sunbathing
on a lazy Sunday afternoon. On the Boston side there are Hatch
Shell concerts, with performances by the Boston Pops, rock and
jazz stars, and spectacular Fourth of July fireworks. Upstream,
there are riverside festivals of music, food, and arts and crafts. Avid
birdwatchers know that the Charles is a favorite haven of indigenous and migrating birds. White domestic geese, Canada geese,

mallards, cormorants, black-crowned night herons, and, here and there, great blue herons may be observed. Bald eagles occasionally soar overhead.

The third weekend in October brings the Head of the Charles Regatta, the world's largest rowing event. Harvard is among the few universities that have at their doorsteps a river suitable for daily crew practices and intercollegiate races. It's not unusual to see Olympic-level crews practicing and racing there. For most of the year sailing races are held downstream, between the Longfellow and Boston University bridges.

The Charles wasn't always the natural asset it is today. Until 1910, when it was dammed at its mouth, the river was tidal, exposing rank-smelling mud flats at low tide. The Charles River Dam Bridge kept it at a constant level, creating a broad and relatively placid freshwater lake almost four miles long. Commercial docks and warehouses on both banks gave way to boathouses and green space. Needless to say, the transformation has been of inestimable benefit to Harvard.

Since access to Boston and Allston is vital to Harvard and the Cambridge community, the bridges crossing the river and its basin are essential economic and cultural conduits. Spans over the Charles have come and gone since 1662, when the Great Bridge— the first of any importance to be built in America—was completed. (Before the construction of the Great Bridge, a ferry at Charlestown, near the mouth of the Charles, was the principal connection with Boston. By order of the General Court of Massachusetts Bay, revenues from the ferry provided Harvard with its first source of regular income.)

Of the nine bridges linking Cambridge with downtown Boston, the Back Bay, and the cities of Brighton and Allston, the Harvard Bridge is the oldest and longest. Opened in 1891, it crosses the basin at almost its widest point and is 2,165 feet in length. Though it is named for John Harvard, the Massachusetts Institute of Technology fronts its Cambridge end. Traditionalists quashed a 1946 campaign to rename it Technology Bridge, but Tech students and alumni still claim a proprietary interest. An urban legend holds that the Harvard Bridge's official length is "364.4 Smoots plus an ear," as measured by MIT fraternity brothers using the five-foot-seven-inch frame of pledge Oliver Smoot, MIT class of 1962, as a calibration unit.

Inspired by the towers and stonework of European bridges, the 1,768-foot Longfellow (aka "Pepperpot" or "Salt and Pepper") Bridge is the river's most picturesque. Designed by Edmund March Wheelwright, class of 1876, it opened in 1906. Its eleven spans support two Red Line subway tracks and four vehicular lanes connecting Cambridge's Kendall Square area with Boston's West End. The bridge is named for Henry Wadsworth Longfellow, LL.D. 1856, poet and professor of romance languages at Harvard.

Closer to Harvard's bailiwick, the 440-foot, Georgian-style Anderson Memorial Bridge stands near the site of the seventeenth-century Great Bridge; it links the core of the University with its athletics facilities and the Business School campus. Another Wheelwright design, it replaced a creaking wooden drawbridge and was opened in 1915. The $300,000 structure was given by the diplomat Larz Anderson, class of 1888, in memory of his father, Civil War general Nicholas Longworth Anderson, class of 1858. Its neoclassical ornamentation includes motifs of peace and war, as well as books, an inkwell, and other instruments of learning. A tablet on the Cambridge side reads

> May this bridge, built in memory of a Scholar and Soldier, connecting the College Yard and playing fields of Harvard, be an ever present reminder to students passing over it of loyalty to country and Alma Mater and a lasting suggestion that they should devote their manhood developed by study and play on the banks of this river to the Nation and its needs.

Though it was not the intent of the donor (an automobile collector and onetime ambassador to Japan), the structure is invariably referred to as the Larz (not the Nicholas Longworth) Anderson Bridge. A small plaque on its downstream side, near the Cambridge end, commemorates the suicide by drowning of the fictional Harvard freshman Quentin Compson, a character in William Faulkner's *The Sound and the Fury* and *Absalom, Absalom!* A similar plaque, with the legend "Drowned in the fading of honey-suckle," was originally put in place by young Faulknerians in 1965. It was lost during repairs to the bridge in 1983, but was then myste-riously replaced by the present plaque, which substitutes *odour* for *fading*. No variant of the phrase can be found in either of Faulk-ner's novels.

A few hundred yards downstream is the smaller-scaled Weeks Memorial Footbridge (1927), providing a shortcut from the river houses to the Business School and athletic fields. Steam and elec-trical lines are enclosed within it. Designed in elegant Georgian Revival style by McKim, Mead & White, the bridge was given by friends of John W. Weeks, a former secretary of war and Massachu-setts senator. Its embellishments, which include decorative seals, are considered exceptional, but the balustrade has been disfigured by graffiti.

Still further downstream is the 330-foot River Street Bridge, built in 1926. Like the Anderson Bridge, it replaced a pile trestle bridge and is supported by three graceful neoclassical arches. Ar-chitect Robert Peabody Bellows, class of 1899, took the Pont Neuf in Paris as his model. Upstream, the Eliot Bridge (1951) is the new-est of Cambridge's bridges, and the westernmost. Close to the Watertown-Cambridge line, it connects with Soldiers Field Road. Similar in style to its near neighbors downstream, it too has three arches. The bridge's name honors both President Charles W. Eliot and his son Charles, class of 1882, a landscape architect who greatly improved the Charles River shoreline and who first proposed the construction of a bridge at the site, known as Gerry's Landing.

Related entries: Allston; Cambridge/Boston; Fictional Harvard; Underground. *Related Websites:* www.cambridgema.gov/~CAC/ community_river.html (Charles River Festival); www.hocr.org (Head of the Charles Regatta).

Clocks

Harvard owns an uncommon number of clocks, a great many of them antiques, from grandfathers to brackets; English, Dutch, and French; musical clocks and banjos; clocks of marble and tortoise-shell, of silver and gold, and of the rarest woods. Generous donors have given valuable clocks to the president's office, to the Fogg Art Museum, and to the Collection of Historical Scientific Instruments. In 1943, fifty notable timepieces from the seventeenth and eighteenth centuries were part of a bequest from Grenville L. Winthrop, class of 1886. With this collection as a core, the University soon appointed an Honorary Keeper of the Clocks at the Fogg Art Museum: Charles Addison Ditmas Jr., an authentic character who served with token remuneration until his death in 2002. It was his task to "keep"—care for, wind, repair, and replace the parts of—more than 200 precious clocks in Harvard buildings.

A gifted amateur, Ditmas lavished affection on his clocks and harkened to the music of their gears. "Clocks are people, and old clocks are very old people," he wrote in an unpublished essay. "Such a demand for patience, quiet acceptance of their quirks, and then the task of gently coaxing from them better behavior! Sometimes, when I have finished, I feel as old as the clock itself."

"These clocks are like my old friends," Ditmas once said. "They speak to me, and I speak back to them."

One Harvard clock that Ditmas did not "keep" was a highly advanced cesium-beam atomic clock developed by a group of physicists that included Nobel laureate Norman Ramsey, Higgins Professor of Physics Emeritus. Atomic clocks measure time in tiny movements of atoms; a second is defined as the time it takes a cesium atom to make 9,192,631,770 oscillations. Another timepiece outside Ditmas's domain was an electric "sun-clock" erected in the early 1990s near the Business School's strikingly modern Class of 1959 Chapel. A golden sphere within a Plexiglas case marks the approximate time by rising to the top of the case at noon and sinking to the bottom at midnight.

High-profile clocks tick away in the towers of Eliot House, Dunster House, Adolphus Busch Hall, and Harvard's neighboring First Unitarian and St. Paul's churches. But if a single clock enjoys pride of place at Harvard, it's the College Clock—installed in the west gable of Massachusetts Hall, facing Harvard Square, in 1725. Fittingly, this clock has been handsomely restored to replicate its eighteenth-century appearance.

Related entries: Characters; Towers.

College Pump

A burnished replica of an older College pump fronts Hollis Hall, in the Old Yard's northwest corner. A water pump was once an indispensable utility and favorite gathering place for denizens of the Yard. Today, most students, faculty members, and tourists pass by the pump without giving a thought to the era it represents.

The earliest survey map of the Yard, made in 1812, shows that what is now thought of as *the* College pump was the northernmost of three that provided water for the College buildings. This pump tapped a well that may have been sunk in 1764, when Hollis Hall was constructed. All three Yard pumps provided water for drinking, cooking, washing, and occasional dunkings of obstreperous freshmen, but the Hollis Hall pump was noted for its pure, good-tasting output, waggishly known as "Chateau de la Pompe."

In the latter years of the nineteenth century the Yard was rocked by sporadic bombings—the nightwork of students with an extra-curricular interest in chemistry and/or anarchy—and the pump took its share of hits. In the winter of 1901, it was destroyed by a dynamite blast that was widely ascribed to the Med. Fac., a notorious secret society. (Coincidentally, that year's Hasty Pudding Show was a three-act burlesque called *The Dynamiters*.) The Harvard Corporation, weary of pranks and concerned about communal hygiene, refused to rebuild the pump and ordered the well sealed.

In anticipation of Harvard's 1936 Tercentennial, Dr. J. Dellinger Barney, class of 1900, a Boston urologist, led a successful drive to restore and reactivate the pump. With appropriate speechifying and versifying, a replica was dedicated during the Tercentenary celebration. The new pump tapped a Cambridge main, and a modern bubbler replaced the communal tin cup of old.

By the late 1960s, the Tercentenary pump was in disrepair. It was finally replaced in 1987, as a 350th birthday gift from Radcliffe to Harvard. William S. Brouwer, a Boston craftsman who had studied at the Graduate School of Design, crafted a faithful and sturdy copy of the ancient pump. A time-delay faucet, actuated by the pump's wooden arm, took the place of the anachronistic bubbler. Today the pump is kept in good working order by Harvard's Facilities Maintenance Department.

"The College Pump" is also the title of a long-running column in *Harvard Magazine,* begun by David T. W. McCord '21, when he assumed the editorship of the *Harvard Alumni Bulletin* (the magazine's former title) in 1940. McCord saw the new column as "a corner reserved for random comment, for the stray line of Harvard verse, the pleasant non-sequitur of academic observation, the simple fragment or phrase." So it remains; and since then "the Pump" has spewed forth its legible liquid more than 700 times.

"Your wooden arm you hold outstretched / To shake with passers-by" is the column's epigraph. McCord found the lines in verses by William Roscoe Thayer, class of 1881—later a scholar of Italian history and editor of the old *Harvard Graduates' Magazine*—that first appeared in the *Harvard Register* of June 1881:

TO THE COLLEGE PUMP
Your wooden arm you hold outstretched
To shake with passers-by;
Your friends are always thirsty ones,
But you are never dry.
A hundred Classes at your lips
Have drunk, and passed away;
And where the fathers quenched their thirst
The sons now quench today.

Related entries: Harvard Magazine; the Yard.

Commencement

Harvard's Commencement has been called the "oldest continuous springtime festival in North America." The first graduating class of nine students "commenced" in 1642, long before the United States was a nation. But the exercises have not been continuous. They were cancelled on nine occasions, either because of the plague (probably smallpox) or Revolutionary War tensions. "Springtime" also requires a qualifying footnote. In the seventeenth century, Commencement was in September—a time when most graduates commenced their careers as clergymen or teachers.

And there's not just one Commencement: the big day involves three separate ceremonial occasions. The first is the morning exercise, held outdoors in the Tercentenary Theatre, when the president awards diplomas *en bloc* to College seniors and degree candidates from the professional schools. At lunchtime and immediately after, advanced degree candidates—those receiving the Ph.D. and degrees in law, medicine, education, and so on—are handed their individual diplomas by the deans of their schools. Graduating seniors receive their diplomas from their house masters. In the afternoon, the Alumni Association holds its annual meeting, again in the Tercentenary Theatre. This conclave includes a report from the president and an address by the speaker of the day, usually a figure of national or world stature who was awarded an honorary degree at the morning exercises. Past speakers have included Secretary of State George Marshall (1947); Russian dissident Aleksandr Solzhenitsyn (1978); King Juan Carlos of Spain (1984, when another regal recipient—Benny Goodman, King of Swing—was also an honorand); German Chancellor Helmut Kohl (1990); and Secretary of State Madeleine Albright (1997).

What almost everyone thinks of as *the* Harvard Commencement takes place on a Thursday morning in early June, when more than 30,000 students, faculty, parents, alumni, dignitaries, and guests gather in the center of historic, leafy Harvard Yard to observe the *rite de passage* from degree candidate to diploma recipient. It's the one time in the academic year when all of Harvard's schools—degree candidates, deans, and faculties—come together in one setting.

It's also the occasion when Harvard's president announces to the senior class, "By virtue of authority delegated to me, I confer on you the first degree in Arts or in Sciences, and admit you to the fellowship of educated men and women." At an earlier stage of the proceedings, the president has stated that he admits recipients of the Ph.D. "to the ancient and universal company of scholars, and entrust to you the free inquiry of future generations." Equally resonant are his words to the Law School's degree candidates, who are told that they "are ready to aid in the shaping and application of those wise restraints that make us free."

The morning exercises are a ritualized series of set pieces that reach far back into Harvard's history. In earlier days, the Sheriff of Middlesex County was invited to Commencement to control unruly and sometimes inebriated students and alumni. The exercises still begin with the exhortation, "Mr. Sheriff, pray give us order." The sheriff solemnly takes center stage, pounds his staff three times on the stone steps, and in his strong Boston accent intones, "The meeting will be in order." It is an opening hard to beat. (On one recent occasion, however, the sheriff had to be chided for faulty syntax. For the prescribed injunction, he had substituted a solecism offensive to the ears of literate Harvardians: "As High Sheriff of Middlesex, this meeting will be in order." A year later the dangling modifier was gone.)

The earliest Commencements featured student orations in Latin, Greek, and Hebrew. Today, three degree candidates deliver an undergraduate Latin Oration, an undergraduate English Oration, and a graduate English Dissertation. Polished by prior coaching, these five-minute speeches are often eloquent, sometimes humorous, and largely free of bromides and clichés. The president then summons his deans to present degree candidates. At the end, as a kind of celebrity climax, he awards honorary degrees; the number ranges from seven to fourteen. By tradition—probably reflecting Harvard's low-church aversion to pomp—honorands are not "hooded with ceremonial attire." They must make do with a brief bow and a quick handshake as they accept their leatherbound diplomas.

Music by the Commencement Choir is an important element of the morning ceremony. Standard selections are anthems of Bach, William Tans'ur, Vaughan Williams, and Randall Thompson. At the conclusion, the entire assembly joins in the Latin words of the Harvard Hymn, and as the assembled company disbands, all of the church bells in the immediate vicinity ring out in chorus. So ends Commencement: not only a graduation exercise, but also an annual handover of responsibility for the University's welfare (in the words of "Fair Harvard") "from the Age that is past, / To the Age that is waiting before."

The Reverend Peter J. Gomes, Pusey Minister in the Memorial Church—whose invocations and benedictions have opened or closed the Commencement exercises for more than 30 years—has noted in an essay titled "These Festival Rites" that

> Someone, observing the rather casual dignity of the day, remarked that Commencement is more like a lawn party than a ballet, and a less charitable but more astute observer suggested that the vast assemblage in formation in the Old Yard was very much like that wonderfully chaotic game of croquet with flamingos and hedgehogs in *Alice in Wonderland.* First-time visitors to the scene are rather horrified at what appears to be rank confusion, but then they remember that this is, after all, Harvard, where conformity, even for self-preservation, has been elevated to the rank of an original sin. That it works at all is a tribute to patience and good will and the general sense that, come what may, the day is to be enjoyed.

Related entries: Bells; Diplomas; "Fair Harvard"; Honorary Degrees; Regalia; Songs and Marches; the Yard.

Consulting

To their traditional functions of teaching, research, and writing, many of today's academics add consulting. Some Harvard faculty members are as noted for outside activities as they are for classroom lectures. There's Alan Dershowitz, Felix Frankfurter Professor of Law, whose long list of celebrity clients in criminal cases includes O. J. Simpson, Mike Tyson, Claus von Bulow, and Michael Milken. There's Jeffrey Sachs, Harvard's former Galen Stone Professor of Trade, who drafted constitutions for Poland, Mongolia, and other former socialist countries in the 1990s. There's Rosabeth Moss Kanter, professor of business administration, who is said to earn upwards of $25,000 a day for talks at corporate meetings, clinics, and retreats. The fast-track lives of such faculty members inevitably expose them to charges that they must be short-changing their students. But when the *Wall Street Journal* accused

Dershowitz of "carrying on a big-money law practice under cover
of a professorship at Harvard," he countered that he taught two
courses per semester, and—excepting religious holidays—had
never missed a lecture in 20 years of Law School teaching.

To keep consulting activity within bounds, virtually all colleges
and universities impose some version of what is known at Harvard
as the "20 percent rule"—meaning that one day of the work week
can be given to external involvements. At the end of each academic
year, Harvard faculty members are required to file reports on their
outside activities, including the fees they've received.

President Derek Bok, who gave much thought to the pros and
cons of academic consulting, concluded that the positives could
outweigh the negatives, especially in the sciences. In *Beyond the
Ivory Tower* (1982), Bok wrote that "by traveling periodically to
corporations, academic scientists carry ideas, recent developments,
and critical judgments from the university to industry and thus encourage the process of technological development . . . At the same
time, consulting can provide useful information to university scientists concerning sophisticated research methods, new forms of
instrumentation, or even employment opportunities for graduate
students. More important still, consultants may discover practical
problems in industry that lead to challenging issues for basic research, as has occurred in fields such as materials science and solid-
state physics."

Among the first academic consultants of the modern era was
Edwin H. Strobel, Bemis Professor of International Law, who took
a leave of absence from Harvard Law School in 1903 to serve as
special adviser to the king of Siam (now Thailand). After his death
in Bangkok in 1908, Strobel was given a state funeral. Professor
Felix Frankfurter, who graduated from the Law School in that
year, served the Wilson, Harding, and Hoover administrations
by sending them bright young lawyers. Frankfurter became a close
friend and informal adviser to Franklin D. Roosevelt, and when
FDR won the White House in 1932, Frankfurter was described
as "a one-man recruiting agency for the New Deal." Roosevelt
was the first president to draw heavily on academic expertise
for a "brain trust." ("The country is being run by a group

of college professors," groused West Virginia Senator Henry Hat-field.)

With the entry of the United States into World War II, Harvard loaned scores of faculty members to government agencies. William L. Langer '15, PH.D. '22, Coolidge Professor of History, served as chief of the research and analysis branch of the Office of Strategic Services; after the war he helped shape regional studies centers that produced research data for government and industry. Many faculty members who stayed in Cambridge did military research. Chemist Louis Fieser developed incendiary bombs and napalm. Applied mathematician Howard Aiken, working with IBM and the navy, built the first large-scale computing machine. As a White House science adviser, President James B. Conant spent more than half his time in Washington and oversaw the top-secret program to plan and build an atomic bomb.

The war effort forged an effective working relationship between universities, government, and industry, and the Cold War institutionalized it. The creation of the National Science Foundation in 1951 reflected the government's new reliance on nonprofit institutions as sources of basic research. Newly developed "area studies" centers fed reports and data to governmental offices and agencies. The Center for International Affairs, founded in 1958, maintained an advisory service for developing countries. The academics associated with such centers logged a lot of travel time in their information-gathering and consulting roles.

After winning the presidency in 1960, John F. Kennedy stocked his administration with so many fellow alumni that Harvard was half-jokingly called "the fourth branch of government." More than a dozen senior faculty members were among the young president's top-level appointees or consultants. JFK saw the United States as a munificent provider of ideas, goods, and services to the free world; through area studies programs, special commissions, and Kennedy's most durable innovation, the Peace Corps, academics from Harvard and other universities shared their expertise on democratization, economic development, education, and health care with national agencies and private organizations on every continent.

In an increasingly global, technology-driven "information economy," the demand for specialists rose. The new environment led Harvard's faculties to review and tighten guidelines governing consultative activity. A policy statement adopted by the Faculty of Arts and Sciences includes this sweeping statement:

> With the acceptance of a full-time appointment . . . an individual makes a commitment to the University that is understood to be full-time in the most inclusive sense. Every member is expected to accord the University his or her primary professional loyalty, and to arrange outside obligations, financial interests, and activities so as not to conflict with this overriding commitment to the University.

Related entries: International Outreach; Research Centers and Institutes; Trademark Protection and Technology Transfer.

Continuing Education

Through the Harvard Summer School, the Extension School, and the Institute for Learning in Retirement, the University opens its resources to thousands of nontraditional students each year.

Summer School. The country's oldest academic summer session began as the outgrowth of a botany course for teachers initiated by Professor Asa Gray in 1871. By the turn of the century, more than 60 courses were offered and enrollment was approaching 800. The school's eight-week programs now enroll some 5,000 students, from every state and more than 90 foreign countries. They range from teenagers in the Harvard Summer Secondary School Program to retirees learning a language or building computer skills. Full-semester credit and noncredit course offerings span more than 30 liberal arts fields, as well as pre-medical, pre-law, and pre-business areas; intensive instruction in foreign languages; English as a second language; visual and environmental studies; expository, creative, and professional writing; and graduate programs in education.

The Summer Secondary School program is a magnet for academically talented sixteen-to-eighteen-year-olds, who enroll to take college-level courses for credit. Its College Choices program offers tours of other New England colleges, along with coaching on the composition of college application essays. The Summer School also administers the Harvard-Ukrainian Summer Institute and a study abroad plan that provides language instruction at outposts in Chile, China, Germany, Greece, and Italy.

Extension School. This large school, now in its centennial decade, has been described as Harvard's greatest community resource. It offers part-time study in the evenings, on an open-enrollment basis, to more than 14,000 students each year. Though more than a third live in Cambridge or Boston, others come from outlying communities and neighboring states, as well as from overseas. Three out of five extension students are women; three out of four have a bachelor's degree, and one out of five has earned a graduate degree. Students may choose from some 560 courses in more than 50 fields, and from a dozen degree or certificate programs. Fewer than ten percent of the school's students, however, seek degrees or certificates. The school's dean explains that "most enroll for a course or two each year, for personal enrichment or professional development."

"Distance learning," via the Internet, gives the school global outreach. Via streaming video and audio technologies, Internet courses instruct students throughout the country and in South America, Europe, the Middle East, and Asia.

The school is based at 51 Brattle Street, just off Brattle Square. With the exception of a few science courses that meet in the Medical Area in Boston, all classes are held within, or near, Harvard Yard. Most are taught at night, when classroom buildings are not being used for regular courses.

Institute for Learning in Retirement. Something of a newcomer, founded in 1977, this program offers its retirement-age members more than a hundred courses and study-group sessions in a typical year. Drawn from a broad spectrum of the Cambridge/Boston community, the membership includes professionals from such fields as law, medicine, the arts, government service, education, engineering, technology, and business. The courses—run entirely by institute members—have recently ranged from "Buckminster Fuller" to "Zoroastrianism," and from "W. E. B. DuBois" to "The Supreme Court in the Twenty-First Century."

The institute's membership has been capped at 500. Classroom space limitations were a factor, says its dean, but so were "the desire to maintain a sense of community and a spirit of collegiality in our comfortable but constrained quarters." The institute has been a model for similar programs throughout the country and the world. When it opened, with an initial enrollment of 92, there were few such initiatives in the United States. Its enrollment has since grown to more than 300.

The activities of the Summer School, the Extension School, and the Institute for Learning in Retirement are overseen by the University's Division of Continuing Education, formed in 1975 as a division of the Faculty of Arts and Sciences. All told, well over half a million people have participated in their programs. Taken together they express what President Charles W. Eliot no doubt had in mind when he stated, more than a century ago, that "it has been too much the custom to think of education as the affair of youth, and even of the earlier years of youth; but it really should be the work of the whole of life."

President Eliot, who lived to be 92, would have been cheered by the work of Mary Fasano of Braintree, Massachusetts. She left school in the seventh grade, toiled as a cotton-mill laborer, raised a family, and started high school at 71. Taking one Extension School course per semester, she went on to become the eldest student in Harvard history to earn a bachelor's degree, receiving her A.L.B. (Bachelor of Liberal Arts in Extension Studies) in 1997, when she was 89.

The continuing education dispensed by the Extension School is complemented by programs offered under the auspices of the Harvard Alumni Association. For the past quarter-century, the HAA's travel-study program has taken groups of alumni to almost every corner of the world, from Alaska to the Fiji Islands, in the company of scholars who serve as lecturers and guides. The HAA sponsors or co-sponsors nearly 40 such trips each year; the tab runs from about $2,000 per person to upwards of $8,000. Three or four times a year, a longstanding "Harvard Comes to . . ." series sends a half dozen faculty members and an upper-level administrator to major cities for day-long discussions of topical subjects. The HAA also holds one or two "Alumni Colleges," devoted to topics both current and historical, each year. These tightly packed colloquia offer alumni an opportunity to return to Cambridge for two days and to engage faculty members in give-and-take. A newer continuing education program, initiated in 2002, is an HAA Internet offering called harvard@home. It disseminates lectures and public addresses given by faculty members and administrators.

For the most part, Harvard's continuing education units are cash cows, bringing in substantial and much-needed revenue for the Faculty of Arts and Sciences.

Related entries: Alumni; Information Technology; Lectures; Virtual Harvard. *Related Websites:* www.dce.harvard.edu (Extension School); www.haa.harvard.edu (Harvard Alumni Association).

Core Curriculum

Since the late 1970s, candidates for the A.B. degree have been required to take a set number of Core Curriculum courses in each of seven broad areas: foreign cultures; historical studies; literature and arts; moral reasoning; quantitative reasoning; science; and social analysis. At the outset, there were some 80 Core courses, two-thirds of them newly organized. A quarter-century later, the number of course listings had doubled.

The development and phasing-in of the Core Curriculum, which took almost eight years, reflected a longstanding assumption that undergraduate education at Harvard should be both general and specific. Degree candidates are expected to have gained exposure to a fairly wide range of subjects and to have studied a particular field in some depth. Finding the best way to impart a truly general education, however, has given rise to much academic debate.

In the early years of the twentieth century, President A. Lawrence Lowell reined in the "free elective" system of his predecessor,

Charles W. Eliot, by imposing distribution and concentration requirements. A student was now required to take a given number of courses in departments outside a chosen area of concentration, though reasonably wide latitude was permitted in selecting those courses.

A signal change in the curriculum occurred soon after World War II. A senior faculty committee, convened in wartime to consider "the objectives of a general education in a free society," issued an influential report in the summer of 1945. Informally known as the "Red Book," it outlined a program of new courses divided into three areas: natural sciences, social sciences, and the humanities. Over the next five years, some 50 new General Education courses appeared in the course catalogue. All undergraduates had to take a specified number of these courses in each area, and for more than a decade they made up some of the College's most popular classes. Among them were Natural Sciences 5 ("The Nature of Living Things"), taught by George Wald, a future Nobel laureate; Humanities 3 ("The Rise of the Greek Classic"), taught by John H. Finley Jr.; Social Sciences 2 ("Western Thought and Institutions"), taught by Samuel Beer; and Social Sciences 11 ("East Asian Civilizations," affectionately dubbed "Rice Paddies") taught jointly by John K. Fairbank, Edwin O. Reischauer, Benjamin Schwartz, and Albert Craig.

By the 1960s, however, it was evident that the intellectual coherence and integrity of "Gen Ed" was unraveling. Critics noted a blurring of distinctions between Gen Ed courses and departmental offerings. Others assailed some for their lack of academic rigor. Administrators of the program found it increasingly difficult to recruit young teachers willing to give large Gen Ed courses outside their departments.

In the mid-1970s, incoming dean Henry Rosovsky urged the Faculty of Arts and Sciences to address the need for curricular reform. During the series of strongly argued debates that followed, two powerful personalities held things together. One was Dean Rosovsky, an economist with a well-honed understanding of academic politics; the other was President Derek Bok. Both felt strongly that Harvard undergraduates deserved a new kind of curriculum to prepare them for the fast-changing worlds of work, learning, and service they would soon enter.

The Core Curriculum took shape in the late 1970s, after almost four years of deliberation and debate. Its rationale would subsequently be explained in the packets sent to first-year students before their arrival. Harvard undergraduates, they would be told, need guidance in achieving the goal of becoming broadly educated; the faculty has a concomitant responsibility to guide them toward the knowledge, intellectual skills, and habits of thought that are the distinguishing traits of what Harvard's Commencement rhetoric calls "the fellowship of educated men and women."

The Core was a new departure. Though some faculty members had argued forcefully for the study of the "traditional canon," the new curriculum was not based on a mastery of ideas in Great Books. It did not prescribe the acquisition of particular bodies of information or the survey of current knowledge in certain fields. The Core did seek to introduce students to the major "approaches to knowledge" in areas that the faculty considered indispensable. Core courses were designed to demonstrate differing kinds of knowledge, explore differing forms of inquiry, suggest differing modes of analysis, and search out differing standards of value. No student was to graduate without some exposure to these various ways of "knowing."

The first Core courses appeared in the 1979–80 catalogue. They were largely new ones, constructed in conformance with specifically prescribed Core guidelines. Many became very popular. Representative of the current range of offerings are:

- Foreign Cultures 48 ("The Chinese Cultural Revolution"), Roderick MacFarquhar.
- Historical Study B-53/4 ("World War and Society in the 20th Century"), Charles Maier.
- Literature and Arts A-41 ("Shakespeare, the Later Plays"), Marjorie Garber.
- Literature and Arts B-51 ("First Nights: Five Performance Premières"), Thomas Kelly.

- Literature and Arts B-54 ("Chamber Music from Mozart to Ravel"), Robert Levin.
- Literature and Arts C-14 ("The Concept of the Hero in Greek Civilization"), Gregory Nagy.
- Literature and Arts C-61 ("The Rome of Augustus"), Richard Tarrant.
- Science A-35 ("Matter in the Universe"), Robert Kirshner.
- Moral Reasoning 22 ("Justice"), Michael Sandel.
- Social Analysis 68 ("Race, Class, and Poverty in Urban America"), William Julius Wilson.

It was not unusual for students to take Core courses out of intellectual curiosity rather than to fulfill curricular requirements. For them the Core Curriculum was an exhilarating and enlightening innovation. But from the beginning there were articulate critics of the Core, and by the late 1990s their number had grown. Some faculty members, especially in the sciences, had never accepted the program's rationale and had expressed concern that the Core's "dumbing down" of serious science might repel gifted students, who would prefer universities with less constricting requirements. Other faculty members claimed they could teach the same courses in the Core as the ones they offered departmentally and said they disliked teaching outside their departments.

Students also complained. Some chafed under constraints that forced them to take courses in unfamiliar terrain. Others criticized the program for offering courses that "lacked depth" or did not adopt a multicultural perspective. It was often said that Core courses enrolled too many students and that sections were poorly taught by indifferently trained graduate students. Finally, some student critics wanted a Core Curriculum that would enable them to engage with more of the Great Books. One *Crimson* editorial bluntly demanded, "Get Rid of the Core."

After periodic committee reviews, changes were made in some of the criteria for new courses and in the rules permitting students to meet Core requirements with departmental courses. With the appointment of a new dean, the Faculty of Arts and Sciences began a two-year curricular review in the fall of 2002. Whatever the outcome, some elements of the Core program seemed likely to survive.

Related entry: Harvard College. *Related Website:* www.courses.fas.harvard .edu/~core.

Crimson

Crimson was not always Harvard's color of choice. For generations, its diplomas were tied with blue ribbon. At the College's 1836 Bicentennial, the decorations were blue and white. "This was probably the survival of a medieval tradition that blue was the proper color of every faculty of Arts," explains the historian Samuel Eliot Morison in *Three Centuries of Harvard.*

Harvard crimson seems to have made its debut at the 1858 Boston City Regatta. College tutor Charles W. Eliot—who would become the University's president eleven years later—rowed in the Harvard boat. Before race day, he wrote later, he and a teammate shopped for silk bandannas for their fellow rowers to wear as distinguishing headgear. The fabric they selected was "of a handsome red hue." One of the bandannas, of a color that most people might accept as crimson, is preserved in the University Archives.

Magenta, a dye introduced in the 1860s, found favor for a time with Harvard's newly organized baseball club and with some of the crews. But in 1875 a majority of the undergraduate body voted to reaffirm the primacy of crimson. The editors of the student paper duly changed its name from *The Magenta* to *The Crimson,* declaring that "magenta is not now, and . . . never has been, the right color of Harvard."

Thirty-five years later, at the start of his presidency, A. Lawrence Lowell took a personal role in determining exactly what "the right color" should be. Working under his direct supervision, dye masters at a Watertown dry-cleaning company produced a hue that the new president dubbed "arterial red." In May 1910, the Harvard Corporation formally approved it as the University's official livery color.

Crimson is now extensively used as a signifier for pennants, doctoral gowns, neckties, football helmets, track singlets, and much else. Yale uses blue in a similar way. The coloristic distinction, however, is not universally understood. In the mid-1990s, the American Honda Motor Company offered car models in "Harvard Blue."

Related entries: Archives; Athletics; Harvard Crimson.

Crimson Key

Tours of Harvard Yard are a specialty of the Crimson Key Society, an undergraduate organization. Founded in 1948, primarily as a welcoming committee for visiting sports teams, the society recruits student guides who like talking about Harvard and its history. During term time, tours for the public depart twice a day from the Information Office in Holyoke Center; tours for the hundreds of official visitors who pass through Harvard each year are arranged through the University Marshal's Office. (The Admissions Office now runs its own tours for prospective applicants, but some of the leaders are Crimson Key members.) International groups make up an increasingly large component of the Crimson Key's public tours; some VIP tours are conducted in languages other than English.

In a typical year, approximately 3,000 visitors take tours during term time; another 12,000 take summer tours, conducted by "Keysters" and other student volunteers. The tours include stops at University Hall, Memorial Hall, the College Pump, Widener Library, and Harvard's three surviving eighteenth-century buildings (Massachusetts Hall, Wadsworth House, Holden Chapel). No tour is complete without a photo-op at the John Harvard statue, one of New England's most-visited tourist attractions.

The Crimson Key also runs tours during registration week, parents' weekends, and reunion week. In 1986, the year of Harvard's 350th anniversary celebration, the organization published a useful *Guidebook to Harvard University.*

Related entries: Admissions; College Pump; Holden Chapel; John Harvard—and His Statue; Massachusetts Hall; Memorial Hall; Wadsworth House; Widener Library; the Yard. *Related Websites:* www.marshal .harvard.edu; www.news.harvard.edu/guide/to_do.

D

Members of the Chun-Sa Troupe, one of Harvard's ethnic
dance groups, performing in Sanders Theatre.

Dance

Not so long ago, a mention of dance at Harvard would have meant house formals or waltz evenings. Those still exist and are usually well attended. But newer forms of dance activity now engage more than 600 students, faculty members, and alumni at centers throughout the University.

A program sponsored by the Office for the Arts offers courses in ballet, bodywork, jazz, modern dance, Pilates (an anatomically based system of body conditioning), tap, and West African dance, as well as improvisation and choreography. These courses sometimes require public performances as part of the curriculum. Most are given in the Rieman Dance Center, housed in the former Radcliffe gymnasium. Students practice and perform there, and occasionally take "Learning from Performers" master classes with professionals from ensembles such as the Paul Taylor Dance Company.

And yes: Harvard does field a ballroom dancing team.

Related entry: Arts. *Related Websites:* www.fas.harvard.edu/~dance; www.harvardballroom.org.

Deans

An old Harvard jest has it that a dean is someone who does not have enough sense to be a professor or enough friends to be president. But don't be fooled. Though there are many high-ranking people in the University hierarchy—the president, five vice presidents, members of the Corporation and Board of Overseers—the deans are among the most powerful in terms of authority, decision-making, and influence.

All ten graduate and professional schools, as well as the Faculty of Arts and Sciences, the College, the Extension School, and the Radcliffe Institute, are headed by deans. They lead their faculties and rule on appointments; they control budgets, raise funds, and set policies for degrees, departments, curriculum, and admission. True, it is the president who, after extensive consultation, appoints the deans themselves, and a dean serves "at the pleasure of the president." So there may be tensions in the power relationship. The president has a platform for leadership in higher education, and the vice presidents have the power to enforce policies of the central administration, but in matters of crucial importance to the schools, it's the deans, with the concurrence of their faculties, who decide major academic issues.

Deans come in varying shapes and sizes, and the schools differ in their nomenclature: there are associate deans, assistant deans, deans of administration, admission, development, finance, financial aid, deans of freshmen, and deans of academic planning, affirmative action, and student affairs. Because it is by far the largest school, the Faculty of Arts and Sciences has the most deans—some 40 or so. A smaller school may have only five or six.

At the highest levels, *the* dean of a school is ordinarily appointed from within a given faculty. There have been exceptions—at the Medical School, for instance—when a faculty member moved to another institution and later returned to become dean. But the usual assumption is that those who know a school from the inside are best qualified to lead it.

Perhaps because of their considerable power, deans receive their share of academic ribbing. At another major university, the saying is that it is the job of the faculty to think; the job of the president to make speeches; and the job of the dean to make sure that the president does not think and the faculty does not make speeches. It is said that a president of the University of Virginia once received a letter requesting a university speaker for an alumni club meeting. To the club's request that he not designate "anyone lower than a dean," the president is alleged to have replied that there was no one lower than a dean. A similar story has it that President A. Lawrence Lowell was asked to provide "a witty dean" for the annual meeting of a regional Harvard Club. Lowell purportedly responded that he was unable to supply such a dean, but that he did have two assistant deans who were half-wits and that he would gladly send both of them. And it was Lowell's successor, James B. Conant, who coined a new collective noun when he spoke of "a gripe of deans."

Related entry: Discipline.

Dental School

In numbers of students, the School of Dental Medicine is the smallest of Harvard's professional schools. But for anyone suffering from a toothache or an impacted wisdom tooth, the training of skilled dentists is by no means a minor matter.

Founded in 1867, Harvard's dental school was the first university-based institution of its kind in the United States and the first to have close ties with a major medical school. For the most part, dentists had been an untrained group, sometimes doing double duty as barbers or handymen. Now, for the first time, the education of dentists could draw on all the scholarly and scientific resources of an urban university. Initially located near the Massachusetts General Hospital in Boston, the school moved to its present location in the Harvard Medical Center in 1909. In addition to establishing high standards of professional treatment, its faculty members introduced a curriculum that required dental students to attend classes with medical students; to take courses in basic science and pathophysiology; and to take part in clinical programs in hospital wards and community health centers. The school's doctoral and postdoctoral programs were modeled on those of the Medical School.

The Dental School's greatest changes began to unfold in 1991. The dean announced a comprehensive revision of the predoctoral curriculum, bringing the school into line with the Medical School's New Pathway program. The new curriculum, he explained, "culminates in the awarding of the D.M.D. after four years of training. This curriculum utilizes the problem-based methodology of learning. Students develop skills in critical thinking and problem-solving to enhance their abilities in clinical diagnosis, treatment, planning, and delivery of clinical care. In addition, the conceptual and technical aspects of dentistry are taught by utilizing a comprehensive approach to patient care, as opposed to a discipline-based or departmental approach. As before, research remains an additional component of the curriculum. Each student conducts a research project over the four-year period."

The school has a student body of just over 200. It has about 40 full-time faculty members, and another 80 or so whose teaching

or advising is part-time. Admission to the school involves a rigorous process of screening and interviews. International and minority students are strongly encouraged to apply. About a quarter of
those who enroll are from abroad, and one-third are minority
members.

The training of dentists today must keep pace with contemporary practice. Thanks to the widespread use of fluoride in public
water supplies, far fewer cavities and tooth-decay problems require attention. Instead, cleaning and preventive measures have
joined oral surgery as the major activities of most dentists. The
current programs of the Dental School reflect these developments.
Beyond these high-level training programs, the Dental School is
particularly characterized by its emphasis on research, focusing on
such areas as implants, new materials, epidemiology, and micro-
biology.

Related entries: Diversity; Medical School. *Related Website:*
www.hsdm.med.harvard.edu.

Dining Services

Harvard is in the food purchasing and distribution business in a
big way. On average, 25,000 meals are served daily during term-
time, in thirteen house dining halls and twelve campus restaurants and catering services in Cambridge and Boston. That works
out to roughly five million meals a year—a total that doesn't include all the fast food sold in Harvard's many grills and cafeterias.
Feeding Harvard requires more than 600 chefs, service staff, dining room attendants, washing machine operators, and supervisors.
The largest food-dispensing operations are the Culinary Support
Group (CSG), off JFK Street in Cambridge, and Memorial Hall's
Annenberg dining commons, a few minutes' walk to the north.

The CSG prepares soups, sauces, marinated meats, composed
salads, and various *mis en place* for the recently renovated finishing kitchens in the undergraduate houses and restaurants. Some of
the victuals are delivered in wagonloads, pulled by electric carts
through a quarter-mile-long network of tunnels that link the river
houses. Computer-based planning controls this delivery system.

Annenberg, opened in 1996, has become the flagship of Harvard dining halls. Some 1,600 first-year students eat there each day. After the completion of Memorial Hall in 1874, its Great Hall served as the College's main dining commons; patronage later dwindled as "eating around" came into vogue, and the commons closed in 1926. In the 1930s the newly built undergraduate houses, each with its own dining hall, took over the task of feeding upperclassmen. Freshmen ate at the Harvard Union on Quincy Street. Memorial Hall was still used for glittering University banquets, including the annual honorary degree dinner in June. Through the generosity of former Harvard parent Walter Annenberg, the space was meticulously restored in the mid-1990s and renamed in honor of the Annenbergs' late son Roger '62.

Fifty years ago, Harvard dining rooms were conventional places where students in coats and ties ate meals of limited gastronomic appeal. Dress codes are now long gone, and each dining room competes for preeminence in serving up varied food styles. In a single month, a house dining room may offer kosher, soul, Asian, Mexican, African, and Caribbean food. Though complaints about "institutional food" are still heard, most students seem pleasantly surprised by the variety and quality of Harvard's menus.

Even so, no University dining hall is likely to match the opulent offerings of a century earlier. At Annenberg Hall's inaugural dinner in 1996, a reproduction of a Memorial Hall menu from the early 1900s was provided as a keepsake. It offered a choice of four soups, including green turtle; four kinds of fish, as well as oysters and clams; twelve broiled items, among them mutton chops; stewed kidneys in wine sauce, tripe, sweetbreads, and pigs' feet; such game delicacies as prairie chicken, reed birds, canvasback duck, quail, partridge, and Lake Erie teal; and lambs' and beef tongues as cold dishes. For carnivores, those were the days of elegant dining at Harvard.

Culinary industry professionals and independent tasters periodically sample the fare served at house and freshman dining halls. In 2003 the Harvard University Dining Services won gold medals in two competitions sponsored by the American Culinary Federation. The same year brought a grand prize for the Dining Services' Crimson Catering menu and a second place for its undergraduate menu from the National Association of College and University Food Services; a Gold Quill Award from the National Association of Business Communicators; and a Leadership Award from *Food Management* magazine.

Related entries: Harvard Union; Houses; Memorial Hall; Underground.
Related Website: www.dining.harvard.edu.

Diplomas

Until the nineteenth century, it was a do-it-yourself proposition: a graduate had to have his diploma drawn up by a local "engrosser," using language specified by the Harvard Corporation. He then submitted it, with a fee, for signing and sealing by the president of Harvard College. In 1813, adopting a practice that Yale had followed for more than a century, the President and Fellows voted to allow the diploma to be printed from an engraved plate and issued "for such charges as the Corporation shall determine."

The first diploma was printed on vellum parchment, with a light blue ribbon affixed by the University's seal in wax. Since then, the design and shape of the baccalaureate diploma have been altered at intervals, most notably in 1860, 1903, 1935, 1961, and 1962. (The format changes are traced in detail in *The Harvard B.A. Diploma, 1813–2000,* a limited-edition monograph by J. F. Coakley '68.) Harvard diplomas were personally signed by the president until the 1890s, when a facsimile signature was substituted. As an economy measure, paper replaced sheepskin in the 1930s.

By vote of the faculty, the language of the diploma was changed from Latin to English in 1961, touching off an April "diploma riot." (Showing that he could dish it out as well as take it, President Nathan Pusey, a classicist, emerged from his study to address the demonstrators in Latin; unmoved and largely uncomprehending, they marched off chanting, "Latin *si,* Pusey *no!*") Aesthetically, Harvard's first English-language diploma was a washout: devoid of ornamentation, no longer in the traditional horizontal format, its unembellished text appeared on a sheet the size of ordinary office paper. To Philip Hofer, the Houghton Library's curator of printing and graphic arts, "it looked like the luncheon menu at the Faculty Club." A year later the dud diploma was supplanted by a horizontal design created by the 78-year-old artist Rudolph Ruzicka. Graduates of the class of 1961 were invited to exchange their underwhelming diplomas for the new model. That version is still in use today; only the signature lines have changed. The A.B. diplomas now bear the facsimile signatures of the president of Harvard and the dean of Harvard College, and the genuine signatures of house masters and co-masters.

Over the past half-century, the production of Harvard's diplomas has been speeded and simplified by evolutionary changes in printing technology. From 1918 until 1960, every A.B. diploma was engrossed by Joseph R. Rosen Jr., a Boston penman who, from autumn until June, labored over his work from 4 A.M. to 10 P.M., bedding down on a cot in his cramped office. With the advent of the English version in 1961, Harvard's Printing Office began producing all diplomas by letterpress, and did so for twenty years. After a relatively short interval in which offset lithography was the method of choice, the Printing Office switched to a computer-based system in 1990. A complex program that integrates data-processing and high-quality electrostatic printing now does the entire job in one long weekend.

Related entries: Arms; Commencement.

Discipline

"When I was first asked to come to this university," fumed President Edward Everett, "I supposed I was to be the head of the largest and most famous institution in America. I have been disappointed. I find myself the sub-master of an ill-disciplined *school*." For two centuries, when Harvard was still small, the president was virtually the only officer to administer student discipline. As the representative of the Corporation, he had to cope with countless infractions of the College's many strict and petty regulations. It was a thankless job, and in Everett's case, three years at it (1846–1849) were enough.

Undergraduate ingenuity and experimentation, coupled with the temptation to put elders to the test, may have stayed fairly constant over the years. But today's standards of acceptable behavior, and the degree of personal freedom now extended to students, would surely have startled President Everett. Just as startling would be the elaborate mechanisms, involving large numbers of University personnel, that are now used to maintain order and decorum.

By the last third of the nineteenth century, the College had grown large enough that the president could no longer act as disciplinarian. The office of dean of Harvard College was established in 1870, relieving the newly installed president, Charles William Eliot, of much formal administrative work, including discipline. Shortly thereafter, the first University-wide statutes were adopted. One of them formalized the rule that each faculty was responsible for enforcing discipline within its own area. That power could be delegated to committees, and that has been done ever since.

At the academic level, the most common infractions involve some form of dishonesty: plagiarism, cheating, fraud, imposture, and such. The most complex and extensive disciplinary machinery for dealing with these transgressions is the College's. Authority resides mainly in the Administrative Board, a large body made up of assistant deans of freshmen, senior tutors of the houses, teaching members of the Faculty of Arts and Sciences, and senior administrators. The dean of the College is chairman. The Ad Board meets weekly throughout the academic year. It follows rules enacted by the faculty, but it also has the option of invoking or deviating from historical precedents that may fall outside those rules.

The Ad Board deals with cases that range from unsatisfactory academic performance, plagiarism, and cheating to alcohol abuse, theft, vandalism, drug dealing, and sexual assault. In a disciplinary hearing, an assistant dean of freshmen or senior tutor presents the facts of the case, both orally and in writing, and represents the student whose case is under review. Lying about an infraction weighs heavily against the accused. Education is a key part of the board's role. Students are expected to gain from the disciplinary experience a fuller understanding of maturity, responsibility, and self-management. Elaborate precautions are taken to protect rights of confidentiality. Names of disciplined students only rarely come to light.

The Ad Board can act in one of four ways: no action; warning; probation for a set limit of time; and requirement to withdraw. The more serious punishments are probation and enforced absence from Harvard. Probation means that a student must be especially conscientious about academic performance and personal conduct. Requirement to withdraw is imposed for the most serious academic and behavioral deficiencies; a year off is the usual penalty. To be readmitted, the student must show that he or she has used the time off productively.

Dismissal or expulsion cannot be delegated to a committee: both call for a faculty vote. Each requires severance from the University, but there is a critical difference. Dismissal does not preclude a changed and contrite student's eventual readmission, should the faculty assent. Expulsion means that the student can never return. Folklore has it that his or her name is expunged from all records, but in fact the registrar's records are never destroyed. Indeed, administrative error has sometimes allowed an expelled student's name to appear in the *Alumni Directory*. In one notorious case, the expellee was a regular at reunions and regional meetings.

Prior to the reforms brought on by the upheavals of the 1960s and 1970s, the Ad Board was viewed as mysterious and arbitrary, in some ways resembling a star chamber. Students never appeared in person. The board saw itself as benign, dispensing judgments in a humane and careful way, pointedly giving students the benefit of the doubt. But the perception among students was different; the meting-out of justice behind closed doors was understandably suspect. This has led to radical changes in the system. Ad Board rules have been liberalized. Students now have the right to appeal a decision. In some disciplinary cases, they may have the option of meeting with the board and the opportunity to have a personal advisor present. Complaints are still heard that the board does not allow cross-questioning, bars lawyers from its proceedings, and does not provide for judgment by peers.

Complementing the Ad Board is the Student-Faculty Judicial Board, created in 1987 to deal with nonacademic disciplinary issues for which the Ad Board's procedures seemed inadequate. Since its inception, this board has been convened only once.

Every graduate and professional school has some sort of formal machinery for dealing with student misconduct. Students admitted to these schools are assumed to be mature and responsible citizens. Much of the disciplinary responsibility falls to administrative deans. Some schools use administrative boards, others committees of the faculty, sometimes including students.

The disturbances of the late 1960s led to a University-wide Statement of Rights and Responsibilities. The fundamental premise is that there are "certain values which are essential to [the University's] nature as an academic community. Among these are freedom of speech and academic freedom, freedom from personal force and violence, and freedom of movement." These values had been severely transgressed by a significant number of protesting students and a few sympathetic faculty members.

Sexual harassment is a newer category of grave misbehavior. Unlike most other offenses, it is defined at length and in great detail. The University and each faculty have adopted detailed definitions of inappropriate interpersonal conduct, whether it involves students only, faculty members and students, or faculty members exclusively. Many of the professional schools have sexual harassment officers. Ordinarily the first recourse is an attempt to resolve the matter informally; failing that, there is access to formal action. This area of misconduct is complicated by the fact that rape and sexual assault are subject to legal action by the Commonwealth of Massachusetts.

Faculty members may be subject to disciplinary action for various kinds of malfeasance, such as financial impropriety, neglect of duty, or sexual harassment. Informal settlement is the most common resolution. In some cases there is a possibility that the American Association of University Professors, always sensitive to potential violations of tenure, may intervene. Every attempt is made to maintain confidentiality. Harvard has ways of handling unpleasantness quietly.

Related entries: Deans; Presidents.

Diversity

Its admissions and financial aid programs, its cosmopolitan ethos, and, yes, its reputation for diversity have made Harvard an ever more diverse place. The process has been helped along by powerful social movements—civil rights, feminism, and gay and lesbian activism; by the liberalization of U.S. immigration laws in 1965; and by concurrent changes in the demographics of the larger society.

Long before diversity became a buzzword, Harvard was known for its heterogeneous mix of students, its eccentric professors and campus characters, and its toleration of what the philosopher William James admiringly called "its undisciplinables." By the end of the nineteenth century, the College had the best-funded financial aid program of any private institution and was using it to assemble an increasingly national student body. Improvements in rail and water transportation made Cambridge accessible to students in far-off states and from abroad; President Charles W. Eliot's refusal to raise tuition fees kept the College open to scholars of modest means. The separate but supposedly equal "Annex," Radcliffe College, was advancing the higher education of women. In the twentieth century's first decade, Harvard enrolled students from all 48 states and 30 foreign countries. A Boston donor had created a $10,000 scholarship fund for students from China; the Chinese Club had 31 members. At a time when Yale, Princeton, and other elite colleges would not accept African-Americans, Harvard did, and it had a dozen or so. The proportion of Jewish students had reached 7 percent and was steadily rising.

The years after World War II brought marked changes in the size and composition of the College, as the G.I. Bill of Rights opened Harvard classrooms to thousands of veterans. Many were from blue-collar or rural backgrounds and often were the first in their families to seek a college education. Other turning points came in the 1960s and 1970s, when the admissions offices of the College and graduate schools responded to the civil rights movement with programs aimed at raising the number of African-American, Hispanic/Latino, and Native American applicants, and when the melding of the Harvard and Radcliffe admissions offices paved the way for a policy change that quadrupled the presence of women in the College. The University's affirmative action program, begun in 1970, increased the presence of women and minority members within every faculty rank and at all administrative staff levels. Harvard also adopted anti-discrimination statutes protecting once-marginal members of the University community: minority members, people with disabilities, and gays and lesbians.

In the wake of the social upheavals of the 1960s and early 1970s, when students sought to express their individuality—and their disdain for the establishment—through nontraditional modes of dress (jeans, muu muus, dashikis), the backgrounds of the students themselves were increasingly nontraditional. "The faces in the Yard," wrote *Harvard Magazine* contributing editor Jim Harrison in a 1986 photoessay, "reveal a range of ethnicity as diverse as the first dozen names in the student telephone book—Aamoth, Aaronoff, Abati, Abbasi, Abbey, Abel, Abercrombie, Abers, Ablow, Abney, Aboudi, Abou-Zamzam." And more nontraditional students were arriving. These were the children of the first generation of Asians and Indians to become U.S. citizens after the passage of the 1965 Immigration Act, which ended the discriminatory quotas that had barred immigrants from the Far East for four decades. These hard-working and accomplished students distinguished themselves academically, and their presence added to Harvard's religious diversity: Muslim, Hindu, Buddhist, and other non-Christian groups grew in size and visibility. Academic rites like the senior-class Baccalaureate, Class Day, and Phi Beta Kappa Literary Exercises began to include invocations, prayers, and hymns from sacred texts such as the Qur'an and Rig-Veda.

Today, Harvard's largest ethnic minority is composed of students whose identity is classified as "Asian/Pacific Islands." In recent years these students have made up about 17 percent of the College's population and about 12 percent of the University's. For students classified as Black/Non-Hispanic, the corresponding figures are 8 percent and 6 percent; for Hispanics, 8 percent and 5 percent; and for Native Americans, 1 percent (College and University). The proportion of students classified as White/Non-Hispanic is now about 45 percent in the College and 41 percent University-wide.

Since the advent of jet travel in the 1950s, the proportion of students coming to Harvard from other countries has risen steadily. About 7 percent of students in the College, and almost 20 percent University-wide, reside outside the United States. Canada, with 492 students, sends the largest number to Harvard, according to tables for the academic year 2002–2003. But China was a perhaps surprising second, with 337 students. Next came South Korea (207), the United Kingdom (174), Japan (134), Germany (124), and India (112). In all, nearly 140 nations were represented. Among the 50 or more ethnic groups with undergraduate and graduate student membership are the Caribbean Club, Hong Kong Club, Irish Cultural Society, Korean Americans for Community and Culture, Persian Society, Philippine Forum, Romanian Society, Teatro Estudiantil Latino, Tibetan Connection, and the Turkish Cultural Society.

Related entries: Aab; Admissions; Affirmative Action; Alumni; Characters; Fashion; Firsts (Men); Firsts (Women); Gay and Lesbian; "Godless Harvard"; Harvard Foundation; International Outreach.

Divinity School

Harvard's second oldest professional school (after the Medical School) was founded in 1816 to prepare candidates for the Christian ministry. Though it was and is nondenominational, its earliest students and faculty members were mostly Unitarian. Today the school views itself as a place where men and women from a wide variety of ethnic, cultural, and religious backgrounds study Christian and Jewish scripture, traditions, and literature alongside other world religious and value systems. Among its almost 500 students and 40 faculty members are members of the Jewish, Muslim, Hindu, and Buddhist faiths. Nearly 60 percent of the student body are women, and almost 10 percent of those enrolled come from countries outside the United States. The school's constituent parts include an interschool Center for World Religions and a program of Women's Studies in Religion. In addition to the *Harvard Divinity School Bulletin,* issued three times a year, the school publishes two scholarly journals: the *Harvard Theological Review* and the *Journal of Feminist Studies in Religion.*

Essentially the smallest of the professional schools, with an endowment of about $325 million (roughly one-quarter the size of the Business School's), the Divinity School occupies five buildings on the University's perimeter, northeast of the Law School, the science laboratories, and the museums. While the school remains a leader among university schools of theology, its status at Harvard sometimes seems problematic. Despite its ties to other faculties in such fields as archaeology, history, languages, and philosophy, the fit between faith and reason in a university setting has not always been a comfortable one. In consequence, the school has been subjected to repeated reviews and reorganizations over the years. Twice, in fact, the University has come close to divesting itself of the school.

The most recent instance was in the 1940s, when President James Conant—facing a vexed financial situation, low student morale, and criticisms that the school was not at the theological forefront—considered transferring it to Oberlin College. In the end, a special commission recommended an ambitious fund-raising effort to invigorate the school. Its state changed for the better with the arrival in 1953 of Conant's successor, Nathan Marsh Pusey. A committed Episcopal layman, Pusey took a particular interest in the Divinity School, spearheading its fund drive and enlarging and improving its faculty. Pusey's most illustrious appointments were the noted theologians Paul Tillich, who received a University Professorship, and Reinhold Niebuhr, who held a visiting professorship for two years.

From the latter part of the nineteenth century until comparatively recently, pastoral training at the Divinity School was clearly subordinate to critical historical study. In the mid-1970s, however, the school began to renew its commitment to educate men and women for service as leaders in religious life and thought, as ministers, teachers, or social activists. There are two principal master's degree tracks—one for students planning to enter the ministry, the other for those with a general interest in religion—as well as a doctoral program in religious and theological studies.

Of the school's handful of buildings, the most notable is Divinity Hall (1825), reminiscent of Bulfinch in its architectural styling. Until the nineteenth century it was the school's only building, providing classrooms, a chapel, library, and dormitory rooms. Andover Hall (1911), a neo-Gothic structure of gray granite, dominates the school's cluster of buildings; it houses faculty and administrative offices, classrooms, and a liturgically neutral chapel. The 500,000-volume Andover-Harvard Theological Library combines with other Harvard collections to form one of this country's largest and strongest theological libraries.

William A. Graham Jr., Murray A. Albertson Professor of Middle Eastern Studies in the Faculty of Arts and Sciences and John Lord O'Brian Professor of Divinity, was named dean in 2002. He is the first layman in the school's long history to hold the deanship.

Related entries: Firsts (Women); "Godless Harvard." *Related Website:* www.hds.harvard.edu.

Dropouts

There are different ways of leaving Harvard. Graduating is generally considered a good one. Dropping out is not necessarily bad. Many talented and subsequently successful students have left the premises, temporarily or permanently, before completing their degrees.

"Stopping out" is a temporary mode of departure. An estimated 15 percent of undergraduates, feeling burned out at some point during their four years of study, opt to take a term or two off. Most return with renewed motivation. Since the 1960s, the dean's office has encouraged stopping out as an antidote to academic malaise.

To be bounced is the least happy way to clear out. To qualify, it helps to be found seriously derelict in academic obligations or to have broken a major College rule or state law. Still, many a fired student has gone on to lead a life of achievement and service.

The most famous of Harvard's dropouts may be William H.

Gates III, founder, chairman, and chief software architect of Microsoft Corporation. He enrolled in 1973 and as a sophomore wrote programming language for what would be the first wave of personal computers. In his senior year he left Harvard to focus on Microsoft, which soon became a high-tech colossus and made Gates the world's richest man. (Considerate of their alma mater, Gates and his business partner Steven Ballmer '77 have been generous donors to Harvard.)

Another renowned dropout was the inventor, businessman, and polymath Edwin H. Land. He entered the College in 1926, stopped out for two years, returned once more, and left for good in 1932 to perform experiments, invent, and found the Polaroid Corporation. The company opened up the field of instant photography with the Polaroid Land Camera, and Land himself eventually held more than 500 American patents.

Unlike Gates and Land, William Randolph Hearst, class of 1886, left under a cloud. As an undergraduate, he is said to have partied a lot and studied little. He also worked on the *Lampoon's* business staff. When the young jokester sent engraved chamberpots to faculty members as Christmas gifts, the recipients took umbrage and Hearst was expelled. A quarter of a century later, the powerful publisher paid for the *Lampoon's* castle-like clubhouse on Mount Auburn Street. And his youthful excesses did not keep the College Admissions Office from accepting later generations of Hearsts.

R. Buckminster Fuller, philosopher, inventor, and designer of the geodesic dome, was bounced from Harvard not once but twice. He entered with the class of 1917. Dropout writers, poets, singers, and actors constitute a class unto themselves. A partial list would include the essayist Logan Pearsall Smith, class of 1888; author, playwright, and poet Gertrude Stein, Radcliffe class of 1897; and a passle of poets: Edwin Arlington Robinson, class of 1895; Robert Frost '01; Wallace Stevens '02; Ogden Nash '24; and Robert Lowell and Delmore Schwartz '39. Among performing artists who didn't stay the course are folksinger Pete Seeger '40; singer and guitarist Bonnie Raitt '72; and actor and screenwriter Matt Damon '92.

Recognizing what Frost, Fuller, Land, Lowell, and other of her lapsed progeny had achieved without a diploma, Harvard later granted them degrees *honoris causa*—as did other institutions of higher learning. On receiving an LL.D. from New England College, in Henniker, New Hampshire, in 1967, the irrepressible Ogden Nash responded in characteristically free-form verse:

> I'd rather, if I dared or dast,
> Conceal my academic past,
> But the horrid truth is bound to pop out;
> You behold in me a Harvard dropout.
> With freshman year my studies ended,
> But since I wasn't fired or suspended,
> I could knock today on the Dean's front door
> And be a full-fledged sophomore.
> But why should I toil two years, or three,
> To gain a simple B. A. degree?
> I needn't be by Brahmins buffeted
> To gain a distinction much more coveted,
> For home in New Hampshire, here in Henniker,
> Are philosophers wise as Plato or Seneca
> Whose sensitive nerves were so unstrung
> By my losing fight with the mother tongue
> That they raised me up beside my betters
> And pronounced me to be a Doctor of Letters.
> How fitting—for letters gave me my start;
> I know most of the alphabet by heart.
> Spurred on by the honor you've done me this fall,
> I'm going to dig in and learn it all.
> You've been kind to this synthetic Yankee;
> Thankee.

Related entries: Discipline; Honorary Degrees; Lampoon.

Dumbarton Oaks

For the historically minded, the name of this Washington, D.C., research center will recall the four-power conference that laid the groundwork for the United Nations in the summer of 1944. For the visually minded, it may evoke the splendors of a secluded Georgetown estate whose formal gardens are a national treasure. For landscape architects and scholars of antiquity and later times, it denotes collections that are unmatched in this country.

The centerpiece of the estate is a historic mansion built in 1800 and acquired by Robert Woods Bliss and his wife, Mildred, in 1919. Bliss, a retired diplomat, collector, philanthropist, and member of the class of 1900, conveyed the property to Harvard in 1940. At his death in 1962, the University received his distinguished collections of sculptures and artifacts from pre-Columbian Mexico, Central America, and South America, as well as his library of pre-Columbian art and archaeology. The collections were housed in a modern wing designed by Philip Johnson '30, B. ARCH. '43.

The Dumbarton Oaks collections, used by scholars from all over the world, represent three fields of specialized interest:

• *Byzantine studies,* bringing together printed and other historical and cultural resources from the fifth and sixth centuries A.D. to the sixteenth century.

• *Pre-Columbian studies,* covering the art and archaeology of Mesoamerica, the Intermediate Era, and the Andes, up to 1492 and extending into the early colonial period.

• *Landscape studies and garden history,* emphasizing exemplary gardens of the western world.

Dumbarton Oaks's elaborate gardens were especially dear to Mildred Bliss, who worked closely with the landscape gardener Beatrix Farrand to enlarge and refine them. ("What a good time we had making our garden pudding," Farrand wrote to Mrs. Bliss.) Making the most of the land's steep elevation, they created terraced lawns, ornamental stairways, and paths winding past pools, a pebble garden, and groves of trees. Plantings of broad-leaf evergreen, yew, holly, and boxwoods abound. Open to the public during daylight hours, this elegant habitat provides a feast for the senses.

During World War II, Dumbarton Oaks was the Washington base for Harvard president James B. Conant, who spent more than half his time as a top-level governmental science adviser. In the spring of 1944 Conant offered the estate to Secretary of State Cordell Hull as the site of talks aimed at planning an international peacekeeping organization to succeed the League of Nations. Hull convened the historic six-week session—attended by delegates from Great Britain, the Soviet Union, China, and the United States—in the music room of the mansion on August 21, 1944.

Related entry: Harvard Elsewhere. *Related Website:* www.doaks.org.

E

A part of Harvard that is now extinct, the octagonal
Thayer Commons railroad station stood near the
Law School. It was demolished in 1883.

Ed School

With the nation facing the greatest teacher shortage in its history, what will it take to form, train, and retain the next generation of teachers? What are the best ways to introduce online and Web-based instruction for students of varying ages? These are a few of the pressing questions under debate at the Graduate School of Education (HGSE).

In most respects the Ed School is one of the University's smallest graduate schools: traditionally, it has had the most meager endowment. Yet the size of its alumni body—roughly 22,000—makes it one of Harvard's Big Three, behind Business and Law. In contrast to the origins of most of the graduate and professional schools, its inception was tentative and diffuse. The Summer School, established five years after President Eliot's installation in 1869, enrolled many teachers who wished to learn more about the subjects they taught and about new educational theories and practices. In the 1890s a non-degree-granting program began under the aegis of the Graduate School of Arts and Sciences; unlike other Harvard graduate programs, it admitted women. In 1906 the Faculty of Arts and Sciences created a "division of education," and in 1920, under President Lowell, it was reborn as an autonomous Graduate School of Education, with its own dean, faculty, courses, and budget.

Yet the new school faced certain challenges from the start. One was what would now be called "mission diffusion." Another was limited financial support and its corollary, budgetary impoverishment. Similar difficulties have afflicted Harvard's other small schools, Divinity and Design.

The School of Education has always had to face the inevitable dichotomy between practice and research. Should it train teachers and other practitioners for vocations in public-school education? Or should it pursue the loftier and more scholarly goal of researching the principles of education and the biological roots of learning, while examining styles of educational administration and public policy? Over time, this persistent tension was to some extent reconciled by various deans and by the interventions of Harvard presidents. President Lowell's successor, James Conant, gave the school strong support because he believed primary and secondary education was the key to preventing the great social upheaval that might occur if equality of opportunity were not made available to all. Under his leadership, and that of some young, strong-minded deans, the school became a nationally recognized center for the training of young teachers, as well as for research in such fields as the psychology of learning, the relation of schools to urban society, the politics of educational policy formation, and the use of new technologies in pedagogy, curriculum development, and counseling. For the foreseeable future, the answer to the school's identity problem appears to be "both/and" rather than "either/or."

There are good reasons for the school's persistent penury. In contradistinction to the alumni of the Business and Law schools, its graduates—largely teachers and administrators—are rarely able to make substantial gifts or grants to the school. Another sticking point is the belief of many that teacher training and education in general should be a responsibility of local, state, and federal government. Government funding of Ed School projects over the years has in fact been significant, but it has also been variable and unpredictable. Taking all of this into account, a recent dean of the school led a capital campaign that raised a record-breaking $111 million, assuring some stability in the early decades of the twenty-first century.

The school currently enrolls some 1,200 students, most of them full-time. Many are teachers or administrators, but some come from related professional fields like community service and educational media. About three-quarters are women; nearly a quarter are minority members; and more than 10 percent are from other countries. The school has the full-time equivalent of 50 faculty members, who give a variety of popular courses, ranging from Howard Gardner's "Cognitive and Symbolic Development" to Sara Lawrence-Lightfoot's "The Sociology of Education: The Culture of Schools."

The school offers two major degree programs, a Certificate of Advanced Study, and non-degree and special tracks.

Related entry: Virtual Harvard. *Related Website:* www.gse.harvard.edu.

Elmwood

The president of Harvard lives at Elmwood, a two-century-old High Georgian-style manse near the intersection of Mount Auburn and Elmwood streets, a mile and a half west of Harvard Square. Elmwood became the official residence when Derek Bok assumed the presidency in 1971. The former President's House at 17 Quincy Street had been an occasional focus for antiwar protests, so Bok and his wife, Sissela, decided to shield their young children from potential disturbances by making Elmwood their home.

The house has had an extraordinary history. Set on a gentle rise with a commanding view of the Charles River salt marshes, it was built in 1767 for Thomas Oliver, class of 1753. Oliver, a Tory, was the son of a prosperous West Indies merchant, an amateur poet, and later lieutenant governor of the province of Massachusetts. In September 1774, seven months before the start of the Revolutionary War, thousands of angry patriots surrounded the house and forced Oliver to resign as presiding officer of the governor's council. A week later, he and his family left Elmwood and moved to Boston. During the siege of Boston in 1776, the Continental Army used the house as a hospital; three years later—along with other fine Tory mansions in Cambridge—it was confiscated and sold at auction as the property of "a notorious conspirator."

In 1787, Elmwood was resold to Elbridge Gerry, class of 1762, a signer of the Declaration of Independence, two-term governor of Massachusetts, and vice president under James Madison. Gerry's name lives on in "gerrymandering," an opprobrious term for a form of political redistricting (which, ironically, he opposed). Gerry took the oath for the vice presidency in his Elmwood study in 1813 and died in office the following year. Gerry's widow sold Elmwood to a Boston clergyman, the Reverend Charles Lowell, class of 1800, in 1818. His youngest son, the poet James Russell Lowell, class of 1838, was born there and made it his home for much of his life.

Lowell described Elmwood as "the seat of [his] inspiration." "It is a pleasant old house, isn't it?" he wrote to the poet and novelist

Thomas Bailey Aldrich, who had leased Elmwood while Lowell and his wife, Frances, were staying in Europe. "Doesn't elbow one, as it were. It will make a frightful conservative of you before you know it. It was born a Tory and will die so. Don't get too used to it. I often wish I had not grown into it so. I am not happy anywhere else." When Lowell was in residence, students were welcomed to Elmwood, and young poets came there for advice. Lowell also entertained a procession of literary figures, among them Charles Dickens, William Dean Howells, and his neighbor Henry Wadsworth Longfellow, who commemorated one of his visits in a poem called "The Herons of Elmwood."

Lowell died in 1891, and the house and most of the adjacent land remained the property of his heirs until 1920. In that year, the archaeologist and art historian A. Kingsley Porter became professor of fine arts at Harvard. For five years he lived at Elmwood, and in 1925 he purchased the estate. Porter held graduate seminars on the top floor, invited students for tea and talk, and maintained the tradition of high-level entertaining. Dinners at Elmwood were always patricianly elegant, and in deference to the past, all downstairs rooms continued to be illuminated by gaslights and candles. After Porter's sudden death in 1933, Mrs. Porter kept Elmwood's doors open to students and faculty friends. When she died in 1962, the house was left to Harvard. Under the terms of Professor Porter's will, the bequest brought with it a $100,000 trust fund for preservation and maintenance.

The Harvard Corporation designated the house as the residence of the dean of the Faculty of Arts and Sciences and as a venue for academic and scholarly conferences. After repairs and restorations, Dean Franklin L. Ford and his family moved in and stayed until 1970, when Dean Ford, a historian, resigned to resume his scholarly research and teaching. With the Bok family in residence the next year, the Office of the Governing Boards took over the former President's House at 17 Quincy Street.

Elmwood's interior has recently been remodeled again, this time in the style of the period in which the house was built, and to suit the activities of President Lawrence Summers—from faculty dinners, to undergraduate discussions, to time with friends and family.

Related entry: Presidents.

Endowment

Harvard's endowment has been described as a large body of water surrounded by a dozen thirsty deans. More concisely, the endowment is

- Worth nearly twice as much (on the order of $20 billion dollars) as the next largest university endowment (Yale's).
- The second or third largest among the nonprofit institutions of the world (yielding primacy only to the Roman Catholic Church and perhaps—depending on the value of Microsoft stock—the Bill and Melinda Gates Foundation of Seattle, Washington).
- Providing capital support of more than $1 million per enrolled student at Harvard.
- Divided into 10,200 individual investment units, more than 85 percent of them restricted accounts for specific schools, programs, faculty chairs, scholarships, and the like.
- Cared for by the Harvard Management Company, an in-house subsidiary.

The history of the endowment is a remarkable success story. Over the centuries, generous alumni, other individual donors, foundations, and corporations have regularly added to it. Most have done so with the intention of strengthening the institution as a whole, and/or supporting specific programs. In the mid-twentieth century, Harvard's endowment was about $215 million, roughly comparable in size to Yale's. But in subsequent decades—thanks in large part to the investment acumen of Paul Cabot, the University's treasurer from 1949 to 1966—Harvard's capital accumulation accelerated. Since the formation of the Management Company in

1974, the endowment's value has grown from just over $1 billion to a level that exceeds the gross national product of a dozen or more developing countries. In fiscal year 2003 it increased by 12.5 percent.

The endowment is an essential source of aid to the University's annual budget, providing stability as well as innovative opportunities. Endowment income currently meets about 28 percent of operating costs—a larger proportion than is now derived from tuition and sponsored research. Its annual injections give Harvard the wherewithal to maintain faculty salaries and student scholarships at the highest and most competitive levels.

But such a boon to the budget is also a bane to the University's public relations. The endowment's celebrated size reinforces the platitude that Harvard is so rich that it doesn't need any more money, and that alumni should thus direct their philanthropy to needier causes. Many faculty members and others also view the endowment as a source of funds that could and should be accessed to meet a variety of needs. A growing chorus of critics has assailed what is seen as miserly annual payout percentages. What may be the loudest howling is heard when the annual compensation of Harvard Management Company executives is published. In good years, a successful investment manager may earn more than $15 million in salary and bonuses—about 30 times what Harvard's president makes.

Two misapprehensions can be readily rebutted. The value of the endowment is indeed substantial—approximating the cost of seven or eight nuclear submarines—but maintaining Harvard's position as a world-class institution requires the level of income generated by a world-class endowment. Otherwise, the University will almost certainly lose its comparative advantage in personnel, facilities, and scholarly resources. Moreover, disbursements from large portions of the endowment are limited under Massachusetts statutes that define quite precisely what Harvard can and cannot do with its nest egg.

The second point—increasing annual payout percentages—is more complex. Several Harvard Business School professors have recently written that the University endowment should not become a kind of ever-increasing bank account; rather, it should be prudently drawn upon to support urgent current needs, such as helping the financially weaker professional schools (Design, Divinity, and Education) and supporting critical programs like scholarship aid. The Harvard Corporation's response has been to reaffirm the goal of keeping endowment spending relatively constant in good times and bad. To guard against the ups and downs of economic cycles, this has meant an annual rate of 4 to 5 percent of the value of the endowment.

While it's true that an able Harvard investment manager may make as much as Boston Red Sox slugger Manny Ramirez, it's also true that individuals—in finance, baseball, and most other lines of work—do not set the market for their skills. The Management Company was conceived and organized by University treasurer George Putnam '49, M.B.A. '51, a great-nephew of A. Lawrence Lowell. President Lowell could scarcely have foreseen that Harvard would spawn the first nonprofit firm to engage in such relatively sophisticated practices as stock lending, and one of the first to exploit computer-based options trading, arbitrage, derivatives, and venture capital opportunities. The Management Company also broke ground by providing investment services to donors making deferred gifts to Harvard. Maneuvering in highly specialized areas of finance requires expertise, and Harvard pays the going rate for astute investment managers. If it didn't, the best of them might be working on Wall Street.

Related entries: ETOB; Fundraising. *Related Website:* vpf-web.harvard
.edu/annualfinancial.

ETOB

Used throughout the University, the acronym ETOB stands for "Every Tub on its Own Bottom." This axiom, coined in the early nineteenth century, is the bedrock of a highly decentralized system of financial management.

In Harvard parlance, a *tub* is a high-level institutional unit—one of the ten faculties, for example, or the central administration.

All told, there are 52 tubs and countless sub-tubs. Each tub is expected to be self-financing: to prepare its own budgets, raise its own funds, and keep itself solvent.

Though the University has no central budget, it does, paradoxically, have a central Budget Office. That office reviews the proposed budgets of the tubs and submits them to the Harvard Corporation, adding its recommendations for approval. The Corporation traditionally approves only individual budgets, not an aggregate for the University as a whole. And although the Budget Office compiles University-wide figures, it does so for informational—not operational—purposes.

In theory, the central administration bears no responsibility for the solvency of any faculty, museum, or other University institution. In actuality, there are times when it does intervene. Examples might include founding a new institute or research center, rescuing a school or program that is experiencing protracted financial trouble, or subsidizing essential activities that cannot otherwise be supported. In some cases the administration acts as banker and makes loans, at interest, to a needy faculty or institution. In other cases it may make outright grants from its own funds.

The smaller schools—Design, Divinity, and Education—are most likely to need periodic help. At the other end of the spectrum is the School of Business Administration. Though the Faculty of Arts and Sciences and the Medical School have larger endowments, the Business School's is spread over a smaller operational unit, and the school has amply demonstrated its ability to attract outside funds from well-heeled graduates and asset-heavy corporations. A faculty's reliance on outside (or "soft") money is an important index of its financial well-being. Outside gifts and grants make up less than one-third of the income stream of the Faculty of Arts and Sciences, with the federal government providing about 13 percent of that amount. In contrast, the School of Public Health receives 84 percent of its income from outside sources, and governmental support accounts for 43 percent of the funding. In general, the Corporation is tough-minded in its insistence on a positive bottom line and in its reluctance to intervene unless the situation is serious indeed.

The development of ETOB as an institutional policy has never been documented in detail. The term evidently originated during the presidency of John Thornton Kirkland (1810–1828). Declining to weigh in on the siting of a new building, Kirkland is said to have stated that "it is our practice here for every tub to stand on its own bottom." The chief justification for the system is that it encourages initiative and self-reliance. It also gives the various faculties the utmost freedom to pursue their academic goals as they see fit. Among the negative aspects of ETOB are the territorial jousting that impedes interaction among faculties and fosters duplication of academic effort. ETOB also means that the central administration has far less authority than it otherwise might. Finally, the system is fussy and bureaucratic; the internal billing and transfer procedures are onerous and at times may be carried to what may seem absurd extremes. But in dollars-and-cents terms, as a means of achieving and maintaining collective financial responsibility, ETOB works well overall. In fiscal year 2002, operating income for the University as a whole was $2.357 billion; expenses came to $2.287 billion, and the books thus showed an unrestricted operating surplus of almost $70 million.

Related entries: Endowment; Fundraising.

Extinct Harvard

Buried in Harvard history is a lost world of pedagogical practices, secret societies, research activities, and physical facilities that have left scant traces of their existence. A few were transitory; others survived for generations. Here are some of them.

The fixed curriculum. For the better part of two centuries, students at Harvard College followed a strictly prescribed course of study. In colonial times, classes were limited to ancient languages (Latin, Greek, Hebrew, and such oriental tongues as Syriac and Aramaic); Aristotelian physics; rhetoric; and divinity. Teaching methods stressed drill and rote memorization. Mathematics and geography were subsequently added to the curriculum, and by the first half of the nineteenth century, upperclassmen could also study history, philosophy, forensics, and certain modern languages. More elective courses were introduced only after the Civil War.

The Hebrew language requirement. Though biblical studies were a central part of the fixed curriculum, Hebrew was never a popular subject, and few students mastered the language. The faculty dropped the Hebrew requirement in 1755.

Social ranking. Until 1769, when an alphabetical system was adopted, the social standing of a student's parents determined the place he occupied in the classroom, at prayers, in the dining hall, and in academic processions.

The five-dollar master's degree. For more than two centuries, any graduate of the College could receive a master's degree after three years of undirected study. In the early nineteenth century, the only qualifications were said to be "keeping out of jail for three years and paying five dollars." One of President Eliot's early reform initiatives was the requirement of an earned master's degree for graduate study. The last of the bargain degrees was granted in 1872.

The Harvard Branch Railroad Line. Linked to the Fitchburg Railroad, the Cambridge spur line was incorporated in 1848 by residents hoping to promote their town as a close suburb of Boston. Its octagonal station was adjacent to the house of Oliver Wendell Holmes, close to the Law School. When the line failed in the Civil War years, the building was renovated as Thayer Commons, an inexpensive dining hall. The structure was torn down in 1883.

The Med. Fac. Most notorious of the secret societies that burgeoned in the nineteenth century, the Medical Faculty Society was formed in 1818 as a spoof on learned societies. At the outset, members wore knee-breeches and wigs at clandestine meetings, bewildered initiates with unintelligible "medical lectures," and awarded honorary degrees with comic Latin citations to public figures, among them presidents Andrew Jackson and Martin Van Buren, the daredevil jumper Sam Patch, and the famous Siamese twins Chang and Eng. In 1824 the society perpetrated a famous hoax by sending a certificate of honorary membership to Tsar Alexander I of Russia. The tsar, thinking that he was being recognized by the Medical School, responded with a gracious message of thanks and a chest of finely crafted surgical instruments. The society's costumed invasions of Cambridge homes led the faculty to suppress the Med. Fac. in 1834, but it was soon revived. The commission of an act that would warrant expulsion from the College eventually became the chief qualification for membership. The group's secret rituals became increasingly grotesque, the pranks more vandalistic. Members were quick to exploit the invention of dynamite, and in the latter years of the nineteenth century the Yard was rocked by sporadic bombings. In 1901, an explosion of great force shattered the old College Pump. Four years later, when a member was caught stealing a bronze memorial tablet from Phillips Brooks House, the Med. Fac. was suppressed for good.

Greek-letter fraternities. Several national college fraternities—Delta Kappa Upsilon, Zeta Psi, Psi Upsilon, Theta Delta Chi, and others—chartered Harvard chapters in the decade before the Civil War. "Fraternities became such a nuisance that the faculty abolished them about 1857," writes Samuel Eliot Morison, "but when the ban was removed in 1865 it was discovered that several had been leading a surreptitious life." A chapter of Alpha Delta Phi, formed in the 1830s, surrendered its charter in 1865 and became the present A.D. Club. Zeta Psi grew into the Spee Club. Other Greek fraternities (including Zeta Tau, with an exclusively Jewish constituency) came and went over the next 70 years, but none survived after World War II. Today the only Harvard organizations with Greek-letter associations are the A.D. Club; the Delphic Club, which began as Chapter Zeta of Delta Phi; the mock-Greek Pi Eta Club, formed in 1865; and the College's Phi Beta Kappa chapter (Alpha-Iota of Massachusetts).

Bloody Monday. This nineteenth-century donnybrook pitted freshmen against sophomores on the first Monday evening of the academic year. Black eyes, nosebleeds, and shredded clothing were taken in stride, along with the occasional concussion or fracture. The antecedent of this ritual rumpus was a rough and artless proto-football game played from the 1820s until 1860, when the faculty outlawed it. Undeterred, underclassmen kept up the tradition—minus the ball. On taking office in 1869, President Eliot ordered the carnage stopped. Diminishing in intensity and violence, it nevertheless went on until 1917. To one former participant, Dr.

Morton Prince, class of 1875, Bloody Monday was "a Homeric battle." Many of his contemporaries, Prince wrote, "looked forward to
the fray with the greatest of glee."

The Lawrence Scientific School. Founded in 1847 by Abbott Lawrence, grandfather of President A. Lawrence Lowell, this large
school offered graduate and undergraduate instruction in the physical and life sciences. It formed the foundation for most of the scientific departments in today's University and trained an impressive
number of educators. Under President Eliot, undergraduate instruction in science and technology was shifted to the Faculty of
Arts and Sciences, and in 1906 the Lawrence School was reconsti-
tuted as the Graduate School of Applied Sciences. That school was
dissolved six years later, in anticipation of a Harvard merger with
MIT. When a court ruling blocked the merger, Harvard started a
new School of Engineering. It survives as a component of the Division of Engineering and Applied Sciences.

The Harvard School of Mines. Though the post-Civil War years
brought a rising demand for mining engineers, a short-lived
School of Mining and Practical Geology suffered from low enrollment. Founded in 1865, the school engaged Raphael Pumpelly, one
of the world's foremost geologist-engineers, as its star faculty member. But when enrollment fell to zero in 1874, the school was
closed.

Veterinary School. Founded in 1882, the Harvard School of Veterinary Medicine was based in Boston. Its facilities included a hospital for the treatment of ailing animals, a dissecting room, a
museum, and a forge, where aspiring vets learned to shoe horses.
Clinical services were provided free of charge. By the turn of
the century the school was languishing, and it was dissolved in
1901.

The Gentleman's C. To the easygoing clubmen who dominated
the College's social structure in the Eliot and Lowell eras, it was an
article of faith that "the gentleman's grade is a C." To aim higher
was to risk being scorned as a "greasy grind." In an occasional
poem composed for a Boston Harvard Club smoker in 1909, Judge
Robert Grant, class of 1873, LL.B. 1879, contrasted the places of the
"C man" and "the poor old scholar" in the College hierarchy:

The scholar in his way's all right. But it comes down to this:
What does one go to college for? Assuredly it is
To study human nature, get an H and a degree.
How best may one accomplish this? By averaging C.
The able-bodied C man! He sails swimmingly along.
His philosophy is rosy as a skylark's matin song.
The height of his ambition is respectably to pass,
And to hold a firm position in the middle of his class.
The middle course is safest. Does not Ovid state it so?
He is one of the old classics and he surely ought to know.
The C man holds the balance in the academic scale
Betwixt the A man at the top and the E man at the tail.
"Avoid probation" is the tag he whispers to the young,
"Or otherwise some college team is likely to be stung.
A skillful choice of studies makes one's afternoons all free;
The chief merit of electives to the man who aims at C."
Such are the words of wisdom he utters from his throne,
For the C man owns the college and sets the college tone.
The man who's busy at his books an hour a day or so
And then jogs to the Stadium or goes out for a row,
If at examination time he pulls a first-rate mark,
The world forgives a genius; that fellow is a shark.
But he who seeks a Summa Cum by unrelenting toil
And hibernating in the Yard consumes the midnight oil,
Who never loafs, who never cuts, and rarely goes to town,
Who picks his courses heedless of the hours when they're set
    down,
Who doesn't care to join a club, or if he does make one,
Selects the literary sort where studious stunts are done,
Who deems a run or a sharp walk sufficient exercise,
Who though he's working overtime competes for some old
    prize,
And when he should be rooting for the ball nine or the crew,
Devours Professor William James who wrote "What Maisie
    Knew,"
That fellow in a moral sense of course may beat the band,
But viewed by an industrial age he's hard to understand! . . .

The Great Depression and World War II brought a new degree of seriousness to undergraduate life, and the Gentleman's C became passé. In recent years, however, critics of grade inflation have given a certain currency to the term "Gentleman's B."

School for Social Workers. Harvard's links to this school, founded in 1904 in partnership with Simmons College, lasted only twelve years. One of America's first social-service programs at a university level, the school offered a one-year course geared to a certificate and an apprenticeship in practical social work. Its social-service interests were shared by the nascent Department of Social Ethics (1906)—the outgrowth of a pioneering course on contemporary social problems (nicknamed "Drains, Drunks, and Divorce") taught by the Reverend Francis Greenwood Peabody, preacher to the University and Plummer Professor of Christian Morals. In 1916 the Corporation ended its support of the School for Social Workers and formed the Department of Sociology.

The 47 Workshop. For two decades, Professor George Pierce Baker's 47 Workshop produced a notable stream of playwrights, actors, and theatrical producers, directors, designers, critics, and teachers. An outgrowth of Baker's English 47, a course first offered in 1905, the workshop was based in Massachusetts Hall; plays written and produced by its members were staged at Radcliffe's Agassiz Theater. Among Baker's star pupils were the playwrights S. N. Behrman and Eugene O'Neill, the scenic designer Lee Simonson, and the novelist Thomas Wolfe. The workshop's classroom and rehearsal stage were destroyed by fire in 1924. When the administration declined to provide funds for new facilities and general support, Baker decamped to head what became the Yale School of Drama.

Geography. The teaching of geography, a fixture of the curriculum in colonial times, was subsumed by the now defunct Department of Natural History in the nineteenth century. The subject was later transferred to the Department of Geology, to the displeasure of many geologists. Geography got a boost in 1930, when Dr. Alexander Hamilton Rice, a wealthy amateur explorer, funded a lavishly equipped Institute of Geographical Exploration (with the proviso that he himself would be its director). Academic bickering over geography's proper place in the University continued, and in 1948 a controversial ruling by President James Conant terminated all courses and research programs in the subject.

Biddies. In undergraduate argot that older alumni will recall, "biddy" meant chambermaid. The term had supplanted "goody," a middle-English contraction of "good-wife" that was current at Harvard for more than two centuries. In the beginning, housekeeping duty was part of the job description of Mistress Eaton, wife of Harvard's first principal, Nathaniel Eaton. In testimony given in 1639, she apologized for her negligence: "And that [the students] made their beds at any time, were my straits never so great, I am sorry they were ever put to it." When the first goody was hired is not a matter of record, but the College apparently had a one-person housekeeping detail until the 1700s. From then on, the staff grew to keep up with the size of the College. That it was increasingly made up of Irish immigrants may explain the terminological shift from goody to biddy. When maid service was ended, as an economy measure, in 1954, one critical alumnus declared that Harvard had lost its "last remnant of gracious living."

Fatigue Lab. Founded in 1927 by the biochemist Lawrence J. Henderson, the Harvard Fatigue Laboratory spawned pathbreaking research on the effects of altitude, heat and cold, nutrition, and physical exercise on body and mind. Experiments were conducted not only in Cambridge but also in the White Mountains, the Nevada desert, and the Mississippi Delta. Scores of bright young physiologists who trained at the HFL later opened their own labs throughout the world. During World War II, under contracts with the army, navy, and air force, the lab did pioneering studies on human factors in aviation and aerospace. It was disbanded in 1947.

The Radcliffe Publishing Procedures Course. Begun in 1947, it started out as a summer crash course for women seeking careers in magazine and book publishing. It was opened to men in 1949. Over the next half-century, the course helped launch the careers of more than 3,500 publishing hopefuls from colleges around the country. After the dissolution of Radcliffe College in 1999, it was transferred to Columbia's Graduate School of Journalism.

Landmark buildings. The Old College was the earliest. Erected in 1642, near the present site of Grays Hall, it was the first college building in the colonies. Modeled after Eton College, the E-shaped building housed classrooms, the College library, a dining commons, and student chambers. It soon fell into disrepair and was abandoned when the first Harvard Hall was completed in 1677.

The twentieth century saw the obliteration of a few distinctive buildings to make way for larger structures. The first to fall was Gore Hall, a Gothic edifice built in 1844 to house the University library. It was demolished in 1913 and replaced by the Harry Elkins Widener Memorial Library, a massive building many times the size of the structure it replaced. Appleton Chapel, built in 1858, was razed in 1931 to make room for Memorial Church. Hemenway Gymnasium (1873), the most elaborately ornamental of Harvard's buildings, succumbed in 1937 and was replaced by a smaller squash facility, also called the Hemenway Gymnasium.

Lawrence Hall, built in 1873 for the now-extinct Lawrence Scientific School, burned down in the spring of 1970. Then the property of the Graduate School of Education, it had been occupied by radical students and homeless people during that year's protest demonstrations. Hunt Hall, constructed in 1895 as the first Fogg Art Museum, was demolished in 1973 to clear space for Canaday Hall, a new freshman residence on the north side of Harvard Yard.

Two post-World War II buildings had relatively brief lives. Allston Burr Lecture Hall, a modern science classroom building erected in 1949, was demolished in 1979, yielding its site to the Sackler Art Museum. Aiken Computation Laboratory (1947), where information technology was nurtured at Harvard, was torn down in 1997 and replaced by the Maxwell Dworkin Laboratory.

Century-old Carey Cage, the first permanent structure built at Soldiers Field, was demolished in 1997 to make way for a new racquets center. Reputedly the world's oldest facility built specifically for baseball, the building was later used by the Business School and the Harvard Varsity Club. Architecturally distinctive, it was Harvard's only half-timbered building.

The Cambridge Electron Accelerator—technically, a 6 GeV electron synchrotron—was constructed by Harvard and MIT in 1962. Its physicists pioneered many of the techniques now used by high-energy colliding-beam facilities. After decommissioning in 1973, it became the High Energy Physics Laboratory, and the electron accelerator was used for cancer therapy. The remaining facilities were demolished in 1999, to be replaced by new science buildings constructed atop an extensive underground parking garage.

Not a Harvard building, but a Harvard landmark for half a century, was the Colonial-style Gulf station at the intersection of Massachusetts Avenue and Harvard Street. Built in 1940, it stood on the former site of Beck Hall, the first in a series of late-nineteenth-century luxury apartment buildings. The Gulf station was torn down in 1988 to make room for the Inn at Harvard Square.

Related entries: Architecture; College Pump; Final Clubs; Fires; Gold Coast; Grade Inflation; Harvard Elsewhere; Harvard Hall; Information Technology; Maps; Radcliffe; Soldiers Field; Underground.

F

The first woman faculty member, Alice Hamilton, was appointed
assistant professor of industrial medicine in 1919. She was a social
reformer and a pioneer in the new field of occupational health.

Faculty Club

The club's neo-Georgian building stands on a Quincy Street plot where Henry James Sr. and his notable family once lived. Designed by Coolidge, Shepley, Bulfinch & Abbott, architects of the contemporaneous residential houses, it opened in 1931. The building was extensively renovated in 1989.

Many academic and administrative departments hold their regular meetings over dinner in the second-floor function rooms. Committees often meet over lunch. Faculty recruitment interviews take place here, and many prospective members spend a night or two in one of the club's dozen third-floor bedrooms. In the first-floor dining area, three separate rooms have tables for two, four, or six, and a "Long Table" for unaccompanied diners who want a quick meal and some friendly banter with colleagues. Downstairs, Harvard's most upscale cafeteria is brightened by theatrical posters of earlier days. For preprandial or postprandial browsing, a spacious and well-lit reading room on the first floor is stocked with current periodicals, domestic and foreign. The reading room, function rooms, and corridors are decorated with paintings from the Harvard Portrait Collection and with archival photographs.

Unlike some universities, Harvard has never withheld support for a heavily subsidized but communally attractive meeting place for faculty members and their guests—though would-be budget-cutters did menace the Faculty Club in the 1970s. To the rescue came President Derek Bok and a cadre of deans, all of whom lunched regularly at the club and often sat at the Long Table, where they exchanged news and views and quashed unfounded rumors. They realized the value of the club in promoting community and collegiality.

For more than a generation, women faculty members—what few there were—had only restricted access to the club and ate in a dining room of their own. The club did not serve alcohol, and coats and ties were mandatory. All this has long since changed. Membership is now open to members of the Harvard community without payment of dues, and to many members of the Cambridge community who have even a tenuous connection with Harvard. Full bar services are available. As one old-timer has noted, the dress code has withered away to a point where "almost any sort of costume that adequately covers the body may be seen."

The extensive (and expensive) renovations of the club's interior transformed the premises from slightly scruffy to handsome and inviting. The cuisine, too, has been upgraded without sending menu prices over the top. Some regulars maintain that the lunches and dinners are the best bargains in town. And yes, the club did serve horse meat for years. The entree was added to the menu, priced at 75 cents, during a wartime food shortage in the winter of 1943–44. Horse steak remained a club staple until 1983, when a new French chef refused to prepare it because the barreled meat shipped to the club was frozen, not fresh.

Related entries: Dining Services; Fashion; Portrait Collection. *Related Website:* www.hfc.harvard.edu.

"Fair Harvard"

Samuel Gilman's "Fair Harvard," written for the bicentennial celebration of September 1836, is the University's anthem. Two verses, the first and fourth, are sung at every Commencement and at many other ceremonial occasions. The Reverend Mr. Gilman, class of 1811, was pastor of the Unitarian Church of Charleston, South Carolina. He borrowed the melody for his ode from an old Irish harpers' air that was already famous as "Believe me, if all those endearing young charms," but words and music did not coalesce until shortly before the celebration. The bicentennial assembly sang "Fair Harvard" with a "deep and holy enthusiasm," and Gilman received an honorary degree at the following year's Commencement.

"Fair Harvard" has been subjected to occasional revisions and unauthorized changes. One graduate recast the first stanza because he thought the first four lines were unsuitable for athletic events. More recently, Radcliffe alumnae and sympathetic male graduates successfully made the case that the first line—"Fair Harvard! Thy sons to thy Jubilee throng"—was outdated. Alternative phrasings were floated, and in 1997 the line was officially changed to "Fair

Harvard! We join in thy Jubilee throng." (Curiously, it was in the
northeast bedroom of Fay House, at 12 Garden Street, Cambridge,
that Samuel Gilman wrote "Fair Harvard." In 1885 that red-brick
building would be purchased to house the future Radcliffe College.)

Here, in Gilman's original version, are verses I and IV:

Fair Harvard! Thy sons to thy Jubilee throng,
 And with blessings surrender thee o'er
By these Festival-rites, from the Age that is past
 To the Age that is waiting before.
O Relic and Type of our ancestors' worth,
 That hast long kept their memory warm,
First flow'r of their wilderness! Star of their night!
 Calm rising thro' change and thro' storm.

Farewell! Be thy destinies onward and bright!
 To thy children the lesson still give,
With freedom to think, and with patience to bear,
 And for Right ever bravely to live.
Let not moss-covered Error moor thee at its side,
 As the world on Truth's current glides by,
Be the herald of Light, and the bearer of Love,
 Till the stock of the Puritans die.

Related entries: Commencement; Songs and Marches.

Fashion

Informed by an acquaintance that he had been singled out as the
faculty's best-dressed man, Barrett Wendell—a famously snobbish
professor of English in the pre-World War I years—is said to have
replied stiffly, "Sir, you do me slight honor."

If the natty professor thought Harvard fashion was at a low ebb
in those days, it's as well that he's no longer around. The relaxation
of the Faculty Club's dress requirements in the early 1970s effec-

tively marked the end of fashion at Harvard. The mere notion of fashion, of course, would have offended the College's Puritan founders. The College Laws of 1655—and every scholar was expected to own a copy—stipulated that "if any Student shall weare long haire . . . the President shall have power to reforme it." Though the earliest statutes said nothing specific about dress, the College Laws of 1734 warned that

> If any Scholar shall go beyound ye College Yar[d] or fences without Coat, Cloak, or Gown, (unless in his Lawfull diversions) he shall be punished by the President, or one of the Tutors, not exceeding Two Shillings. And If any shall Presume to put on or wear Indecent Apparell, he shall be punished According to the Nature and degree of the offence, by the President or one of the Tutors; but If he wears womens Apprell, he shall be liable to publick admonition, degradation or Expulsion.

The academic gown, a throwback to medieval times, had only recently been adopted. Samuel Eliot Morison, in *Three Centuries of Harvard*, notes that the gowns "might be of any bright color, like those of eighteenth-century Oxonians." The latter years of the eighteenth century, writes Morison, brought another dress-code change:

> In 1786, partly to enforce authority and partly to lessen competition in expensive dress, the Corporation forbade students to wear silk and prescribed a uniform coat of blue-gray, with waistcoat and breeches of the same, or nankeen, olive, or black, and distinctions to mark the different classes: plain buttonholes and no buttons on cuffs for freshmen; buttons on cuffs for sophomores; "cheap frogs to the button holes" *except* those on the cuffs for juniors; frogs all over for seniors. . . . Gold and silver lace, cord, and edging were forbidden. The students loathed this livery, and evaded it as far as they dared; after efforts to enforce it by dreadful penalties, the class distinctions were abandoned for a time; but the blue-

gray tailed coats, cut much like dress coats of today, and scholar's gown, remained *de rigueur* for some years. Around 1822 an Oxford gray coat with "skirts reaching to the bend of the knee" and a great-coat "with not more than two capes were required."

The Corporation had ruled in 1816 that "night gowns" could be worn "within the limits of the college or town of Cambridge." (Dressing gowns, explains Morison, were accepted as casual attire in those days.) No scholar, however, was allowed to appear in shirt-sleeves.

The whole body of old student laws was abolished in the mid-nineteenth century. A new latitude in matters of dress, and the proliferation of social clubs in the decades after the Civil War, helped usher in an era of sartorial elegance and, sometimes, foppery. One's tailoring, after all, spoke volumes about one's fitness for an exclusive club. Expensive attire had a parallel in the luxurious appointments of the Gold Coast apartment buildings that sprang up on Mount Auburn Street in the 1890s. For the next sixty years or so, undergraduate standards in dress and manner would be set by clubmen who had come to Harvard from Andover, Exeter, and the "St. Grottlesex" schools and who would buy their rigs at the eponymous Andover Shop, J. Press, or "the Brothers" (Brooks Brothers). For clothes of much the same cut, but at lower prices, a cost-conscious student could shop at the Harvard Cooperative Society—or buy clubmen's castoffs at Max Keezer's.

Compared with the dizzying whirl of women's fashions in hats and clothing, the masculine cycle has always seemed to unreel in slow motion. But changes occur. High collars went out of style after World War I; with the influx of veterans after World War II, government-issue khakis displaced gray flannels as the trouser of choice. White duck pants and saddle shoes had by then had their day in the sun. The same thing could be said for hats, which went through a process of devolution. At the turn of the century, students were no longer wearing top hats, as their fathers and grandfathers might have done, but most would have owned a high-crowned, curly-brimmed derby, as well as a straw hat for spring and summer wear. A decade later, the checked golf cap, worn well forward over the nose, was in favor. In the 1920s—after an interval when fashion demanded a hat artfully teased to look hopelessly torn, crumpled, and dirty—a well-dressed undergraduate would sport a gray homburg, bound with a narrow black tape around the brim. Fedoras in shades of brown or green would become popular in the 1930s, and the straw boater would continue to enjoy sporadic revivals. By the 1940s and 1950s, going hatless would be socially acceptable; and by the 1960s, the language of hats, for both women and men, would go mute. In the Age of Aquarius, the new mode of self-expression, up top, would be *hair.*

The last great fashion shift of the century came late in the 1960s. Student radicals of the time spoke of changing the system, but what they actually achieved was a revolution in fashion and taste. For centuries, cultural patterns had been set by society's wealthiest and most prominent members. The ideology of the 1960s reversed that. Patterns in dress, speech, music, and dance now were set at the other end of the social scale. Well-off students of earlier generations had dressed much as their fathers had; those not so well off usually tried to blend in. Now dressing down was the watchword. Some clubmen might hold the line, but legions of male undergraduates rejected the traditional jacket-and-tie ensemble as the uniform of the conformist establishment, opting instead for the uniform of a laborer or a woodsman: blue denim jeans, sweatshirt, boots. The power structure capitulated, and coat-and-tie rules, once strictly enforced at house dining halls, were abrogated without much of a fuss.

Coat-and-tie rules also came under assault at the Faculty Club and at the Harvard Clubs of Boston and New York, where resistance was stiffer. The Faculty Club solicited its patrons' views, and the pages of its guest book showed this vote for the status quo from one of the faculty's best-dressed men, the classicist and former Eliot House master Professor John H. Finley Jr.:

> Though drawn by Lysippus and Myron,
> And often displayed by Lord Byron,
> The masculine throat

Is small object of note:
It looks brighter with tighter attire on.

Which brought this pointed rejoinder from Penelope Laurans,
then a Ph.D. candidate in English:

True, Byron was shockingly bred.
Still, at Harvard (have I been misled?)
I've been brought up to note
That what's outside the throat
Matters less than what's inside the head!

The club finally relaxed sartorial standards for its diners. The
small print now reads, "Appropriate attire is required at all meals."
   Related entries: Characters; Diversity; Faculty Club; Final Clubs; Gold
Coast.

Fictional Harvard

"I should say that Harvard yields no good materials for fiction,"
wrote the philosopher and cultural critic George Santayana, who
knew the place both as a graduate of the College and as a faculty
member. His dim view has not kept others from having a go. Harvard has been the setting for hundreds of novels and short stories,
from *The Belle of Boston: or, the Rival Students of Cambridge* (1844)
to *The Dante Club* and *Harvard Yard,* both published in 2003.
   Like the institution itself, the Harvard novel had small beginnings. The earliest specimens are thin novelettes with predictable
plots and purple prose. In *The Belle of Boston,* set in the 1820s, the
upright Philip Percy contests with his classmate, the dissipated
Southerner George Thornton, for the affections of a girl "with
flowing tresses, and a face radiant with love and beauty." In the
town-gown brawl that climaxes Joseph Holt Ingraham's *Bruising
Bill* (1845), undergraduate Edward Cassidy has his head broken
by Bill, an apprentice printer, but the two are then reconciled.
Hammersmith: His Harvard Days (1878), by Mark Sibley Severance,

class of 1869, is a more ambitious and variegated novel, laced with
the undergraduate argot of its day and with colorful accounts
of football games, rowing races, Class Day, and college pranks.
Modeled on Thomas Hughes's *Tom Brown at Oxford, Hammersmith* sold well. "Neither Mr. Hughes nor Mr. Severance is a first
or even second rate novelist," declared a contemporary reviewer,
but "both are very successful as historians of their boyhood experience."

Quite so. Whatever their literary shortcomings, these early stories and novels are historically important because they preserve
daily details of college life in times now distant from our own.
Nelly Brown; or, the Trials, Temptations and Pleasures of College Life
(1845), by the pseudonymous Tim Whippoorwill, describes a "de-
bauch," with undergraduates tippling champagne, playing cards,
and breaking a College rule by smoking in the Yard. The first Harvard novel written by an alumnus—*Fair Harvard: A Story of American College Life* (1869), by William Tucker Washburn, class of
1862—depicts a brutal hazing ritual; a rooftop gunpowder explosion, disrupting a faculty meeting; and a secret session of the notorious Med. Fac.

Tales of college pranks, romances, and athletic feats—especially
with "Harvard" in the title—were much in vogue from the 1890s
until the outbreak of World War I. Those years saw the appearance
of *Harvard Stories,* by Waldron Kintzing Post, class of 1890; *Forbes
of Harvard,* by Elbert Hubbard; *Harvard Episodes, The Diary of a
Freshman,* and *Sophomores Abroad,* by Charles Macomb Flandrau,
class of 1895; *Jarvis of Harvard,* by Reginald Wright Kauffman; *Philosophy 4,* by Owen Wister, class of 1882, LL.B. 1888; *The Count at
Harvard,* by Rupert Sargent Holland '00; *Brown of Harvard,* by
Rida Johnson Young and Gilbert Payson Coleman; and *Henry of
Navarre, Ohio* and *Pepper,* by "Holworthy Hall." Most of these authors were recent graduates when their books were published.

A few writers explored almost untrammeled literary terrain.
Harvard Episodes has its share of pranks, but it also hints at the
presence of a gay subculture. A generation earlier, *Two College
Friends* (1871), by Frederick W. Loring, class of 1870, had traced the
romantic attachment of two Civil War-era undergraduates, Ned

and Tom, who leave Harvard to fight with the Union army. *The Cult of the Purple Rose* (1902), by Shirley Everton Johnson, class of 1895, described a coterie of aesthetes inspired by Oscar Wilde and Aubrey Beardsley; in a somber climax, one of the cultists kills himself.

The output of Harvard fiction fell off in the years after World War I, but the literary quality improved and the accounts of college life became more frank. With unprecedented infusions of liquor and sex, *Wild Asses* (1925) traced the college careers of five dissimilar members of the class of '23, three of them veterans. The youthful author, James G. Dunton '23, had been an ambulance driver in the war. *Not to Eat, Not for Love* (1933), often cited as the best of all Harvard novels, was the work of young George Weller '29, later a noted foreign correspondent. Thomas Wolfe's *Of Time and the River* (1935) and William Faulkner's *The Sound and the Fury* (1929) and *Absalom, Absalom!* (1936) contained extended Harvard sequences. Wells Lewis '39 was a senior when he published *They Still Say No* (1939), about a girl-crazy freshman; the son of Sinclair Lewis, he would be killed in action in France in 1944. J. P. Marquand '15, the most successful novelist of his era, satirized cold-roast-Boston insularity in his Pulitzer Prize-winning *The Late George Apley* (1937), and did it again in *H. M. Pulham, Esquire* (1941). The varsity athlete, a favorite figure in the Harvard fiction of earlier days, made a comeback in *The Crimson Road* (1938), *Fuller at Harvard* (1939), and *Colonel of the Crimson* (1940), by Robert Smith Playfair '36, and in *The Iron Duke* (1938) and *The Duke Decides* (1939), by John R. Tunis '11. These were juvenile novels, but with crisp narration and authentic settings. The same period also saw the earliest Harvard detective novels: *Harvard Has a Homicide* (1936) and a sequel, *Reunion with Murder* (1941), by Timothy Fuller '36.

Not until after the war, with the publication of Helen Howe's *We Happy Few* (1946) and May Sarton's *Faithful Are the Wounds* (1955), did women arrive as writers of Harvard fiction. The principal character in Sarton's novel, a liberal professor who commits suicide during the McCarthy witch hunts, strongly resembles the literary historian F. O. Matthiessen, who leapt to his death from a

Boston hotel window in 1950. A second-generation Harvard author made his debut in 1953, when John Phillips Marquand Jr. '46, writing as "John Phillips," published *The Second Happiest Day*. Its central chapters portrayed the wartime militarization of the University. As war and witch hunts faded into the past, the fancies of young Harvard authors lightly turned to thoughts of love. College romance (with more explicit sex than ever before) informed the themes or subplots of *Fume of Poppies* (1958), by Jonathan Kozol '58; *Love with a Harvard Accent* (1962), by "Leonie St. John"; *Love Story* (1970), by Erich Segal '58, PH.D. '65; and *The Paper Chase* (1971), by John Jay Osborn '67, J.D. '70. The critics might cavil—*Love with a Harvard Accent* left the *Harvard Alumni Bulletin*'s undergraduate reviewer "with the disappointing feeling that there is still to be written a worthwhile novel about the way Harvard and Radcliffe students live"—but those books sold, and *Love Story* and *Paper Chase* were made into top-grossing films.

The Harvard fiction published in subsequent years would almost fill a five-foot shelf. Among the many titles are *Ham Martin, Class of '17* (1971) by Edward Streeter '14; *A Darkening Green* (1974), by Peter S. Prescott '57; *The Last Convertible* (1978), by Anton Myrer '44; *Class Reunion* (1979) and *After the Reunion* (1985), by Rona Jaffe '51; *Splendor & Misery: A Novel of Harvard* (1983), by Faye Levine '65, ED.M. '70; *The Class* (1985), by Erich Segal; *Harvard, John: A Story of the Sixties* (1987), by Harrison Livingstone, A.B.E. '70; Anne Bernays's *Professor Romeo* (1988); John Kenneth Galbraith's *A Tenured Professor* (1990); and *The Student Body: A Novel* (1998) by "Jane Harvard" (a consortium of four collaborators).

Harvard crime novels are now a subgenre unto themselves. Timothy Fuller's pioneering whodunits have been followed by *The Morning After Death* (1966), second-to-last of the 21 Inspector Strangeways novels by "Nicholas Blake" (the British poet C. Day Lewis); *The Memorial Hall Murder* (1978), third in Jane Langton's Homer Kelly series; *Death in a Tenured Position* (1981), fifth of 14 Kate Fansler novels by "Amanda Cross" (Carolyn G. Heilbrun); Victoria Silver's *Death of a Harvard Freshman* (1984) and *Death of a Radcliffe Roommate* (1986); John Minahan's *The Great Harvard*

Robbery (1988); *A Darker Shade of Crimson* (1998) and *Blue Blood* (1999), by Pamela Thomas-Graham '85, M.B.A. '89, J.D. '89; *The Dante Club* (2003), by Matthew Pearl '97; and *Harvard Yard* (2003), by William Martin '72.

Readers interested in sampling some representative Harvard fiction might begin by picking from the following list.

Harvard Episodes. Charles Flandrau's 1897 skewering of college snobs and butterflies irked old grads and was regarded by some as scandalous. Flandrau's seven loosely linked stories may not form a true novel, but no matter.

Philosophy 4. In this lyrical little novel, Owen Wister—known for his classic western *The Virginian*—neatly captured what Michael J. Halberstam '53, writing in a 1969 issue of *The American Scholar,* would call "the hearty pipe tobacco, manly tweeds, and the unexamined life" of turn-of-the-century Harvard clubmen. Sophomores Billy and Bertie, the central figures, are engaging airheads.

Not to Eat, Not for Love. The coming of age of young Epes Todd is George Weller's theme, but his canvas is broad. Halberstam again: "Weller shows us Harvard changing [in the late 1920s] from what was basically an advanced Eastern finishing school with a few intellectual students and professors to a great intellectual factory with a few finishing school students still caught in its gears. Weller's students are not boys, but young men. They are questioning, cynical, amused and amusing, but they are exactly like Flandrau's tennis-flanneled youngsters in not caring about what they are taught, why, or by whom."

Harvard Has a Homicide. Eccentric graduate student Jupiter Jones comes across the body of Professor Singer, late of the fine arts department. Uncovering scandal at every turn, and "with the maximum of liquor and the minimum of effort," Jupiter eventually helps close the case. Timothy Fuller, Harvard's first mystery writer, writes wittily and incorporates many cameos of 1930s Cambridge.

H. M. Pulham, Esquire. The 25th reunion report of the title character is the framing device for J. P. Marquand's account of a hardshell Bostonian's losing battle to escape his stifling New England heritage and live a little.

Love Story. To a *Harvard Bulletin* reviewer, the nation's best-selling novel for more than a year was simply "undiluted escapism . . . in which college days are happy, women are pure and faithful and men are strong and sensitive, and America is a country untroubled by social tensions." That said, Erich Segal's 1970 narrative of the star-crossed love of a Harvard hockey star and a dying Radcliffe student is still a rather good read.

The Last Convertible. "The Fusiliers"—five classmates who arrived at Harvard, as did author Anton Myrer, in 1940—soldier on through a world war and its aftermath. The many characters in this coming-of-age novel are skillfully drawn.

The Dante Club. The perfervid imagination of Matthew Pearl '97 has created a serial murderer who draws inspiration from Dante's *Inferno,* and a posse of Dante translators—Oliver Wendell Holmes Sr., Henry Wadsworth Longfellow, James Russell Lowell, and the publisher J. T. Fields—who join forces with an African-American Boston policeman to run the killer to ground.

Harvard Yard. In another historical thriller, Boston rare-book dealer Peter Fallon tracks down the autograph manuscript of a lost Shakespeare play left by the bard to—of all people—the infant John Harvard. Much of the book unfolds in the past; author William Martin '72 is obviously a Harvard history buff.

Related entry: Hollywood's Harvard.

Film Archive

I Often Think of Piroschka. The Death Ship. A Call Girl Named Rosemarie. Film without a Title. The Last Days of the Golden Donut. If you missed any of these offbeat pictures, you might catch them at a Harvard Film Archive screening. And if cinema classics are more to your taste, the Film Archive's regular showings also offer works by such masters as Ingmar Bergman, Luis Buñuel, Alfred Hitchcock, John Huston, John Ford, Fritz Lang, and Orson Welles.

Based at the Carpenter Center for the Visual Arts, the Harvard Film Archive (HFA) stores some 9,000 films in climate-controlled vaults in Southborough, Massachusetts. About 6,000 are prints and 3,000 are videotape masters, DVDs, or in other video formats. Preservation is HFA's watchword: saving rare film from rapid deterioration was the stated mission of filmmaker and faculty member Robert G. Gardner '48 when he founded the archive in 1979.

Among the HFA's holdings are 35mm prints of feature films by cinema's foremost practitioners, as well as documentaries, experimental films, and animation. Showings are held in the Carpenter Center's basement-level theater or in an adjoining screening room. In term time and during the summer, the HFA offers a variety of film series. Cinema buffs welcome these opportunities to view familiar or *recherché* films on a wide screen, with state-of-the-art projection and ambient sound—and at a nominal cost of admission.

In recent years, HFA showings have focused on works from the international and independent cinemas. The exhibition series includes retrospectives of noted directors and actors, surveys of important periods and movements, and in-depth explorations of historic themes and contemporary issues. Filmmakers and actors sometimes introduce their own work. As an affiliate of the International Federation of Film Archives, HFA also has access to film prints from a network of more than a hundred film repositories.

HFA films are available for analysis by students in Visual and Environmental Studies and for use in other undergraduate courses.

Related entries: Arts; Brattle Theatre; Carpenter Center. *Related Website:* www.harvardfilmarchive.org.

Final Clubs

Some see the undergraduate "final" clubs as snobby, elitist, discriminatory sites of male raucousness and drunken revelry—"*Animal House* on the Charles." Others, more tolerantly, see them as relatively innocuous refuges for students who value an old-fashioned form of camaraderie. Because some of the clubs now open their doors to non-members for parties and dances, they may seem more acceptable to unclubbed undergraduates than they once did.

The history of Harvard final-clubdom dates from 1791, when

the Porcellian Club (originally the Argonauts) was organized. The term *final*—often mistakenly rendered as *finals*—is used because roughly ten of the most patrician clubs once formed the top rung of a social ladder that began with the Institute of 1770. From an assortment of "waiting" clubs at the next level, the final clubs would select a dozen or so initiates in each year's junior class. As distinguished from the less exclusive social or thematic clubs, like the Hasty Pudding, Pi Eta, or the Signet Society, the final clubs imposed rigid standards of clubbability: family, social class, money. Through the generosity of wealthy graduates, each had substantial premises of its own, occupying some of the choicest real estate in the Harvard Square area.

What went on inside wasn't widely known. Part of the ethos of joining a club was keeping mum about its activities. A member might talk in generalities to an outsider about elegant lunches and dinners, about postprandial brandy and cigars, about formal and informal debates on literature, morality, and politics. That the club was sometimes the scene of all-night parties and all-day drinking contests might not be mentioned, though tales of such doings have always persisted. Rumor also has it that club libraries maintain files of term papers and examinations culled from undergraduate courses. Supposedly A-graded papers are thus available for unprincipled members to copy, perhaps revise, and submit as their own.

All of the clubs have traditionally held fall-term "punches" to size up prospective members, followed later by a rowdy initiation dinner. Initiation fees and annual dues have traditionally been geared to those with the wherewithal to afford them, but a few scholarships were always there for candidates who were socially acceptable but financially strapped.

"The clubs are not the best preparation for living in a democratic society," wrote the Harvard historian Samuel Eliot Morison, a clubman himself, "yet many of their graduates have been faithful servants to the University, to the Republic, and to learning." Franklin D. Roosevelt, Sadruddin Aga Khan, and West Virginia Senator Jay Rockefeller belonged to the Fly Club. T. S. Eliot is said to have composed verses "to the boys" of his Fox Club; Bill

Gates '77 was a later member. J. P. Morgan Jr. helped found what is now the Delphic. John F. Kennedy and his brothers joined the Spee. A list of past members of the Porcellian, the most prestigious club, reads like a Boston/New York Social Register. Oliver Wendell Holmes, Theodore Roosevelt, Harold Vanderbilt, and any number of Cabots, Lowells, Saltonstalls, and Searses were "Porkers."

In recent years, the status and character of the final clubs have changed. Social position became a less important credential in the 1970s, a time of marked change in the racial, ethnic, and class composition of the student body; additional scholarship funds helped open membership to a wider range of prospects. By admitting non-members to weekend parties, the clubs positioned themselves as havens from the under-21 drinking laws of the Commonwealth of Massachusetts. Rambunctious rituals of binge drinking increased; so did incidents of public intoxication and indecent exposure. Police were summoned; repeated floutings of College rules against underage alcohol consumption vexed deans and house staff members. The year 1984 was a turning point. Because all of the clubs remained closed to women, the College administration cut off their access to such University services as heating, electricity, and the Centrex telephone system. The clubs were on their own.

Attrition and mergers have reduced the roll of final clubs to eight: the A. D., at 1 Plympton Street; the Delphic, 9 Linden Street; the Fly, 2 Holyoke Place; the Fox, 44–46 JFK Street; the Owl, 30 Holyoke Street; the Phoenix-S. K., 72 Mount Auburn Street; the Porcellian, 1324 Massachusetts Avenue; and the Spee, 76 Mount Auburn Street. "From 1878, when the A. D. purchased a house of its own," notes Professor Morison, "every final club has shaken down its graduates for a house, each new one surpassing the last in size and luxurious appointments." The half-dozen red-brick Georgian Revival clubhouses situated on Mount Auburn Street add picturesquely to the ethos of Harvard's Gold Coast and blend well with the styling of nearby Lowell House and its soaring bell tower. The oldest of the Gold Coast houses is the Fly Club's, built in 1899; its fine columned portico faces discreetly away from the street. The clubhouses of the Phoenix-S. K. and the defunct Iroquois Club (now the headquarters of Harvard's Office for the Arts) are of 1915 vintage; the Spee Club's squarish neo-Georgian house dates from 1931. What may be the most distinctive house was built for the now-extinct D. U. club. This handsome building, at 45 Dunster Street, would be at home in Colonial Williamsburg. Its architects, Perry, Shaw, and Hepburn, were in fact the designers of Williamsburg (and, later, of Harvard's Houghton Library). Part of the building's ground floor has long been tenanted by J. Press, the Ivy League clothier.

The final clubs are still all-male, though the election of women is debated from time to time. In the past decade or so, five all-female clubs—the Bee, Isis, Pleiades, Seneca, and the Sabliere Society—and three Harvard-based sororities have come into existence. At this writing, none has rooms of its own; members borrow or rent space from the final clubs, the houses, or local restaurants for their events.

Essentially a vestige of the past, the final clubs now vary in solvency and apparent staying power. Animal House? Many clubbies would regard the label as slighting. But had he not been president of the Spee Club, could the late Doug Kenney '68 have scripted that classic frat movie?

Related entries: Gold Coast; Hasty Pudding Show; Lampoon; Signet Society.

Fire

Like most long-lived institutions, Harvard has been severely scorched by fire. Its costliest and most spectacular conflagrations occurred in 1764, when Harvard Hall burned to the ground, and in 1956, when flames consumed the clock tower of Memorial Hall.

The Harvard Hall fire—described by the historian Samuel Eliot Morison as "the worst disaster in the history of the College"—broke out on a frigid January night. To avoid a smallpox epidemic in Boston, the General Court of Massachusetts had been meeting in the hall during Harvard's winter vacation. A fire left smoldering on a hearth overheated a floor beam, and by the small hours of the morning the building was ablaze. In a raging snowstorm, 75-year-old President Edward Holyoke and provincial governor Francis Bernard directed a bucket brigade, but the most they could do was quench secondary fires ignited by flying sparks. The 5,000-volume College Library, housed on the hall's second floor and considered the best in America, was destroyed, except for some 400 books that were out on loan or not yet unpacked. Also lost were most of the College's earliest records, along with scientific equipment, portraits, stuffed animals and birds, and other museum pieces.

The College escaped further serious fires until 1845, when a curious circular structure, built just two years earlier to shelter a cyclorama depiction of ancient Athens, burned down. The post-Civil War era brought more fires, beginning with the Great Boston Fire of 1872. On hearing that the commercial district was menaced by fire, President Charles William Eliot sped by horse carriage to the State Street office of Harvard's treasurer. Cramming securities and financial records into carpetbags, he removed them to the safety of Cambridge. But the great fire did destroy properties in which Harvard had investments.

In January 1876 a coal fell from a grate and set fire to the living room, theater, and library of the Pi Eta Club, one of Harvard's early fraternities, on the top floor of Hollis Hall. The roof of the building caved in, and the hall's water-drenched rooms below were uninhabitable for the rest of the academic year. To safeguard other Yard dormitories, the College fitted some with brick firewalls. That may have helped to contain a coal fire that broke out in Stoughton Hall three years later. The lead firefighter on that day was the ever-reliable College janitor, Austin Kingsley Jones, who set down his overworked garden pump only once—to ring the morning recitation bell at the height of the blaze.

In later decades, serious fires damaged another Yard dormitory, Thayer Hall; the Law School's Dane Hall; a new Medical School building in Boston; and Boylston Hall's chemical laboratories. In 1899 an unfinished University boathouse burned to the ground. The worst of the College's dormitory fires occurred in February 1905: Thayer Hall again was the site. A low fire in a grate ignited a painter's pot of varnish; instead of dropping it from a window, the man sought to carry the flaming pot down a hallway. When the intense heat forced him to drop it, the corridor caught fire and convection currents drew the flames up stairwells to floors above. Thayer residents who were trapped in their rooms extricated themselves by sliding down what would now be regarded as primitive rope fire escapes. Luckily no one died. Because Thayer's interior partitions were mostly of brick, the fire was confined to the building's north entry, but all the rooms in that part of the structure were gutted. Other fires damaged the Randall Hall dining commons in 1911; parts of Massachusetts Hall in 1924; and the upper stories of Claverly Hall in 1951. (Two mysterious Claverly fires within three days raised suspicions of arson.)

But the fire of the century began on the afternoon of September 6, 1956, when the tower of Memorial Hall burst into flame during a renovation project. Firefighters rushed from the Cambridge fire station, directly across the street, and hoisted a 100-foot extension ladder, only to find that their water pressure was insufficient to reach the upper part of the tower. The fire burned for twelve hours. All that remained the next morning was the tower's brick base, some smoldering timbers, and the great bell, cracked and ruined. An unattended blowtorch was thought to have ignited the conflagration.

Harvard's last trials by fire came during the riotous springs of 1969 and 1970. Using books, papers, and furniture as kindling, antiwar protesters tried to torch a Shannon Hall office used by the University's naval ROTC unit in May 1969. The would-be arsonists "did such a rotten job you almost feel sorry for them," said an officer attached to the ROTC unit. A year later, in May 1970, firefighters battled an early-morning fire that razed Lawrence Hall, a 123-year-old building last used by the Graduate School of Education. The dilapidated structure, adjacent to the Law School, had been scheduled for demolition. Shortly before the fire, in the spirit of the times, radical students and street people had appropriated it as the headquarters of a "Free University."

In earlier days, a serious fire almost always spurred stepped-up prevention and preparedness measures. After the Harvard Hall disaster, the General Court bought the College a £100 "water engine." The Hollis Hall fire of 1876 led to the installation of a water main in the Yard. After the 1879 Stoughton fire, the Harvard Corporation gave the city of Cambridge a $3,000 chemical engine, a novelty at the time. In the wake of the 1905 Thayer Hall fire, the College added exterior fire escapes to the larger Yard dormitories. Over the years, stricter fire codes required Harvard to equip or retrofit its buildings with advanced fire detection and suppression systems.

Fires have also prompted notable acts of generosity and, in some cases, improvements to Harvard's physical plant and/or collections. Assuming responsibility for the Harvard Hall fire, the General Court paid for a new building, and the present Harvard Hall opened two and a half years after the fire. The Province of New Hampshire contributed funds to restore the College Library; hundreds of graduates sent volumes from their own libraries; and from England, Thomas Hollis V—a grandnephew of Harvard's great eighteenth-century benefactor—shipped many thousands of books. When the University boathouse burned in 1899, a $50,000 gift from the Harvard Club of New York allowed work on a new structure (of brick, not wood) to start immediately. The New York club had also funded the boathouse that went up in smoke. After the Massachusetts Hall fire, which burned out the roof as well as lecture rooms, laboratories, and the classroom and rehearsal stage of Professor George Pierce Baker's 47 Workshop, the building was reconfigured as a freshman dormitory with large, comfortable suites.

The Memorial Hall tower was a different story. As its own insurer, the University set aside a repair fund of $313,000, representing the estimated cost of replacing the tower. But in an era that would become rather notorious for deferred maintenance, the replacement of the tower was postponed indefinitely. By 1974, Memorial Hall's centennial year, the repair fund's principal had more than doubled. The fund was not restricted to tower repairs, however, and much of it was eventually spent on renovations to other parts of the building. A series of gifts and pledges from alumni and friends kept alive the possibility that the tower would someday rise again, and in 1999 it did, thanks to a contribution of $2 million from one of Harvard's most generous donors, Katherine Bogdanovich Loker. The tower's restoration—in its original form, without later embellishments—marked the completion of the $2.6 billion University Campaign, which Mrs. Loker co-chaired. The project cost came to $4 million.

Related entries: Architecture; Bells; Clocks; Extinct Harvard; John Harvard—and His Statue; Libraries; Memorial Hall; Towers.

First Year

Just making the cut is a coup: only one out of ten Harvard College applicants gains admission. Yet registration week can be chastening. You were a high school valedictorian? So were about half of your 1,650 college classmates. Played three sports and captained a team? So did most of the varsity hopefuls you'll meet here. Won a Trivia Bowl contest? Say hello to your new roommates. They did too.

If the cast of characters seems a bit daunting, so is the range of academic and extracurricular opportunities. But most entering freshmen soon find that the first year is structured to allow the utmost leeway for self-discovery, while providing safety nets for those who may need them. As the *Official Register of Harvard University* states, "There is no 'freshman program'; students make their own decisions about the level and pace at which to start their undergraduate study." All first-year students must take a one-semester course in Expository Writing and fulfill a foreign-language requirement; other than that, the study-card choices are wide open. Outside the classroom, many extracurricular programs in the arts, public service, and intramural athletics are specifically tailored for first-years. Freshman intercollegiate teams are a thing of the past, and all students are eligible for Harvard's 41 varsity squads, for the many club teams, and for most of the College's 250-plus student-run organizations and social groups.

First-year students must be housed at Harvard. Rooming groups, assembled by the Freshman Dean's Office with an eye to affinities and shared interests, are assigned to one of seventeen residence halls in and around Harvard Yard. Four of those halls are among Harvard's oldest buildings; all seventeen have recently been refurbished. Ethernet connections in every suite provide access to Harvard's high-speed data network, the University Library's online catalog, HOLLIS, and, through the Internet, the outside world.

The Yard's residence halls are divided into units known as entries or entryways, consisting of 20 to 40 students and overseen by a proctor—a graduate student or University officer who rooms in the hall, serves as an academic adviser, and supervises the organized activities of his or her entry. Upperclassmen called prefects also assist first-years in making the transition to college life. All freshmen gather for meals in Annenberg Hall, the handsomely restored refectory of Memorial Hall. Loker Commons, on Memorial Hall's lower level, offers fast food at off-hours, along with pool tables, video games, and Internet access.

Freshmen (and upperclassmen) typically take four courses per semester. Course choices are usually made in close consultation with an academic adviser. A special perquisite for first-year students is the Freshman Seminar program, in which small groups of students work with a faculty member on a specialized research subject. Topics range from the particular ("Calculating Pi") to the general ("Tragedy"), and from the earthbound ("Research at the Harvard Forest") to the ethereal ("'Are We Alone?' The Idea of Extraterrestrial Intelligence from the Scientific Revolution to Modern Science Fiction").

More than half the members of each entering class ordinarily qualify for Advanced Standing, allowing them the option of completing requirements for the A.B. degree on an accelerated basis. Few students, however, elect to graduate ahead of schedule— though each year a handful take advantage of the program to pursue a fourth-year master's degree in their chosen field of study.

Freshmen having difficulty with coursework can consult the Bureau of Study Counsel, which provides peer tutoring as well as programs aimed at improving reading skills, study habits, and time management. The International Office serves the needs of students from other countries. The University Health Services offers mental health and emotional counseling, physical fitness and nutritional programs, and round-the-clock medical services.

Freshmen are expected to declare a field of concentration by the end of the year. At about the same time, they are randomly assigned to one of Harvard's twelve residential houses, where they will spend three years as upperclassmen.

A year of study at Harvard College is costly: for a freshman registering in 2003, the sticker price for tuition, room, board, and fees was more than $40,000. Fortunately, a $95 million financial aid budget and a need-blind admissions policy enable the College to draw students from all economic strata. Each year, about 70 percent of undergraduates receive various forms and combinations of aid: scholarships, grants, loans, and term-time employment; the average financial aid package is worth more than $24,000. The upshot is a representative first-year class remarkable not only for its kaleidoscopic mix of interests, activities, and accomplishments but also for its range of social, geographic, ethnic, and religious backgrounds.

Lexical note: though the *Harvard Crimson* hews to the politically correct *first year,* the terms *freshman* and *first year* are used without distinction in publications of the Freshman Dean's Office, the Admissions Office, and in the *Official Register of Harvard University.* The once popular *frosh,* however, is now largely obsolete.

Related entries: Admissions; Core Curriculum; Dining Services; Houses; UHS. *Related Website:* www.fas.harvard.edu/~fdo (Freshman Dean's Office).

Firsts (Men)

Who were the first graduates of Harvard College? Who received the first honorary degree? Who was the first Native American graduate? The first African-American? The first Ph.D.? Who was the first Harvard man to become president of the College? The first to be president of the United States?

The nine members of the College's first graduating class, in 1642, were Tobias Barnard, Samuel Bellingham, Nathaniel Brew-

ster, John Bulkley, George Downing, William Hubbard, Henry
Saltonstall, John Wilson, and Benjamin Woodbridge. All of their
surnames still appear in the *Harvard Alumni Directory*. After graduation, Bulkley and Downing became the College's first teaching
fellows. Downing had a picaresque political career in Britain, becoming the first Harvard graduate to be elected to Parliament
(from Edinburgh, in 1654) and to be knighted (in 1660). Saltonstall was the first Harvard man to become a physician, taking
M.D. degrees from the University of Padua in 1649 and from the
University of Oxford in 1652.

Leonard Hoar, of the class of 1650, was the first Harvard graduate to serve as president of the College (1672–1675). His predeces-
sors, Henry Dunster and Charles Chauncy, were Cambridge University men.

The College's first Native American graduate was Caleb
Cheeshateaumuck, class of 1665. A member of the Wampanoag
tribe, from Martha's Vineyard, he attended Harvard's short-lived
Indian College and died of tuberculosis within a year of his graduation. (The Indian College expired as well, and Harvard had almost no other Native American students until the latter years of
the twentieth century.)

David Denison, of the class of 1690, was the first Harvard man
to lose his life in war. After graduating, he joined Sir William
Phips's expedition to assault French Canada; he was killed, or perhaps died of disease, on that ill-fated venture.

The first scholar to hold an endowed chair at Harvard was Edward Wigglesworth, class of 1710, a young cleric whose deafness
had kept him from getting a parish. A gifted teacher, Wigglesworth
was named to the Hollis Professorship of Divinity when it was
funded in 1721 by the London merchant-philanthropist Thomas
Hollis.

Harvard's first Jewish faculty member was (at least arguably) Ju-
dah Monis, A.M. 1720, who taught Hebrew for almost 40 years.
"Arguably" because, before his appointment in 1722, Monis converted to Christianity in a public ceremony in the College hall. A
contemporary account called him "the first Jewish Christian in
North America." Nitza Rosovsky's *The Jewish Experience at Har-*

vard speculates that by 1886, when Harvard observed its 250th anniversary, "perhaps a dozen Jews had graduated from the College"; but the identity of the first Jewish graduate is uncertain. The distinguished educator Horace Meyer Kallen '03, PH.D. 1908, may have been the first Jew to have taken undergraduate and graduate degrees in the Faculty of Arts and Sciences. In 1985, economics professor and former dean Henry Rosovsky—Nitza Rosovsky's husband—became the first Jew named to the Harvard Corporation. Lawrence Summers, installed in 2001, is the first professing Jew to hold the presidency.

Benjamin Franklin, awarded an honorary M.A. in 1753, is often cited as Harvard's first honorary-degree recipient. Franklin was appointed colonial deputy postmaster general in that year, and on his later diplomatic missions to London he procured books for the College Library, as well as scientific apparatus for John Winthrop, Hollis Professor of Mathematics and Natural Philosophy.

John Adams, class of 1755, America's first minister to Great Britain, was the first graduate to become president of the United States. Elected in 1796, he served for one term. The first Harvardian to hold a cabinet post was Timothy Pickering, class of 1763, secretary of state under Adams and his predecessor, George Washington. Harvard's first U.S. senators were Tristram Dalton, class of 1755, and Caleb Strong, class of 1764. Both were from Massachusetts and were members of the first Senate, convened in 1789.

John Quincy Adams, class of 1767, son of John Adams, and the sixth president of the United States, was the first president of the Alumni Association, organized in 1840. Then in his seventies, Adams held the office until his death eight years later. (He was not the only former U.S. chief executive who would preside over the HAA; Theodore Roosevelt, class of 1880, did so as well.)

Harvard's Graduate School of Arts and Sciences, established in 1872, granted its first Ph.D. degrees in 1873. They went to William Byerly (mathematics) and Charles Whitney (history), both members of the class of 1871. The first Harvard graduate to earn a Ph.D. at another institution was Jeremiah Dummer, class of 1699, who took a doctorate at the University of Utrecht in 1703.

Beverly Williams, who applied in 1847, was the first African-American admitted to Harvard College, but he died of tuberculosis before entering. Richard T. Greener, class of 1870, was the College's first black graduate. Born in Philadelphia, he grew up in Boston, attended Phillips Academy in Andover, Massachusetts, for a year, and after graduating from Harvard held a chair of philosophy and sacred literature at the University of South Carolina. He later became dean of the Howard University Law School. As secretary of the Grant Memorial Association, he raised funds for the construction of Grant's Tomb; he also served as U.S. consul in Bombay and in Vladivostok.

Harvard's most famous African-American graduate is W. E. B. (William Edward Burghardt) Du Bois, class of 1890, who in 1895 became the first black to receive Harvard's Ph.D. His dissertation was titled *The Suppression of the African Slave Trade to the United States of America, 1638–1870.* Du Bois was a teacher, scholar, editor, activist, organizer of international congresses, and co-founder of the National Association for the Advancement of Colored People. He dedicated his life to solving "the twentieth century's problem of the color line." As Du Bois grew older, he became convinced that the crimes of racism in America called for radical solutions. He joined the Communist Party in 1961, and, increasingly pessimistic about the prospects for racial harmony in America, renounced his citizenship and emigrated to Ghana. He died there, at 95, just before the March on Washington in 1963—a landmark event in the peaceful revolution he had long worked for.

Other firsts, some of them grist for trivia contests:

- The Reverend George Burroughs, class of 1670, was the first alumnus to be hanged—at Salem, Massachusetts, for witchcraft, in 1692. (Burroughs was not the last Harvard graduate to end up on the gallows. John White Webster, class of 1811, Erving Professor of Chemistry and Mineralogy, was hanged in 1850 for the murder of Dr. George Parkman, class of 1809.)
- Jonathan Trumbull, class of 1727, was the first graduate to govern a state (Connecticut, 1769–1784), and—150 years

later—to have a Yale undergraduate college named for him (as governor, Trumbull was an ex officio member of the Yale Corporation).

- James B. Connolly, class of 1899, was Harvard's first Olympic medalist. At the first modern Olympics in 1896, he won the hop-hop-and-jump event.

- Theodore Roosevelt, class of 1880, LL.D. '02, was the first alumnus to win a Nobel Prize. For his role in mediating an end to the Russo-Japanese War, he was awarded the Peace Prize in 1904. Erving Professor of Chemistry Theodore William Richards, class of 1886, PH.D. 1888, was the first faculty member to gain a Nobel. He won the 1914 Chemistry Prize for his work in determining atomic weights.

- The name of Raktaprachit Aab, class of 1913, A.M. 1914, of Bangkok, Thailand, came first in the eighteen editions of the *Harvard Alumni Directory* published between 1910 and 1990. He died, at 96, in 1989.

- Wayne Johnson '44 was the first and only Harvard athlete to win a letter at Yale. After winning two football H's, he earned his Y as Marine trainee at Yale in 1943. (Because of wartime restrictions, Harvard and Yale did not compete in football that year.)

- Dr. John Jeffries, class of 1763, was Harvard's first aeronaut. He crossed the English Channel by balloon in 1785. More than two centuries later, the University's first astronaut would be Harrison Schmitt, PH.D. '64, who took part in the sixth lunar landing and stayed on the moon for a record 75 hours. Astronaut Jeffrey Hoffman, PH.D. '71, was the first Harvardian to walk in outer space. On his maiden voyage on the STS-51-D mission in 1985, he and his colleagues had to suit up and maneuver in space to repair and reactivate a satellite that had unexpectedly failed. "To commemorate five good years at Harvard," Hoffman took with him on his flight a small *Veritas* banner. He later donated it to the University.

Related entries: Aab; Alumni; Degrees; Extinct Harvard; Native American Program; Nobel Laureates; Presidents.

Firsts (Women)

Who were the first women professors at Harvard? What was the first Harvard College class to include women members? What about the Medical School? The Law School? Who was the first woman to receive a Harvard honorary degree? You don't have to be a radical feminist to be interested in such questions. In certain cases, however, the answers are a bit embarrassing to Harvard. For an institution that prides itself on being a pacesetter, the dates of some of these "firsts" for women are surprisingly late.

Williamina Paton Fleming, who would become the most famous female astronomer of her time, was the first woman to hold a Harvard Corporation appointment. An internationally known expert on stellar spectra, she was named Curator of Astronomical Photographs at the Harvard Observatory in 1898. The first woman to hold a professorial rank was Alice Hamilton, who was named to an assistant professorship in the Medical School's newly created department of industrial hygiene in 1919. Many male professors strongly objected to this break in tradition, and Hamilton herself learned that the Harvard Corporation was "far from enthusiastic" about it. Under the terms of her appointment, she could not use the Faculty Club, sit on the Commencement platform, or apply for football tickets. Her investigations and teaching revolutionized the field of occupational health, but when Dr. Hamilton retired in 1935 she was still an assistant professor. After retirement she served the Department of Labor as a consultant, remaining professionally active until she was 80; in her nineties, she actively protested the Vietnam War. She died in 1970, aged 101; in 1995 the U.S. Postal Service honored her with a definitive stamp.

Not until 1948, when the constitutional historian Helen Maud Cam left the University of Cambridge to join the Faculty of Arts and Sciences, did Harvard appoint a woman to a full professorship. Professor Cam was a groundbreaker in more ways than one: she regularly attended Morning Prayers, the first female to do so since the institution of the service in 1638. In 1956, the astronomer Cecilia Helena Payne-Gaposchkin became the first woman to be advanced to a full professorship from within the faculty's ranks.

The Medical School's first tenured woman full professor was the psychiatrist Grete Bibring, appointed in 1961. The Law School's first tenure appointment was that of the international tax authority Elisabeth Ann Owens in 1972. Helen Vendler, PH.D. '60, a scholar of English and American literature, was the first woman to receive a University Professorship; she was appointed to the A. Kingsley Porter chair in 1990.

The early 1980s saw the first appointments of women to graduate school deanships. Patricia Albjerg Graham, a historian of American education and former Radcliffe vice president, was named dean of the Graduate School of Education in 1982; the anthropologist Sally Falk Moore was appointed dean of the Graduate School of Arts and Sciences in 1985. The first woman to attain vice-presidential status was Sally H. Zeckhauser, who became administrative vice president in 1987. She had previously been president of Harvard Real Estate, Inc., formed in 1979 to manage more than $100 million worth of residential and commercial real estate in Cambridge, Boston, and Allston. By 1997, three of Harvard's five vice presidents were women.

The first woman candidate for overseer appeared on the ballot in 1970. She was Helen Homans Gilbert '36, a Radcliffe trustee. She finished fifth out of ten candidates, and six years later became the first woman to serve as president of the senior board. Judith Richards Hope, J.D. '64, was the first woman elected to the Harvard Corporation. She served from 1989 to 2000.

Harvard granted more than 2,000 honorary degrees before conferring one on a woman. That landmark event came in 1955; the recipient was Helen Keller, Radcliffe class of 1904. She had also been the first deaf and blind student to receive a college degree. A later honorary-degree recipient, Barbara Ward, Lady Jackson, became the first woman to address a Harvard Commencement audience in 1957. Lady Jackson was then assistant editor of *The Economist*.

At the undergraduate level, women were first permitted to attend Harvard classes in 1943—but officially they attended Radcliffe College. That finally changed in the early 1970s, when a "non-merger merger" made Harvard responsible for most of the academic administration of women at the College. (On Harvard's behalf, it might be noted that the College had been the first major all-male institution to derive a workable educational formula to accommodate women in its classrooms.)

The major graduate and professional schools were slow to open their doors to women students. The Medical School's first class to include women—twelve of them—graduated in 1949. The Business School accepted its first women M.B.A. candidates that same year. The first women Law School graduates took their degrees in 1953. The Divinity School did not admit women until 1965. Women students weren't granted the Harvard Ph.D. (as distinct from the Radcliffe Ph.D.) until 1963.

Faye Levine '65 was the first woman to serve as executive editor of the *Crimson.* Over the next dozen years, women rose to leadership positions in virtually every undergraduate organization. Even the *Lampoon* finally succumbed, electing Lisa Henson '82 as the first woman president in the magazine's 106-year history.

"Brains before beauty" has long been an unofficial but generally accepted axiom informing the admissions decisions of the graduate and professional schools. But what about "brains *and* beauty"? Admitted to Harvard Law School, Erika Harold won the Miss Illinois contest and put her academic career on hold so that she could compete in the Miss America Pageant in September 2002. There she sang an aria from *Carmen,* did well on a contemporary-culture quiz, and, at the end of the evening, walked downstage to be crowned the new Miss America. The record suggests that this achievement was another Harvard first. Two recent graduates of the College—Laurie B. Gray '03 (Miss Rhode Island) and Nancy A. Redd '03 (Miss Virginia)—were among the top ten Miss America finalists a year later, garnering more than $20,000 apiece in the course of state and national competitions.

Related entries: Firsts (Men); Radcliffe; University Professors.

Fountains

Harvard has *one* first-rate fountain: a pleasingly mystic assemblage of druidical stones and water vapor, situated north of Harvard Yard, between Memorial Hall and the undergraduate Science

Center. It consists of 150 large field stones from western Massachusetts, arranged to form a slightly lopsided circle about 60 feet in diameter, along with 70 spray jets, which, in timed cycles, can produce dense mist about five feet in height. When the sun is out,
its refracted light yields a rainbow in the horizon of mist. The
fountain can be lighted at night; in winter it operates with low-
pressure steam. Anonymous donors gave this remarkable water-
work to Harvard in 1984. The planners included Peter Walker, ad-
junct professor at the School of Design, and his SWA Group, a
Boston firm. Walker explained that the planners had aimed to create the feeling of "mist at the bottom of a crashing waterfall, but
without the crashing," and to provide a venue that would "encourage sitting, playful entry, and even, in the summer heat, immersion." At the time of its dedication, a news release made reference
simply to "An Original Fountain." Robert and Grace Tanner were
eventually revealed as the imaginative donors, and it is now officially called the Tanner Rock Fountain.

Harvard has other, older fountains, but they disappoint. The
courtyards of Hilles Library and the de Gunzburg Center for European Studies once had them, but they are rarely if ever in working
order. The Class of 1876 Fence (1910), behind Holworthy Hall, includes a memorial fountain, but its dimensions are bird-bath-like,
and it doesn't run. The Classes of 1887–1888 Gate, near Canaday
Hall, incorporates a horse-trough-sized piece of plumbing that
doesn't run either. Two shallow pools in front of William James
Hall once afforded a summer dipping-place for Cambridge youngsters, but when emptied they became depositories for rubbish, and
in time were filled in to serve as flower beds.

Related entries: Gates; the Yard.

Fundraising

Harvard's fundraising prowess can be credited largely to the loyalty
of its alumni, to the financial successes that many have enjoyed,
and to the solicitational skills developed over the years by staff
members and volunteers. In annual surveys taken by the *Chronicle*

of Higher Education, Harvard perennially leads all universities in alumni contributions, as well as in overall fundraising.

That level of achievement takes organization. Across all of Harvard's schools, some 600 staff members are involved in alumni affairs and development work. This includes a range of increasingly specialized areas: major gifts, principal gifts, corporate and foundation giving, annual funds, planned giving, donor relations, communications, alumni clubs and events, reunions, gift processing, computer support, and more. In recent times, the overall development effort has brought in more than $500 million a year in unrestricted and restricted gifts and grants.

The University Development Office (UDO), under the broader umbrella of Alumni Affairs and Development, oversees and coordinates many of the fundraising activities of Harvard's faculties, research centers, and allied institutions. The Harvard College Fund, established in 1926, is the most visible of the University's many fundraising platforms. The fund produces about one-fifth of Harvard's total income from gifts and grants, and its solicitation methods and organization have been widely emulated.

The fund started out with a cadre of 70 class agents who canvassed classmates for unrestricted gifts for current use within the Faculty of Arts and Sciences. In the late 1930s it became the first alumni fund to enlist 10,000 givers in a single year. By 1957, when annual contributions broke the million-dollar mark, the number of donors had risen to 19,000. In later years, the fund's operations became more complex and professionalized. Mailings were supplemented by telephone solicitations. A senior gift program was begun. A class endowment program—enabling donors to make retained life-income gifts to Harvard—was added, along with a parents' fund, a corporate matching-gifts program, and "associates" groups for larger donors. The fund's directors also took a new approach to reunion giving. A major class gift at the time of the twenty-fifth reunion had been traditional since 1902, but such gifts were omitted from the fund's annual totals until 1949. Since the 1970s, the fund has put increased emphasis on reunions other than the twenty-fifth. Its leaders now set annual goals for non-reunion classes, and for classes that have passed the fiftieth reunion. The strategy has worked amazingly well. Collectively, post-fiftieth classes now come up with as much as $40 million a year. One sixtieth-reunion class recently gave $20.6 million, the largest of that year's class gifts; with a donation of more than $18 million, the fiftieth-reunion class also outstripped the twenty-fifth, which gave $13.8 million.

The roster of Harvard College Fund volunteers now exceeds 5,000 and includes increasing numbers of women, minorities, and undergraduates. Some 2,500 are active in a given year; more than half take part in the fund's "phonathons." Solicitation is no longer confined to unrestricted gifts. A change in crediting rules in 1984 opened the way for capital gifts earmarked for endowment, building needs, libraries, professorships, or financial aid.

Since the earliest years of the twentieth century—when the first campaign took in $2.4 million, making Harvard the first institution of higher education to raise as much as a million dollars in a single try—the University's major fund drives have set the standard (and consistently raised the bar) for other universities. The last great fundraising effort of the century was Harvard's first university-wide appeal: the $2.1 billion University Campaign, announced in 1994. By that time other universities had launched billion-dollar campaigns, but no educational institution had sought $2 billion or more. When the final tally was finished early in the millennial year 2000, more than 174,000 alumni and friends had contributed $2.6 billion.

The next major campaign—almost surely the most ambitious yet—will doubtless be mobilized when Harvard completes a complex planning process for the extensive new facilities to be built on its properties in Allston.

Related entries: Allston; Alumni; Reunions. *Related Website:* www.haa.harvard.edu/hcf (Harvard College Fund).

G

"The guardhouse," Harvard's smallest—and, on a cost-per-square-foot basis, most expensive—structure, stands behind Johnston Gate, the main vehicular entrance to the Yard.

Gates

The brick-and-ironwork Memorial Fence, erected at the start of the twentieth century to enclose Harvard Yard, incorporates 26 ornamental gates donated by College classes, clubs, or individuals from 1890 to 1995. Though thousands pass through them daily, few pause to examine the architectural detailing of these portals or to read their inscriptions.

The Johnston Gate (1890), the main entrance to the Yard, is the oldest and most elaborate. Built with funds bequeathed by Samuel Johnston, class of 1855, a Chicago businessman, it was the first Harvard commission of the great Charles Follen McKim, whose architectural firm would plan the Harvard Union, Harvard Stadium, and the Medical School and Business School campuses. The gate's stone pillars, between Massachusetts and Harvard Halls, are inscribed with records of Harvard's founding, including this passage from *New Englands First Fruits* (1643), the earliest printed account of the College:

> After God had carried us safe to *New England*, and wee had builded our houses, provided necessaries for our liveli-hood, rear'd convenient places for Gods worship, and setled the Civill Government: One of the next things we longed for, and looked after was to advance *Learning* and perpetuate it to Posterity; dreading to leave an illiterate Ministery to the Churches, when our present Ministers shall lie in the Dust.

Though the Yard is normally closed to car traffic, the Johnston Gate is the main entrance for maintenance, delivery, and security vehicles. It is also the first University structure to have been built with a high-quality brick, custom-made to replicate the type used in early College buildings, known to masons as Harvard brick.

The Class of 1875 Gate (1900), closer to the heart of Harvard Square, bears an injunction from the Book of Isaiah: "Open ye the gates that the righteous nation that keepeth the truth may enter in."

The Class of 1857 Gate (1901), between Lehman Hall and Wadsworth House, the Yard's second oldest building, opens into the Yard from Massachusetts Avenue. Its Latin inscription is from an ode of Horace: "Felices ter et amplius, quos inrupta tenet copula nec malis divulsus querimoniis suprema citius solvet amor die." ("Thrice happy and more are they whom an unbroken bond unites and whom no sundering of love by wretched quarrels shall separate before life's final day.")

The McKean Gate (1901) faces the Porcellian Club's quarters on the other side of Massachusetts Avenue. Given by the Porcellian, oldest of the elite final clubs, it bears the club's emblem, a boar's head, above the arch. The gate is named for the Reverend James McKean, class of 1794, the founder of the club (and Harvard's Boylston Professor of Rhetoric and Oratory from 1809 to 1818).

The Class of 1890 Gate (1901), also on Massachusetts Avenue, leads into the Yard through a Wigglesworth Hall archway. "Enter to grow in wisdom" is inscribed on the street side; within are the words "Depart, better to serve thy country and thy kind." Both legends were composed by President Charles William Eliot.

Set in a curved retaining wall at the corner of Massachusetts Avenue and Quincy Street, the Class of 1880 Gate (1901) bears the names of distinguished classmates Theodore Roosevelt and Robert Bacon (a former secretary of state, ambassador to France, and fellow of Harvard College). This locked gate has led nowhere since 1949, when the construction of Lamont Library blocked it off.

On the far side of the Yard, north of the Johnston Gate, the Class of 1870 Gate and Sundial (1901) front Harvard's third oldest building, Holden Chapel. Facing Cambridge Common, this gate is also locked; two nearby gates were closed when Lionel and Mower Halls were completed in 1926. On the base of the elegant little 1870 sundial are the haunting words, "On this moment hangs eternity."

The Class of 1876 Gate (1900), also known as the Holworthy Gate, is the Yard's principal opening to the northwest. It gives access to the Music Building, the Law School campus, the undergraduate Science Center, and other science buildings. Nearby is a much newer gate, added in 1995 as part of a $2.3 million restoration of the Memorial Fence. A quarter-century earlier, the demolition of Hunt Hall (to make space for a freshman dormitory) had left a conspicuous gap in the fence. The new gate and 180 feet of adjoining brick and ironwork completed the enclosure of the 22-acre Harvard Yard; the gate was formally dedicated in 1997 to mark the twenty-fifth anniversary of the opening of freshman residence halls to women. The gate's slate plaque quotes the poet Anne Bradstreet, a seventeenth-century citizen of Cambridge and early Harvard parent: "I came into this Country where I found a new World and new manners at which my heart rose." Though the dedicatory theme had not been thought of when the gate was planned, architect Michael Teller presciently transformed the original fencing's militaristic rows of ornamental spear tips into gentler rows of tulips.

Further east, the picturesque Gates of the Classes of 1887 and 1888 (1906) form the Yard's only double-entry portal. Around the corner, on Quincy Street, are two relatively late additions to the Memorial Fence: the Class of 1885 Gate (1914), facing the Fogg Art Museum and opening into Sever Quadrangle, and the Eliot Gate (1936). Given by the class of 1908, the last to graduate during Charles Eliot's 40-year presidency, the Eliot Gate stood at what was once the north entrance to the driveway of the President's House. On it are the words of Edward Cotton, an Eliot biographer: "He opened paths for our children's feet to follow. Something of him will be a part of us forever."

The Dudley Gate (1915), a conspicuous clock tower marking the south entrance to the President's House driveway, was demolished, along with the driveway, after World War II. Across Quincy Street, the Hallowell Gate (1928), a gift of the class of 1901, leads into the Harvard Union complex (now the Barker Center for the Humanities).

Ornamental gatework is a part of the older residential houses and of Radcliffe Yard. Of the several gates in the fence enclosing Soldiers Field, the Newell Gate—a memorial to Marshall Newell, class of 1894, an admired football player and oarsman—is the most distinctive. Just south of the Anderson Bridge, this gate forms the principal pedestrian entrance to the athletics complex.

Related entries: Architecture; Final Clubs; Guardhouse; Holden Chapel; Houses; Soldiers Field; Wadsworth House; the Yard.

Gay and Lesbian

Like most institutions of higher education today, Harvard has a range of groups based on sexual orientation. For undergraduates, the principal one is the Bisexual, Gay, Lesbian, Transgendered, and Supporters Alliance (BGLTSA). Graduate and professional schools have similar associations; for alumni, faculty, and staff, there's the Harvard Gay and Lesbian Caucus (HGLC), with local chapters in many U.S. and foreign cities and an overall membership of more than 2,500.

The existence of these formal organizations would have been hard to imagine in earlier times, when members of the University community who were attracted to persons of the same sex had to be highly circumspect. Some hid their feelings even from themselves. Others might socialize at gay bars in Boston or clandestine gatherings in Cambridge—but with caution, since exposure could bring ostracism or even disciplinary action. In one long-buried disciplinary case, a five-member administrative board investigated homosexual activities involving a handful of Harvard students, a young philosophy instructor, and a few outsiders, following the suicide of a College sophomore in 1920. Citing "unspeakably gross acts," the board ordered seven undergraduates and a Dental School student to leave Harvard; the instructor was fired. The dental student took his own life, and one of the banished undergraduates did so years later. (Records of the inquiry remained secret until 2002, when an enterprising *Crimson* reporter secured their release and meticulously reconstructed the case.)

In the wake of the social and political upheavals of the 1960s, prevailing attitudes started to change. New York City's 1969 Stonewall Riot was the rallying point that brought the gay movement into the open, and not long after it a Harvard-Radcliffe Gay Students Association was formed. Its purpose was primarily social. The aims of the Gay and Lesbian Caucus, organized in 1983, were explicitly political. Over the years its members successfully lobbied to include sexual orientation in the University's antidiscrimination policy statement; to extend Harvard benefits to same-sex partners; and to end University involvement with ROTC, since that program excluded openly gay, lesbian, and bisexual students. The HGLC also created a foundation to support gay and lesbian interests at Harvard and Radcliffe; established a public service fellowship and a resource center; published a literary quarterly and a newsletter; and sponsored readings, lectures, and social events. The HGLC continues to advocate the appointment of gay, lesbian, bisexual, or transgendered tutors and proctors in the residential houses and freshman dormitories; to work for the election of gay and lesbian alumni to the Board of Overseers and the board of directors of the Harvard Alumni Association; and to encourage the academic study of gay and lesbian history and concerns. The HGLC admits students as non-voting members. An annual dinner meeting takes place at the Faculty Club on Commencement Day.

Significant milestones for Harvard's gay and lesbian community have included the election of an openly gay man, Thomas Parry '74, to the Alumni Association's board of directors in 1995; the election, two years later, of the first openly gay candidate for the Board of Overseers, Sheila Kuehl, J.D. '78, then speaker pro tem of the California State Assembly; the acceptance of same-sex commitment ceremonies by Memorial Church, announced in 1997; and the appointment in 1998 of same-sex partners, Professor Diana Eck and the Reverend Dorothy Austin, as masters of Lowell House.

Among the Harvard and Radcliffe alumni who have been at the forefront of the gay rights movement at the national level are Frank Kameny, PH.D. '56, who in the late 1950s filed the first gay antidiscrimination lawsuit after being fired as an army maps service astronomer because of his sexual orientation; Massachusetts representative Barney Frank '61, J.D. '77, the most articulate Congressional exponent of gay rights; and New York District Court Judge Deborah Batts '69, J.D. '72, who was named to the federal judiciary by President Clinton in 1994 and remains, at this writing, its first and only openly gay member.

Related entries: Fictional Harvard; Reunions; ROTC. *Related Websites:* www.hcs.harvard.edu/~queer (Harvard BGLTSA); hglc.org (Gay and Lesbian Caucus).

Gazette

What's new at Harvard? There are many ways to find out: read the daily *Crimson,* the weekly *Independent,* or the bimonthly *Harvard Magazine;* log on to the University's Webpage; or subscribe to "Harvard in the News," a daily email digest put out by the News Office.

If weekly reading suits you best, the most comprehensive and authoritative medium is the *Harvard University Gazette.* This official publication is delivered free during the academic year to faculty, staff, undergraduate residences, and other locations throughout the University; outsiders may subscribe for $25 a year ($32 beyond the United States). The *Gazette* puts out 36 issues a year and distributes upwards of 31,000 copies per week. Copies are available without charge at the Holyoke Center information office. Two special issues, recapping each semester's major features and reports, are sent free to alumni each year.

First published in 1906, the *Gazette* survived for many years as a small-circulation broadsheet that was essentially an academic calendar. In 1969—a time of student protest and discord, when communicating the University's point of view was seen as an imperative—the *Gazette* was recast as a tabloid newspaper. Since then it has continued to expand, presenting more consistent news coverage and more feature articles, improving its layouts and typography, and in recent years increasing its use of four-color illustrations.

In addition to covering significant University issues and events, the *Gazette* carries summaries of discussions and votes at faculty meetings; the texts of memorial minutes presented at those meetings; profiles of faculty and staff members; a coming-events calendar; athletic schedules and summaries; "This Month in Harvard History"; police-blotter records; obituaries; and "Opportunities," a listing of job descriptions and salary grades for open positions within the University.

Related entries: Harvard Crimson; Harvard Magazine. *Related Website:* www.harvard.edu (the University's home page).

Gilbert & Sullivan

Little Buttercup, Nanki-Poo, the Duke of Plaza-Toro, Jack Point, Reginald Bunthorne, Mad Margaret, and others of their ilk have been doing turns on the Agassiz Theatre stage for almost half a century, under the aegis of the Harvard-Radcliffe Gilbert & Sullivan Players. Each year the Cambridge Savoyards present an operetta in early December and another in early spring; the troupe's impresarios tout their December offering as the best-attended, biggest-budgeted show—with the largest cast, crew, and pit orchestra—of any fall production at Harvard.

Since 1956, the company's inventive producers have been recycling a dozen works from the G&S canon (omitting only the great collaborators' first effort, *Thespis,* a largely lost work, and their last, *The Grand Duke,* generally rated as substandard). HRG&SP is an undergraduate organization, though some of its productions have featured alumni and/or professional directors and singers from the local arts community. The opening night of a show's nine-performance run is a black-tie affair; the run ends with "hack night," when cast members traditionally take unbridled liberties with their lines. At intervals, the G&S Players have forsaken the canon: they offered Johann Strauss Jr.'s *Die Fledermaus* in 1969; a musical adaptation of Charles Dickens's *The Mystery of Edwin Drood* in 1993; and George and Ira Gershwin's *Of Thee I Sing* in 1999.

The first G&S performance at Harvard may have been a concert version of *The Pirates of Penzance* at Sanders Theatre in 1896, sixteen years after the operetta's première. Other productions were mounted sporadically until 1950, when the Winthrop House

Drama Society launched an annual series. Members of the group formed the Harvard Gilbert & Sullivan Players in 1956, and "Radcliffe" was added to the organization's charter in 1991.

The G&S Players made do with piano accompaniments until 1960, when a Loeb Drama Center production was staged with full pit orchestra. The disciplined playing of what is now a 50-piece unit has become a musical strong point of the company. A 1975 production of *Iolanthe* had an orchestra whose members included Christopher Wilkens, former assistant conductor of the Cleveland Orchestra, as principal oboe; violinist Lynn Chang '75, a winner of the International Paganini Competition, as assistant concertmaster; and Yo-Yo Ma '76, soon to be world-famous, as principal cello.

Related entries: Arts; Music. *Related Website:* www.hcs.harvard.edu/ ~hrgsp/.

Glass Flowers

Preserved at the Museum of Natural History on Oxford Street, the world-renowned Glass Flowers are one of Harvard's two most popular tourist attractions, drawing an estimated 120,000 visitors a year. (The other magnet for tourists is the John Harvard statue.) These elegant blown-glass models—more than 4,000 in all—constitute what has been called "the Sistine Chapel of the glass world." Delicate, beautiful, amazingly realistic, they were crafted by Leopold and Rudolph Blaschka, a father-and-son team of German glass blowers, between 1887 and 1936.

The Glass Flowers are more formally known as the Ware Collection of Glass Models of Plants. Viewers should not expect dazzling arrangements or beautiful bouquets. Each model is a scientific specimen, soberly displayed in a glass case, labeled and organized in taxonomically correct order, and representing almost 850 botanical species. Lilies, roses, pines, cacti, and fungal bodies are just a few of the horticultural samples rendered in glass. Some are shown in magnified models—as much as four times life-size, or even larger—demonstrating such botanical basics as insect pollination, plant reproductive cycles, and plant diseases.

Professor George Lincoln Goodale, founder of Harvard's Botanical Museum, commissioned these remarkable feats of glass modeling in the 1880s as an improvement on the traditional but inexact wax and papier-mâché replicas used for botanical teaching and research. The Blaschkas, whose family had been fashioning artistic glass reproductions for four centuries in and around the village of Hosterwitz, near Dresden, had mastered the technique of developing subtle colors in glass, completing their works—which were sometimes supported by wire armatures—with paint, enamel, and animal glues. The arrival of the Glass Flowers at Harvard elicited universal acclaim for the beauty of the objects themselves and for their great potential as teaching tools.

Botanical teaching methods have changed: the Glass Flowers are now considered more of an artistic curiosity than a learning device. Over the years, the deleterious effect of ultraviolet lighting and the harmful vibrations from viewers' feet have taken a toll on the more delicate models. This has necessitated a massive and costly restoration program, requiring an estimated 15,000 hours of conservation work, mostly off-site, by highly trained specialists. For some time to come, only a portion of the Glass Flowers will be exhibited while the full collection is cleaned and repaired.

In addition to his work on the Glass Flowers, Rudolph Blaschka created glass models of sea anemones, sea cucumbers, cuttlefish, jellyfish, squids, slugs, and other marine invertebrates for the Museum of Comparative Zoology.

Related entries: John Harvard—and His Statue; Museums. *Related Website:* www.hmnh.harvard.edu/exhibitions/glassflowers.html.

God's Acre

Mossy headstones in the Old Cambridge Burying Ground are the oldest remaining link with Harvard's first years. In fact, the burial field predates Harvard: records of an early town meeting in 1635 include an order "that the Burying Place be paled [fenced] in." Cambridge, then called Newtowne, was still being settled, and the creation of a "schoale or colledge" was almost two years away.

God's Acre can be entered from Garden Street, opposite Cam-

bridge Common, close to the heart of Harvard Square. Its plot—
actually about two acres in size—is bounded on the north by historic Christ Church (Episcopal) and on the south by the First Parish Church (Unitarian). Here lie the remains of the town's first
leaders: a provincial governor, judges, scholars, and nine Harvard
presidents—Dunster, Chauncy, Oakes, Rogers, Leverett, Wadsworth, Holyoke, Willard, and Webber.

The Old Burying Ground is also the resting place of Thomas
Shepard, the most powerful evangelical preacher of his time and a
member of Harvard's first Board of Overseers, assembled in 1642;
of Stephen Daye and Samuel Green, the first College printers; and
of Jonathan Belcher, class of 1699, provincial governor of Massachusetts and New Hampshire, later governor of New Jersey. The
formidable Henry Flynt, class of 1693, a tutor for 55 years and fellow for 61, lies here, as does the first Hollis Professor of Divinity,
Edward Wigglesworth, class of 1710.

Fourteen minutemen who died in the battles of Concord and
Lexington are buried here. The "Dana tomb," from a later era,
holds the remains of Chief Justice Francis Dana, class of 1762; the
painter Washington Allston, class of 1800; the poet Richard Henry
Dana, class of 1837, and other members of the Dana family.

Latin inscriptions on some of the grave markers, almost illegible
today, memorialize youths who died while still in college. One
was Thomas Spear *(Singulari Temperantia Sobrietate et Humilitate
Juvenis)*, only sixteen at his death in 1723. Noah Merrick and
Charles Cutter both drowned *(Lacu Cantabrigiensi casu submersi)*,
in 1762 and 1779 respectively. John Holyoke, son of President Edward Holyoke, succumbed in 1753, just two years after taking his
degree.

Though the oldest headstones are severely eroded, some are of
surprising thickness. A few reveal the outline of a winged skull,
with such legends as *Memento Mori* and *Fugit Hora*. Here and
there, visitors to God's Acre are still reminded that

Death is a Debt to Nature Due;
As I Have Paid It, So Must You.

Related entries: Firsts (Men); Harvard Hill; Presidents.

"Godless Harvard"

From Harvard's earliest days, religion and religious services have been a meaningful—if variable—presence in the lives of students and faculty. In the seventeenth century, religion in its Puritan form was pervasive: in frequent services of prayer and daily Bible readings, and in the course curriculum, lectures, language requirements, observances of holy days, and the Commencement exercises. The College's first stated mission, after all, had been "to advance learning, and perpetuate it to Posterity; dreading to leave an illiterate ministry to the churches, when our present ministers shall lie in the dust," and the College statutes of 1646 had ordained that "Every one shall consider the mayne End of his life and studyes, to know God and Jesus Christ which is Eternall life."

That College was a rather far cry from the one that late-nineteenth-century detractors sometimes derided—in Cotton Mather's eighteenth-century phrasing—as "godless Harvard." It was true that in the liberalizing regime of President Charles W. Eliot, Harvard had been the first of America's religiously founded colleges to abandon compulsory chapel, in 1886. But morning prayers, Sunday services, and courses in religion continued to be an integral part of College life for the next century and beyond.

In recent decades, a religious groundswell has been evident in the College and some of the professional schools. Largely driven by student interests, this new and deeply personal concern with religion draws on all of the traditional faiths and many belief systems outside the mainstream. An assistant dean of the College has stated that the parents of incoming first-year students increasingly inquire about religious resources. "In fact," says the dean, "the second most frequently asked question is 'where do Harvard students attend church, synagogue, temple, or religious services of various kinds?'" (The most frequent parental question, not surprisingly, concerns the availability of financial aid.)

Signs of renewed religious interest at Harvard are plentiful. At registration, growing numbers of students return religious preference forms. Student attendance is up at Memorial Church, Harvard Hillel, the Catholic Student Center, the Islamic Society, and other churches and centers near Harvard Square. Some of the College's largest enrollments are in courses dealing with the Bible, Christian ethics, the spread of Islam, religion in America, and other religious topics. Many undergraduate houses have informal religious study groups that are organized and led by students.

Diversity, pluralism, and varieties of spiritual experience characterize religious life at Harvard today—a circumstance that is underscored by the roll of chaplains in the University's United Ministry. There are almost 30 chaplaincies—and the number is larger if one takes into account various subdivisions (the Orthodox, Conservative, and Reform branches of Judaism, for example). The chaplaincies serving Harvard students are:

Baha'i Association
Baptist (American)
Baptist (Conservative)
Baptist (Southern)
Boston-Cambridge Ministry in
    Higher Education
Buddhist Community
Campus Crusade for Christ
    (interdenominational)
Catholic Student Center /
    St. Paul's Church
Chabad House (Jewish)
Christian Science Organization
Church of Jesus Christ of
    Latter-Day Saints
Episcopal
Hindu Fellowship
Hillel Foundation (Jewish)

Humanist
Intervarsity Christian Fellow-
    ship
Islamic Society
Lutheran Campus Ministry
Memorial Church (Protestant
    nondenominational)
Orthodox Christian Fellowship
    (Eastern rites)
Presbyterian
Religious Society of Friends
    (Quakers)
Swedenborgian
Unitarian Universalist
United Church of Christ (Con-
    gregationalist)
United Methodist
Zoroastrian Association

All of these ministries sponsor programs to help students deal with personal crises and issues of spirituality or ethics. According to many chaplains, students often come to them saying, "I want to get to know my religion better," or "I need help to grow in what I believe is most important in my life." In addition to offering such support, members of the United Ministry are committed to a collaborative code of non-proselytization and respect for the religions of others. This means that they oppose all forms of religious harassment and manipulation and will assist any student who becomes the target of "destructive religious groups."

The many activities of the Divinity School, with its Center for the Study of World Religions; the Harvard Business School's architecturally stunning nondenominational chapel; Professor Diana Eck's Pluralism Project, documenting the growing presence of Muslim, Buddhist, Hindu, Sikh, Jain, and Zoroastrian communities in the United States; and the popular undergraduate courses long taught by Professor of Divinity Harvey Cox, Professor Eck, Professor James Kugel, and the Reverend Professor Peter J. Gomes, Pusey Minister in the Memorial Church and Plummer Professor of Christian Morals, are other notable features of Harvard's religious landscape.

The continuing existence of morning prayers in Memorial Church—a tradition that harks back to the College's founding— may be symbolic of religion generally at Harvard. The service takes place from 8:45 to 9:00, Monday through Saturday during term time. Speakers from virtually every faith, and from all parts of the University and outside it, address the congregation; on occasion the president of Harvard, or a dean, may occupy the pulpit.

Related entries: Divinity School; Gates; Memorial Church; Music. *Related Website:* www.memorialchurch.harvard.edu.

Gold Coast

This three-block cluster of residence halls and clubhouses on Mount Auburn Street may have lost some of the glitter it had when it got its sobriquet. But the Gold Coast remains an architecturally intriguing and historically evocative quarter of the College.

The grandly scaled buildings lining the north side of the street were planned in the 1890s and are emblematic of an era that the

social and literary critic Henry Seidel Canby called the Age of
Confidence. Over the first two decades of Charles W. Eliot's presidency, from 1870 to 1890, the College's enrollment had doubled,
but no undergraduate dormitories had been added since 1871.
"The Corporation," as Samuel Eliot Morison has written, "left the
housing of the new increment to private capital." Beck Hall, built
where the Inn at Harvard Square now stands, was the first of 20
luxury apartment houses erected between 1876 and 1904. Claverly
Hall, constructed in 1892, started the trend to Mount Auburn
Street. Stolid buildings named Dana Chambers, Randolph Hall,
Apley Court, Russell Hall, and Westmorly Court filled out the
Gold Coast over the next eight years. The Lampoon castle, set on a
triangular lot facing Randolph Hall, added an impish architectural
fillip in 1910.

At a time when many Yard dormitories still lacked central heating and plumbing above the basement, the new residence halls
offered suites with private baths and steam heat. And more:
Randolph Hall, with its Queen Anne turrets and Flemish gables,
had its own quadrangle, tennis court, and squash courts.
Westmorly Court had its diamond-leaded window panes and oak
wainscoting. Claverly, Randolph, and Westmorly had indoor
swimming pools. There were uniformed doormen and even but-
lers. For wealthy students, the Gold Coast became the epicenter of
undergraduate life. Its denizens could dine at "waiting" or "final"
clubs just a block or two away. Playing fields and boathouses were
within a few minutes' walk. A tunnel connected Claverly Hall to
the Lampoon and the Fly Club across the street. Franklin D. Roosevelt '04 was one of many well-heeled freshmen who were drawn
to the newly completed halls. (He and his Groton schoolmate,
Lathrop Brown, secured a first-floor suite in Westmorly Court,
now Adams House B-17, where they roomed for four years.) Suites
in Claverly Hall were so coveted that would-be residents had to be
elected in freshman year.

"The Corporation did nothing to meet this competition in
the way of providing modern conveniences in the Yard," noted
Professor Morison, "and the only residential halls that the College erected—the highly unattractive Conant, Perkins, and Walter

Hastings—were so far from the new centre that only freshmen, law, and graduate students would live in them." Not until 1914, with the opening of three freshman residence halls in the early years of President A. Lawrence Lowell's administration, did the College start to catch up with undergraduate housing needs. Its next step was to acquire Gold Coast properties during and after World War I. In 1916 Harvard obtained Randolph Hall in a swap for College House, an aging Harvard Square building that combined student housing and street-level stores. Required residence in the new freshman halls, coupled with a 35 percent drop in war-time enrollment, soon made the private residence halls increasingly unprofitable. By 1920 the College had purchased six of them, including Claverly Hall and Westmorly Court, on favorable terms. A decade later, when the residential house system was born, Claverly was ceded to Lowell House and was also used to absorb overflows from other houses. Westmorly and Randolph became components of Adams House.

Of the seven original houses, urbane Adams was thus the only one to keep its distance from Georgian Revival styling. Its ornate interiors are pleasingly esoteric. The entrance lobby of the tower block—erected in 1931 on the site of the old Russell Hall—is in Italian Renaissance style. Above the wrought-iron balustrades and torchères of the main staircase is an intricate Moorish dome. The library boasts cherrywood paneling and a barrel-vaulted ceiling. Bainbridge Bunting's *Harvard: An Architectural History* compares the house dining hall to "the pump room of an eighteenth-century British spa." Some of the elegance of the old Gold Coast lives on at Adams House.

Related entries: Architecture; Final Clubs; Houses; Lampoon.

Governance

Responsibility for Harvard's corporate well-being is vested in two distinct governing bodies, both dating from the seventeenth century: the Board of Overseers and the President and Fellows, also known as the Harvard Corporation. Of the two, the latter is decidedly the more powerful; and since 1650, when the Corporation was chartered, the statutory duties of the Overseers have been far from clear. Yet for all its idiosyncrasies, this venerable machinery has served the institution surprisingly well for more than three and a half centuries.

The Overseers. The composition of the Honorable and Reverend Board of Overseers—an antique term still used on some formal occasions—has changed from time to time, but since 1865 it has consisted of 30 elected members. Broadly, the board's mandate is to monitor the life of the University to ensure that the institution fulfills its charter obligations as a place of learning; to provide advice and counsel; and to consent to certain acts of the Corporation. Visiting committees have long been a principal device for exercising oversight. There are now about 60, assigned to all of Harvard's schools, departments of the Faculty of Arts and Sciences, the library system, and various other entities.

Members serve six-year terms. Five are elected annually, from a slate chosen by a committee of the Harvard Alumni Association. All degree-holders, except those holding Harvard appointments, are eligible to vote. The electorate now numbers more than 200,000; from 15 to 20 percent cast votes in a typical year.

The founding of the Board of Overseers dates from an act of the General Court of the Massachusetts Bay Colony in 1642. This board supplanted an earlier board of *inspectores,* appointed in 1637 to manage the opening of the infant college. The newer board, designed to govern an institution that was now a going concern, had 22 members: the governor and deputy governor; the magistrates of the colony; the ordained ministers of Cambridge, Boston, and four surrounding towns; and the president of the College. Nowhere in the act of 1642 is the word *overseer* used, but it does appear in the Charter of 1650.

The Board of Overseers typically meets five times a year. Much of its business is conducted in standing committees, where members interact with representatives of the administration and faculties. A significant use of the Board's counsel-and-consent authority comes in connection with the election of a new president of the University or the selection of other new Corporation members.

The Corporation. The smaller of the two governing boards, the Harvard Corporation has retained virtually the same form since 1650. It is the oldest chartered corporation in North America. The seven members include the president and treasurer and a self-perpetuating body of five fellows, who serve open-ended terms. Until quite recently, the Corporation was actively involved in much of the day-to-day management of the University, and in effect was a combined multiple executive and board of trustees. With the evolution of a larger administration, and with far less Corporation involvement in everyday affairs, "multiple executive" has become a less applicable term.

The powers of the Corporation are formidable. All University property, including the endowment, stands in its name. Every faculty is subject to its ultimate control. All degrees are officially voted by the President and Fellows, and all appointments are made by their designees. Investment and budgetary matters, and the disposition of University property, are technically within the Corporation's purview, though the oversight of the endowment is the direct responsibility of the Harvard Management Company and its board.

The inability of the Board of Overseers to deal efficiently with the ordinary business of the College brought the Corporation into being. In mid-seventeenth-century Massachusetts, assembling the Overseers was a major task, and with the exception of the president, almost none of its members had an adequate grasp of institutional affairs. With the creation of the Corporation in 1650 the General Court sought to give Harvard the kind of autonomy enjoyed by colleges within the universities of Cambridge and Oxford. But the new structure differed from the English model in one important respect: the continued existence of the overseeing senior board.

The Corporation meets approximately eleven times a year, usually for about five hours, and holds a two-day retreat in the summer. The president of Harvard chairs the meetings. The agenda may include budgetary analyses, fundraising, tuition rates, and other economic issues; capital project reviews; investment and endowment concerns; and long-range financial planning. Regular reports, written and oral, are given by deans and heads of University institutions. One of the Corporation's paramount duties is to choose, with the advice and consent of the Overseers, the president of Harvard. It acts as a confidential sounding board to the president, and, in a larger sense, reinforces the office by complementing and enlarging the president's strengths.

Until the late eighteenth century, the Fellows of Harvard College were drawn from the faculty. Since then, members have come primarily from the legal and financial professions. The Corporation's first woman member, Judith Richards Hope, J.D. '64, joined the board in 1989 and served until 2000. As of 2004 the fellows included a corporate chief executive officer; a senior partner of a management consulting firm; a historian and former university president; a lawyer who had been the State Department's chief legal officer; the former director of the Congressional Budget Office, now the president of a nonprofit policy institute; and an executive who served as secretary of the U.S. treasury (President Lawrence Summers). It included one woman and one minority member. Three were graduates of Harvard College; with the exception of President Summers, none was from the Cambridge/Boston area.

Related entries: ETOB; Firsts (Women); Presidents.

Grade Inflation

You'll hear differing theories about the causes, and differing views about what to do about it. But there's general agreement that grade inflation has been endemic at Harvard College—more so, in fact, than at many other selective institutions.

The proportion of seniors graduating with honors has risen steadily since the mid-1940s, when just under one-third earned summa cum laude, magna cum laude, or cum laude degrees. The high-water mark came in 2001, when a record 91 percent of seniors took honors. The comparable figures at Yale and Princeton were 51 percent and 41 percent. Were Harvard students really that much smarter? Or did Yale and Princeton have (ahem) higher standards? Whatever the answers, a grading spectrum that had once ranged from A to F was now running the gamut from A to B. And with more As than Bs: in 2001, 48 percent of *all* undergraduate grades were As or A-minuses, while 40 percent were within the B range.

Grade inflation is a national problem, and faculty members have dithered about it for years. When the number of Harvard summa degrees soared from 79 to 115 in 1996, the Faculty of Arts and Sciences moved to cap the proportion at 5 percent of the graduating class (roughly 85). In the fall of 2001, the dean for undergraduate education relayed a faculty committee's conclusion "that grade inflation has become a serious problem . . . and that steps should be taken to combat it." She released data that affirmed what was already recognized: that grades in the humanities were "notably higher" than in the natural and social sciences. The faculty soon passed legislation aimed at stiffening grading standards, achieving consistency among academic divisions, and limiting the distribution of honors within departments.

Even before the new rules took effect, administrators reported that the inflationary trend might have peaked. In the academic year 2001–02, for the first time in recent decades, the College's mean grade declined slightly from the previous year.

Some faculty members and many students have argued that since admission to the College becomes more competitive each year, the increasing competence of entering students naturally drives up the mean grade. But since Yale's and Princeton's admissions processes are equally selective, what accounts for the far smaller percentages of students earning honors at those institutions? In any event, many Harvard faculty members doubt that today's students are significantly brighter or more accomplished than those of past generations.

That grade inflation is in part a legacy of the 1960s is a widely held view. Its adherents argue that during the Vietnam war, many faculty members relaxed their grading standards so that male students would not lose draft deferments. Indeed, the late 1960s seem to have been a defining moment in the history of grade inflation at Harvard: in 1969, average SAT scores for entering freshmen declined, but grades in the A-to-B range showed a 10 percent increase. A reduction in the average size of classes and sections—obviously a good thing in itself—is a more recent factor. The data issued by the dean for undergraduate education showed that grades increased as class size diminished ("an unintended but understandable consequence of closer involvement by faculty with students").

Whatever the underlying causes, grade inflation may at last be abating. Awarding honors to 91 percent of a class does raise questions about the stringency of the College's academic standards. And Don Alhambra de Bolero, the Grand Inquisitor in Gilbert and Sullivan's *The Gondoliers,* did have a point when he sang, "In short, whoever you may be / To this conclusion you'll agree / When every one is somebodee / Then no one's anybody!"

Related entries: Admissions; Gilbert & Sullivan; Ivy League.

GSAS

In many categories, Harvard is the first and oldest. In graduate education, however, it must defer to Yale and Johns Hopkins. The first Ph.D. in the United States was conferred at Yale in 1861. Harvard awarded its first Ph.D. (in mathematics) to William Byerly more than a decade later, in 1873. And although Harvard established a small Graduate Department in 1872, it wasn't until 1889–90—long after Yale and Hopkins had organized such schools—that what is now Harvard's Graduate School of Arts and Sciences took shape.

Today the GSAS enrolls more than 3,200 students pursuing advanced degrees—mostly Ph.D.s and A.M.s—in some 53 separate programs, ranging from anthropology to East Asian languages and civilization to physics and sociology.

Harvard's creation of a Graduate Department in 1872 reflected the farsighted leadership of perhaps its greatest president, Charles W. Eliot. Early in his administration, Eliot recognized that Harvard could never equal the great European universities, and especially the German universities, without a faculty and a program that awarded advanced degrees. Typically, his thinking and proposals stimulated instant opposition. Some decried the cost, maintaining that the University had insufficient funds to teach undergraduates properly. A Graduate Department, these critics held, would inevitably weaken and diminish education in the College. President Eliot, however, declared that the graduate school "will strengthen the College. As long as the main duty of the faculty is to teach boys, professors need never pursue their subjects beyond a certain point. With graduate students to teach, they will regard their subjects as infinite, and will keep up that constant investigation which is so necessary for the best teaching."

Overall, GSAS receives more than 10,000 applications a year; about 11 percent of those applicants are accepted. A large proportion of graduate students receive some form of financial aid. In contrast to the College, graduate students are seen as financially "free-standing," and parental resources are not usually taken into account in granting financial aid. In recent years, the school's annual budgets for financial assistance—both unrestricted and restricted funds—have amounted to a staggering $30 million. This doesn't include more than $14 million in sponsored funds from outside institutions. Increasingly, the best potential graduate students are offered so-called merit scholarships as an enticement. Other scholarships are tailored to minority members and special classes of student. GSAS administrators take pride in the diversity of the student body, which includes a large proportion of international enrollees (now more than 25 percent of the total).

In the social sciences and the humanities, students ordinarily take two years of course work—four courses per term in residence—and then, while working as teaching fellows in undergraduate courses, begin research for their doctoral dissertations. Graduate students often apply for and receive traveling fellowships to study abroad. The elapsed time for the completion of Ph.D. requirements in these areas can vary from five or six years to as much as eight or ten years. In fields where multiple language competencies are needed, the length of time may be extended. Recent reform proposals have stipulated that time limitations be imposed as graduate students fulfill their requirements, similar to those of the Law School (three years for the J.D.) and Business School (two years for the M.B.A.).

Most course work in the sciences occurs in laboratories where experiments and research are done under the supervision of senior faculty members. The length of time required to complete the Ph.D. in such fields as chemistry, physics, or biology is generally four to five years. The Ph.D. dissertation in the sciences also is different in that students, sometimes working in teams, perform experiments and then present their results in jointly authored journal articles.

The heavy teaching load assumed by Harvard graduate students has been a sensitive issue. Claims are heard that the University exploits its graduate students and deprives undergraduates of meaningful contact with senior faculty members. At Yale and Princeton, it's said, undergraduate courses are mostly taught by regular faculty members, not graduate students. Harvard's answer is that graduate students here teach sections in big courses, in which large numbers of undergraduates attend lectures by senior faculty and then benefit from intense learning sessions in sections of fifteen to eighteen students, led by fresh, enthusiastic young teaching fellows on the threshold of their academic careers. Almost all graduate students avail themselves of the opportunity to improve their teaching skills by attending sessions at the Derek Bok Center for Teaching and Learning. Videotaping of sections, counseling by senior advisors, and micro-teaching evaluations (getting teaching fellows to present a five-minute unit of teaching and then critiquing the relative strengths and weaknesses) are all part of the Bok Center's program.

Graduate school life has never been easy for young men and women who must work long hours, often in isolation and without recognition, as they pursue studies that may come to seem remote from "real world" issues. Stress over grades, covert and overt competition with one's peers, a pervasive atmosphere of survival of the fittest, and the appearance, if not the reality, of preoccupied faculty advisors often lead to anxiety and alienation. One tragic symptom is the incidence of suicide among graduate students at Harvard and other universities. The GSAS administration has responded by providing counseling through the University Health Services and by reviewing the advising system.

Related entries: Deans; Diversity; Firsts (Men); Firsts (Women); Life Raft; UHS. *Related Website:* www.gsas.harvard.edu.

GSD

Preparing architects, landscape designers, and urban planners for a rapidly changing environment is a complex mission. Harvard's Graduate School of Design (GSD) must deal with sweeping trends like globalization; such evolving technologies as computer-aided design; the uses of new materials and construction methods; and the political and economic imperatives of environmental responsibility. All this makes for a stimulating intellectual milieu, but also for a highly challenging one that requires the capacity to accommodate varied perspectives and input from different disciplines.

The GSD offers three kinds of degrees in distinct but related fields. Professional programs prepare graduates for entry into the practice of architecture, landscape design, and urban planning; post-professional degree programs cater to the needs of established practitioners; and the school's doctoral programs provide opportunities for research and scholarship that will undergird future teaching and advance the work of design professionals.

In addition to these degree programs, the GSD sponsors a range of other instructional and research programs and centers:

- The Loeb Fellowship Program, in which nine to twelve mid-career professionals annually pursue independent study.
- The Executive Education Program, offering customized courses for higher-level executives and practicing designers.
- The Career Discovery Program, a six-week summer program that assists young professionals in sorting out career opportunities.
- The Center for Design Informatics.
- The Center for Urban Development Studies.
- The Joint Center for Housing Studies.
- The Real Estate Academic Initiative.
- The Center for Technology and Environment.

The GSD has a faculty of almost 100—including visiting scholars from all over the world—and an enrollment of more than 550. Faculty members are often leading practitioners in their fields:

their day-to-day experience in dealing with clients, funding agencies, and political players adds a critical dimension of authority and credibility to their teaching.

The GSD has existed as such since 1936, making it the second youngest (after the Kennedy School of Government) of Harvard's professional schools. However, its roots go back to 1874, when Professor Charles Eliot Norton admitted architectural history into his College fine arts courses. Undergraduates were later permitted to study for the degree of bachelor of science in architecture; through the efforts of leaders in the field like Frederick Law Olmsted Jr. and Charles Eliot, a similar field of study was created in landscape architecture. The Faculty of Arts and Sciences eventually transferred these degree programs to the graduate level. In 1936, President James Conant melded Harvard's free-standing activities in architecture, landscape architecture, and city planning into a single Graduate School of Design. Its first dean was Joseph Hudnut, whom Conant wooed away from Columbia's School of Architecture.

Hudnut was a convinced modernist. One of his first moves was to appoint the famous German Bauhaus innovator Walter Gropius as chair of the department of architecture; Gropius, in turn, brought in Marcel Breuer, another noted modernist. These exponents of International Style changed the school's orientation and trained such future architectural heavyweights as Philip Johnson '27, Edward Larrabee Barnes '38, I. M. Pei, and Paul Rudolph. The GSD was recognized as a major stronghold of avant-garde architecture and design; it was also known for its introduction of the studio method, an innovative instructional approach built around the collaborative efforts of groups of students, structured project assignments, and interdisciplinary techniques.

The Spanish-American modernist Josep Lluis Sert succeeded Hudnut in 1953. During his deanship the GSD intensified its focus on urban environments, reestablishing a department of city planning and instituting the nation's first degree program in urban design. More recently, the school has introduced courses on responsible land and property development and has collaborated with the Kennedy School on joint course offerings and degree programs. It has also worked closely with the Faculty of Arts and Sciences to provide for undergraduate-level study of the built environment.

Related entry: Kennedy School of Government. *Related Website:* www.gsd.harvard.edu.

Great Salt and Other Relics

Harvard's oldest piece of silver plate is known as the Great Salt. Made in London, it was brought to New England in 1638 by Elizabeth Glover, who married Henry Dunster, the College's first president, three years later. On Mrs. Dunster's death, just two years after her marriage, the piece was given to the College by her brother.

The surface of the oddly shaped salt cellar has a hollowed trough and three scrolled cusps. In a time when salt was a relatively costly and valued commodity, an elegant container of this sort would have been set at the head of the table. In later years, the Great Salt was invariably placed wrong-side-up, because its flanges were assumed to be legs. ("The three cusps or curlicues on the Great Salt are not legs, but hooks on which to hang napkins," noted Professor Samuel Eliot Morison, whose word was law in such matters, but today it is generally agreed that they were meant to support a plate of fruit.)

The Great Salt is one of eight pieces of historic sterling silver plate that Harvard usually keeps under lock and key. Among the others are the Stoughton Cup, made by the Boston silversmith John Coney for Lieutenant Governor William Stoughton, class of 1650, and presented to outgoing President Increase Mather at the Commencement of 1701; the Holyoke Cup, a "caudle cup" once owned by Edward Holyoke, Harvard's president from 1737 to 1769; and the handsome Dunster Tankard. (Engraved with the initials *H.D.* and once thought to have belonged to President Henry Dunster, it was actually made about 80 years after Dunster's death in 1659.)

Other sacred relics, displayed only during presidential inaugurations and other festive occasions, include:

- The College Charter, granted by the Great and General
  Court of the Massachusetts Bay Colony in 1650, thus estab-
  lishing what is now the oldest corporation in the Western
  Hemisphere.
- Book I of the College records (1639–1795).
- The almost-triangular and astonishingly knobby President's
  Chair, crafted by an anonymous artificer of Puritan times and
  used in every presidential inauguration since 1737.
- The boxed College seals (1843, 1885).
- The outsized keys to the College, given "with a pious mind"
  (so reads an inscription on the key ring), by William Gordon
  Stearns, class of 1824, for the inauguration of Edward Everett
  in 1846.

The documents, seals, and keys to the College are stored in the
University Archives. The President's Chair and some of the silver
plate are usually on display in the Fogg Art Museum; the chair is
also used by the president at each year's Commencement exercises.
The rest of the silver is kept in the vaults of the Fogg.

Related entry: Archives.

Guardhouse

The University's smallest building is a neo-Victorian gate lodge,
five feet square and twelve feet high, just inside Harvard Yard's
Johnston Gate. Known as the guardhouse, it was installed in 1983
for an overall outlay of $57,000. More than half of that sum
underwrote the restoration and landscaping of adjacent terrain,
which was previously hot-topped; the construction cost of the di-
minutive wooden structure itself came to $21,000, or $840 per
square foot.

The lodge was designed to shelter a guard regulating traffic at
the Yard's main vehicular entrance. A structure of similar size had
once stood on the same site, but that was before the Cambridge
Historical Commission became the final word on proposed alter-

ations to Harvard Yard and its buildings. The architectural firm of Graham Gund Associates, headed by Graham Gund, M. ARCH. '68, M.A.U. '69, floated a hundred designs for the guardhouse before hitting on one that fully satisfied the commission.

The final result is a happy and harmonious addition to the Yard. The lodge's arched windows echo those of nearby Harvard Hall; its walls take their light-brown shade from the stout columns of Memorial Church, just visible 200 yards away. The walls are textured with a raised-diamond pattern that discourages postering. And to foil nocturnal mischiefmakers who might seek to make off with the little building, its footings are embedded in granite.

Related entries: Architecture; Gates; the Yard.

H

The 1893 Hasty Pudding Show was titled *Hamlet, or the Sport, the Spook and the Spinster.* This is the oldest surviving photograph of a Pudding Show kickline.

Harvard Advocate

For undergraduates with literary ambitions, the *Advocate* has often been an important springboard. Its history begins in 1866, making it not just Harvard's oldest surviving publication but also "the nation's oldest continuously published collegiate literary and arts review." Past presidents have included the poets Wallace Stevens '01 and Conrad Aiken '11; Malcolm Cowley '19 and James Agee '32, who became influential critics; and A. Whitney Ellsworth '57, founding publisher of *The New York Review of Books*. (Among former presidents who did *not* pursue literary careers were the great jurist Learned Hand, class of 1893; John H. Finley Jr. '25, classicist and longtime master of Eliot House; and Daniel Ellsberg '52, PH.D. '63, the economist and military strategist who made public the Pentagon Papers.) James Laughlin '36, later a pioneering publisher, held the title of Pegasus (literary editor), as did the poets Robert Bly '49 and Donald Hall '50.

Edwin Arlington Robinson, T. S. Eliot, E. E. Cummings, Robert Fitzgerald, Howard Nemerov, Norman Mailer, and Adrienne Rich all contributed to the *Advocate* as undergraduates. So did Theodore and Franklin Roosevelt, John Reed, and Leonard Bernstein. Some of their letters and memoirs reflect the pride they felt when the magazine accepted a poem or short story. The *Advocate* has also carried work by many established writers, among them William S. Burroughs '36, Henry Miller, Marianne Moore, Ezra Pound, Sir Stephen Spender, Richard Wilbur, and William Carlos Williams.

Published four times a year, the *Advocate* includes short stories, poetry, literary and art criticism, photographs, and interviews with notable figures in the arts. It accepts advertising, sells for $5 a copy, and charges $25 for a year's subscription. About 50 undergraduates are listed as editorial and business staff members.

A board of trustees—made up of former staffers and headed by the lawyer and novelist Louis Begley '54, LL.B. '59—helps out, as needed, with financial and administrative problems. Not long ago, when the magazine fell on hard times in managing both its funds and its relations with Harvard's real estate office—landlord of its premises at 22 South Street—there was talk of ceasing publication. The trustees came to the rescue and stability was restored. The *Advocate* remains an essentially student-run publication, dedicated to the continuation of its tradition of literary and artistic creativity.

Related entry: Arts. *Related Website:* www.hcs.harvard.edu/~advocate.

Harvard College

In common usage, "Harvard College" signifies the oldest component of the University: the liberal arts college. Confusingly, the University's chief governing body, the Harvard Corporation, is legally called the President and Fellows of Harvard College. But that ancient title quite accurately suggests that the College is Harvard's geographic and spiritual heart. And the heart of the College itself is Harvard Yard and its 30-odd buildings, on or around a plot of land known to seventeenth-century settlers as Cow-yard Row.

Established by the General Court of the Massachusetts Bay Colony in the fall of 1636, English-speaking America's first college got off to a faltering start two years later, with a student body of about a dozen young scholars and a tyrannical miscreant, Nathaniel Eaton, as master. A few weeks after the first classes began, John Harvard, a young Puritan minister, died at nearby Charlestown, leaving half his estate and his library of more than 400 books to the fledgling college—then simply called "the college at Cambridge." In 1639 the General Court voted "that the Colledg agreed upon formerly to be built at Cambridg shalbee called Harvard Colledge."

The College now has some 6,650 male and female students, from all 50 states and six continents, and representing a spectrum of socioeconomic, ethnic, and religious backgrounds that is unsurpassed by any comparable institution. It has more than 80,000 living alumni. Historically, their continuing involvement has been a vital factor in endowing professorships, buttressing financial aid programs, attracting "nontraditional" applicants, supporting undergraduate organizations and teams, and maintaining and enlarging the College's physical plant. Over the years, engaged alumni have helped monitor and guide the affairs of the College as members of the Board of Overseers, through service on Overseers' Visiting Committees and committees of the Harvard Alumni Association, and as volunteer interviewers for the Admissions Office. One index of alumni loyalty is the progress of the Harvard College Fund, established in 1926. In recent times its annual appeals have realized as much as $100 million, and new giving records are set each year.

The College has been part of the Faculty of Arts and Sciences since 1890. Though it provided "coordinate education" to women in conjunction with Radcliffe College, Harvard College remained all-male until the 1970s, when the residential and tutorial systems of both colleges were consolidated, their admissions offices were unified, and a policy of equal access was adopted for future entering classes. A full merger of Radcliffe and Harvard was effected in 1999, and today almost half of the College's students are women.

Related entries: Admissions; Alumni; Diversity; Fundraising; Governance; Houses; John Harvard—and His Statue; Radcliffe; the Yard. *Related Website:* www.college.harvard.edu.

Harvard Crimson

The *Crimson* is Harvard's only daily newspaper. There are many undergraduate papers and magazines: the *Independent, Current, Diversity & Distinction, Perspective, Salient,* and more: out of 226 officially recognized student organizations in one recent count, 26 were publications. But none compares to the *Crimson* for frequency, for comprehensive reporting, for provocative editorials and enterprising special features.

Many members of the community start their day with the *Crimson.* "Cambridge's Only Breakfast Table Daily" has an estimated readership of 10,000. Free copies are distributed to undergraduate residence halls; others must subscribe, buy single copies at local newsstands, or check the *Crimson's* online edition, which claims more than a million hits a week.

The late Professor David Riesman—himself a former *Crimson* editor—once described the publication as "quite simply the best undergraduate newspaper in America." Some faculty members and administrators would disagree: a few have been so burned by reading what they deemed to be distortions of their words that they have stopped speaking to *Crimson* reporters. But journalistic objectivity remains a *Crimson* ideal.

The paper was born on January 24, 1873, as a biweekly called *The Magenta*. The first issue bore the motto "I won't philosophize and will be read." It was renamed in 1875, when Harvard's athletic teams adopted crimson as their official color. For a time the publication was little more than an unofficial register of College activities. Later on, sports dominated its columns. Gradually the *Crimson* became a full-service newspaper, with op-ed pages, arts sections, columns by writers from many political persuasions, and editorials expressing the majority and dissenting views of its editors. Since 1925 the *Crimson* has also published its candid and sometimes snide *Confidential Guide* to College courses.

Any student can try out—in *Crimson* parlance, *comp*—for positions on the editorial and business staffs. Though the paper may not be a major moneymaker, in most years it pays a fairly substantial dividend to top editors. A *Crimson* credential has helped countless staffers obtain media positions in "the real world." (A former *Crimson* chairman claimed to have given currency to the phrase by instituting a regular column under that title.) The pages of *The New York Times, Washington Post, Los Angeles Times,* and *The New Republic* often carry the bylines or syndicated columns of ex-*Crimson* writers. Among staff members of earlier times who went on to attain distinction in journalism or in public life were Franklin D. Roosevelt '04, Walter Lippmann '10, Joseph Alsop '32, David Rockefeller '36, Theodore H. White '38, and John F. Kennedy '40.

The *Crimson* is the nation's second oldest college paper (only the *Yale Daily News* has enjoyed a longer life span). Its headquarters is a neocolonial brick building at 14 Plympton Street, built in 1915.

Related entries: Crimson; Gazette; Harvard College. *Related Website:* www.thecrimson.com.

Harvard Elsewhere

Harvard's writ runs well beyond the confines of Cambridge. The Business School campus and the Soldiers Field athletics complex are across the Charles River in Allston. The University now owns far more land there than in Cambridge (more than 340 acres, as against 220), and that property will be extensively developed for academic purposes in coming years. The Medical School has been in Boston since 1810; the schools of Dental Medicine and Public Health are also based there. In Jamaica Plain, two miles south of the Medical School campus, is the pastoral parkland of the Arnold Arboretum, a site of horticultural and botanical research since 1872. Harvard now owns the former U.S. Arsenal in Watertown, two miles upstream from Soldiers Field and the Business School. Purchased in 2001 for $162 million, the newly renovated building houses the Business School's publishing division and other tenants.

Overlapping suburban Concord, Carlisle, and Bedford is the Museum of Comparative Zoology's 750-acre Concord Field Station. The Harvard Depository is in Southborough, 25 miles west of Cambridge; it stores more than 60 percent of the University Library system's holdings. In neighboring Marlborough is the New England Primate Research Center, a Medical School outpost. Further west, in Petersham, is the 2,500-acre Harvard Forest. The forest includes other tracts in Phillipston, Royalston, and Hamilton.

The University owns the Artemas Ward Homestead, a 1727 house in Shrewsbury, Massachusetts, that was once the home of the Continental Army's first commander-in-chief, a member of the Harvard class of 1748. It is now a museum. In Maine, the William Dean Howells Memorial House at Kittery Point and the Kendall House on an island in Northeast Harbor are available for the academic or recreational use of members of the University. Red Top, a 21-acre estate in Ledyard, Connecticut, is the training quarters for the men's crews' annual Thames River boat race with Yale. The property was purchased by rowing alumni in 1881.

Further afield are three research centers: the Center for Hellenic

Studies and the collections and libraries of Dumbarton Oaks, both in Washington, D.C., and the Center for Italian Renaissance Studies at the Villa I Tatti, outside Florence. The Business School has field offices in California's Silicon Valley, Buenos Aires, São Paulo, Hong Kong, Tokyo, and Paris. The ancient city of Sardis, in western Turkey, is the site of a Harvard-led archaeological exploration.

The University had other foreign outposts in earlier days. In 1889 the Harvard Observatory built a station near Lima, Peru, on a hill that was renamed Mount Harvard. Its equipment was soon shifted to Arequipa, Peru, and in 1927 the station was transferred to Bloemfontein, South Africa, where Harvard astronomers worked until University funding ended in the 1950s. In the 1920s, the Medical School had a School of Tropical Medicine with research stations in the Panama Canal Zone and in Soledad, Cuba.

Harvard's name is found in certain places with which the University has no formal connection. There are towns named Harvard in Massachusetts, Illinois, Iowa, Nebraska, and Idaho. The oldest is Harvard, Massachusetts, incorporated in 1732 and named by Josiah Willard, class of 1698. (His father, Samuel, was Harvard's acting president from 1701 to 1707; his grandson, Joseph, was president from 1781 to 1804.) The town is situated about 25 miles northwest of Cambridge; its population of 5,000 includes a number of Harvard faculty and staff members. The Oak Ridge Observatory of the Harvard-Smithsonian Center for Astrophysics is located there.

Harvard, Illinois, is in dairy country. It was founded in 1856 and named by one E. G. Ayer after his home town of Harvard, Massachusetts. Harvard, Nebraska, founded seventeen years later, is in grain country. Harvard, Iowa, was called Grainville when it was laid out in 1879; it was renamed following the discovery that there was already a Grainville, Iowa. Harvard, Idaho, was named in 1906 and is in Latah County, which boasts eight towns named for colleges, among them Princeton, Yale, Stanford, and Vassar.

At 14,420 feet, Mount Harvard (not to be confused with the one near Lima) is Colorado's third highest peak. It is 223 feet taller than nearby Mount Princeton and 224 feet taller than Mount Yale. In the vicinity of Alaska's Prince William Sound are glaciers named Harvard and Radcliffe (and others named Amherst, Bryn Mawr, Dartmouth, Lafayette, Smith, Wellesley, and Williams). Harvard Glacier is more than 23 miles long; Radcliffe Glacier is steeper and shorter.

The University's Office for Technology and Trademark Licensing takes firm action against educational institutes—and there have been many—that attempt to appropriate the Harvard name for commercial ends. Certain other usages are accepted as innocuous. Describing Stanford University as the Harvard of the West is usually seen as complimenting both institutions. Rice University is sometimes called the Harvard of the Southwest. Duke and Emory vie for the right to be known as the Harvard of the South. Nicholls State University T-shirts bear the legend *The Harvard of the Bayou.* But make no mistake: there's really only one Harvard.

Related entries: Allston; Arnold Arboretum; Business School; Dental School; Dumbarton Oaks; Extinct Harvard; Harvard Forest; Libraries; Medical School; Observatories; Sardis; School of Public Health; Soldiers Field; Trademark Protection and Technology Transfer; Villa I Tatti.

Harvard Forest

Almost 3,000 acres of forests, ponds, wetlands, and diverse plantations outside the town of Petersham, Massachusetts, make up the primary holdings of the Harvard Forest—another part of the University that's remote from the Harvard Square area. But the forest is not very distant. From Cambridge it's just 65 miles west on Route 2.

The Harvard Forest has offices, laboratories, greenhouses, and museum and seminar space in the typical New England community of Petersham. Research projects generally focus on ecology and conservation, with an emphasis on the history and evolution of the forests of central New England. Specific studies have dealt with soils and the development of forest site concepts; the biology of temperate and tropical trees; forest ecology and economics; and ecosystem dynamics. The Fisher Museum—named for Richard Fisher, the forest's first director—contains a remarkable collection of 23 three-dimensional dioramas. Each presents an aspect of central New England forests. Altogether, more than 40 professionals and support staff work at Petersham. Affiliated with the forest are noncontiguous plantations of pine, hemlock, and conifers in Hamilton, Massachusetts, and the virgin forest of Pisgah in southwestern New Hampshire.

The forest was deeded to Harvard in 1907 by the owners of the land. Further gifts from abutting owners simplified the boundaries and secured the approaches. The forest is the nation's oldest demonstration tract and silviculture research laboratory.

The Harvard Forest administers graduate programs in forestry in the Faculty of Arts and Sciences; faculty members also offer courses in various departments such as Organismic and Evolutionary Biology and Earth and Planetary Sciences, as well as in the Freshman Seminar Program. The forest's operations are funded from an endowment and from government and private foundation grants.

Related entries: Arnold Arboretum; Harvard Elsewhere. *Related Website:* harvardforest.fas.harvard.edu.

Harvard Foundation

Spurred by the civil rights movement, the enrollment of African-Americans in predominantly white institutions doubled during the 1970s. From 1971 to 1976, Harvard College conferred degrees on more than 300 black graduates, exceeding the number graduated over the previous century. But the recruitment and admission of more black students did not ensure a fulfilling educational experience for all. Even the most academically and socially successful often said that they felt they were *in* Harvard but not *of* it. For the growing number of students from segregated or partially segregated backgrounds, the College could seem an alien place. By the end of the decade, black undergraduates were demanding a University-funded Third World center, modeled on centers recently formed at such institutions as Brown, Princeton, Stanford, Tufts, and Yale.

President Derek Bok appointed a student-faculty committee to weigh the pros and cons of creating a multicultural center. The chairman was the Reverend Peter J. Gomes, B.D. '68, minister in Memorial Church and Plummer Professor of Christian Morals. As an alternative to what might be seen as a haven for minority members, the committee's report proposed a foundation to promote racial understanding through cultural interaction. Advocates of a Third World center opposed the plan, but Bok approved the report and named a Medical School professor, Dr. S. Allen Counter Jr., to direct the Harvard Foundation for Intercultural and Race Relations.

The foundation began life in a small room in University Hall. Dr. Counter, an African-American neuroscientist who had done field work in Africa, Asia, and South America, proved an indefatigable organizer. Working closely with undergraduates, he developed a lecture series, forums, and cultural programs for the Harvard community. "Cultural Rhythms," a University-wide performance and food festival, quickly became an annual fixture.

The foundation now has office space in Thayer Hall. Its staff continues to sponsor film and lecture series; to hold annual conferences on ethnic studies and on advancing minorities and women in science and engineering; and to host an annual Ivy League-wide Cinco de Mayo celebration. Its diverse list of guest speakers in recent years includes three secretaries of the United Nations; actors Jackie Chan, Andy Garcia, Jimmy Smits, and Denzel Washington; Archbishop Desmond Tutu; and the Supreme Court justices of the Navajo Nation.

Related entries: Affirmative Action; Diversity. *Related Website:* www.fas.harvard.edu/~harvfoun.

Harvard Hall

Erected on the site of two earlier Harvard Halls, the College's fifth oldest building has been used continuously for lectures and classes since its opening in 1766. With its prominent white cupola (where the College bell once hung), this dignified red-brick structure stands on the north side of the College's original quadrangle, facing the oldest of Harvard's surviving buildings, Massachusetts Hall.

Work on the first Harvard Hall, also known as the Old College, began in the summer of 1638, but the structure was not completed until 1642. A wooden building with gables, dormers, and a rooftop tower, it was described in a contemporary pamphlet as "too gorgeous for a Wilderness, and yet too mean in others apprehensions for a Colledg . . . It hath the conveniences of a fair Hall, comfortable Studies, and a good Library." Only five years after its completion, however, President Henry Dunster was lamenting the "yearly decays of ye rooffe, walls, and foundation," and by 1679 the hall was reported to have "fallen doune, a part of it." The remaining parts were demolished, and the building was replaced by a second Harvard Hall, completed in 1677. This one combined medieval and Renaissance architectural features and was built of brick. As with the first Harvard Hall, all College activities—instruction, chapel, library, dining commons, and chambers—were housed in this single building. It was consumed by fire during a raging storm on the night of January 24, 1764. This catastrophic event also destroyed virtually all of the 5,000 volumes composing the College library.

The General Court of Massachusetts, which had been meeting in the hall while the College was out of session, voted funds for a third Harvard Hall. Designed by provincial governor Francis Bernard, the building took two years to construct. It too had a chapel, library, and dining commons but did not provide quarters for students or tutors, making it America's first collegiate building devoted solely to academic uses. The second floor was the site of Harvard's first museum, described by a nineteenth-century College librarian as "containing reptiles in alcohol, stuffed skins of beasts and birds, and miscellaneous curiosities which were a great attraction to the country census and a great weariness to the showman, the librarian." The hall's interior was hung with paintings, the library had rich woodwork, and the dining commons was ornate. Bainbridge Bunting's *Harvard: An Architectural History* hails the hall as "the most sophisticated American college building before Bulfinch, though its importance has been overlooked by architectural historians."

When chapel and commons were shifted to University Hall in 1815, Harvard Hall's first floor was converted to classrooms, a "mineralogical cabinet," and laboratories, while the entire second story was given over to the College Library. Later additions significantly changed the configuration of the building. A center pavilion was built in 1842; in 1870, in a move to provide lecture and library space for the science department, the spaces on either side of the pavilion were filled in with one-story additions. This alteration was done with sensitivity and respect for the integrity of the original building; the architects were Ware and Van Brunt, who were planning Memorial Hall and Weld Hall at the same time. In 1968 the interior of the hall was extensively rebuilt to meet stricter fire-safety requirements. This work was also carried out with commendable regard for the fine old building's eighteenth-century character.

This historic structure is now a thoroughly up-to-date facility, with video- and audio-equipped classrooms and comfortable seating.

Related entries: Architecture; Bells; Extinct Harvard; Fire; Libraries; Science Museums.

Harvard Heroes

Many Harvard occasions honor stellar students or faculty members. Since the mid-1990s, the University has also recognized outstanding staff members—officially hailed as Harvard Heroes—for their achievements. They work in a variety of offices and sites:

Alumni Affairs and Development	Human Resources
	Office of the President
Arnold Arboretum	Planning and Real Estate
Faculty Club	University Dining Services
Financial Administration	University Health Services
Government, Community, and Public Affairs	University Information Systems
	University Library
Harvard Magazine	University Operations Services
Harvard University Press	University Police Department

In mid-June, when the majority of students and faculty are gone and academic Harvard is relatively quiet, almost a thousand members of these central administration units gather in Sanders Theatre to celebrate the achievements of a new cadre of Harvard Heroes. Each unit selects the individuals—or in some cases, teams—to be honored. The ceremony is brief and joyous, with carefully crafted introductions of awardees, a video collage of faces and voices, and a congratulatory talk by the president. The event ends with a reception in Annenberg Hall, featuring music by the Harvard Heroes All-Star Garage Band.

As President Lawrence Summers put it at one recent ceremony, "Harvard does not forget those who labor long, well, and quietly to make the University a well-run, fair, and humane place."

Related entries: Gazette; Outings and Innings.

Harvard Hill

One of the University's least-known outposts is a gentle rise at the junction of Amaranth Path and Rose Path in Cambridge's venerable Mount Auburn Cemetery. The Harvard Corporation purchased this hillock in 1833 as a resting place for the rare faculty member, alumnus, or student who had no family plot. Almost 40 now lie there.

Among the first to be remembered on Harvard Hill was John Hooker Ashmun, class of 1818, Royall Professor of Law, who died in 1833. His remains are under one of the lot's two sarcophagus-shaped monuments. The other memorializes John Thornton Kirkland, Harvard's fourteenth president, whose remains are actually in the Lodge family tomb on Oxalis Path. Grave markers of later decades memorialize Henry Lyman Patten, class of 1858, killed in the Civil War; Louis François de Pourtalés, Count Neuchâtel, who died soon after receiving an honorary degree in 1880; Evangelinus Apostolides Sophocles, University Professor of Ancient, Byzantine, and Modern Greek; and Christopher Columbus Langdell, the Law School's first dean.

In recent years these nineteenth-century figures have been

joined by a number of faculty members or administrators whose service to Harvard seemed to make Harvard Hill a particularly appropriate burial site. Among them were William Alfred, Lowell Professor of the Humanities Emeritus; Karl W. Deutsch, professor of government; Charles A. Ditmas Jr., honorary keeper of the clocks; Archie C. Epps III, dean of students; Nathan I. Huggins, professor of Afro-American studies; John R. Marquand, A.M. '63, secretary of the Faculty of Arts and Sciences; University Professor Robert Nozick; and W. C. Burriss Young '55, A.M. '56, associate dean of freshmen.

Interment at the Hill requires Corporation approval. Because of diminishing space, burials are now restricted to cremated remains. The hill commands a fine view of the University: Memorial Hall, William James Hall, the towers of the river houses, and Harvard Stadium stand out in the distance. A handsome monument, erected in 1996, is inscribed, "My race being run, I love to watch the race.—John Masefield, Litt. D. 1918." The inscription continues: "This peaceful spot was acquired in 1833 by the President and Fellows of Harvard College for members of Harvard's family. Here they lie within view of a place they loved."

Related entries: Clocks; God's Acre; Harvard Elsewhere. *Related Website:* www.mountauburn.org.

Harvard Magazine

A bimonthly publication with a circulation of 230,000, *Harvard Magazine* has been in existence under one title or another for more than a century. It is written by people connected with Harvard, about matters concerning Harvard, and for a Harvard-related readership. As such, it could be insufferably parochial. Yet *Harvard Magazine* is by no means a house organ for the Harvard administration, or a narrowly focused publication of interest only to graying alumni. Partly because Harvard is such a large institution, with internationally known faculty, students from all over the world, and research projects at the leading edges of most fields, the magazine's articles almost always appeal to the proverbial "general reader."

Admittedly, each issue includes class notes; obituaries of alumni, faculty, and staff; and regular columns called "The College Pump," "The Browser," and "John Harvard's Journal," all of them Harvard-specific. But a typical issue also contains articles of broad general interest. Recent examples might include such titles as "Saving Culture from the Nazis," "Mind, Brain, and Behavior," "A Splendid Little War" (about the pivotal roles that three of Harvard's most prominent alumni—Henry Cabot Lodge, William Randolph Hearst, and Theodore Roosevelt—played in the runup to the Spanish-American War), "Democracy's Prospects" (a forum on problems of governance in American institutions), and "The Professionalization of Ivy League Sports."

At least three cover articles have drawn national attention and scores of letters. One argued the theory that the earl of Oxford wrote the plays attributed to Shakespeare. Another was a critique of the way the Sistine Chapel ceiling had been restored. The third was by a gay alumnus who described his mostly unhappy experiences at Harvard College. That one brought a mailboxful of letters from readers, some provoked by the author's sexual orientation, some angered by Harvard's accepting him, and some chastising other writers for their intolerance.

The magazine has a rich heritage. Founded in 1898 as the *Harvard Bulletin,* it supported itself through paid subscriptions and took an independent tack on controversial issues facing the College. In 1910 the title was changed to *Harvard Alumni Bulletin;* the present title was adopted in 1973. Shortly thereafter, in response to changes in publishing economics, the magazine reduced its frequency from monthly to bimonthly, dropped its paid-subscription policy, and, in partnership with the University administration, expanded its complimentary mailing list to include the majority of University alumni and officers. To help ensure the magazine's continued editorial independence, the editorial and business staffs developed an effective program of voluntary support. About one-third of the publication's revenue stream is derived from readers' monetary contributions; advertising income and University funding cover the remaining operating costs.

Since 1936, a regular column written by an undergraduate writer has been a fixture of the magazine. Authors of "The Undergraduate" are selected through competition, and many have later distinguished themselves as professional journalists. Among the best known are former *New York Times* columnist J. Anthony Lewis '48; *Newsweek* columnist Robert J. Samuelson '67; *Slate* editor and "Crossfire" panelist Michael Kinsley '72; Anne Fadiman '74, essayist and editor of *The American Scholar; New York Times* reporter David Sanger '82; and freelance writer and critic Adam Goodheart '92.

In the field of magazine journalism, the reputation of *Harvard Magazine* remains high, and it continues to set a brisk pace for its peer publications at other universities.

Related Entries: Alumni; Gay and Lesbian. *Related Website:* www.harvard-magazine.com.

Harvard Neighbors

To newcomers, Harvard can seem an unwelcoming place. Its remaining Proper Bostonian types have been around a long time, and some of the non-New Englanders have adopted the cold-roast-Boston manner. Breaking into old, settled groupings—the Faculty Club's Long Table, the inner circle of an academic department, a social club, or (especially) a private luncheon or dining group—is notoriously hard.

The programs of Harvard Neighbors, a volunteer organization, are designed to warm up this chilly scene. Founded in 1894 as a faculty wives' group called the College Teas Association, Harvard Neighbors is now open to all faculty and staff members and their spouses or partners. Its mission is to create a sense of community among new and older members. In addition to an array of lectures, lunches, teas, exhibitions, and family outings, Harvard Neighbors sponsors many interest-group meetings. Among them are:

Adventures in Art	Jane Austen Reading Group
After Five	Japanese Culture
Afternoon Bridge	Knitting and Crocheting
Art, Creativity, and Meaning	Language Conversations
Bookgroups	(German, Italian, Japanese)
Cinephiles Unite	Quilting Bee
A Community of International	Self-guided Autobiography
Women	Tennis
Creative Needleworks	Watercolor Workshops
English Conversation	Women's Chorale
Infant and Toddler Playgroup	Yoga

The Neighbors' offices are in the basement of 17 Quincy Street, the home of Harvard's Governing Boards. Dues are nominal. When the College Teas Association was organized, its stated purpose was "to consider the best way of promoting social intercourse among the ladies belonging to the University." Today, by bringing together men and women from disparate parts of the institution, the services and programs of Harvard Neighbors help to decomplexify a "multiversity," melding its various outposts into a genuine community.

Related entry: Cambridge/Boston. *Related Website:* www.neighbors.harvard.edu.

Harvard Student Agencies

The motivating idea for Harvard Student Agencies (HSA) originated in 1957, as a result of two emerging problems at the College. The first was a tuition increase that threatened to outpace available scholarship funds and force students to find their own financing. The second was the all-too-evident fact that many enterprising undergraduates were running small-scale businesses out of their rooms. That imperiled Harvard's real estate tax exemption. Some way had to be found to let student entrepreneurs earn money to help meet the rising cost of tuition. Out of these dilemmas, the concept of forming an umbrella group for student businesses—legal for Harvard, and potentially lucrative for students—was born.

The new corporation's aims, as stated in its charter, were "to conduct and supervise enterprises for the benefit of students . . . who are in need of financial assistance to defray the expenses of their education; to provide opportunities for such students to be gainfully employed; . . . to provide [business] experience for its members."

Almost half a century later, HSA generates work opportunities for more than 800 students, and maintains a permanent staff that provides training in entrepreneurship, mentoring, and continuity from year to year. All told, HSA revenues come to $6 million annually. The organization supplies many valuable services to the Harvard community and beyond, including:

- Renting all kinds of equipment: microfridges, refrigerators, TVs, VCRs, fans, telephones, and more.
- Operating a cleaning agency for laundry and linen leases, dry cleaning and shirt services, and bulk linen rentals.
- Providing summertime storage for students' personal effects.
- Running a temporary job agency for students (interested applicants are offered a legendary bartending course, whose graduates—as many as 50 per month—receive a "Doctor of Mixology" degree).
- Retailing Harvard insignia items.
- Promoting college-authorized, direct-to-student advertising for outside business clients.
- Organizing alumni, faculty, and corporate sponsors to help students with their business plans and careers.

Let's Go Publications, with a list of more than 60 titles—some in French and other languages, including Polish—is HSA's largest enterprise. Aimed at "a new breed of traveler, the student on a (low) budget," the *Let's Go* guides have proved popular with travelers of every breed. Geographic diversity rules: there are *Let's Go* books for Europe, China, Egypt, the Middle East, Peru and Ecuador, Israel, and Southwest USA, and city guides to Amsterdam, Barcelona, Boston, New York, London, Paris, Prague, San Francisco, and other tourist magnets. Each title points readers to the hippest backstreet cafés, the best bargain restaurants, the cheapest lodgings that aren't fleabags, and the most fabulous beaches. HSA also publishes *The Unofficial Guide to Life at Harvard, The Harvard Guide to Career Week,* and most recently, *The Guide to Getting In.* (The focus of that last one is gaining entrance to institutions of higher education.) Let's Go Publications' list expands yearly: it is available on the HSA Website.

Related Websites: www.letsgo.com; hsa.net

Harvard Union

A handsome, block-wide Georgian Revival building completed in 1901, the Harvard Union now forms the core of the Barker Humanities Center, dedicated in 1997. It was the gift of one of Harvard's great benefactors, Major Henry Lee Higginson, class of 1855, A.M. (hon.) 1882, who conceived it as a "house of fellowship" for students who couldn't afford to belong to a Gold Coast social club. The Spanish-American War was ending when Higginson proposed his gift of $150,000 to construct the Union, and it was designated as a memorial to the eleven Harvard men who had lost their lives in the war. Their names were inscribed at the entrance to the building's manorial living room; the last name was that of Sherman Hoar, class of 1882, the model for Daniel Chester French's statue of John Harvard. Downstairs was a deck gun from the cruiser *U.S.S. Harvard.*

The Union provided dining rooms, meeting rooms, libraries, and a place for dances and entertainments, but within a few years its membership began to tail off. Three decades later, when the house system was formed, "unclubbed" upperclassmen could take their meals in house dining halls as sumptuous as the Union's, and the Union was made into an eating and meeting place for freshmen. It functioned as such until 1996, when the former dining commons of Memorial Hall was reincarnated as a freshman dining hall. Over the protests of traditionalists, the Union was remodeled to create offices and classrooms for academic departments in the humanities.

The transformation drew formerly scattered departments together, but at the price of partitioning a palatial interior that was a masterwork of McKim, Mead & White, the architects of Harvard Stadium, the Medical School campus, and the Harvard Club of New York City (which has architectural affinities with the Union). The Union's exterior remains as commanding as ever, and the interior retains chandeliers ornamented with antlers of horned animals shot by loyal alumnus Theodore Roosevelt. Still, many who knew the Union in its earlier state feel that something precious has been lost.

Related entries: Dining Services; Extinct Harvard; Gold Coast; John Harvard—and His Statue; Memorial Hall.

Harvard University Press

Whether one's interests lean toward the history of Boston sports and the Moog synthesizer, or gnosticism and Walter Benjamin, Harvard University Press's display room in Harvard Square is a congenial place to browse and talk shop. Many names and faces of distinguished Harvard faculty members appear on the handsome book jackets in the window, and the authors themselves often drop by to thumb the well-stocked shelves and pick up a bargain or two.

Harvard has been a home to printing since 1643, when Henry Dunster, first president of Harvard College, inherited a printing press, plates, and paper from his wife, Elizabeth Glover. But it was not until 1913 that the Corporation established the entity known as Harvard University Press. By the 1930s, the Press had evolved into a publisher of "scholarship plus"—not only highly specialized academic tomes but also books for the general intellectual reader. This mission still characterizes the Press today.

In the 1970s, HUP's director, Arthur J. Rosenthal (founder of Basic Books) launched dynamic new lists in science and psychol-

ogy and expanded the number of paperback titles—successful
strategies that many other university presses would soon imitate.
Carol Gilligan's *In a Different Voice* (which has sold over 600,000
copies) and E. O. Wilson's *Sociobiology* are just two of the many
books that caused ripples far beyond the banks of the Charles.

By 1990, when William P. Sisler of Oxford University Press
(USA) took over as director, global markets were changing rapidly
and new adaptations were required. The rise of online booksellers,
the increasing power of bricks-and-mortar chainstores, the loss of
many independent bookshops, the decline of the monograph, and
the influence of multimedia demanded that the Press and its business partners reinvent themselves for survival in the new millennium. With MIT and Yale, HUP built a state-of-the-art distribution center, Triliteral, to give its customers around the world the
highest level of service; and in partnership with Acme Bookbind-
ing it pioneered a print-on-demand program to make available in
original editions key works that have long been out of print, such
as the Adams Papers and the works of Ralph Waldo Emerson.
HUP was one of the first university presses to adopt worldwide
pricing, as well as innovations in editing and production that gave
it the capacity to bring time-sensitive projects to market within a
season.

In 1949 a bequest from Waldron Phoenix Belknap Jr. established
the Belknap Press imprint "for books of long-lasting importance,
superior in scholarship and physical production, chosen whether
or not they might be profitable." This prestigious imprint can be
found on such recent publications as *Late Antiquity: A Guide to the
Postclassical World; The Harvard Guide to African-American History;
The Harvard Dictionary of Music; The Harvard Guide to Women's
Health; The Kennedy Tapes; The Poems of Emily Dickinson;* Helen
Vendler's *The Art of Shakespeare's Sonnets;* T. M. Scanlon's *What We
Owe to Each Other;* and Stephen Jay Gould's *The Structure of Evo-
lutionary Theory.*

Related entries: Lectures; ZephGreek. *Related Website:* www.hup.harvard
.edu.

Hasty Pudding Show

Hasty Pudding Theatricals, once the thespian arm of one of Harvard's earliest social clubs, touts itself as America's oldest dramatic institution. The annual Hasty Pudding Show, featuring hairy-legged actors in drag, a kickline, and ribald ad-libbing, traces its ancestry to 1844, when a student named Lemuel Hayward produced and starred in *Bombastes Furioso,* an English farce.

The Hasty Pudding Club had been founded in 1795. Its bylaws decreed that meetings be kept secret; required a patriotic oration on George Washington's birthday; and ordained that "members in alphabetical order shall provide a pot of hasty pudding [a mix of corn meal, water, and salt, consumed with milk or molasses] for every meeting." In the club's earliest years, members regaled one another with poetry recitations, orations, and song. In 1800 they began holding mock trials, and in 1844 young Hayward hit on the idea of staging a play instead of a trial. A few clubmates took female parts (defying a College ordinance that if a student "wears women's apparel, he shall be liable to public admonition, degradation, or expulsion"), and a tradition was born.

The Pudding broke fresh ground in 1855 with a musical setting of Henry Fielding's mock-heroic *Tom Thumb, a Tragedy.* In the mid-1860s its dramatists began to concoct their own scripts, and they soon offered public performances. Senior Owen Wister's 1882 rehash of *Dido and Aeneas* was a box-office bonanza: it played in Boston, New York, and Philadelphia and helped finance a new clubhouse at 12 Holyoke Street. Since the opening of the building in 1888, its stage has been the venue for an original musical comedy every winter (with the exception of two wartime years in the 1940s). Harvard purchased the clubhouse in 2000, but the terms of the sale allowed Hasty Pudding Theatricals to stay on. (In 2003 the Hasty Pudding Club found new premises in a former University building at 2 Garden Street. The club and Hasty Pudding Theatricals had for some time been administratively separate.)

Over the years, the Pudding Show has been a stepping-stone for undergraduates who would achieve success on Broadway and in Hollywood—among them Robert Benchley '12, Robert Sherwood '18, Alan Jay Lerner '40, and Jack Lemmon '47. Salacious humor, atrocious puns, and absurd situations remain hallmarks of the high-testosterone productions. Characters have borne such evocative names as Belle Bottoms (and her daughter Ophelia), Maximillian Bucks, Willy Cracker, Giovanna Dance, Mel O'Drama, Chaim Pistove, Amanda Pleaseme, Ivan E. Rexionne, Hal E. Tosis, Sonya Vabitzsch, and Curtis Interruptus. Recent show titles have set the punning tone: *Bewitched Bayou, Keep Your Pantheon, A Thousand Clones, Witch and Famous, Between the Sheiks, Saint Misbehavin', A Tsar Is Born, Fangs for the Memories, It's a Wonderful Afterlife.*

All undergraduates are eligible to try out for the Pudding Show. Direction, set and costume design, and much of the staging are now largely the domain of professionals, but the casts are still decidedly amateur—and all-male, though in recent decades women have assisted backstage, run the front office, and even written scripts. Each year's show draws a total audience of ten or twelve thousand; more than 40 performances are presented in Cambridge, New York, and Bermuda. To generate buzz for the show, Hasty Pudding Theatricals awards replica pudding tureens to its Man and Woman of the Year: among those honored in recent years have been actors Harrison Ford, Jodie Foster, Anjelica Huston, Paul Newman, Sarah Jessica Parker, Julia Roberts, Susan Sarandon, and Bruce Willis, along with director Martin Scorsese.

Related entries: Arts; Final Clubs; Gilbert & Sullivan.

Hillel

Near the end of World War II, Jewish faculty members and students founded a community center for services and programs. Since the population of Jewish students was not large, a relatively small number were involved at the outset: it's said that only four attended the first meeting. In the postwar years, however, the percentage of Jewish students in the College and graduate schools grew substantially. The community center, called Hillel, moved from its original location on Massachusetts Avenue to larger but more distant premises on Bryant Street, near the Divinity School. By the late 1960s, increasing numbers of Jewish students were turning more overtly to Jewish traditions to support their efforts at self-definition during their undergraduate and graduate years. In response, Hillel began to offer more worship opportunities, more kosher food, more lectures, study groups, softball teams, and other programs.

Unlike most Hillel organizations on other college and university campuses, Harvard Hillel was not identified with a particular branch of Judaism. Led by Rabbi Ben-Zion Gold, it eagerly welcomed Jews of all denominations, including those who were skeptical about older, orthodox traditions. The resulting size of its constituency posed perennial space problems.

In the 1990s, thanks to the generosity of many families—especially the Rabbs, Riesmans, and Lippers—a new center was built on Mount Auburn Street, near the College's river houses. The striking building, designed by the Israeli architect Moshe Safdie and named in honor of Henry Rosovsky, professor of economics and former dean of the Faculty of Arts and Sciences, houses the Riesman Center for Harvard Hillel. Worship spaces, meeting rooms, dining facilities, and study rooms attract hundreds of Jewish students of every cast. Safdie understood the fluid nature of Harvard's Jewish community and designed rooms that could be used for multiple purposes.

As its mission statement notes, Harvard Hillel today is "centered on students' active and self-conscious choice to be Jewish, to explore the relevance of Jewish tradition to their own lives . . . and to contribute with force and vision both to the Jewish community and the world at large." In a sense, Hillel has become a microcosm of American Jewish life: a place of diversity, openness, tolerance, deep respect for learning, and justified self-confidence.

Related entries: Architecture; Firsts (Men); "Godless Harvard." *Related Website:* www.hillel.harvard.edu.

Holden Chapel

"In terms of adaptive use at Harvard, Holden Chapel holds the record," states Bainbridge Bunting's *Harvard: An Architectural His-*

tory. Though the College was founded to train ministers, a century passed before it acquired a free-standing chapel. But within less than a generation of its completion in 1744, notes Bunting, "Holden Chapel was abandoned for religious uses." With the opening of Harvard Hall in 1766, prayer services moved to a larger chapel on the hall's first floor, and elegant little Holden was successively used as a military barracks, a firehouse, and a storeroom for salvaged lumber. From 1783 to 1810, it housed Harvard's nascent Medical School. In 1850, after years of disuse, it was renovated as a lecture hall; a lower floor was made into a museum. Fitted with a stage in 1870, the lecture hall was then used for plays and student orations. Elocution and music classes were held there, and Holden Chapel later became the home of the Harvard Glee Club, the Collegium Musicum, and the Radcliffe Choral Society. These groups still rehearse there.

The initial gift of £400 for the chapel's construction came from Jane Holden, the widow of a prominent English Dissenter, member of Parliament, and director of the Bank of England. The building was and is a gem of High Georgian styling. Richly ornamented, small but majestic in its proportions and scaling, it struck a completely new note in Harvard architecture. Like other eighteenth-century College buildings it faced westward, away from what is now the Old Yard. The arms of Madam Holden, ensconced in handsomely carved scrollwork, appeared over the entrance pediment. In 1880, accepting the fact that most of those using the chapel approached it from the Yard, College officials had a new entrance cut on the building's east wall, and the west door was blocked up. A duplicate coat of arms was placed over the pediment of the east wall in the 1920s.

Holden forms the north side of a small quadrangle, bounded by Hollis, Harvard, and Lionel Halls. In the nineteenth century, this plot of land and the great elm tree that once stood there were the rallying point for Bacchanalian Class Day rites at Commencement time.

Related entries: Architecture; Gates; Harvard Hall.

Hollywood's Harvard

The quintessential Harvard movie, for better or for worse, may be *Love Story,* based on the best-selling novel by Erich Segal '58, PH.D. '65, and released in 1969. This sticky-sweet weepy, which received seven Academy Award nominations, follows the college careers of Oliver Barrett IV (Ryan O'Neal), a WASP hockey star, and Jenny Cavilleri (Ali MacGraw), a Radcliffe music concentrator from a blue-collar family. They frolic in the Yard, in class, and in bed, and eventually marry, only to find that Jenny is terminally ill. The dialogue includes the much-parodied line "Love means never having to say you're sorry." At Freshman Week screenings, *Love Story* invariably elicits mirthful hoots and brash commentary. *The Paper Chase,* set at the Law School and filmed three years after *Love Story,* offers better acting and is a perennial Harvard Square favorite.

Needless to say, Hollywood had discovered Harvard long before Paramount Pictures filmed *Love Story* and 20th Century Fox made *Paper Chase.* More than two dozen films, of decidedly varying quality, have featured Harvard protagonists or Harvard itself as the *mise en scène.* Here's a quick overview, with ratings given by the co-authors of this book (four stars are tops):

★★★An adaptation of the 1909 play *Brown of Harvard* was filmed in 1917; a remake, scripted by Yale man Donald Ogden Stewart, followed nine years later. William Haines played the obnoxious Brown, who competes with the studious McAndrews (Francis X. Bushman Jr.) for athletic laurels and the favor of a professor's daughter. John Wayne makes his film debut in the uncredited role of a football player; location shots show Harvard Square, Widener Library, Memorial Hall, the Hasty Pudding Club, and Harvard Stadium. This silent film is easily the best of the early Harvard movies.

★★In addition to the sensational manslaughter trial of the actor Roscoe ("Fatty") Arbuckle, the year 1922 brought the release of two Harvard-related films. In the Rockett Film Corporation's *Keeping Up with Lizzie,* young Harvard grad Dan Pettigrew (Edward Hearn) won the ambitious Lizzie Henshaw by unmasking a phony count who tried to purloin her dowry. In Paramount's *The*

Young Rajah, Rudolph Valentino played a Hindu princeling who became a star Harvard athlete and lost his heart to a Brahmin, Molly Cabot (Wanda Hawley).

★★Other early films with Harvard protagonists were *Birthright* (Micheaux Film Corporation, 1924), with Peter Siner as an idealistic black graduate facing bigotry and brutality in a southern town; *Forever After* (First National, 1926), with Lloyd Hughes as a wounded war veteran who had been forced to leave Harvard because of his impractical father's financial reverses; and Frank Capra's *For the Love of Mike* (First National, 1927), with Ben Lyon, Claudette Colbert, and closing footage of a Harvard-Yale boat race.

★★In *Flight* (Columbia, 1929), a talkie directed by Capra, Lefty Phelps (Ralph Graves) botches a play in the Harvard-Yale game, joins the Marines, and is sent to quell an uprising in Nicaragua. Lost in the jungle, he is rescued by his pal Williams (Jack Holt), who also lets Lefty have the girl they both love.

★★★King Vidor's *H. M. Pulham, Esq.* (MGM, 1941) was a sophisticated and faithful adaptation of J. P. Marquand's 1941 bestseller. As in the novel, the plot unfolds in flashbacks as stuffy Boston banker Harry Pulham (Robert Young) writes an entry for his Harvard 25th reunion report. Hedy Lamarr, Viennese accent notwithstanding, is appealing as the career girl from Iowa who almost brings him out of his shell. In the strong cast are Charles Coburn, Bonita Granville, Ruth Hussey, Van Heflin, and (in her first bit part) Ava Gardner.

★★The last of the prewar Harvard films was *Harvard, Here I Come* (Columbia, 1941), with former world light-heavyweight boxing champ "Slapsie Maxie" Rosenbloom as a rough diamond who wins an athletic scholarship to Harvard but can't cut it academically. Slapsie Maxie, who had retired from the ring in 1939, would go on to make more than 20 films in his second career as an actor/entertainer.

★★★Bob Hope's *Son of Paleface* (Paramount, 1952), a sequel to his *Paleface* (1948), reintroduced Harvard and Hollywood. Hope played a tenderfoot Harvard grad who heads west to claim an inheritance, only to encounter a mountain of debt and the mountainous *poitrine* of Jane Russell, well cast as Calamity Jane. The helpful intercession of Roy Rogers and Trigger ensures the triumph of Hope over adversity.

★★ *The Thomas Crown Affair* (MGM, 1968) was a representative 1960s caper movie, adapted by Alan Trustman '52, J.D. '55, from his own novel. Steve McQueen was cast against type as a wealthy, Harvard-trained multimillionaire who planned bank heists for diversion; Faye Dunaway was an insurance investigator who couldn't keep from falling for him. Their romance heated up in a famously sexy chess match. A 1999 remake—with Pierce Brosnan and Rene Russo, but without the chess—still feels like a 1960s movie.

★★★The box-office success of *The Paper Chase* (20th Century Fox, 1973) gave it legs as a television sitcom. Based on a novel by John Jay Osborn '67, J.D. '70, who co-wrote the script, the adaptation had Timothy Bottoms as a first-year Law School student suffering under the despotic Professor Kingsfield (John Houseman), while forming a romantic attachment to the prof's daughter (Lindsay Wagner). Authentic-sounding student banter and an affecting love subplot bolster this film, but its greatest strength lies in Houseman's Oscar-winning performance as Kingsfield. His chilly aloofness and stern, didactic classroom manner unforgettably depict old-style—and now long-gone—teaching methods.

★To wring more tears and more cash from the plot line of *Love Story*, Paramount issued *Oliver's Story* in 1978. Ryan O'Neal's still-grieving widower falls for a woman as rich as he is (Candice Bergen); Ray Milland reprises his role as Oliver's insufferably snobbish father; and the audience snores.

★★The Harvard Medical Area was the venue for two late-1970s films, *Coma* (MGM/United Artists, 1978) and *The House of God* (United Artists, 1979). *Coma* was a treatment of Robin Cook's 1977 novel of that name, published while Cook was enrolled at the Kennedy School of Government; the director was the prolific author and screenwriter Michael Crichton '64, M.D. '69, who later created the TV series *ER*. Geneviève Bujold played Susan Wheeler, a medical student who wants to find out why "Boston Memorial" patients with minor ills are slipping into irreversible comas. The cast includes Richard Widmark as Susan's mentor and Michael Douglas as a sympathetic fellow student. *The House of God,* never commercially released, took its title (a riff on the name of Harvard's affiliated Beth Israel Hospital) and its shapeless plot from a 1978 novel by Stephen Bergman '66, M.D. '70, writing under the pseudonym Samuel Shem. Though the book's worldwide sales have reached almost two million, the film's overworked, oversexed interns are caricatures, and much of the black humor falls flat.

★★*A Small Circle of Friends* (United Artists, 1980) marked the directorial debut of Rob Cohen '77, one of the film industry's "baby moguls" of the time. Shot in Cambridge and Los Angeles, it tracks the intertwining lives of three Harvard College students during the tumultuous 1960s. Brad Davis, Jameson Parker, Karen Allen, and Shelley Long, looking old for their parts, head the cast. Cohen may have had in mind a Cambridge counterpart of François Truffaut's classic *Jules et Jim* (1962), but the resemblance was lost on the critics, who reviewed his film coolly.

★★*Soul Man* (New World, 1986) was the first Harvard picture since *Birthright,* filmed some 60 years earlier, with a racial theme. Aspiring applicant Mark Watson (C. Thomas Howell) resorts to darkening his skin with tanning pills in order to win a scholarship reserved for an African-American candidate. James Earl Jones plays Professor Banks, a law lecturer, and Julia Louis-Dreyfus makes an early, pre-*Seinfeld* film appearance. The underrated Howell does amusing impressions of Stevie Wonder and the artist formerly known as, well, The Artist Formerly Known as Prince. A silly comedy, but funnier and less offensive than one might have expected.

★★★*Reversal of Fortune* (Warner Brothers, 1990) is *sui generis:* a Harvard-related film that is not pure fiction. Based on a book by Alan Dershowitz, Frankfurter Professor of Law, its central figure is the Danish-born socialite Claus von Bulow, twice tried in the mid-1980s for the attempted murder of his wife, Sunny. Jeremy Irons is Von B., Glenn Close is Sunny, and Ron Silver is Dershowitz, who served the defense as a consultant. The Dersh's son Elon co-produced.

★★★With gross receipts of more than $260 million, *The Firm* (Malofilm, 1993) ranks as the most commercially successful of Harvard-related films. In this adaptation of John Grisham's best-seller, Tom Cruise played Mitch McDeere, a Law School graduate who unwittingly signs on with a corrupt Memphis firm. To foil his crooked bosses and elude menacing FBI agents, Mitch devises a plan whose intricacy does credit to his Harvard credentials. The strong supporting cast includes Gene Hackman, Jeanne Tripplehorn, Holly Hunter, David Strathairn, and Wilford Brimley.

★★★Two later films, *Just Cause* and *Legally Blonde,* also had Law School ties. In *Just Cause* (Warners, 1995) Sean Connery played a Harvard law professor who returns to the courtroom to aid a black Floridian (Blair Underwood) convicted of a rape/murder. With the redoubtable Laurence Fishburne cast against type as a cigar-chomping sheriff (and George Plimpton '48 in a cameo role), the film perhaps deserved better notices than it got. That can't be said of *Legally Blonde* (MGM/United Artists, 2001), which had a predictable plot and too many blonde jokes. Admitted to Harvard Law School, preppie Warner Huntington III (Matthew Davis) dumps beautiful, blonde, bouncy Elle Woods (Reese Witherspoon) and reconnects with an ex-girlfriend (Selma Blair). Determined to win Warner back, Elle enrolls at the Law School. Before you can say "Alan Dershowitz," she finds herself holding the key to a celebrity murder case. As if.

★★Harvard Yard was the setting for the equally far-fetched *With Honors* (Warners, 1994). Joe Pesci played Simon, a homeless man who sleeps in a Harvard boiler room and discovers an honors thesis dropped through a grate by Monty (Brendan Fraser), a klutzy, self-absorbed senior. Simon offers to barter the thesis, page by page, for material goods, and an unlikely friendship develops. Any thesis-writer of the 1990s would surely have had a copy on his or her hard drive, but that seems not to have troubled the screenwriters or director Alek Keshishian '86, whose own honors thesis earned him a *summa.* The story line was inspired by the real-life example of Damon Paine, a homeless man taken in by the residents of Harvard's Sacramento Street co-op, whose lives he made, if not miserable, *not fun.*

★★★Though its locus was MIT, *Good Will Hunting* (Miramax, 1997) included sequences filmed at Harvard. The Oscar-winning script was the work of Matt Damon '92, who played the title role, and Ben Affleck. Will Hunting, a combative young janitor from South Boston, is an untutored math genius who prefers barroom brawls to Bayesian analysis. Robin Williams, as his volunteer therapist, won an Oscar for best supporting actor; Minnie Driver played Skylar, a pre-med student from Britain whose attentions help Will mature. The protean George Plimpton pops up again, briefly, as a psychologist. The film garnered nine Academy Award nominations and has grossed more than $230 million worldwide.

★Three more recent releases—*How High, Harvard Man,* and *Stealing Harvard*—brought the Harvard-based film genre to a new low. In the stupefyingly crude teen movie *How High* (Universal, 2001), Staten Island potheads Silas and Jamal (rappers Method Man and Redman, respectively) toke up on weed of supernatural potency, ace their SAT tests, are hailed as geniuses, and are recruited by the fatuous Chancellor Huntley to diversify Harvard's undergraduate mix. A semester of smoking and skirt-chasing ends when the dopers exhaust their stash and turn to (what else?) grave-robbing. "*How High,*" noted one of the film's more charitable critics, "makes *Legally Blonde* look like a Preston Sturges masterpiece."

Drug use also pervades *Harvard Man* (Cowboy Pictures, 2002). Its hero, Alan Jensen (Adrian Grenier), is a philosophy concentrator and captain of the basketball team. Seduced by a sexy Boston College cheerleader (Sarah Michelle Gellar), whose father is a Mafia don, Alan also has it on with his philosophy prof (Joey Lauren Adams) and is tripping on LSD when he takes the floor for the crucial Dartmouth game. When a point-shaving scheme goes bad, he must outsmart the cheerleader, her dad, and the FBI. (*Hoop Dreams* meets *The Firm?*) Filmed in three weeks in Toronto and Cambridge, at a cost of $5.5 million, *Harvard Man* was confected by Harvard men: writer-director James Toback '66 and producer Michael Mailer '87 (son of Norman '43).

The preposterous *Stealing Harvard* (Columbia, 2002) features Jason Lee as John Plummer, a *naïf* who must keep a forgotten promise to put his niece Noreen (Tammy Blanchard) through college if she can get in. When she's admitted to Harvard, John turns to his dimwit friend Duff (the unfunny Tom Green), and they commit petty crimes to raise the $29,879 required to defray the tuition bill. The (non-Harvard) film makers dithered about the name of this idiotic picture: *You Promised, Stealing Stanford,* and *Say Uncle* were all considered. (The most fitting title, *Dumb and Dumber,* was already taken.)

★*Prozac Nation* (Miramax, 2004) is based on Elizabeth Wurtzel '89's memoir of her freshman-year crackup and her ensuing addiction to Prozac. Galt Niederhoffer '97 co-wrote and co-produced this draggy, druggy film, rated R for "language, drug content, sexuality/nudity, and some disturbing images." Christina Ricci (over)plays the unsympathetic heroine-memoirist.

One Hollywood film that makes no mention of Harvard—*Casablanca* (Warners, 1942)—has a special place in the hearts of filmgoing Harvardians. This Bogart/Bergman classic has found favor with nearly three generations of students and is regularly and reverently screened at the Brattle Theatre during end-of-semester exam weeks. Few students graduate without experiencing its mysterious and stress-dispersing magic.

With rare exceptions, Harvard bars commercial filming on its premises. Producers therefore film "Harvard scenes" at more lenient institutions. *Paper Chase* and *Legally Blonde* were filmed at the University of Southern California. For *Mona Lisa Smile* (Columbia Tristar, 2003)—with Julia Roberts as a protofeminist Wellesley fine arts professor, c. 1953, who makes side trips to Harvard—the filming locations included Wellesley, Columbia, and, yes, Yale, where Sterling Library stood in for Harvard's Widener.

As a matter of policy, the Office of the University Provost and the Office for Technology and Trademark Licensing do not contest the use of Harvard's name in movies, assuming that audiences should be able to tell fiction from fact.

Related entries: Brattle Theatre; Fictional Harvard; Film Archive; Trademark Protection and Technology Transfer.

Honorary Degrees

Each year Harvard confers more than 6,000 earned degrees, as well as a few that are awarded *honoris causa.* Categorically, the "degrees

in course" range from the bachelor's, conferred since 1642, to the
Ph.D. in Biological Sciences in Dental Medicine, approved in
2001. (Before World War II, there were about 30 separate advanced
degrees; the number has since grown to more than 160.)

The climax of the annual Commencement exercises comes
when a dozen or so eminent figures rise in turn from their chairs
on the platform to receive honorary degree citations from the president and accept the plaudits of the audience. World leaders, scholars, scientists, humanists, artists of all kinds, jurists, business leaders, educators, entertainers, and every so often a virtually unknown
"spirit" who has labored quietly and without much recognition to
do good in some troubled part of the world—all are represented
on Harvard's two-and-a-half-centuries-long roll of honorary degree
recipients.

Who chooses these people? How does the selection process
work? What are the criteria? All members of the University community—faculty, students, staff, alumni—are annually invited to
propose candidates. Nominations are sent to a committee made up
of selected members of the Corporation, the Board of Overseers,
and senior faculty. This group meets periodically to build a list of
candidates for the Commencement two years hence. Its recommendations must be approved by both the Corporation and the
full Board of Overseers. By proposing or vetoing names, Harvard's
president exerts considerable influence on the selection process.

The committee's deliberations are secret, complicated, and often
political in the broadest sense. Increasing efforts go into creating a
list that reflects diversity: in fields of scholarship, areas of public
life, gender, race, national origin, politics, and extent of public recognition. Discussions are often heated and sometimes resolved by
Washington-style horse trading. The committee chair, usually a senior member of the Corporation, moderates the discussions.

Once the committee decides, some rather unusual if typically
Harvardian conditions of award and acceptance come into play.
Honorary degrees are not awarded in absentia: an invited candidate must agree to receive his or her award in person. At intervals,
honorary degrees have been awarded "out of season"—that is, during other parts of the year when the recipient was in Cambridge.
So honored, among others, were British Prime Minister Winston

Churchill, in September 1943, and South African President Nelson Mandela, in September 1998. At Harvard's Tercentenary celebration in 1936, no fewer than 62 degrees were awarded out of season. (Today it is mind-numbing to imagine the tedious reading of citations for so many people in a single ceremony. But as one commentator noted, never before had any academic platform held so many of the world's intellectual leaders.) The justification for out-of-season awards is obvious: the eminence of the recipients, their busy schedules, and the strong desire to recognize them during their lifetimes.

Another Harvard tradition is secrecy: the identities of honorary degree recipients are not officially revealed until Commencement Day. Candidates are urged to maintain silence about their pending honor, and if reporters (especially from the *Harvard Crimson*) demand confirmation, a noncommittal reply is encouraged. Though occasional leaks occur, the secrecy condition is usually observed.

The identity of one honorand is normally revealed in advance— usually about two months ahead of Commencement. This is the speaker at the afternoon meeting of the Alumni Association. Officers of the HAA single out one individual from the honorary degree list and invite him or her to deliver the address. This recipient represents all the honorands with a toast at a formal dinner the night before Commencement and at the Chief Marshal's Spread the next day. One of the most celebrated speeches ever given at Harvard was the outlining of a plan for the economic recovery of Europe by Secretary of State George C. Marshall in 1947. Other Commencement speakers of the past half-century have included Adlai Stevenson, then U.S. representative to the U.N., in 1965; Aleksandr Solzhenitsyn, Russian novelist, in 1978; Carlos Fuentes, Mexican author and diplomat, in 1983; German chancellor Helmut Kohl in 1990; and Václav Havel, president of the Czech Republic, in 1995.

Harvard's first honorary degree went to Benjamin Franklin in 1753. The College subsequently honored the mathematician John Winthrop in 1773, George Washington in 1776, and after that many great figures who helped found the Republic: John Adams, the Marquis de Lafayette, Thomas Jefferson, John Jay, Samuel Adams, Alexander Hamilton, and John Hancock. Over more than two centuries, honorary degrees have been conferred on fourteen U.S. presidents—sometimes before the man was elected to office, as with Franklin D. Roosevelt, then governor of New York (1929); Dwight D. Eisenhower (1946); and John F. Kennedy, then a Massachusetts senator (1956). President Ronald Reagan was considered for a degree in conjunction with Harvard's 350th anniversary in 1986, but politics prevailed and the idea was dropped.

The first woman recipient was Helen Adams Keller, Radcliffe class of 1904, who was honored in 1955. Her citation read: "From a still, dark world she has brought us light and sound; our lives are richer for her faith and her example." Not every award has been greeted with acclaim. University officials received many letters of protest after an award to Walt Disney in 1938 (on the grounds that he was merely a Hollywood cartoonist who made films for children), and after awards to Mohammed Reza Pahlevi, Shahinshah of Iran, in 1968, and to Benazir Bhutto '75, prime minister of Pakistan, in 1989. Both soon fell into political disfavor in their home countries. Harvard is generally cautious about awarding honors to current political leaders or to controversial figures. Offers of honorary degrees are rarely turned down, but noteworthy exceptions, for reasons other than frail health, have been Jean-Paul Sartre, Ingmar Bergman, Katherine Hepburn, and Ted Williams.

Related entries: Commencement; Diversity; Firsts (Men); Firsts (Women).

Houghton Library

To President Charles W. Eliot, Widener Library was "the heart of the University." A current faculty member has his own metaphor for the Houghton Library: he calls it the Fort Knox of Harvard. This rare book and manuscripts library is the stronghold where the University safeguards some of its most precious treasures: scarce first editions, ancient illustrated books, priceless manuscripts.

To list even a few of the Houghton's manuscripts and first editions is to conjure up the names of major figures in western civilization: Galileo, Samuel Johnson, John Keats, Percy Shelley,

Antoine-Laurent de Lavoisier, Aleksandr Pushkin, Emerson and Thoreau, Hawthorne and Melville, Emily Dickinson, Amy Lowell, Oliver Wendell Holmes Sr., William James, Leon Trotsky. The uniqueness of the collections at Houghton lies both in their completeness and in a special regard for the author's milieu. For example, the library not only has about half of all the existing manuscripts of Keats's works; it also has many manuscripts and books of members of Keats's literary circle, along with Keats's annotated copy of Shakespeare's plays and poems. Similarly, it owns manuscripts of some of Melville's works, first editions of almost all his books, and his own Shakespeare, with Melvillian marginalia.

The Houghton also has box upon box of manuscripts, drafts, correspondence, photographs, and other memorabilia left by twentieth-century literary figures. If a scholar proposes to write on Edwin Arlington Robinson, T. S. Eliot, Robert Frost, Bertolt Brecht, Delmore Schwartz, Dylan Thomas, Vladimir Nabokov, or John Updike, he or she must visit the Houghton to study materials unavailable elsewhere.

The library also has specialized collections associated with its Department of Printing and Graphic Arts; the Woodberry Poetry Room; the Harvard Theatre Collection; the Theodore Roosevelt Collection; and the Harry Elkins Widener Memorial Collection. Secreted in some of these collections are illuminated and calligraphic manuscripts of the fifteenth century, rare architectural drawings from the past four centuries, and valuable representative samples in the history of printing and typography, as well as daguerreotypes, early prints, and photographs, and archives of audio and video recordings of poets reading their works.

The Houghton opened in 1942. It was the gift of Arthur Houghton, a relatively young, bookish, and prosperous Harvard graduate from an upstate New York family that derived its fortune from glassware. Houghton was never known to travel without a book or two in his pocket, and he donated many of his collections to the library. From its earliest years to the present, it has been blessed with the leadership of gifted directors and curators, like William Jackson, William H. Bond, Philip Hofer, Rodney Dennis, and Eleanor Garvey—all of them "grand acquisitors," individuals of exquisite taste and a remarkable ability to secure valuable books and manuscripts for Houghton's collections.

The last Harvard building to be styled in the traditional red-brick neo-Georgian manner, Houghton Library stands near the center of the Yard, cheek-by-jowl with kindred library buildings. Its curators mount revolving exhibitions, and on any given day faculty members, graduate students, visiting scholars, and under-graduates can be seen working side-by-side in the main reading room. Whether scholars-in-the-making or scholars-already-made, all seem to delight in being able to lay their (gloved) hands (*very* carefully) on original manuscripts and rare books of incomparable worth.

Related entries: Architecture; Libraries; Z Closet. *Related Website:* hcl.harvard.edu/houghton.

Houses

At Yale they're called colleges. Many other institutions settle for dormitories or residence halls. But Harvard has houses, and it's in these twelve complexes of neo-Georgian and contemporary build-ings that most upperclassmen eat, sleep, study, organize intramural athletics, and participate in social, cultural, and community service activities. If there's a single distinguishing aspect of the Harvard College experience, it's house life.

The nine river houses, located on or near the Charles, are Ad-ams, Dunster, Eliot, Kirkland, Leverett, Lowell, Mather, Quincy, and Winthrop. The three Quad houses, originally built around the Radcliffe Quadrangle, north of Harvard Square, are Cabot, Cur-rier, and Pforzheimer. There's also a thirteenth house, Dudley, to which Harvard's 120-odd nonresident undergraduates and all grad-uate students in Arts and Sciences are attached. Lehman Hall, its headquarters, looks out on Harvard Square.

Though the house system was instituted in 1930, the notion of housing students in residential colleges had been broached as early as 1871. For many years there was debate and general dissatisfaction over letting students find their own lodgings in Cambridge, with the wealthiest congregating on Mount Auburn Street's Gold Coast and poorer and minority students consigned to cheaper, drearier dwellings beyond Harvard Square. Well before he became president in 1909, Abbott Lawrence Lowell had envisioned new residential communities within the College, modeled on those of Oxford and Cambridge. "What we want," he told a Yale audience in 1907, "is a group of colleges, each of which will be national and democratic, a microcosm of the whole university."

But Lowell actually wanted more. He wished to embed some major educational reforms in the future houses, and this meant providing space in each of them for resident tutors, tutorial instruction, and a library. His ideal was "self-education," with the student, not the course, as the essential unit of learning, and with students of different backgrounds and interests learning as much from each other as from classroom instruction. In Lowell's view, such interactions could occur only in residential colleges.

In the 1920s, Lowell sought outside funding for his plan, but with scant success. In January 1929, however, he received a stunning pledge of more than $11 million to fund seven undergraduate colleges. There are various legends about how this came to pass. The evidence suggests that Edward Harkness, a Yale graduate, had been ired by his alma mater's delay in taking him up on an offer to fund the construction of residential colleges in New Haven. In the fall of 1928, Harkness called on Lowell, and—while Yale was still temporizing—a deal was struck. Mindful that a former Princeton president, Woodrow Wilson, had been a prominent advocate of the college system, the *Yale Record* would describe the upshot as "a Princeton plan done at Harvard with Yale money."

Four neo-Georgian freshman residence halls built earlier in Lowell's presidency formed the main architectural elements of Kirkland, Winthrop, and Leverett Houses. Two former Gold Coast residence halls provided components of Adams House. Lowell, Eliot, Dunster, and another part of Adams House were built from the ground up. The architect was Charles A. Coolidge, class of 1881, who had planned Lowell's freshman residence halls, the Medical School quadrangle, the Law School's Langdell Hall, and the campus of Stanford University. To the new river houses he applied the red-brick, neo-Georgian styling of the freshman residences. Some critics have dismissed the architectural look of the houses as derivative. But the historian Walter Muir Whitehill surely had it right when he praised Lowell House as a "masterpiece of creative eclecticism"—a description that could extend to other river houses.

Those seven houses opened in the early 1930s. Quincy House, adjoining Lowell and Leverett, was added in 1958. The twelve-story Leverett Towers, completed a year later, broke sharply with the neo-Georgian styling of the original houses and was Harvard's first experiment with high-rise design. Mather House, a 21-story high-rise, went up on the far side of Dunster House in 1971. In that same year, Harvard and Radcliffe entered into an agreement that opened the river houses to women and merged three Radcliffe Quadrangle residence centers into the house system, bringing the total of residential houses to twelve.

Much administrative work of the College is delegated to the houses. All are led by masters and (usually) co-masters, the former always a tenured faculty member or senior administrator. They set the standards and tone of house life. Under the masters are Allston Burr Senior Tutors, who act as administrative deans and also teach, and 20 or more resident tutors, largely graduate students, who advise, counsel, coach, and help out in other ways. The student-to-tutor ratio is roughly 20:1. The house office keeps the records of all of the 300–400 students living in the house. Tutors handle advising and letter-writing for fellowship and professional-school candidates—a function that falls to the central dean's office at most colleges.

The dining halls are central to the communal life of the houses, and following the pattern of British colleges, all have Junior Common Rooms (JCRs) and Senior Common Rooms (SCRs) as well. Students hold meetings and social events in the JCRs, and faculty associates meet regularly in the SCRs to discuss house affairs and hear occasional talks about their colleagues' research and teaching. The houses also provide a locus for art, film, and drama societies, chamber music and opera groups, publications, public service initiatives, and intramural sports teams. Each year more than 300 house teams contest in approximately 850 matches and tourneys in almost 30 different sports. Competition for the Straus Cup, awarded annually to the house with the best won-lost record, is always keen.

In earlier days, house masters combed lists of freshman applicants to select rising sophomores they wanted for the house. Information gleaned from interviews figured importantly in the process. This eventually led to house stereotyping. Eliot became known as the preppy house, Winthrop as the jock house, Adams as artsy, Lowell as intellectual. To some extent the stereotypes conformed to reality, and for the most part, each house came to value and even flaunt its particular ascription. For a time, the College dean's office sought to make the composition of the houses more heterogeneous by imposing caps for geographic and school backgrounds, fields of concentration, and the like. But by 1972, the winds of change and egalitarianism were blowing strongly. The result was a more equitable system in which the masters relinquished their powers of selection and students ranked all twelve houses in order of preference. The ranking system was later modified, but certain houses still continued to maintain a characteristic profile, and a few had disproportionate numbers of minority members and varsity athletes. In the mid-1990s, administrators made a final effort to end what President Lowell would have seen as a subversion of the house plan: a system that allowed, at least to some extent, the self-segregation of students by interest and background. The cure for this ailment (still debated in some quarters today) was full, computer-based "randomization." This denied both students and masters any chance to express a preference. The newly designed computer program made assignments that factored in only one parameter, gender, thereby ensuring that each house had a mix quite similar to that of the overall student body.

In one important respect, the transition to house life still affords a significant choice to freshmen who have bonded during their first year at Harvard. In March, first-year students are given the option of consolidating their applications for house assignments with those of friends—of either sex, and with an upper limit of eight. Friends can thus stay together for three more years. Such "blocking group" applications are sifted through a computerized process. Though they can no longer state preferences, most undergraduates come to accept and feel proud of the house they're assigned to.

Curricular reforms come and go, but the invention and refinement of the house system stands out as the most far-reaching innovation in the history of Harvard College. As one College dean puts it, the house plan is a twelve-carat jewel in Harvard's crown.

Related entries: Allston; Architecture; Athletics; Charles River; Gold Coast.

I J K

John Harvard's statue, cast in bronze by Daniel Chester French, was
unveiled in 1884. Since no likeness existed, the sculptor took
a recent graduate, Sherman Hoar, as his model.

Information Technology

It drives advanced research, opens up new instructional opportunities, knits the University community together, and quickens the tempo of institutional life. The computer revolution had its Harvard beginnings during World War II; within half a century, it had profoundly affected every part of the institution.

The unveiling of Professor Howard Aiken's Mark I Automatic Sequence Controlled Calculator in 1944 was a landmark event in the history of IT. Built with the help of IBM and based on standard IBM punch-card technology, the Mark I was 50 feet long, weighed five tons, and took three to five seconds to do a straightforward multiplication exercise. It was soon outdated by all-relay calculators like Aiken's Mark II, and by third- and fourth-generation computers with electronic components. Professor Aiken gave the University's first computer-science course in 1952, and by the 1960s Engineering and Applied Sciences was the faculty's fastest-growing division. Though an Office for Information Technology (OIT) was created to coordinate planning and operations, computing at Harvard evolved in typically decentralized fashion, with schools and departments developing their own computer platforms and databases. By the late 1980s, almost a dozen different internal networks were in use. Carrying out the directives of a faculty committee on information technology, the OIT planned and installed a high-speed data network, bundled with a new, high-capacity telephone system. Utilizing 10,000 miles of copper and fiberoptic cable, the $30 million project was completed by the mid-1990s. Connecting residential facilities, faculty offices, and classrooms University-wide, it supported email and electronic bulletin boards, file transfer, interpersonal communications, and computer-based instructional programs. In 1993, when Harvard Yard buildings were tied into the network, members of the class of 1997 became the first in Harvard history to be bonded electronically. By plugging his or her computer into a wall jack, a freshman could be in instant touch with fellow students, faculty members, or the roughly 15 million computer users then linked globally by the Internet.

Increasingly powerful computers, along with the Internet's

global reach and information-gathering prowess, had a catalytic effect on scholarly research in every academic field, condensing the time required to produce and evaluate new findings. Connectivity also reshaped instructional programs. Students could send their assignments to electronic "drop boxes" and receive emailed responses from their teachers. Faculty members held electronic office hours; study groups worked together online. Within five years, more than a thousand courses within the Faculty of Arts and Sciences had their own Websites, and many provided multimedia "courseware" for interactive learning programs.

Information technology gave a new dimension to Harvard's teaching mission. Via the Internet, the Extension School now offers "distance education" courses that can be viewed by students anywhere in the world. Registered students, including those in the Boston area, have the option of attending lectures delivered on campus or watching them online. Students in distance education courses complete the same coursework and receive the same credit as students taking the courses locally. The schools of Business, Education, Law, and Medicine are among the graduate and professional schools that sponsor an increasing variety of interactive learning programs.

Many of Harvard's libraries, museums, and collections now offer searchable databases and online exhibits. From the Alumni Association's Harvard Gateways site, one can download videos on a range of Harvard-related subjects. The HAA also puts out an electronic newsletter, *Harvard Monthly;* the University News Office compiles a daily email digest. The URL www.harvard.edu is an entry point for virtually all University sites.

All of the University's schools maintain computing support units to assist students, faculty, and staff members. University Information Systems (UIS) is Harvard's central information technology office. Its Center for Training and Development gives courses in word processing, database design and management, Webpage design, computer graphics, desktop publishing, and more. For those outside the immediate University community, the Extension School has a wide spectrum of evening courses in computer programming, systems administration, networking, database development, and multimedia.

At the undergraduate level, computer science is among the 41 standard fields of concentration. With a teaching faculty of about a dozen, this small but growing program typically enrolls about 75 concentrators. Some combine computer studies with other fields, such as economics, linguistics, mathematics, physics, or psychology. Harvard's computer science and electrical engineering facilities are now housed in the state-of-the-art Maxwell Dworkin Building, opened in 1999 and funded by a $20 million gift from Microsoft executives William H. Gates III and Steven Ballmer, both members of the class of 1977. (The building—"Max Dorks" in undergraduate parlance—is named in honor of the donors' mothers, Mary Maxwell Gates and Beatrice Dworkin Ballmer.) Near the Law School, this striking building stands on the site once occupied by the Aiken Computation Laboratory, where information technology was nurtured at Harvard (and where Gates, as a sophomore, worked around the clock to write a programming language for the first generation of personal computers).

Related entries: Continuing Education; Dropouts; Gazette; Virtual Harvard. *Related Websites:* www.digital.harvard.edu; www.harvard.edu; www.haa.harvard.edu/ath; www.harvard.edu/infotech.

International Outreach

Harvard is an increasingly international institution. Nearly one in five full-time students now comes from outside the United States. Though the proportion of foreign students in the College hovers at around 8 percent, some of the graduate and professional schools, like the schools of design, government, and public health, draw more than one-third of their students from other countries. Harvard hosts more than 2,500 postdoctoral researchers and visiting faculty members from abroad, a large proportion of them in the Medical Area. No other academic institution has so many. Today's faculty searches are almost always worldwide in scope.

Many of Harvard's research centers focus on regional areas in diverse parts of the world. At both graduate and undergraduate levels, courses with an international orientation abound. Foreign

Cultures is one of seven major areas in the undergraduate Core Curriculum. The Faculty of Arts and Sciences offers instruction in some 54 foreign languages, among them Arabic, Armenian, Croatian and Serbian, Czech, Ethiopian, Mongolian, Nepali, Pali, Persian, Polish, Portuguese, Sanskrit, Swahili, Thai, Tibetan, Turkish, Ukrainian, Urdu-Hindi, Uzbek, and Vietnamese. Though opportunities for undergraduate study abroad have been relatively limited in the past, the Faculty now has an Office of International Programs and a Standing Committee on Out-of-Residence Study; both are working to expand such opportunities. "While it is true that teaching is at the heart of what goes on at Harvard College," wrote Dean William C. Kirby in a letter to the faculty, "it is also true that not all of the education that a student receives must take place in Cambridge, Massachusetts."

Alumni living outside the United States are the fastest-growing branch of the Harvard family. The total is expected to reach 40,000 in the near future. The most recent edition of the *Alumni Directory* had Harvardians living in 184 countries. Some 70 of those countries have Harvard clubs. In addition to England, Canada, France, Japan, and Germany—which have (in that order) the largest concentrations of alumni—there are Harvard clubs in such places as Bulgaria, Croatia, Egypt, Finland, Indonesia, Israel, Pakistan, Peru, Saudi Arabia, and Ukraine. In these countries and others, graduate and professional school alumni predominate. Though Europe still has the largest proportion of international alumni (nearly 40 percent), the Pacific Rim can claim almost 20 percent and is moving up fast. All told, the Harvard population of Japan, Taiwan, the People's Republic of China, Hong Kong, Singapore, Malaysia, and South Korea has almost quintupled in the past quarter-century.

Though most of Harvard's research centers and programs are Cambridge-based, its Center for Renaissance Studies is located at the Villa I Tatti, outside Florence, Italy; the University also supports an archaeological field station at Sardis, in western Turkey. To aid its researchers working overseas, the Business School has field offices in Argentina, Brazil, France, Hong Kong, and Japan.

Despite its increased international ties, Harvard remains an American university—a point often reiterated by presidents past and present. It attracts international students partly because it is representative of America and because its traditions are rooted in the life of the nation. But the numerical growth of its international student body may be gradual in the future. Since class size is not elastic and larger numbers of foreign students would mean reduced access for American applicants, 20 percent may effectively prove to be a University-wide ceiling for international registration.

Related entries: Aab; Business School; Core Curriculum; Harvard Elsewhere; Museums; Sardis; Villa I Tatti.

Ivy League

More than a decade before formal league play was organized, the *New York Herald Tribune* sportswriter Stanley Woodward used the phrase "ivy colleges" to describe nine schools—Brown, Columbia, Cornell, Dartmouth, Harvard, Pennsylvania, Princeton, the U.S. Military Academy at West Point, and Yale—that had nurtured the game of football, had engaged in longstanding athletic rivalries, and had buildings with ivy-covered walls. That was in the fall of 1933. Associated Press sports editor Alan Gould has been credited with the first use of "Ivy League" in February 1935.

Concerned about the professionalization of college football, eight college presidents met in 1945 to sign an "Ivy Group Agreement" (West Point was not represented). Affirming that their football programs should be "in fitting proportion to the main purpose of academic life," the presidents ruled out athletic scholarships, pledged to uphold joint standards for financial aid and eligibility, and formed a standing committee whose members included the colleges' directors of athletics. In 1952, the Ivy Group voted to abolish spring football practice and banned postseason games; two years later its members agreed to extend their policies to all intercollegiate sports and announced the inception of formal Ivy League football competition. Round-robin play began in the fall of 1956.

In subsequent decades, the Ivy Group created formal programs for women's teams; reluctantly accepted a National Collegiate Athletic Association ruling that made freshmen eligible for varsity teams; restored limited spring football practices (also reluctantly); and adopted an "academic index" that pegged admissions standards for athletes to grade point averages for the schools' students as a whole.

Despite the league's relatively strict standards, the eight schools have succeeded in attracting accomplished student-athletes and achieving a high level of competition and parity. Princeton now boasts the largest number of league championships in all sports, followed closely by Harvard. Next, in descending order, come Pennsylvania, Yale, Cornell, Dartmouth, Brown, and Columbia. Former Ivy athletes have gone on to distinguish themselves in the professions, business, entertainment, politics, and occasionally in professional sports. In one recent season, there were nine former Ivy Leaguers on National Football League rosters.

The Ivy Group—now officially known as the Council of Ivy Group Presidents—maintains an office staff in Princeton, New Jersey. "Ivy League," however, has achieved currency as a shorthand term for the eight participating institutions in the aggregate, and as a descriptive denoting a more or less acceptably elitist manner and a conservatively natty style of dress. It thus lends itself to an adjectival formation, as in "That fellow doesn't look *Ivy* to me."

Related entry: Athletics. *Related Website:* www.ivyleaguesports.com.

Jazz

Jazz didn't come into its own at Harvard until the 1970s. True, many College clubmen of the 1920s and 30s were avid fans, wearing out Bix Beiderbecke and Jack Teagarden 78s on their wind-up Victrolas. True, too, that composer Johnny Green '29 wrote "Body and Soul," which became an all-time hit when tenor saxophonist Coleman Hawkins recorded it in 1939; and that Count Basie and Jimmy Rushing waxed early-1940s recordings of "Harvard Blues" (lyrics by George Frazier '32) that are rediscovered from time to time. It's also true that a Chicago-style Dixieland band called the Crimson Stompers—led by Larry Eanet '52 on valve trombone, with classmates Bill Dunham and Walt Gifford on piano and drums—enlivened the Cambridge-Boston jazz scene in the early

1950s. But over the first half-century of the Jazz Age, Harvard produced few jazz instrumentalists, and though it spawned some important composers, none paid much heed to jazz-related idioms until Frederick Rzewski '58 wrote "Les Moutons des Panurge," a bouncy jazz-gamelan piece, in 1969.

Then things started to change. Thomas Everett, appointed as Band Director in 1971, was surprised to find no organized jazz activity at Harvard. A bass trombonist who had played with jazz groups, Everett rounded up enough "bandies"—a saxophonist, a trumpeter, a sousaphonist who also played electric bass, a guitarist, and a drummer—to play at an Adams House dance. Everett recalls the gig as a disaster, but his group stayed together and was bolstered by the addition of members like Stephen Sacks '75, a music concentrator who would earn a *summa* for Harvard's first jazz-related dissertation (on Charlie Parker). On the College mixer circuit, on occasional dates at other schools, and at a memorable free concert at Sanders Theatre in 1974, the Harvard Jazz Band began to take off. Today it's still flying high—and indeed there are now two jazz ensembles, known as the Sunday Band and the Monday Band.

The Jazz Band's liftoff coincided with the creation of Harvard's Office for the Arts (OFA). Through its Learning from Performers program, its Jazz Masters series, and its arts grant and lesson subsidy programs, the OFA brought notable jazz artists to Harvard and helped support the Jazz Band's activities. A collaboration between the OFA and the Department of Afro-American Studies led to "The Jazz Tradition," a course taught by Everett. The OFA's first Jazz Masters concert, in 1980, honored pianists Bill Evans and John Lewis. Lewis, an original member of the Modern Jazz Quartet, had been commissioned to compose a piece that he titled "The Gates of Harvard"; it was premiered by the Bill Evans Trio and the Harvard Jazz Orchestra. The Jazz Masters series later brought Benny Carter, Gerry Mulligan, Clark Terry, J. J. Johnson, and other jazz greats to Harvard.

Jazz now has a place in the College curriculum. Having given a popular Core Curriculum course on chamber music, the pianist and Mozart scholar Robert Levin '67, Robinson Professor of the Humanities, went on to create Core courses on jazz and the Swing

Era. Ingrid Monson, a former jazz trumpeter, now holds the Quincy Jones chair of African American Music, a joint appointment of the Music Department and the Department of Afro-American Studies. She too has taught a Core course, "Sayin' Something: Jazz as Sound, Sensibility, and Social Dialogue." As a resource for students and faculty members researching jazz-related subjects, the Morse Musical Collection in Hilles Library contains audio and video recordings of workshops, interviews, and performances featuring jazz musicians.

Another indicator of the increasing presence of jazz in Harvard life is the list of younger alumni who have become well known in jazz circles. Among them are trumpeter, composer, conductor, and arranger Bob Merrill '81, the founder, in his Harvard days, of the Hasty Pudding Club's "Jazz at the Pudding" series; tenor saxophonist and composer Don Braden '85; saxophonists Anton Schwartz '89 and Joshua Redman '90; and vocalist Sara Lazarus '84 (who also plays tenor sax). In recent years, the Harvard Club of Boston has sponsored a February Combo Jazz Fest in which Harvard students are featured. The University's rather staid honorary-degree process has also taken increasing note of jazz musicians. To sustained applause on Commencement Day, Harvard has honored such artists as Benny Goodman (1984), Ella Fitzgerald (1990), Benny Carter (1994), and Quincy Jones (1997).

Related entries: Arts; Music. *Related Website:* www.digitas.harvard.edu/ ~jazzband.

John Harvard—and His Statue

The real John Harvard is a shadowy figure. No portrait has come down to us; important details of his life are missing. There is no record of his shipboard passage to New England. We don't know just how long he lay ill before his early death, at 30, in 1638. We do know, however, that he was the first benefactor of the country's first college and that in posthumous acknowledgment of his bequest of half his estate and his substantial library the Court of the Massachusetts Bay Colony ordered "that the college agreed upon formerly to be built at Cambridge shall be called Harvard College."

John Harvard was born in Southwark, not far from London Bridge, in 1607. His father was a butcher; his mother's family came from Stratford-upon-Avon, where his grandfather was a butcher, maltster, and yeoman. (The family home on Stratford's High Street, with its Elizabethan half-timbered architecture, is now maintained as a museum.) Both families were relatively prosperous and well-connected; there has been speculation that the Harvard family in London knew William Shakespeare and attended his plays.

Young John was educated at St. Saviour's Grammar School, Southwark, where he studied grammar, the classics, and the Bible. When he was seventeen, tragedy struck the Harvard family five times in two months, as the plague took four of his brothers and sisters and then his father. At 20, having decided to enter the ministry, John enrolled in Emmanuel College, Cambridge, then a seedbed of Puritan zeal. He received his B.A. in 1632 and his M.A. three years later; married Ann Sadler, the sister of a classmate; and emigrated with her to the Massachusetts Bay Colony in the summer of 1637, a little over a year after their marriage. Having come into a small inheritance from his mother, he evidently devoted much of it to buying books, which he brought with him to the New World.

The Harvards settled in Charlestown, where John began a brief career as minister and teacher. His fellow townsmen doubtless thought well of him. He was learned and had a notable library. The proposal to build a college in the wilderness of Newtowne—later Cambridge—engaged his interest. But in the summer of 1638 he died "of a consumption." He left no written will but did express a wish that half his estate—779 pounds/12 shillings/2 pence—and his more than 400 books be left to the new college not far from Charlestown. John Harvard "sacrificed a life of comparative ease and security to do his part toward building a New England where men might lead the good life," wrote the College's master historian, Samuel Eliot Morison, in *The Founding of Harvard College* (1936). "And the one deed which has given glory to his name perhaps did more in its consequences to bring future generations within reach of the true and good, than all the efforts of the more gifted and prominent founders of New England."

Daniel Chester French's much-photographed bronze statue of John Harvard, cast in 1884, is essentially a creation of the sculptor's imagination. It was the gift of Samuel J. Bridge, an elderly Boston businessman and longtime benefactor of the College. President Charles W. Eliot had reservations about the commission, noting that "such attempts to make portrait statues of those of whom there are not only no portraits, but no records or recollections, are of very doubtful desirableness. Such a course tends to the confusing and confounding of historical truth, and leaves posterity unable to decide what is authentic and what is mere invention."

On viewing the work in progress, however, Eliot was swayed. "It moves one," he told French's father, "which is . . . an indication of merit." French himself explained that "in looking about for a type of the early comers to our shores, I chose a lineal descendant of them for my model in the general structure of the face." His model was Sherman Hoar, class of 1882. "He has more of what I want than anybody I know," wrote French. "Of course I shall not make it a portrait of him." The statue was initially situated outside Memorial Hall. When it was unveiled, a *New York Times* critic conjectured that John Harvard himself "would certainly have smiled with pleasure if he had foreseen the luck that was to befall his memory . . . in finding his statue in the hands of so able a sculptor as Mr. French. . . . The casting is a triumph of foundry work, the ideal or inner beauty of the face and figure make it a very remarkable and imposing piece of art."

At least partly at French's urging, the statue was transferred to its present site in front of University Hall in 1923. By then the artist had completed America's greatest public sculpture, the majestic seated figure of Abraham Lincoln in the Lincoln Memorial.

One of New England's most frequently photographed objects, the John Harvard statue is rivaled only by the Museum of Natural History's Glass Flowers as a Harvard tourist attraction. The sides of its granite pedestal bear a seal similar to the official one of Harvard College, and the seal of Emmanuel College, Cambridge; an inscription reads, *John Harvard, Founder, 1638.* Tour guides like to call it "the statue of three lies": it is not an authentic portrait of its subject; John Harvard did not found the College; and the actual date of the founding was 1636.

The toe of John Harvard's left shoe has been buffed to a high shine by passersby who have heard that rubbing it brings good luck. Tourists and students sometimes clamber up to be photographed in John Harvard's lap. Pumpkins have been put over his head at Halloween. On the eve of the Harvard-Dartmouth football game, Hanover rowdies have painted him green; on the eve of the Yale game, New Haven rowdies have painted him blue. Despite such indignities, John Harvard gazes westward, unfazed. The classic quatrain of David T. W. McCord '21, published in the *Harvard Alumni Bulletin* in 1940, captures the indomitable spirit of French's sculpture:

> "Is that you, John Harvard?"
> I said to his statue.
> "Aye—that's me," said John,
> "And after you're gone."

Related entries: Glass Flowers; Libraries; Statues and Monuments.

Kennedy School of Government

In its fourth decade, the Kennedy School is still the new kid on the Harvard block. Like some kids, it has been described as dynamic, fast-growing, excitingly alive. New buildings, programs, and faculty members, rising enrollments, larger budgets—these expansionist signs have been evident in the school's formative years. Such growth has now slowed, however, and the heady days of rapid institutional enlargement appear to be over. There have even been cutbacks in programs and staff. In this respect, the K-School has become more like Harvard's other professional schools.

Some 800 students are enrolled; the faculty numbers more than 90, counting junior and senior people and joint appointments. A

one-year degree program, Mid-Career Master in Public Administration (M.P.A.), enrolls about 210 students; a two-year Master in
Public Policy program (M.P.P.) enrolls another 200. Many of the
world's major political figures have spoken at the John F. Kennedy
Jr. Forum (originally the ARCO Forum), in the atrium of the
school's main building. The school's activities are centered in a
masterfully designed four-building quadrangle just off John F.
Kennedy Street, near the heart of Harvard Square.

How did this school originate? According to former Harvard
president Derek Bok, on whose watch much of its growth took
place, it took a variety of "lucky, maybe once-in-a-century, circumstances" to make it all possible. First there was the spirit of the
times in the mid-1960s. The ethos of the Kennedy years helped
make government service a worthy ideal for students and faculty
alike; rigorous training for public service seemed an academic imperative. Harvard also had a remarkable cadre of senior faculty
members who could claim significant government service backgrounds and strong ties to Washington in their current work. They
included such figures as John T. Dunlop, Thomas Schelling, Richard Neustadt, Howard Raiffa, Don K. Price, and Milton Katz.
These scholars began meeting informally to discuss the possibility
of expanding the existing Graduate School of Public Administration, a small and thinly funded school established in 1936 with a
gift from former New York congressman Lucius N. Littauer, class
of 1878.

The assassination of President John F. Kennedy in 1963 was another factor. As early as 1962, the president had considered various
sites in Cambridge for his yet-to-be-built library and museum.
Though they admired Kennedy, many faculty members and Cambridge neighbors opposed a location near Harvard Square because
of the likely increase in traffic congestion. Eventually the library
and museum were built at Columbia Point, on Boston Harbor.
They were opened, with considerable fanfare, in 1979. Meanwhile,
a Charles River site near Harvard Square, formerly a subway yard,
became available. Political deals were struck, funds were raised,
and everything came together to provide a home for the new
school, almost contiguous to the College.

Leadership at the top, and major policy decisions at all levels, were crucial in the school's early years. Presidents Pusey and Bok both supported the idea of a school that would serve society's need for proficiency and integrity in public service. A young professor of politics, Graham T. Allison '62, PH.D. '68, was named dean of the school. He made his mark by attracting high-level faculty and energetically raising funds for buildings, programs, and endowment. Most major policy issues were effectively decided at an early date, though not without controversy. The option of merging the new school with the Business School (as had been done at Yale and Stanford) was resoundingly rejected. Joint appointments for faculty members from other Harvard schools would be encouraged. And despite recurring allegations of liberal partisanship— Yale man George H. W. Bush, during his 1988 campaign, seemed to have the school in mind when he accused his Democratic opponent, Michael Dukakis, of deriving his ideas from "Harvard Yard's boutique"—the school would strive to maintain a policy of inviting faculty members and speakers with differing political viewpoints.

One other key decision was made early on. The school would seek to draw students and faculty from all over the world. Today, about 45 percent of students hold foreign passports, and much of the curriculum has a distinctly international focus.

The school sponsors almost a dozen research centers and many more institutes and research projects (some come and go), as well as at least a dozen executive and special short-term training programs. The centers include:

Belfer Center for Science and International Affairs

Carr Center for Human Rights Policy

Center for Business and Government

Center for International Development

Center for Public Leadership

Hauser Center for Nonprofit Organizations

Shorenstein Center on the Press, Politics, and Public Policy

Joint Center for Housing Studies

Taubman Center for State and Local Government

Wiener Center for Social Policy

Each center sponsors programs focusing on such research topics as energy, technological innovation, developmental challenges in Africa, environmental and natural resource management, and women and public policy. The Kennedy School has numerous fellowship programs as well. Four of the best known are the Mason Fellows Program, for officials and professionals from developing countries; the Heffernan Visiting Fellows, for short visits by distinguished public servants; the Wexner Fellows Program, for young Israeli government and non-governmental officials; and the McCloy Scholars Program, for young German professionals in business and public management.

The school is home to the Institute of Politics (IOP), a student-oriented (and to some extent student-run) organization, established in 1966 to encourage Harvard students to commit themselves to politics and public service. Another goal is to strengthen ties among scholars and political communities. Study groups, seminars, special conferences, debates, and speaking appearances by major political leaders focus on current issues. Anyone attending events at the IOP or the John F. Kennedy Jr. Forum will sense that when it comes to politics at Harvard, this is where the action is.

Related entries: International Outreach; Underground. *Related Website:* www.ksg.harvard.edu.

L

The *Lampoon*'s impish clubhouse, a miniature sixteenth-century
Flemish castle, decked out for a "Worst Actress" award
to Natalie Wood in 1966.

Lamont Library

Undergraduates sometimes call it "Lament" Library, but there's nothing lamentable about Harvard's first modern building, opened in 1949. Designed by Coolidge, Shepley, the firm that planned the College's residential houses, Lamont looks from the outside like a relatively prosaic example of what was called International Style; though its unadorned red-brick walls and white trim help relate it to Harvard's older buildings, the boxy exterior does not make a telling architectural statement. But Lamont's interior is something else: inviting and airy, it makes extensive and inspired use of blond wood, glass, and natural light. The fifth-level Woodberry Poetry Room, a deftly executed essay in Scandinavian style by the Finnish architect Alvar Aalto, seems as contemporary as it did the day it was finished.

The world's first stand-alone undergraduate library, Lamont contains almost 190,000 volumes and has alcoves and reading room chairs for 1,100 users. In partnership with the Radcliffe Quadrangle's Hilles Library, Lamont keeps on reserve most of the books required for humanities and social sciences courses; Cabot Library serves undergraduate needs in the natural sciences. Lamont's collections include a large number of videos, mostly documentaries and feature films, as well as CD-ROMs that are available for circulation.

Lamont stands in the southeast corner of Harvard Yard, on a sloping site formerly occupied by the historic Dana-Palmer House. It was funded in part by a gift of $1.5 million from Thomas W. Lamont, class of 1892, chairman of J. P. Morgan & Co. and a Harvard Corporation member. The full construction cost was $2.5 million. Until 1967, the use of Lamont was restricted to male students.

In addition to the Poetry Room, the library houses the fifth-level Farnsworth Room, devoted to recreational reading; a Language Resource Center on level six; electronic-learning facilities on levels five and three; and, below ground level, a Government Documents and Microforms collection and a Center for Students with

Disabilities. Tunnels connect Lamont with the semi-subterranean Pusey Library and with Widener Library.

Related entries: Architecture; Libraries; Underground. *Related Website:* www.hcl.harvard.edu/lamont.

Lampoon

Its Webpage calls it "the world's oldest humor magazine." Founded in 1876, the *Lampoon* laid a firm claim to that descriptive when its prototype, the British magazine *Punch,* folded in 1992 at the ripe age of 151. (*Lampoon* editors marked the occasion by flying to London for a valedictory dinner with the expiring publication's staff.)

In its early days, the *Lampoon* published work by such budding writers as Owen Wister, class of 1882; George Santayana, class of 1886; and Robert Benchley, class of 1912. Along with the cartoonist Gluyas Williams '11, Benchley was among the few who actually made their names as humorists. Until he was expelled from the College, William Randolph Hearst, class of 1886, was on the business board. The *Lampoon's* style of humor in those adolescent years was vaudevillian: "Did you take a bath recently?" "No, is one missing?" During Benchley's editorship, the first parody issue appeared. Phony issues of the *Harvard Crimson* became a staple; *Lampoon* pranks and stunts, especially during an interval known as "Phools' Week," continue to provide other outlets for college humor.

The *Lampoon's* sporadic issues appear roughly five times a year, sell for $4 a copy, and offer a mix of stories, cartoons, satires, poems, and parody. But for members, the *Lampoon* is more than a publication. Their headquarters is an amusingly eccentric pocket-sized castle that has proven as congenial a setting for social functions as it has been for satiric writing. Built in 1909 between Mount Auburn and Bow Streets, it was designed in mock sixteenth-century Flemish style by Edmund March Wheelwright, class of 1876, a *Lampoon* founder who became city architect of Boston and designed the Longfellow and Anderson bridges. Hearst paid for the building; the Boston art patroness Isabella Stewart Gardner donated antiques and advised Wheelwright on the acquisition of other treasures. The castle's interior walls are lined with some 7,000 Delft tiles, reputedly the largest such assemblage outside the Netherlands. Entrance to the castle is limited to *Lampoon* members and occasional guests.

Over the years the *Lampoon* has gone through various transitions. When the young Marxist John Reed '10 was an editor, he cleansed the magazine of salacious slapstick and local Harvard humor, preferring social satire and scathing political commentary. The magazine would later come under the spell of the nascent *New Yorker's* style and content: it featured short fiction, cartoons that were sometimes droll and occasionally pointed, and vignettes that aspired to sophistication. In the late 1930s the editors introduced an annual series of "Movie Worsts," brief glosses of films so bad that they were fun to watch.

Lampoon parodies have sought to skewer many established publications, from the now-defunct *Literary Digest* to *Cosmopolitan, Mademoiselle, The New Yorker, Newsweek, People, Playboy,* and *USA Today.* (Even the *Harvard Alumni Bulletin* was once treated to a sendup.) Benchley started it with a parody of the old *Life,* a humor magazine edited by Edward S. Martin, class of 1877, a founding editor of the *Lampoon.* A generation later, a 1935 *Esquire* parody—with a full-color drawing of a nude, captioned "What the well-dressed bride will wear"—was banned by Boston postal authorities.

In the late 1960s, the editors spun off books and a national magazine. Parody books had titles like *Bored of the Rings,* a Tolkien takeoff; *The Harvard Lampoon's Guide to College Admissions* sold well. In 1969, veteran 'Poonsters Henry Beard '67, Rob Hoffman '69, and Doug Kenney '68 started the *National Lampoon,* which became a munificent source of royalties for the mother publication. In the 1970s and 1980s, *National Lampoon* was the most widely read publication on college campuses, reaching a peak circulation of 850,000. Kenney also co-wrote the 1978 hit movie *Animal House,* one of the highest-grossing film comedies ever. Today's *National Lampoon* operates under a license from the *Lampoon* (which owns the registered trademark for the name *Lampoon*—a relatively rare instance in which a corporate entity has successfully trademarked an English word).

Lampoon credentials have helped many younger alumni find lucrative work in films and television. On the writing staffs of such durable TV shows as *Saturday Night Live, Seinfeld,* and *The Simpsons,* former 'Poonies have always been strongly represented. Al Jean '81 is the current executive producer of *The Simpsons,* a show whose writing staff over the years has included almost two dozen *Lampoon* alumni. James Downey '74 was for many years head writer of *SNL;* Dennis McNicholas '94 is currently the show's co-head writer. On his staff are at least five recent *Lampoon* grads.

Among alumni of previous generations whose humor enlivened the pages of the *Lampoon* were Elliot Richardson '41, ll.b. '44, later a diplomat and cabinet official; George Plimpton '48, author and sometime actor; actor Fred Gwynne '51; and the novelist, critic, and poet John Updike '54. (Perhaps oddly, Richardson, Gwynne, and Updike were best known in their *Lampoon* days as cartoonists.) More recent *Lampoon* alumni have included Conan O'Brien '85, a *Saturday Night Live* writer before he became the eponymous ('Poonymous?) host of NBC-TV's *Late Night with Conan O'Brien;* Andy Borowitz '80, a frequent *New Yorker* contributor; TV producer Tom Werner '71, now a co-owner of the Boston Red Sox; and Lisa Henson '82, the *Lampoon*'s first woman president, now a Hollywood film producer.

Related entries: Gold Coast; Harvard Crimson. *Related Website:* www.harvardlampoon.com.

Law School

Addressing 700 candidates for law degrees at each year's Commencement, the president declares that these men and women are ready "to pursue those wise restraints that make us free." (Until the 1980s, the text read "those wise restraints that make *men* free.") It is always a memorable moment.

The Law School is one of Harvard's heavyweight professional

schools. Its more than 1,800 full-time students, 80 full-time professors (as well as numerous lecturers and adjuncts), seventeen research programs, and ample endowment make it an imposing presence on the Harvard scene. The titans of American jurisprudence
who have taught there in the past include Oliver Wendell Holmes
Jr., Louis D. Brandeis, Felix Frankfurter, and Joseph Story. Among
its eminent deans have been Christopher Columbus Langdell, the
first to hold the office, and Roscoe Pound, Erwin Griswold, and
Derek Bok. Of the nine justices sitting on the Supreme Court at
the start of 2004, five attended the school: Stephen Breyer, LL.B.
'64; Ruth Bader Ginsburg, '57-'58; Anthony Kennedy, LL.B. '61;
Antonin Scalia, LL.B. '60; and David Souter '61, LL.B. '66.

Many past and present faculty members have literally written
the books in their fields of expertise: Austin Scott on trusts, James
Casner on estate taxes and planning, Louis Loss on securities regu-
lation, Samuel Williston on contracts, Phillip Areeda on antitrust
legislation, Roger Fisher on negotiation and conflict resolution,
and Laurence Tribe on constitutional law.

Founded in 1817, the Law School opened its doors as the first
educational institution of its kind in North America. Two professors taught six students. By 1826, Harvard's law library held 584 titles. The curriculum was intensely practical and highly parochial
in its devotion to Anglo-Saxon common law. It took many decades
for the school to begin to rival the venerable law faculties of Europe.

Over the past two centuries, the story has been one of rapid institutional change in terms of the numbers and kinds of students
and faculty members, courses taught, library acquisitions, and endowment growth. In 1899, the faculty voted to admit a female student, but the Harvard Corporation overruled the decision. Not
until 1950 did the school admit women. Today they make up
about 45 percent of each class, and a growing number of senior and
junior faculty members—including Professor Elena Kagan, appointed to the deanship in 2003—are women. Until well after
World War II, the majority of students were from the eastern seaboard; only a few came from abroad. Students now enroll from all
50 states and from more than a hundred countries worldwide.
There are more than 260 course offerings, and the library contains

more than two million books and manuscripts. With a $400 million capital fundraising drive under way, the school's endowment is expected to reach $1 billion by the end of this century's first decade.

For students, the core of the Law School experience is the three-year Juris Doctor (J.D.) program, which enrolls about 1,600. A much smaller number are in the Master of Laws (LL.M.) and Doctor of Juridical Science (S.J.D.) programs. Many novels, memoirs, films, and TV programs have sought to depict the life of a 1L (first-year student). The best and most vivid is the 1973 film *The Paper Chase,* in which John Houseman plays the intimidating Professor Kingsfield. Some razor-sharp intellectual combat takes place in his classroom, and Kingsfield justifies his sometimes cruel questioning by insisting that "you come here with a headful of mush and you leave thinking like a lawyer." In recent years the school has made a concerted effort to diminish emotional stress while maintaining its famed intellectual rigor—for example, by reducing the size of required courses—and this sort of Socratic jousting has been somewhat softened in 1L and 2L classes. But intellectual parrying, "cold calling" (randomly choosing a student to answer a pointed question), and cross-examining students' arguments continue to be part of many professors' pedagogical repertoires.

The terrors of the first year, sometimes likened to Marine boot camp, usually prove temporary. In addition to their course work, many students avail themselves of opportunities to do various kinds of public service work. A majority of each graduating class has either worked in a voluntary practice organization or for credit in the school's many clinics. Many also work on law journals. The school has ten of them: probably the most prestigious, open by election to a select group of students, is the *Harvard Law Review,* published monthly from November to June, with a circulation of 8,000. Others help run the Harvard Law School Forum, a lecture series that features distinguished speakers from many fields. Another important activity is the annual Ames moot court competition. These student-run mock trials have been held for nearly a century. Real-life cases are researched and argued by students before outside judges. The final round is often adjudicated by senior federal judges (sometimes including Supreme Court justices), and the proceedings are streamed to worldwide audiences via the Internet.

A listing of the school's research centers and programs suggests the wealth of issues under study:

Berkman Center for Internet and Society

Civil Rights Project

East Asian Legal Studies Program

European Law Research Center

Fund for Tax and Fiscal Policy Research

History Project

Human Rights Program

International Tax Program

Islamic Legal Studies Program

Olin Center for Law, Economics, and Business

Labor and Worklife Program

Program on Corporate Governance

Program on Empirical Legal Studies

Program on International Financial Systems

Program on Negotiation

Program on the Legal Profession

Project on Justice in Times of Transition

A priority of Dean Kagan is to tighten "ties to the legal profession, which . . . increasingly over the years—at all law schools—have been attenuated." Law schools, she has said, have tended to isolate themselves as academic and scholarly enclaves, "even as the practice of law has become more commercial and market-driven." Dean Kagan's own experience in law firms and with the federal government—she was a White House advisor in the late 1990s—should help her lead the school in this direction.

Related entries: Hollywood's Harvard; International Outreach; Public Service; Virtual Harvard. *Related Website:* www.law.harvard.edu.

Lectures

Harvard has been described in many ways, but one phrase is undeniably apt. It is a "place of talk," and that covers conversation, debates, panel presentations, roundtable discussions, brown-bag lunch meetings, midnight bull sessions, tutorials, sections—and lectures. Almost everyone seems to be talking or making speeches at least some of the time.

The University has always been able to attract nationally and internationally recognized speakers to its many forums and lecture series. These series are a special genre, often named after a distinguished Harvard figure, varying in the frequency of lectures delivered, and usually administered by a faculty committee that selects the speaker and arranges the event. More than a hundred lecture series exist at the schools and in many academic departments. These are some of the most noted:

• *The Godkin Lectures.* Established in 1903 in memory of Edwin L. Godkin, editor and publisher of *The Nation,* this series features national and world speakers who address "the Essentials of Free Government and the Duties of the Citizen." The series is now administered by the Kennedy School of Government. Past speakers have included Adlai E. Stevenson, Erik Erikson, Daniel Patrick Moynihan, C. Everett Koop, and Kofi Annan.

• *The Charles Eliot Norton Lectures.* This prestigious series, which carries with it a visiting professorship in the Faculty of Arts and Sciences, was established in 1925 in memory of a renowned professor of fine arts who taught at Harvard from 1874 to 1898. The lecturers come from fields encompassing "all poetic expressions": language, music, fine arts, and architecture. Speakers have included T. S. Eliot, Robert Frost, Igor Stravinsky, Leonard Bernstein, Thornton Wilder, Northrop Frye, Helen L. Gardner, Frank Stella, Harold Bloom, Nadine Gordimer, and George Steiner.

• *The Oliver Wendell Holmes Jr. Lectures.* Supported by a bequest from the Holmes estate, this series began in 1941 at Harvard Law School. Speakers have included Learned Hand, William J. Brennan, Stephen Breyer, Ronald Dworkin, and Cass Sunstein.

• *The Dudleian Lectures.* Named after Judge Paul Dudley and administered by the Divinity School, this is by far the oldest lecture series: the first Dudleian lecture was presented in 1755 by President Edward Holyoke. His topic was "The Proof of Natural Religion." Speakers have included William Ellery Channing, William Ernest Hocking, Paul Tillich, Reinhold Niebuhr, and Cardinal (of Milan) Carlo Martini.

• *The William E. Massey Sr. Lectures.* Endowed by an anonymous donor to honor this Virginia businessman and philanthropist, these lectures focus on the history of American civilization. Distinguished past lecturers have included Eudora Welty, Toni Morrison, Gore Vidal, Maxine Hong Kingston, E. L. Doctorow, and John Demos.

• *Nathan I. Huggins Lectures.* Sponsored by the W. E. B. Du Bois Institute for Afro-American Research, the Huggins Lectures in recent years have included such speakers as Lani Guinier '71, David Brion Davis, and Thomas C. Holt.

Most of Harvard's series have free-speech requirements that oblige controversial speakers to answer questions after their lectures and prohibit protesters from disrupting the speaker. Particularly at the Kennedy School of Government, where contentious political views are often aired, speakers and audiences have always had to abide by strictly enforced rules, guaranteeing free speech to both speakers and protesters. Many of the lecture series appear in somewhat revised or slightly expanded form as books published by Harvard University Press.

Related entry: Harvard University Press. *Related Website:* www.hup.harvard.edu.

Libraries

What may now be the world's largest and best university research library had its start in 1638, when John Harvard, a young minister who had recently settled in nearby Charlestown, left his collection of more than 400 books—largely theological—to the newly established college in Cambridge. By the time the Harvard library's first catalog appeared, in 1723, its holdings had grown to 3,500 volumes. All but 404 were lost, however, when Old Harvard Hall burned down in the winter of 1764. (Only one book from John Harvard's library, John Downame's *Christian Warfare*, survived the calamitous fire; it had been on loan and was overdue.) Happily, an appeal for donations soon rebuilt the collection. Thanks in large part to continuing gifts of books and collections, to endowment funds, and to other restricted gifts, the Harvard University Library now contains more than fourteen million volumes. The total does not include manuscripts, microforms, music scores, sound recordings, visual collections, ephemera in the millions, or half a million maps and charts.

The Harvard University Library (HUL) is actually an aggregation of almost a hundred separate libraries—of the graduate and professional schools, of research centers and museums, of academic departments and residential houses, each with its own staff and acquisitions. The Harvard College Library, maintained by the Faculty of Arts and Sciences, is itself a conglomerate of eleven major libraries whose collections number more than nine million volumes. Of these, the Harry Elkins Widener Memorial Library is the largest. A distinctive aspect of Widener, and of many libraries in the University system, is that its book stacks are open to qualified users. In general, anyone affiliated with the University may have access to Harvard libraries.

As a central administrative unit in a largely decentralized institution, the Harvard University Library seeks to coordinate, advise, and strengthen the multiple resources it exists to serve. It sponsors an online catalog, HOLLIS, that can be consulted by anyone who has access to the Internet. To ease pressing space problems in its central libraries, it maintains a vast depository in Southborough, Massachusetts; that facility can retrieve and deliver a book to Cambridge or Boston in a day. One of HUL's pressing concerns is the preservation and conservation of library materials. This endless task is funded primarily by fees and assessments on Harvard's various faculties and other users.

In addition to the eleven major libraries, the Harvard College Library is comprised of 21 departmental libraries and 24 specialized research and office libraries. Widener, the flagship library that dominates Harvard Yard, is weighted toward research materials in the humanities and social sciences. Littauer Library holds major collections in economics and government; outside of Asia, the Harvard-Yenching Library is the largest academic library for East Asian research. Outstanding departmental libraries in fine arts and music are complemented by outstanding theater and poetry collections. Scientific collections are distributed through a dozen libraries. The biggest are the Cabot, a general science library for undergraduates and graduate students; the botany libraries; the Ernst Mayr Library (natural history); and Tozzer Library (anthropology).

Two libraries for undergraduate use date from the middle years of the twentieth century. Lamont in Harvard Yard and Hilles in the Radcliffe Quadrangle hold almost 200,000 books each. Originally for Radcliffe students, Hilles serves the three residential houses—Cabot, Currier, and Pforzheimer—north of the Yard. The ten river houses have libraries ranging from 10,000 to 20,000 volumes.

Most of the Harvard College Library's rare books and manuscripts are in Houghton Library, adjoining Widener and Lamont. The underground Nathan Marsh Pusey Library, completed in 1976, is linked to Widener and Lamont by underground passages and houses the Harvard Theatre Collection, the Harvard Map Collection, the University Archives, some overflow collections from Widener, and faculty offices.

The graduate and professional schools have their own substantial libraries, financed by the schools and administratively responsible to their deans. How handsomely these facilities are supported depends on the financial strength of their schools, both in unrestricted and restricted funds, and on the interests and priorities of their deans.

The Harvard libraries' great variety of bookplates bear witness to the generosity of many generations of bibliophiles. The greatest of the early benefactors were members of the Hollis family of London—wealthy business and professional men, and Dissenters whose interest in Harvard reflected a desire to assist an institution that would set an example of broadmindedness toward all religious sects. Their benevolence has been perpetuated through gifts of books, the establishment of Harvard's first permanent book fund, the endowment of two professorships, and through the adoption of the acronym HOLLIS (Harvard Online Library Information System) for the library system's digital catalog.

In addition to an unceasing need to preserve brittle, worn, and

sometimes mistreated books, librarians of every era have struggled
with space problems. By the late 1830s, Harvard's book collection
had grown to 40,000 volumes, more than could be shelved in
the second-floor library of Harvard Hall. The construction of the
University's first dedicated library building—Gore Hall, a Gothic
structure inspired by the chapel of King's College, Cambridge—
was supposed to provide adequate book storage for the next 75
years. Within two decades, Gore's shelves were full, and new wings
had to be added. By 1913, when Gore and its annexes were razed to
make way for the immense new Widener Library, the College Library owned a half million volumes. The holdings in Widener
alone have since increased by more than a factor of ten.

Faced with an endless barrage of new books, periodicals, and information embedded in nonprint media, today's librarians can no
longer hope, as some of their forerunners did, to collect everything
worth collecting. The infinitely expandable resources of the Internet are now crucial to the capture, retrieval, and use of information
and new ideas. Just how the ultimate interface will be effected—
that is, how billions of words can be digitized for Internet storage,
how the Dewey Decimal System and Google can be made to shake
hands, just who should be setting the agenda—is not yet clear.

Related entries: Architecture; Fire; Harvard Elsewhere; Harvard Hall;
Houghton Library; John Harvard—and His Statue; Lamont Library;
Maps; Radcliffe; Underground; Widener Library. *Related Website:*
lib.harvard.edu.

Life Raft

At Harvard, as elsewhere, terrible things sometimes happen to
good people. Life-threatening illness or death may occur without
warning, disrupting the lives of students, faculty, and staff, or those
of families or friends. Shock and pain seem overwhelming. Where
to turn?

Compassionate and trained advisers are available to members
of the Harvard community through Life Raft, a drop-in group

sponsored by the University Health Services. Noontime meetings are held weekly; emergencies are handled through individual counseling or by telephone. Discussions are confidential and free of charge. Talking with others may ease the burden of isolation and help restore balance to torn lives.

Related entry: UHS. *Related Website:* www.huhs.harvard.edu.

A musical offering in Memorial Church: a holiday
concert by the Kuumba Singers.

Maps

Harvard's Map Collection, the nation's oldest, is one of America's largest centers of maps, atlases, geographic sketches, terrestrial and celestial globes, and cartological references. The origin of the collection is a story of zealous acquisition, institutional dispersal, and later reconsolidation.

In 1818, a German historian sold his collection of 10,000 maps of America to Harvard. They became the core of the Harvard Library's Map Collection, which grew in numbers and quality for the next century and a half. Other collections were formed in the Department of Geography and the Harvard Institute of Geographical Exploration, and they experienced parallel growth. Then, in a controversial action in 1948, President James Conant announced that both the department and the institute would be abolished. Reduced course enrollments, an unproductive faculty, and the termination of a concentration in the field had made it evident that the department was sinking. Geography, in Conant's view, was a subject better suited to elementary and secondary schools.

Critics of the move argued vainly that with America involved in an international cold war and increasingly linked to nations all over the globe, Harvard should strengthen its teaching and research in geography, topography, land exploration, and mapping. But the decision stood, and what remained of geography at Harvard was parceled out to the departments of geology, history, and government. Physical resources, primarily the extensive map collections, were transferred to the Map Collection in Widener Library.

With these and subsequent acquisitions, that collection now numbers over 400,000 sheet and wall maps; 6,000 atlases, with texts in many different languages; 5,000 geographical reference works; and many terrestrial and celestial globes. Two priceless treasures are globes crafted by the sixteenth-century geographer Gerard Mercator. One, a well-preserved terrestrial globe, dates from 1541; the other, a celestial globe made in 1551, is based on the Ptolemaic star system but also reflects the theories of Copernicus, c. 1543. Both have been beautifully restored and are on permanent display.

All kinds of maps—very old, not-so-old, brand new, computerized, interactive digital—reside in the collection. One of its great
strengths is in maps of the age of exploration in the fifteenth
through the seventeenth centuries. Another is in maps of security-
conscious countries like North Korea, China, and Turkey, and of
remote places like inner Asia, the Pacific Islands, and the Arctic
and Antarctica. A third strength is in maps of contemporary subjects, such as traffic volume, flood occurrences, helicopter-route
charts, gas pipelines, hazardous waste sites, seismic activity, and
even microbreweries. A computerized geographic information system enables users to create their own maps of any location, based
on such factors as the incidence of crime, median income of residents, or cause-of-death statistics. In many ways, the Map Collection has become both a library museum and a computer laboratory.

Related entries: Extinct Harvard; Libraries. *Related Website:*
www.hcl.harvard.edu/maps.

Medical School

Five imposing marble buildings in Boston's Longwood Medical
Area form the architectural core of the nation's third-oldest medical school. And at least five distinctive attributes set this school
apart from others at Harvard:

- It was established in the late eighteenth century, a generation
  before the University's other professional schools.
- It is relatively distant from the center of Harvard.
- Though its student enrollment is small, the school's roster
  of interns, residents, postdoctoral fellows, voting faculty, and
  faculty appointees approaches 16,000, far larger than any
  comparable body within the University.
- Its M.D. students may be the most ethnically diverse group at
  Harvard (almost half are nonwhite), and it has the most visiting scholars from other countries (more than 1,100).
- The school's research, teaching, and clinical activities are conducted in affiliation with some eighteen institutions in the

Boston area, and the whole ethos and style of interdisciplinary learning and teaching at the Medical School is singular and complex.

The school as a whole is much larger than the Program in Medical Education (PME), which has about 730 students in its four-year M.D. program. But the PME forms the core educational experience. Another 475 doctoral candidates are enrolled in the school's Ph.D. program, some of them in the Harvard-MIT Health Sciences and Technology Division, which focuses on the molecular science that underlies modern medicine.

Admission is rigorously selective. Nearly 2,000 candidates compete for about 190 places in each year's entering class (including programs in Dental Medicine and Health Sciences and Technology). About half those admitted are women, and diversity of background, ethnicity, color, nationality, age, and interests play into the final selection process. "The consensus is strong at Harvard Medical School that the education of a physician is enhanced by diversity of the student body," states the school's admissions bulletin.

In the mid-1980s, the faculty began a radical restructuring of the traditional curriculum. The resulting New Pathway Program offers a novel form of training geared to lifelong learning and in-depth knowledge of advanced medical procedures and information technology. All students are taught not only the fundamentals of biomedical and clinical science but also the interpersonal skills and techniques that will help make them caring physicians.

In small groups, first-year students examine patients, analyze problems, uncover relevant research in libraries and computer-based resources, and develop habits of independent study and resourcefulness. One guiding principle of the program is an emphasis on the patient-doctor relationship; another is understanding the social context of health care and preventive medicine. A third is appreciating the extraordinary prospects for treatment created by accelerating progress in all branches of the biological sciences.

Each student is randomly assigned to one of four academic societies. (Another 30 students in Health Sciences and Technology belong to a fifth society.) These groupings provide the framework for each student's educational experience. Each is led by a master, associate masters, educators, senior fellows, tutors, preceptors, and advisors. Members of a society share classroom, tutorial, laboratory, and study space, and eventually cohere as a close-knit team, working and learning together. Those who experience the "total immersion" approach of the New Pathway Program are often wearied and sometimes overwhelmed by it. Yet few complain of curricular or instructional inadequacies.

After two years of intensive coursework, third-year students begin clerkships in medicine, surgery, pediatrics, and obstetrics/gynecology. In the fourth year, they take clerkships in more advanced areas—neurology, psychiatry, radiology—and engage in laboratory and field research. Many also take part in Advanced Biomedical Sciences, a program with seminars that address the interface between the basic sciences and clinical practice. Some move on from this program to specialized research projects in hospitals and laboratories.

The school's affiliated hospitals and institutions include:

Beth Israel Deaconess Medical Center
Brigham and Women's Hospital
Cambridge Hospital
Center for Blood Research
Children's Hospital Boston
Dana-Farber Cancer Institute
DVA Medical Center Brockton/West Roxbury
Harvard Pilgrim Health Care
Joslin Diabetes Center
Judge Baker Children's Center

Massachusetts Eye and Ear Infirmary
Massachusetts General Hospital
Massachusetts Mental Health Center
McLean Hospital
Mount Auburn Hospital
Schepens Eye Research Institute
Spaulding Rehabilitation Hospital
University Health Services

Founded in 1782, the Medical School started out in the basement of Harvard Hall, moving to Holden Chapel a year later.

Since Boston had more physicians (and patients) than Cambridge, its premises were transferred there in 1810. The present campus was dedicated in 1906; the white marble buildings—four of them identical in design, though differing in internal function—were the work of Shepley, Rutan, & Coolidge, the firm that also planned the Law School's contemporaneous Langdell Hall.

Related entries: Dental School; Firsts (Women); Holden Chapel; School of Public Health; Warren Museum. *Related Website:* www.hms.harvard.edu.

Memorial Church

At the heart of Harvard Yard, facing Widener Library, stand Memorial Church and its soaring tower. As the Reverend Professor Peter J. Gomes, its longtime minister, has observed, that is just where it should stand, both geographically and symbolically. "The positioning of the church," says Mr. Gomes, "serves to remind us that education is of very little moment without the cultivation of the spirit; that the purpose of education is never simply the accumulation of facts, but also the embedding of learning in the sphere of the whole person—mind and heart, body and spirit."

The College's earliest students said their prayers in rooms that are now long gone. Holden Chapel, built in 1744, was the first separate place of worship; services were later held in University Hall's second-floor chapel (now the Faculty Room), and then in Appleton Chapel, on the site now occupied by Memorial Church. After World War I, President A. Lawrence Lowell resolved to honor Harvard's war dead with a new church. Funded by alumni donations (after a lengthy wrangle over proposed designs), Memorial Church was dedicated on Armistice Day, November 11, 1932.

Colonial in style, the church was designed by Coolidge, Shepley, the firm that planned the contemporaneous Harvard houses. Its exterior responds to Widener Library's stately but ponderous facade with two Doric colonnade porticos, topped by a graceful 170-foot bell tower and spire. Mr. Gomes—the Pusey Minister in the Memorial Church and Plummer Professor of Christian Morals—likes to quote Professor Howard Mumford Jones's description of the building: "Emily Dickinson above, but pure Mae West below." Within, the spacious nave is illuminated by splendid arched windows. Notable for the quality of its woodworking, and evoking the spirit of an American Protestant meeting house, it seats 1,200.

On the marble walls of the adjoining Memorial Transept—designed by the sculptor Joseph Coletti in a coldly formal style that is out of key with the rest of the building—are the names of Harvard's 373 World War I dead. A frieze bears an inscription composed by President Lowell: "While a bright future beckoned, they freely gave their lives and fondest hopes for us and our allies, that we might learn from them courage in peace to spend our lives making a better world for others." In the center of the transept is "The Sacrifice," Malvina Hoffman's tomblike sculpture of a woman grieving over a fallen knight. Hewn from Caen marble, it was commissioned by the widow of Robert Bacon, class of 1880, in memory of her husband and other Harvard men who died in the war.

On the south wall of the church proper, carved on tablets of cream-colored marble, are the names of 697 alumni, students, and faculty members who died in World War II. Plaques on the north wall list the names of some 40 Harvard men who died in the Korean conflict and the Vietnam War. A bronze plaque also records the names of four graduates who died fighting on the German side in World War I, with the Latin inscription, "Academia Harvardiana non oblita est filiorum suorum qui diversis sub signis pro patria spiritum rediderunt" ("Harvard has not forgotten her sons who under opposite flags gave their lives for their country, 1914–1918"). Another plaque, recently added, memorializes three Radcliffe College alumnae who died in service as World War I nurses.

Memorial Church is essentially Protestant and nondenominational; other major faiths have their own places of worship near the Square. But since this church is seen as a repository of Harvard traditions, members of other faiths often use it for weddings, memorial services, or commitment ceremonies. It has thus become a truly ecumenical place, welcoming all. It is also the site of choral concerts and academic lecture series. Each June, the apron in front of its south portico becomes the dais for the Commencement exercises.

The church has a loyal congregation of students, faculty members, and greater Boston residents. Its Sunday services begin at II A.M. and services perpetuate a tradition of presenting "preaching of a high order," not only by resident clergy—most notably the Reverend Mr. Gomes himself—but also by world religious leaders. These have included Paul Tillich, Reinhold Niebuhr, Martin Luther King Jr., and Hans Küng, as well as archbishops of Canterbury, cardinals, Jewish rabbis, and leaders of nonwestern faiths. Appleton Chapel, in the east end of the church, carries on the venerable tradition of morning prayer, a fifteen-minute service on weekdays in term time.

Memorial Church is known for stirring organ music and fine choral singing. On Sundays the University Choir performs Bach chorales or anthems by Handel, Mozart, Brahms, Stanford, and composers of recent eras. The list of University organists and choirmasters is a distinguished one, beginning in 1862 with John Knowles Paine, later America's first professor of music. A 4,500-pipe tracker-action organ replaced the church's original instrument in 1967. Built by Charles B. Fisk '49 and noted for its tonal brilliance, it was at the time of its construction the largest American organ of its kind to have been built in the twentieth century.

Though Memorial Church is not one of Harvard's older structures, a building block more ancient than the College itself is part of its fabric. Embedded in a wall near the main entrance is a stone from St. Saviour's Church, near Southwark Cathedral in London, where John Harvard was baptized on November 29, 1607.

Related entries: Architecture; Bells; Commencement; "Godless Harvard"; John Harvard—and His Statue; Holden Chapel; Houses; Music. *Related Website:* www.memorialchurch.harvard.edu.

Memorial Hall

Henry James memorably described it as a "great bristling brick valhalla," dispensing "laurels to the dead and dinners to the living."

To the Mississippi lawyer Basil Ransom, hero of James's *The Bostonians,*

> the ornate, overtopping structure was the finest piece of ar-
> chitecture he had ever seen. . . . He thought there was rather
> too much brick about it, but it was buttressed, cloistered,
> turreted, dedicated, superscribed, as he had never seen any-
> thing; though it didn't look old, it looked significant; it cov-
> ered a large area, and it sprang majestic into the winter air.

And it still does. If Harvard has one singular landmark building,
it's Memorial Hall. With its buttresses and turrets, its soaring
tower—only recently rebuilt after a devastating fire in 1956—and
its parti-colored slate roofing, this massive structure stands just
north of Harvard Yard, on a triangular plot called the Delta. A
multi-use building long before that term was invented, Memorial
Hall has a huge and magnificent refectory where first-year students
dine daily, and a classically proportioned auditorium that is con-
stantly engaged for lectures and concerts.

Memorial Hall was conceived as a monument to Harvard's Civil
War soldiers who gave their lives for the Union cause. Within three
years of the war's end, a group of alumni had raised more than
$350,000—about one-sixth of the University's endowment at the
time—toward the cost of the building. That sum was enlarged by a
$50,000 bequest from Charles Sanders, of the class of 1802, to
fund a "hall or theatre." The Great Hall and the memorial transept
were completed in 1874; Sanders Theatre, a polygonal auditorium
at the building's east end, opened two years later. The tower was
finished in 1878, and the building was then turned over to Harvard.

The architects, selected by competition, were William Ware,
class of 1852, and Henry van Brunt, class of 1854. Strongly influenced by what is now called Ruskinian Gothic style, their design
was cathedral-like in both mass and configuration. Van Brunt,
however, maintained that its form was "purely accidental and [had]
no significance of sentiment whatever." The young architects drew
heavily on English models. The hammerbeam trusses supporting

the roof of the Great Hall resemble those of London's Westminster Hall. Sanders Theatre, at the other end of the building, was inspired by Christopher Wren's Sheldonian Theatre at Oxford. Between these two sections of the building is its spiritual center, the lofty memorial transept. Vaulted in wood, it has large stained-glass rose windows at each end, like the transept of a cathedral. On the walls are tablets recording the names and places of death of 136 fallen alumni and students; above the tablets are painted inscriptions, in Latin, from the Bible, Plautus, Cicero, Horace, Ovid, and Bacon.

Memorial Hall was the largest academic building of its time. In 1897, the roof of the bell tower was replaced by a more elaborate structure housing four clocks, the gift of the class of 1872. The Great Hall, adorned with tapestries, portraits, and marble busts, became a tourist attraction. During the late decades of the nineteenth century, its ample windows were filled with commemorative stained glass given by College classes from 1844 to 1880. Representing a broad range of designers, manufacturers, and techniques, the windows are a virtual museum of American stained glass. John La Farge's "Battle Window," depicting warriors of the ancient world, and Sarah Wyman Whitman's "Honor and Peace" are among the most noted.

The Great Hall served as the College's principal dining commons until 1925, and Commencement exercises were held in Sanders Theatre from 1876 until 1922. But in later years, Memorial Hall was allowed to languish. The loss of its tower in 1956, and the Harvard administration's apparent reluctance to replace it, compounded the indignity. Finally, after decades of neglect, the building's fabric was refurbished in a $50 million renewal project begun in the late 1980s.

A spectacular restoration of the Great Hall, underwritten by the publisher and philanthropist Walter Annenberg, has returned the space to its original function as a dining commons—this time for the freshman class. The hall now bears the name of the Annenbergs' son Roger '62; an unfinished window on the south wall will be completed in his memory. A $10 million gift from Katherine Bogdanovich Loker transformed the building's lower level—formerly a dusty warren of cramped offices for undergraduate organizations and a few College administrators—into a student center with fast-food services and other appurtenances. Mrs. Loker also made a grant of $2 million to help meet the cost of replacing the hall's burned-out tower. When a new spire was hoisted into place in the summer of 1999, the resurrection of Memorial Hall was complete.

As America's only surviving Ruskinian Gothic building, Memorial Hall richly deserves its position in the National Register of Historic Places. Even more important is the essential role it fills in the daily life of the Harvard community.

Related entries: Architecture; Bells; Dining Services; Fire; Sanders Theatre; Towers. *Related Websites:* www.fas.harvard.edu/~memhall.

Music

The musicality of today's Harvard might not suit the College's Puritan founders, who had scant use for musical instruments and barely tolerated anything more than the chanting of simple hymns. But music is a constant in the lives of today's Harvardians. Students troop to—and perform in—concerts and recitals at Sanders Theatre, Paine Hall, Houghton Library, the residential houses, the nearby Longy School of Music, and Boston's Symphony Hall. They play quartets at faculty members' homes and find rehearsal spaces where they can practice or jam with friends. They listen to music on WHRB while they study, and they walk to class wearing headphones.

Harvard's major choral groups—the Harvard Glee Club, Collegium Musicum, Radcliffe Choral Society, University Choir, and Commencement Choir—carry on a vocal tradition that goes back at least to 1771, when the "young gentlemen of the College" sang an anthem at a formal reception for Governor Thomas Hutchinson. The Glee Club, founded in 1858, is America's oldest college chorus. It began a transition from "college songs" to more serious music in the pre-World War I years, under Archibald T. ("Doc") Davison '06, PH.D. '08. The men of the Glee Club first joined their voices with those of the Radcliffe Choral Society at a carol service in 1912, and in 1917 the combined groups formed the first college chorus to sing with the Boston Symphony. In the summer of 1921 the Glee Club made a seven-week concert tour of France, Switzerland, and Italy, described as the first attempt by a "sizeable college group . . . to establish an aesthetic contact with Europe." The club had its first extended national tour with its Radcliffe counterpart in 1954; that was followed by a European visit in 1956 and a round-the-world tour in 1961. Collaborations with the Boston Symphony were an annual event from 1917 until the mid-1970s. These performances secured the high reputation of these two choral groups.

Among the College's premier instrumental ensembles are the Harvard-Radcliffe Orchestra—which traces its ancestry to the Pierian Sodality, a band formed in 1808—and the famous and irrepressible Harvard University Band. Organized in 1919 as an outgrowth of the undergraduate banjo club, the Band invented the "scramble style" that is now the modus operandi for Ivy League marching bands. The band is known for its gigantic bass drum, introduced in 1927, and for the splendor of its sound. The Harvard Wind Ensemble, affiliated with the band, gives concert performances of contemporary wind literature, from octets to symphonic band works. Other instrumental groups include the Bach Society and Mozart Society orchestras; the Baroque Chamber Orchestra; the Harvard Pops Orchestra; the Brattle Street Chamber Players; the Sunday and Monday Jazz Bands; and two percussion groups, the Harvard University Drummers (THUD) and Han Ma-Eum, a Korean drum troupe.

The redoubtable Gilbert & Sullivan Players present two operettas a year. The College also has a floating number of house opera, chamber music, rock music, and sing-along groups, formally or informally organized. The more durable organizations hold auditions at the start of each academic year. Substantial time commitments are required for rehearsals (at least three hours a week, and in some cases much more) and for performances (often four or five hours a week, usually on weekends). Members often pay modest

fees to cover dues and expenses and are sometimes expected to help
with fundraising.

A perquisite of membership in some groups is the chance to
tour and perform throughout the country and abroad. The Harvard-Radcliffe Orchestra, with nearly a hundred members, has
made summer tours to Europe, Russia, Southeast Asia, and Latin
America. The Krokodiloes, the oldest of Harvard's a cappella singing groups, and the Radcliffe Pitches, a women's group, have made
six-week world tours in the summer. (According to a promotional
flyer, the Kroks' twelve tuxedo-clad singers have sung on six continents.) Other a cappella groups include the Callbacks, Din and
Tonics, Fallen Angels, Kuumba Singers, LowKeys, Mizmor Shir,
Noteables, Opportunes, Under Construction, and Veritones.

At the professional level, Sanders Theatre and the Music Department's 437-seat John Knowles Paine Concert Hall are frequently used by local or touring orchestras or chamber groups.
The Music Department oversees the Blodgett Artist-in-Residence
program, which in recent years has brought the New World Quartet, the Mendelssohn Quartet, and the Ying String Quartet to
Harvard for regular concerts at Houghton Library, Paine Hall, and
all of the houses. The Office for the Arts sponsors a Jazz Artist-in-
Residence program that has imported such guest artists as trumpeter Dave Douglas and percussionist Max Roach. Houghton
Library's quarter-century-old chamber music series has presented
scores of notable ensembles and soloists, among them the Ying,
Borromeo, Lydian, and Melos quartets; pianists Malcolm Bilson
and Robert Levin; guitarists Eliot Fisk and Hopkinson Smith; and
baritone Christopheren Nomura.

In addition to the choral music sung at daily and Sunday services by the University Choir, the Memorial Church sponsors
chamber music recitals in its Pusey Room. The church's Thursday
Lunchtime Recital series in Adolphus Busch Hall features internationally known organists performing on the hall's Flentrop organ.

The Music Department offers undergraduate and graduate
courses on music history, theory, composition, ethnomusicology,
jazz, and world music, as well as credit for classes in conducting,

orchestration, chamber music performance, and historical performance practice. A primary resource for musical study at Harvard is the Eda Kuhn Loeb Library, with more than 160,000 books and scores, and more than 60,000 recordings. The Morse Music Library, in the Hilles Library penthouse, serves as a media center for the undergraduate music curriculum; in addition to books, its collections include some 6,000 scores, more than 7,000 sound recordings, and 1,500 video recordings in DVD, CD, LP record, and tape-cassette formats.

Many musicians who later gained international reputations have passed up study at a conservatory for the broader experiences afforded by Harvard College and the Cambridge/Boston cultural milieu. Among them have been the composers Virgil Thomson '22, Elliott Carter '30, D. MUS. '70, and John Adams '69; conductor-composer Leonard Bernstein '39; harpsichordist Igor Kipnis '52; pianists Ursula Oppens '65 and Robert Levin '68; cellist Yo-Yo Ma '76; jazz trumpeter Bob Merrill '81; and jazz saxophonist Joshua Redman '91. And though Harvard may not (yet) be thought of as an incubator of rock musicians, alumni who've played with well-known groups include Jerry Harrison '71 (Talking Heads), Tom Morello '86 (Rage Against the Machine), and Rivers Cuomo '98 (Weezer).

Related entries: Adolphus Busch Hall; Arts; Gilbert & Sullivan; Houghton Library; Jazz; Memorial Church; Sanders Theatre; Songs and Marches; WHRB. *Related Websites:* www.fas.harvard.edu/~ofa (Office for the Arts); www.music.fas.harvard. edu (Music Department).

A Nobel laureate, chemist Dudley Herschbach, uses the
college pump to show students why Aristotle and Galileo
were puzzled by some aspects of hydraulics.

Native American Program

Soon after its founding, Harvard began what turned out to be a cyclical relationship with Native Americans. In the 1650 Charter of Harvard College was a stated commitment "to the education of the English and Indian youth of this country in knowledge and godliness." Harvard's first president, Henry Dunster, was devoted to this mission: he wanted the College to be "the Indian Oxford as well as the New English Cambridge." The upshot was the establishment of an Indian College on the perimeter of Harvard Yard, near the site of today's Matthews Hall.

Dunster was surely motivated by a desire to bring the "heathens" to Christ, but he also hoped to invigorate the College's faltering fundraising efforts. He was mindful of the potential donors, in London and elsewhere, who were ready and willing to provide funds for the education and conversion of Indians.

Soon five Indians were enrolled in the College. Though most succumbed to disease and early deaths, one from the Wampanoag Tribe—with the euphonious name of Caleb Cheeshahteaumuck—graduated in the class of 1665 and thus became Harvard's first Native American alumnus. At about the same time, the College printing press produced North America's first Bible: an Algonquian translation of the Testaments by the preacher John Eliot.

This relatively promising connection between the College and Indian culture was not sustained. The decrepit Indian College was torn down in 1698, and for the next 270 years there was no significant Native American presence at Harvard. Only in the 1970s, with the rising interest of ethnic and national groups in their roots and heritage, did an American Indian Program emerge, this time "to prepare American Indians to fulfill positions of leadership in schools." An increasing number went on to earn Harvard degrees—among them authors, administrators, directors of Indian education, tribal leaders, and an assistant secretary for Indian Affairs. By 1990, the focus had changed once again with the founding of the Harvard University Native American Program. Its mission was to train Native American leadership across many disciplines:

education, law, medicine, public health, business, and government. This program is thriving.

Courses relating to Native American subjects are taught in the Anthropology Department, the School of Education, the Kennedy School of Government, and the Law School. The Native American Program sponsors a range of intellectual and social activities, including a film series, forums, monthly pot-lucks, a yearly powwow, and art exhibitions. It also administers a University-wide recruitment initiative to advance the professional training and career opportunities of Native Americans.

Related entries: Affirmative Action; Diversity; Harvard University Press. *Related Website:* www.ksg.harvard.edu/hunap.

Nieman Fellows

Many Harvard fellowship programs are small and relatively obscure. The Nieman Fellowships for Journalism are known far and wide, perhaps because media people are good at spreading the news.

In the mid-1930s, Harvard received a $1 million bequest from Agnes Wahl Nieman in memory of her husband, Lucius Nieman, founder of the *Milwaukee Journal.* The funds were to be used "to promote and elevate the standards of journalism and educate persons deemed especially qualified for journalism." Confronting the choice of establishing a school of journalism or developing a different kind of program, President James B. Conant was skeptical. After consulting with publishers, editors, and faculty members, he proposed a program of endowed fellowships for journalists: one that would "offer newspaper reporters the opportunity to take the better part of a year off and participate in the intellectual life of the university." Part of the Nieman bequest would also underwrite a microfilmed collection of daily newspapers.

Archibald MacLeish, a distinguished literary figure, accepted the curatorship. From a pool of 309 applicants, ten men were selected for the first year of the fellowships in 1939. "Here is the University," said President Conant in his welcoming speech. "Take it." He encouraged the fellows to explore all parts of Harvard, attend any course in any school, use any library, talk to any professor. The program earned immediate and strong acclaim.

Over the years the Nieman Foundation has added women, foreign journalists, and non-print-media professionals as mid-career fellows. Out of approximately 250 applicants, about two dozen are now selected each year. Among the distinguished journalists who have held fellowships in past years are former *Atlantic Monthly* editor Robert Manning '46; J. Anthony Lewis '57, former *New York Times* columnist; Robert Caro '66, biographer of Robert Moses and Lyndon Johnson; *Boston Globe* columnist Ellen Goodman '74; Jerelyn Eddings '85, former director of a journalism training center in South Africa; Geneva Overholser '86, columnist, former editor of the *Des Moines Register* and former *Washington Post* ombudsman; Dai Qing '92, Chinese journalist whose forceful writing in opposition to the Three Gorges Dam had a powerful effect on the government; and Chris Hedges '99, former *New York Times* foreign correspondent.

The Walter Lippmann House is the Nieman Foundation's home. The Georgian-style building on Francis Avenue, acquired in 1979, was renamed for Walter Lippmann '10, LITT.D. '44, one of America's foremost twentieth-century journalists. Fellows gather there at least twice a week to hear guest lecturers and discuss current issues. Many find this the most stimulating part of their time at Harvard.

Related Website: www.nieman.harvard.edu.

Nobel Laureates

Since 1901, one measure of institutional eminence has been the representation of faculty members and graduates in the pantheon of Nobel Prize winners. How many Nobel laureates does Harvard have, and how does its total stack up against those of its academic rivals?

The answer depends partly on who gets counted. Do we include all current and former faculty members? Do we count those who are no longer living, like the physicist Percy Bridgman or the biochemist George Wald? What about the molecular biologist James D. Watson, who left Harvard to head Long Island's Cold Spring Laboratory; the physicist Steven Weinberg, who left to accept a chair at the University of Texas; or the economist A. Michael Spence, who left to become dean of Stanford's business school? What about non-faculty members, like Theodore Roosevelt, class of 1880 (peace prize, 1906), or T. S. Eliot, class of 1910 (literature prize, 1948)?

Nobel Prizes are awarded in the fields of chemistry; medicine or physiology; physics; literature; peace; and (since 1968) economics. At this writing, some 40 current or former faculty members have won Nobels. The faculty's first laureate was Theodore Richards (the father-in-law of President James B. Conant), who in 1914 won the chemistry prize for his work on atomic weights. Twenty years passed before another Nobel came Harvard's way. But between the early 1930s and the early 2000s, fourteen faculty members won the prize in medicine and physiology; nine won the physics prize; five won the prize in chemistry; six won the prize in economics; and three won the peace prize (Henry Cadbury, for his chairmanship of the American Friends Service Committee; Ralph Bunche, for negotiating a Middle East armistice; and Bernard Lown, for his work as a founder of Physicians for Social Responsibility).

The 1995 award for literature went to Seamus Heaney, then Harvard's Ralph Waldo Emerson Poet in Residence. But peace and literature may not be Harvard's strong suits. It's the economists who now seem to garner the most Nobel Prizes. Since 1971, a half dozen have gone to current or former members of the economics department. (Trivia buffs take note: they did not receive the "Nobel Prize in economics," as news stories often style it. The award is properly called the "Bank of Sweden Prize in Economic Sciences in Memory of Alfred Nobel.")

The institution that whelped Harvard, the University of Cambridge, remains the world leader in faculty Nobel laureates, with roughly 80. Among American institutions, the University of Chicago claims more than 70; Columbia and MIT follow, with about

60 apiece. Then comes Harvard, followed at a respectful distance by Princeton, Cornell, Johns Hopkins, California Institute of Technology, and Stanford. Yale, with fewer than ten laureates, is not (yet) a contender.

Related Website: www.nobel.se.

Observatory Pinafore, a parody of *H.M.S. Pinafore* put on by Harvard
Observatory staffers in 1929, featured a star turn by astronomer
Cecilia Payne (later Payne-Gaposchkin, second from left)
in the role of Josephine.

Observatories

The sometimes cloudy skies of Cambridge aren't always conducive to exploring the heavens. But the Harvard College Observatory (HCO) on Observatory Hill, at 60 Garden Street in Cambridge, remains a popular place for stargazing on the third Thursday of every month throughout the year. On those evenings, the Harvard-Smithsonian Center for Astrophysics (CFA) sponsors free programs, open to the public, of lectures and then telescopic viewing of the skies from the Observatory roof—if the weather obliges. When it does, visitors may see Saturn, Jupiter, or objects like the Orion Nebula up close, through the Observatory's nine-inch Clark refractor telescope and also through three portable telescopes, all eight-inch reflectors. Attendance at these viewings often reaches more than 200, and many visitors find them an awe-inspiring experience.

Founded in 1839, the HCO provides research facilities for faculty and students in the department of astronomy in the Faculty of Arts and Sciences. The HCO and the Smithsonian Astrophysical Observatory together form the CFA, which involves more than 300 scientists engaged in astrophysical research. These scientists have pioneered in the development of instrumentation for observatories on the ground and in space, covering virtually the whole electromagnetic spectrum.

At the Harvard-Smithsonian Center's Oak Ridge Observatory in Harvard, Massachusetts, astronomers search for evidence of planets around other stars and for signals from extraterrestrial beings. On the eighth floor of Harvard's Undergraduate Science Center, a small but well-equipped observatory is used primarily by students.

In the first half of the twentieth century, Harvard astronomical stations made observations in Peru and, later, in South Africa.

Related entry: Harvard Elsewhere. *Related Websites:* cfa-www.harvard.edu; cfa-www.harvard.edu/hco/.

Ombuds

Following a series of protests aimed at securing a "living wage" for Harvard's lower-paid workers, President Lawrence Summers announced in the summer of 2002 that he would appoint an ombudsman to help resolve academic disputes, supervisor-employee conflicts, instances of perceived discrimination, and similar problems. Early in 2003 he appointed Henry Ehrenreich, Clowes Research Professor of Science, as the first University Ombudsperson. Lydia Cummings, a professional mediator with 24 years' experience as a Harvard administrator, was named to assist him.

A physicist, Ehrenreich had been a member of the faculty since 1963. The new office was to report to Harvard's provost, while remaining independent of any specific administrative structure. The office's services, said Ehrenreich, would supplement but not replace existing mechanisms for addressing grievances within the University's various faculties and staffs. Though the University Ombuds Office was new, the professional schools in the Medical Area have had an ombudsperson since 1991. The University Ombudsperson chairs a University-wide Ombuds Council, which is designed to serve as a forum and resource for those serving ombuds roles or the equivalent in the various schools.

Related Website: www.universityombuds.harvard.edu.

Outings & Innings

The program's name is apt and descriptive. Outings & Innings offers a mix of leisure and recreational activities—Red Sox games, other sporting events, concerts, museums, films and plays, theme parks—to Harvard faculty and staff members, at discounted ticket prices. Money-saving coupons and special deals for travel and lodging, restaurants, services, and merchandise are also part of the mix. A monthly calendar of O&I events appears in the *Harvard Community Resource,* published by the Office of Human Resources.

Launched in 1976, Outings & Innings was a sign of the University's increased concern for the well-being and job satisfaction of its employees—and a somewhat belated response to a successful campaign to unionize support staff members. Under administrative vice president Sally H. Zeckhauser, the first woman named to a high post in the central administration, what had been the Personnel Office put on a more human face and developed programs to help employees balance work and personal responsibilities. Professional counselors were engaged to provide guidance and referrals on child care and elder care; on managing personal and family issues; and to help solve workplace problems. That a relaxing evening at Symphony Hall or Fenway Park might have a beneficial effect on both family life and workplace performance was not lost on Zeckhauser and her staff.

Related Website: http://atwork.harvard.edu/perks.

P

A presidential trio: James B. Conant (1935–1953), Nathan M. Pusey
(1953–1971), and Derek Bok (1971–1991). This photograph, taken
in 1971, was the first since 1861 to show more than two
Harvard presidents together.

Phillips Brooks House

Generations of students have enriched their educational experience by volunteering to work—often for long hours, and late at night—in public service programs organized and coordinated by the Phillips Brooks House Association (PBHA). These varied programs are open to all undergraduates and graduate students; they engage an estimated one-third of all undergraduates each year. Some examples:

- Helping out at homeless shelters.
- Tutoring inmates in prisons.
- Teaching English as a second language.
- Mentoring Cambridge and Boston area youth.
- Providing literacy training.
- Working with the elderly, hospitalized, deaf, victims of domestic violence, refugee families, summer camps for poor children, and many other service activities.

Phillips Brooks House is a large brick building in the northwest corner of Harvard Yard. To help students find service work that suits them, the Harvard Public Service Network helps potential volunteers explore various options and pick the project that feels right to them. Also housed at PBH are the offices of groups like House and Neighborhood Development (HAND), which supports local programs in the vicinity of the residential houses. At PBH, the morale of students and administrators is consistently upbeat. Many alumni look back on PBHA service as the high point of their Harvard years.

Founded at the start of the twentieth century, PBH was named for the renowned preacher Phillips Brooks, class of 1855. As rector of Trinity Church in Boston's Copley Square, Brooks used his pulpit to preach the social gospel and to support the antislavery movement. (He also wrote hymns and carols, of which the most famous is "O Little Town of Bethlehem.") In his long and continuing attachments to Harvard—he was a two-term Overseer, a member of the Board of Preachers, a leader of morning prayers, and a counselor of students—Brooks strongly encouraged religious activism among students. Just before his death in 1893, he proposed "a new building within the College Yard for the use of the various religious societies." Alumni and students readily took up the idea of naming the new social service building and association in his memory. Phillips Brooks House opened in 1900.

Originally designed to promote "Christian good works," the programs of PBHA gradually moved in more secular directions, a development that fostered the involvement of students of differing faiths and creeds. During World War I, volunteers worked closely with the Red Cross, and in the Great Depression they enrolled in groups set up to help the unemployed and the poor. In World War II, large numbers of students worked in hospitals and sold war bonds. In the 1960s, President John F. Kennedy was said to have used the PBHA-designed Project Tanganyika as a model for the Peace Corps; later, PBHA projects served as models for the National Service Corps, now Americorps.

Participation in PBHA activities fell off in the late 1960s and 1970s. Antiwar protests and political dissent diverted traditional streams of idealism. But the 1980s saw a turnaround. Students of those years displayed a renewed enthusiasm and dedication. Volunteers of recent decades have revived and reaffirmed the spirit of Phillips Brooks, and today PBHA programs thrive as never before.

Related entry: Public Service. *Related Website:* www.pbha.org.

Portrait Collection

The more than 1,200 paintings, sculptures, and drawings in the Harvard Portrait Collection constitute a cross-section of New England tastes in portraiture from pre-Revolutionary times to the present. The collection's holdings are scattered throughout the University. The subjects, for the most part, are prominent figures in Harvard history: presidents from Increase Mather to Derek Bok, deans, faculty members, benefactors, illustrious alumni. Aesthetically, the collection's particular strengths are in American colonial painting and nineteenth-century American sculpture. Among the painters represented are John Singleton Copley, John Trumbull, Gilbert Stuart, William Morris Hunt, Lilla Cabot Perry, John Singer Sargent, Joseph DeCamp, Charles Hopkinson, Ellen Emmet Rand, and Gardner Cox. The list of sculptors includes Horatio Greenough, William Wetmore Story, Edmonia Lewis, Augustus Saint-Gaudens, Frank Duveneck, Daniel Chester French, and Walker Hancock.

The College is thought to have acquired its first portrait in 1680, when the Harvard Corporation commissioned a drawing of the English Puritan theologian William Ames. That likeness and an unknown number of others were destroyed in the great Harvard Hall fire of 1764. After the fire, the Corporation engaged John Singleton Copley, then in his late twenties, to make full-length portraits of three benefactors—Thomas Hollis, Nicholas Boylston, and Thomas Hancock—who had endowed the College's first professorships. These were hung in the new Harvard Hall. The collection's earliest portrait sculpture, a plaster cast of a bust of William Pitt, Earl of Chatham, was the gift of Benjamin Franklin in 1769.

Portraits from the collection are on view in more than a hundred buildings on both sides of the Charles River, but the central exhibition point is the Faculty Room of University Hall. This historic room currently contains about 30 paintings and 15 busts, spanning more than three centuries. The earliest painting, dating from about 1700, is an anonymous artist's warmly toned portrait of William Stoughton, donor of Harvard's first Stoughton Hall. X-ray analysis of another early work has revealed an oddity: beneath the likeness of Benjamin Wadsworth, president of the College from 1725 to 1737, is a portrait of another man, wearing a flowing scarf of a style that came into fashion about 1690. At the other end of the timeline is Jason Bouldin's 1996 portrait of Derek Bok, president from 1971 to 1991. To signify that it was painted after the end of Bok's presidency, Bouldin placed in the background, unoccupied, Harvard's sixteenth-century President's Chair.

Eight of the Faculty Room portraits are the work of Charles Hopkinson, "court painter of academia." The prolific Hopkinson, class of 1891, produced almost 850 portraits; nineteen of his sitters were college and university presidents. His painting of the bearded

Shakespearean expert George Lyman Kittredge, Gurney Professor of English Literature from 1917 to 1936, may be the liveliest of Hopkinson's Faculty Room portraits. The walls of the room remained a male preserve until 1995, when the Faculty of Arts and Sciences commissioned a portrait of the British medieval historian Helen Maud Cam, the first woman named to a tenured professorship at Harvard. Jacob Collins's painting of Cam, who joined the faculty in 1948, has since been joined by Patricia Watwood's portrait of the astronomer Cecilia Payne-Gaposchkin, the first woman promoted to a full professorship from within the faculty's ranks.

Outside the Faculty Room, major holdings of the Portrait Collection are on view in Annenberg Hall; at the Fogg Art Museum; at the Barker Center for the Humanities; in the residential houses; and at the schools of Business, Divinity, and Medicine. Conspicuously hung in the Harvard Union, the Barker Center's core building, is John Singer Sargent's masterly portrait of Henry Lee Higginson, one of Harvard's greatest benefactors. Eight feet in height, it shows Higginson slouched on a leather chair, his Civil War cavalry cloak thrown across his lap.

Not all the sitters depicted in the Portrait Collection had Harvard ties. The Museum of Comparative Zoology has George P. A. Healy's painting of John James Audubon. The Harvard Observatory has a copy of Justus Sustermans's portrait of Galileo. A fragile portrait of Geoffrey Chaucer is in the Houghton Library; one of Charles Dickens is in the Barker Center. Antonio Sasso's copy of a portrait of Oliver Cromwell hung in the former President's House at 17 Quincy Street; it is currently in storage.

The curator of the Portrait Collection is based at the Fogg Art Museum. Because of its significance as a historical resource, the collection receives requests for loans, information, and reproduction rights from all over the world. Its most frequently reproduced paintings are Copley's 1783 likeness of John Adams and Robert Feke's portrait of a youngish-looking Benjamin Franklin, c. 1746.

Related entries: Art Museums; Fire; Firsts (Women); Great Salt and Other Relics; Harvard Hall; Memorial Hall; Statues and Monuments. *Related Websites:* lib.harvard.edu/archives/0055.html; www.cshgallery.org (Hopkinson).

Presidents

Harvard presidents of recent times have shown remarkable staying power. Since the Civil War, the United States of America has had 26 presidents; at Harvard, where the chief executive serves without term limits, there have been just eight, averaging nineteen years in office. All told, Harvard has had far fewer presidents (27 since 1640) than has the nation (43 in a span of 214 years, at this writing).

But lengthy presidential terms are a relatively new trend at Harvard. In earlier times, the College changed presidents almost as often as a sinking dot com. In the mid-seventeenth century, it used up three—Leonard Hoar, Urian Oakes, and John Rogers—in fewer than a dozen years. In the two decades prior to the Civil War, five Harvard presidents came and went.

Harvard's earliest presidents assumed formidable workloads. They taught classes, led daily prayer services, examined applicants for admission, recorded expenses and issued receipts, and administered discipline. Their rowdy students needed plenty of that, and occasionally the scholars got the upper hand. Take the case of Leonard Hoar, the third of Harvard's presidents and the least likely, if only because of his surname, to have a residential house named after him. According to a contemporary account, the Reverend Mr. Hoar's pomposity led students "to Travestie whatever he did and said, and aggravate everything in his behaviour disagreeable to them, with a Design to make him Odious." His students eventually left in a body, his tutors resigned in disgust, Hoar relinquished his post, and the College almost closed down for good.

Almost a century later, in 1780, protesting students petitioned for the removal of President Samuel Langdon, dispatching a delegation to inform him that "as a man of genius and knowledge we respect you; as a man of piety and virtue we venerate you; as a President we despise you." Langdon resigned, and the remorseless students took up a collection to speed him on his way. Small wonder that President Edward Holyoke—dying in office at 80, in 1769—had declared on his deathbed that "if any man wishes to be humbled and mortified, let him become President of Harvard College."

In more recent times, the lengthy terms served by Harvard presidents have suggested a greater degree of job satisfaction. The University's most durable leader, Charles William Eliot, stayed the course for 40 years (1869–1909). Four who followed him—Abbott Lawrence Lowell (1909–1933), James Bryant Conant (1933–1953), Nathan Marsh Pusey (1953–1971), and Derek Bok (1971–1991)—averaged two decades in office. Neil Rudenstine, who succeeded Bok, served for ten years. Though Rudenstine outlasted many university presidents of his time, his was the shortest term for a Harvard president since that of the Reverend Thomas Hill (1862–1869).

The president's influence on Harvard's corporate well-being surpasses that of any other individual or board within the institution. Exerting the quiet force of his personality, Eliot reformed the almost-moribund schools of law, medicine, and divinity; created the Graduate School of Arts and Sciences; instituted a system of free electives for undergraduates; and reshaped admissions policy to make the composition of the student body more nationally representative. A. Lawrence Lowell gave the modern University much of its physical form and was an articulate spokesman for American higher education. In their own ways, Conant, Pusey, Bok, and Rudenstine continued and advanced the planned diversification of Harvard's student population that Eliot had begun.

Harvard's president, as a 1939 *Alumni Bulletin* editorial put it, "must hold in mind not only all of the activities of the University, but also its broad policies in relation to contemporary and future developments in society at large. He is expected to show imagination and a statesmanlike outlook." Over the past quarter-century, with the advent of multi-million- and billion-dollar capital campaigns, fundraising has claimed an ever-larger portion of his (and other university presidents') time. But in addition to campaign-driven speechmaking and acting as "closer" in the unending quest for major gifts, the president must also have a thorough understanding of his ten faculties' educational objectives. He is called on to preside over two governing boards, to chair committees weighing senior- or tenured-faculty appointments, and to consult with other officers of the University on matters of ever-increasing complexity. To alumni and the public, he is Harvard's principal spokes-man. The job obviously calls for a wide range of analytic, manage-rial, and political skills.

Since 1650, the selection of the president has been the responsi-bility of the Harvard Corporation; the Board of Overseers must approve the choice. What had long been an essentially closed sys-tem has been somewhat democratized in recent years. At the outset of the last three presidential searches, the Corporation's Senior Fel-low circulated a letter to all members of the Harvard community soliciting nominations. A joint committee of Corporation Fellows and Overseers sifted the responses and made recommendations to both governing boards. (During the two most recent searches, students protested their exclusion from the selection process, not-ing that their peers at Princeton and other institutions had sat on presidential selection committees. The authorities were unmoved. "Many people will be consulted," a former president of the Board of Overseers told the *Crimson.* "But I don't see that the kindergar-ten needs to run the school." Predictably, her words drew fire from *Crimson* editors.)

For almost two centuries, all of Harvard's presidents were Con-gregational or Unitarian clergymen. Thomas Hill was the last in that line. The seven presidents who have served since then have all been academics, and there has been a certain rough balance in their disciplines. Eliot and Conant were chemists; Lowell had been a professor of government; Pusey's field had been classics, Bok's la-bor law, and Rudenstine's Renaissance literature. Harvard's current president, Lawrence H. Summers, is an economist. A few presi-dents held important nonacademic offices before assuming their posts. John Leverett (1708–1724) had been speaker of the Massa-chusetts House, a judge, and the provincial government's envoy to New York. Josiah Quincy (1829–1845) had been mayor of Boston. The Reverend Edward Everett (1846–1849) had been four times governor of Massachusetts, as well as Minister to the Court of St. James's. President Summers had been U.S. secretary of the treasury.

The personal backgrounds of Harvard's twentieth-century presi-dents reflected the increasing democratization of the University as a whole. Eliot and Lowell came from aristocratic Boston families;

both had fathers who had served on the Harvard Corporation. Conant was also a Bostonian, but his father was a photoengraver and part-time building contractor; Conant himself, class of 1914, was the first member of his family to go to college. Pusey, the first Harvard president born west of the Adirondacks, was the son of an Iowa schoolteacher. Bok, raised in California, attended Stanford before enrolling at Harvard Law School; he was the first president since Charles Chauncy (1654–1672) whose credentials did not include a Harvard baccalaureate degree. Rudenstine, a Princeton graduate with a Harvard Ph.D., had been the first in his family to finish high school; his father was a Connecticut prison guard, his mother a waitress. Like Bok and Rudenstine, Summers is the product of a college other than Harvard. He earned his bachelor's degree at MIT before taking his Ph.D. at Harvard.

Between 1672 and 1862, nine Harvard presidents died in office. Others stepped down with visions of enjoying a tranquil old age. (According to Samuel Eliot Morison, Josiah Quincy retired to Boston but humorously complained that after the nocturnal clamor of Harvard Yard, the "'unearthly quiet' kept him awake.") For some, fresh undertakings beckoned. Increase Mather (1685–1701) and his son Cotton, both disaffected with Harvard, helped start a new college to the south, later known as Yale. Edward Everett served briefly as secretary of state in the administration of Millard Fillmore and gave the main address at Gettysburg in November 1863. Conant resigned to become high commissioner to Germany; his successor, Pusey, remained in the educational field as head of the Andrew W. Mellon Foundation. Bok served as chair of Common Cause, and Rudenstine chaired a nonprofit enterprise called ArtSTOR, formed to gather and distribute digital images in the arts, architecture, design, and related fields.

What are Harvard presidents paid? Perhaps surprisingly, surveys taken by *The Chronicle of Higher Education* have shown that the world's richest university trails the front-runners in presidential pay. The top earner in one recent survey ran the University of Pennsylvania: she drew down more than $800,000 in salary and benefits. Next came the former president of Princeton, who had been paid more than $700,000, including some $200,000 in deferred compensation paid when he retired. Yale's president received upwards of $612,000. In that same year, his last as president of Harvard, Neil Rudenstine earned just over $421,000. Even with the president's Elmwood residence, town car, and other perks factored in, Harvard paid its chief executive substantially less than the mega-salaries received by some of his Ivy League peers.

Experts on executive compensation attribute the rapid growth of higher education's so-called "$500,000 Club" to the relative thinness of the talent pool and the strategic importance of presidential fundraising skills. "When you do the math," one has said, "would you pay somebody $500,000 who could help you raise a billion? The return is a no-brainer." Former Harvard president Derek Bok, however, has argued that many university presidents are overpaid and that all of them reap too much credit for achievements attained through teamwork. "Almost everything that matters in an institution—the quality of education, the creativity of the faculty, even the amount of money raised—is the work of so many hands that no one can be certain of the president's role in obtaining the final results," he has written. "A huge presidential salary tends to exacerbate tensions that too often exist between faculty and administration," Bok adds. "When hard times come and faculties are asked to assist in making cutbacks, presidents with huge salaries are not likely to inspire much sympathy or cooperation."

Related entries: Elmwood; Fundraising; Governance.

Prodigies

Students entering the College are normally seventeen or eighteen years old, and exceptions nowadays tend to be at the upper end of the age range. But Harvard has nurtured more than a few prodigies who enrolled in early adolescence—or even before.

Paul Dudley may have been the youngest scholar in Harvard history. The son of provincial governor Joseph Dudley, class of 1665, Paul was ten when he was admitted, and two months short of fifteen when he graduated in 1690. "He appears to have been a normal undergraduate," states *Sibley's Harvard Graduates,* "with no unusual fines and only one large bill for broken glass." Dudley later studied law at the Inner Temple in London. As attorney general of the Massachusetts Bay Colony, he cleared the coast of pirates but was a controversial political figure. For the last 33 years of his life, he was the colony's autocratic chief justice.

Cotton, Nathaniel, and Samuel Mather—sons of the Reverend Increase Mather, the College's sixth president—were other early prodigies. Cotton, the oldest, entered Harvard at twelve and was fifteen when he graduated in 1678; his brothers took their degrees at sixteen. Cotton excelled in ancient languages and amused himself during church sermons by taking notes in Latin. As an adult, and no doubt as a child, he seems to have been an insufferable prig. "I am able with little study to write in seven languages," he declared; "I feast myself with the sweets of all the sciences which the more polite part of mankind ordinarily pretend to." Posted over his study door was a warning to visitors: "Be short." Mather supported the Salem witch trials of 1692 and later interested himself in the Collegiate School of Connecticut, which was renamed Yale at his suggestion. Mather was offered Yale's rectorship but declined it: he wished to be president of Harvard. He was passed over, however, on three occasions. "The Corporation of our miserable College do again . . . treat me with their accustomed Indignity," he wrote in 1724, after the third rebuff.

A more appealing prodigy was Truman Henry Safford, class of 1854. As a child in Royalton, Vermont, he received so much publicity as a "lightning calculator" that he was invited to Boston to be examined by a committee of the American Academy of Arts and Sciences. At the behest of President Edward Everett and Professor Benjamin Peirce, Harvard's foremost mathematician, the Safford family moved to Cambridge so that Truman could prepare to enroll in the College. Entering at sixteen, he fulfilled his degree requirements in two years. Safford had a passionate interest in astronomy: after graduation he divided his time between the Harvard Observatory and the Nautical Almanac Office, then based in Cambridge. His contemporary Simon Newcomb, a colleague at the Nautical Almanac, remembered him as "the most wonderful genius in the office . . . a walking bibliography of astronomy, which one only had to consult to learn in a moment what great astronomers of recent time had written on almost any subject, where their work was published, and on what shelf of the Harvard Library the book could be found." Safford went on to teach at the University of Chicago; as the first director of Chicago's Dearborn Observatory, he discovered 108 nebulae. At Williams College, where he later taught astronomy and mathematics and was college librarian, it was said that "he could tell the position of every book without leaving his seat, and when observing with the transit . . . he did not need a Nautical Almanac, since he remembered the places of all of the stars in it."

Harvard was home to a constellation of prodigies in the years before World War I. One was Norbert Wiener, PH.D. '13, whose father was Leo Wiener, professor of Slavic languages and literature. After graduating from Tufts College at fourteen, Norbert completed his Harvard doctorate in philosophy at eighteen, writing his dissertation on mathematical logic. Long associated with MIT, this formidably contentious and famously absent-minded genius helped create the new field of information theory and founded the interdisciplinary science of cybernetics.

Four prodigies were enrolled in the College during that era. One was Cedric Houghton '13, who died soon after graduating. The others were Adolf A. Berle Jr. '13, Roger Sessions '15, and William James Sidis '14. Berle, who matriculated at the age of thirteen, took an LL.B. from the Law School in 1916. He traveled to Paris with the American delegation to the Versailles Peace Conference, practiced corporate law in New York City, and became a key member of President Franklin D. Roosevelt's "Brain Trust." As assistant secretary of state for Latin American affairs, he took part in many inter-American conferences, and in 1961, at the outset of the Kennedy administration, he headed a task force that recommended the creation of the Alliance for Progress. Sessions, who would become a major composer and composition teacher, also entered the College at thirteen; by then he had already composed his first opera. Half a century later, he returned to Harvard to receive an honorary degree and, soon thereafter, to deliver the Charles Eliot Norton Lectures.

Sidis, the youngest of the group, had been discovered by the press when, at the age of eight, he was identified as the world's youngest high schooler. Though he qualified for admission to Harvard at nine, he was not allowed to matriculate for another two years. By then he was fluent in six languages. Sidis took the mathematics department's most advanced courses; he earned As in math, physics, and French, but got Cs in economics, English, and philosophy. A decade after his graduation, the *New York Herald Tribune* revealed that the "boy brain prodigy" was now a back-office calculator operator in Manhattan. Sidis, who wished only to be left alone, went from job to job, sometimes working as a translator. In 1925 he published a book that anticipated the theory of black holes; physicists and astronomers ignored it. His next book was about collecting streetcar transfers, his consuming hobby. Sidis later moved to Boston's South End, where his desire to live in seclusion was spoiled by a *New Yorker* profile cruelly titled "April Fool" (his birth date was April 1, 1898). Years later the magazine paid a reported $500 to settle a malicious-libel suit brought by Sidis. Within three months of the settlement he died, at 46, of a cerebral hemorrhage.

School of Public Health

Only one of Harvard's professional schools directly addresses issues of life and death on a global scale: the School of Public Health (HSPH). The worldwide spread of AIDS, mass epidemics like SARS and other diseases of puzzling origin, the growing use of tobacco in underdeveloped countries, and terrorist access to deadly toxins—such threats underline the importance of the school's ongoing programs.

Founded in 1922 and always closely linked to the Medical School, the HSPH offered America's first graduate training program in the nascent field of public health. From the outset, the school's mission has been to explore ways to prevent disease and to promote the health of peoples throughout the world. This objective is pursued by a faculty of about 200 (nearly 65 are tenured), and about 825 students enrolled in four degree-granting programs. International students form more than a quarter of the school's enrollment, and women make up 60 percent of the student body. Perhaps more than any other professional school at Harvard, the curriculum and research at the HSPH is fundamentally multi-disciplinary. Diseases and cures are studied in the broadest possible context, drawing on all the medical sciences, quantitative disciplines (epidemiology and biostatistics), social sciences (economics, government, and sociology), and even the humanities (ethics and philosophy). A listing of its centers suggests the range of study at the school:

AIDS Institute
Biostatistics in AIDS Research
Cancer Prevention
Continuing Professional Educa-
   tion
Health Communication
Health and Human Rights
Injury Control

Occupational Health and
   Safety
Population and Development
   Studies
Radiation Sciences and Envi-
   ronmental Health
Risk Analysis

Risk analysis and decision science are relatively new fields of research with sophisticated methods of sorting out and analyzing the risks, costs, and benefits of various health measures. For example, should annual mammograms for women under 50 be paid for out of public funds when clinical evidence confirms high rates of false-positive results? Should expensive antiretroviral drugs be provided to individual AIDS patients in countries where mass preventive policies might have more lasting benefits? Assessing risks and determining the consequences of different policies, under conditions of considerable uncertainty, are the concerns of scholars in this exciting new area.

Historically, the HSPH can boast a long list of distinctive achievements. Philip Drinker, a faculty member at the School, developed the iron lung in 1927. Harvard's first female faculty member was Alice Hamilton, founder of the field of occupational medicine. She was initially appointed to the Medical School's new department of industrial health in 1919; she taught at HSPH until 1935. Three scientists affiliated with the HSPH have received Nobel Prizes: Thomas Weller, Bernard Lown, and Amartya Sen. At least six directors of the Centers for Disease Control and Prevention in Atlanta have been HSPH graduates. Faculty members at the school have identified a distinctive type of HIV that causes most AIDS/HIV infections in West Africa. Closer to home, binge drinking among college students, youth violence and prevention, and gun safety are current public health problems under scrutiny at the HSPH. The term "designated driver" was coined at the school.

Related entries: Firsts (Women); Medical School; Nobel Laureates. *Related Website:* www.hsph.harvard.edu.

Public Service

The term "public service" means different things at different schools. At the Kennedy School of Government, it is likely to suggest some form of government service or work in public institutions. At the College and certain professional schools, it evokes more specific themes: voluntarism, commitment and sacrifice, social action, community needs, the plight of the neglected and forgotten.

This element of dedicated service to others runs through most of the programs of the professional schools, and especially of those in the College. As one undergraduate puts it, "I read in Plato's *Apology* that Socrates claimed the unexamined life was not worth living. As far as I'm concerned, it's the uncommitted life that is not worth living—uncommitted to helping others." Some students have described their work in homeless shelters, inner-city schools, homes for the elderly, and prison libraries as "the best courses at Harvard," though no academic credit is given for such work. Says one regular volunteer at a homeless shelter, "When I arrive at the UniLu [the University Lutheran Church near Harvard Square] on Tuesday nights for my shift, the stresses of everyday life at Harvard become almost insignificant. Outside the Harvard community I am so fortunate to be in, I reconnect with the real world and am reminded of the great inequalities that pervade our society."

An estimated one-third of all undergraduates are actively engaged in community service programs at any given time. Students can learn about work opportunities from the office of the dean of the College (where there is now an assistant dean for public service) and from the Harvard Public Service Network, based in Phillips Brooks House (PBH). The Phillips Brooks House Association (PBHA) is the College's largest mostly-student-run service organization; it coordinates more than 70 different programs.

On registration day, first-year students attend an activity fair, where many public service organizations try to recruit them as volunteers. All are also invited to take part in the Freshman Urban Program, an intensive community-immersion experience during Freshman Week. Another program, House and Neighborhood Development (HAND), is administered through the College's twelve residential houses; it mobilizes more than 300 volunteers to work in public schools and community service groups in local neighborhoods. Then there is CityStep, which sends undergraduates into fourth- and fifth-grade classrooms to teach dance and movement. Other independent initiatives—like the Office of Career Service Programs, the Harvard Program for International Education in High Schools, and the Stride Rite program—offer incentives for service beyond the undergraduate years.

The graduate and professional schools provide students with chances to use their developing skills on behalf of the local community. Law School students provide legal counsel to low-income clients. Medical School students dispense health care to indigent patients. Divinity School students complete hundreds of hours of voluntary field work in pastoral counseling and in local church work. The Kennedy School of Government has an Office of Community and Public Service, which supports summer work in low-paying positions at nonprofit organizations. Probably the most extensive community outreach program is at the School of Public Health. Students there engage in many elementary and secondary school projects, staffing food pantries, health maintenance programs, HIV/AIDS and youth violence discussion groups, and environmental protection conferences.

To assist and encourage talented graduate and professional school students who plan to pursue careers in public service, the University offers grants under a recently established Presidential Scholars program. Under a new fundraising policy, contributions to a University Graduate Student Aid Fund will be used to expand the Presidential Scholars program and to support public service-related research and teaching across the University. In addition, a new Harvard Educational Loan Program (HELP) now offers loans at below-market rates to all graduate and professional school students—international as well as domestic—in degree programs relating to public service.

Hundreds of former students who engaged in public service work at Harvard and Radcliffe have gone on to serve the global community as Peace Corps volunteers. When President John F. Kennedy founded the corps in 1961, Harvard was one of the first institutions to provide facilities, faculty, and administrative support for its training programs. Among private universities, it is outranked only by Stanford in the number of Peace Corps volunteers it has produced—almost a thousand at last count. An alumnus, Mark D. Gearan '78, was director of the Peace Corps from 1995 until 1999, when he left to become president of Hobart and William Smith Colleges.

Related entries: International Outreach; Phillips Brooks House; School of Public Health. *Related Websites:* www.seo.harvard.edu/compubservice (Community and Public Service home page); www.fas.harvard.edu/~pbh (Harvard Public Service Network); www.pbha.org (Phillips Brooks House Association); hcs.harvard.edu/~hand (HAND).

Lining Quincy Street, Harvard's avenue of the arts, are (left to right)
the Fogg Art Museum, the Carpenter Center for the Visual Arts,
and the Harvard Faculty Club.

Quincy Street

Harvard's avenue of the arts, once a quiet residential street, is now lined by a dozen of the University's most-visited buildings. Among them are three fine arts museums, the Carpenter Center for the Visual Arts, Memorial Hall's Sanders Theatre, the Faculty Club, and the Barker Center for the Humanities. Unhappily, Quincy Street is also a thoroughfare for delivery trucks and is part of a major bus route.

Just over a quarter-mile in length, this one-way street runs north-south and forms the eastern border of Harvard Yard. North of the Yard, at the intersection of Quincy and Cambridge streets, is a striking architectural mélange: the soaring polychromatic mass of Memorial Hall (1878); the rear of the city of Cambridge's Georgian Revival fire station (1933); the starkly modernist George Gund Hall (1969), home of the School of Design; and James Stirling's cheekily postmodernist Sackler Museum (1985). Here one can see why Stirling—whose boxy building borrows design elements from Memorial Hall and Gund, though not from the fire station—called the Quincy Street vicinity "an architectural zoo."

On the west side of a long block between Broadway and Massachusetts Avenue, facing the Yard and its brick fencing, are the neo-Georgian Fogg Art Museum and its postmodernist add-on, Werner Otto Hall (1990); the French modernist master Le Corbusier's fantastic Carpenter Center, conceived (as one architectural critic put it) as "a threat to the old Quincy Street . . . a manifesto"; the Faculty Club, a derivative Georgian Revival building; and the Harvard Union, a noble one by Charles Follen McKim that was remodeled in 1997 as the nucleus of a center for the humanities.

On Quincy Street's Harvard Yard side, proceeding northward again, are Lamont Library, Harvard's first large building in the modern idiom (1949); the Georgian Revival Loeb House (originally the President's House, now used by the Office of the Governing Boards); and the Sever Quadrangle's large red-brick structures: Emerson Hall, the philosophy building; Sever Hall, a classroom building designed by the great H. H. Richardson; and Robinson Hall, now home to the history department.

Until the twentieth century, Quincy was a street of frame houses, most of them owned or rented by faculty members. An earlier President's House, built in 1860 and lived in by presidents Felton, Hill, and Eliot, was torn down in 1911 and replaced by a brick residence of much larger proportions (now Loeb House). The house of Henry James Sr., where the younger Henry, William, and Alice James grew up, stood on the present site of the Faculty Club. Almost all of the street's frame houses were eventually demolished or moved, and just two have survived. Sparks House (1838), a Greek Revival dwelling that is now the home of the preacher to the University, was relocated to 21 Kirkland Street—a distance of about 400 feet—in 1968, to make way for Gund Hall. The Dana-Palmer House (1822), a Federal-style structure that once served as Harvard's observatory, was moved across Quincy Street after World War II to permit the construction of Lamont Library. President James Conant and his family had lived there during the war, allowing the navy to use the President's House. Dana-Palmer is now Harvard's principal guest house. In its six splendidly appointed bedrooms, many notable heads—including those of Dean Acheson, Konrad Adenauer, the Dalai Lama, Marianne Moore, and Adlai E. Stevenson—have slept in comfort.

Related entries: Architecture; Carpenter Center; Faculty Club; Fire; Fogg Art Museum; Harvard Union; Libraries; Museums; Memorial Hall; Sanders Theatre; the Yard.

RACONTEURS

"Many's the time, Mrs. Willis, this rascal of yours had to put me to bed, and—ha-ha—if it isn't giving him away, vice- versa. What a time we used to have, you old scoundrel! Remember the night you decided to start training to swim the Channel by diving into the fountain in your dress suit, and . . ."

R

A reunion vignette by Gluyas Williams '11, from a
1938 issue of *The New Yorker*.

Radcliffe

As a women's college, Radcliffe no longer exists. But the memory of its distinguished service in the cause of women's higher education lives on in many minds, and indeed in some of the traditions of Harvard College. Moreover, its successor—the Radcliffe Institute for Advanced Study—is now an integral and dynamic part of the University.

Radcliffe College. Third-youngest of the Atlantic seaboard's Seven Sisters colleges, Radcliffe was founded in 1879 as "The Society for the Collegiate Instruction of Women." In popular usage, it was soon called "the Harvard Annex." At the outset, almost 40 Harvard teachers provided instruction to a student body of about 50 women; the first president was Elizabeth Cary Agassiz, wife of the naturalist and Harvard professor Louis Agassiz. In 1893, in the course of negotiations aimed at cementing relations between the Annex and Harvard, the young college was renamed for Ann Radcliffe, Lady Mowlson, who in 1643 had donated £100 to fund Harvard's first scholarship. Radcliffe College was chartered by the Massachusetts legislature the next year.

In the decades that followed, progress in achieving equal access to all of Harvard's resources came only slowly. The University's leaders resisted the idea of coeducation, preferring the term "coordinate education." But coeducation got a lasting foothold in 1943, when the faculty opened certain upper-level courses to Radcliffe juniors and seniors. "Joint instruction" was such a success that within a few years all Radcliffe students were admitted to Harvard courses. Even so, equal opportunities for women to use Harvard's undergraduate library, to reside in the houses, and to participate in virtually all extracurricular activities were not secured until the late 1960s and 1970s. When the Harvard and Radcliffe admissions offices were united in 1975, near-parity in admissions and financial aid became a realistic goal.

This path to progress was marked by recurring frictions and administrative skirmishes. When an outline for an institutional merger was broached in 1971, the resulting arrangement was soon tagged as a "non-merger merger." Radcliffe administrators and alumnae, for the most part, did not wish to see their college's identity effaced. The upshot was a quarter-century-long standoff that was confusing even to insiders. Though women applied to Harvard for admission, and earned Harvard degrees, their diplomas were signed by the presidents of both institutions. To the vexation of Harvard administrators, Radcliffe continued to claim a measure of authority over the education of women. One telling sign of the way the wind was blowing against Radcliffe as an independent entity was the increasing tendency of women undergraduates to think of themselves as Harvard students. In intercollegiate athletic competition, for example, only the women's crew chose to compete (and continues to compete) under the Radcliffe name.

In 1999, after more than two years of strained negotiations, a genuine merger was achieved. The agreement stipulated that women undergraduates would be enrolled only at Harvard; that Radcliffe College and its board of trustees would legally disappear; that Harvard would absorb the college's former endowment and property; and that Radcliffe's existing research organizations would be subsumed by a new and enlarged Radcliffe Institute for Advanced Study. This new creation was conceived as a world-class multidisciplinary research institution with a strong commitment to the study of women, gender, and society.

Three established research facilities—the 80,000-book Schlesinger Library, the Murray Center, and the Bunting Institute, created in 1960 to promote the professional achievement of talented women—were folded into the new institute. Led by its own dean, the Radcliffe Institute took its place beside Harvard's nine other schools or faculties.

In the wake of the merger, it's probably fair to say that most women at Harvard now feel that it is better for Radcliffe to have moved within the ambit of the University—with a real voice, presence, budget, and dean—than to be marginalized by an administrative fiction that provided the guise of independence without the substance of power.

Attached to the Radcliffe Institute are these centers and programs:

• *Radcliffe Institute Fellowship Program.* Forty to fifty fellowships, funded by stipends from the institute or from independent sources, are awarded annually. Appointments are generally for one year and are open to both women and men. The stated aim is to bring together "outstanding individuals . . . from all over the world to do their own research and to interact with one another in ways that transform them and the knowledge they create." Undergraduates are invited to participate as research partners with fellows, and to attend their events.

• *The Arthur and Elizabeth Schlesinger Library on the History of Women in America.* This library, a national resource, contains major collections of books, letters, diaries, photographs, and other documents on the history of women and the culinary arts. Its holdings include 80,000 volumes and 13,000 linear feet of manuscripts.

• *Murray Research Center.* This center's holdings consist of reports, interviews, and histories of "lives over time," assembled by the Harvard psychologist Henry A. Murray '15. These richly documented case studies, supported by quantitative and qualitative data, illuminate stages of human development and maturation.

• *Outreach Programs.* The institute sponsors a robust program of lectures, seminars, and conferences for scholarly audiences and for the public, including major conferences on such subjects as African-American Women's History, and Women, Money, and Power.

• *Office of Alumnae Services.* Mindful of its roots in Radcliffe College, the institute's Office of Alumnae Services recognizes and serves alumnae through ongoing support of Radcliffe Day and class reunions for the classes of 1962 and earlier. It also supports a program that matches undergraduates with alumnae mentors.

Drew Gilpin Faust—a leading historian of the Civil War and the American South who had previously held a chair at the University of Pennsylvania—was named founding dean of the institute in 2001. She has a tenured appointment in the Faculty of Arts and Sciences. There are three other senior academic positions: a dean for science, a dean for social science, and the Pforzheimer Director of the Schlesinger Library. Each is held by a senior faculty member.

Related entries: Admissions; Athletics; Harvard College; Libraries; Research Institutes and Centers. *Related Website:* www.radcliffe.edu.

Rebellions and Riots

The terms overlap meanings. A rebellion is an open defiance of constituted authority. A riot is a violent disturbance of the public peace. A riot can spark a rebellion, and a rebellion can foment rioting. Over a span of three centuries, Harvard had its share of both.

The last serious riot occurred in the spring of 1970, a year after the last of the rebellions. With the United States mired in the Vietnam War, rising protests against Harvard's ties to the military were climaxed by a forcible occupation of University Hall in April 1969. When local and state police were called in to remove the occupiers, a ten-day student strike ensued. The escalation of the war heightened tension levels on university campuses throughout the nation. In April 1970, a four-hour riot rocked Harvard Square. Many of the area's growing number of hangers-on and street people took part in smashing windows, looting storefronts, and battling police. Forty policemen and 35 Harvard students were treated for injuries. The riot was said to be the worst civil disturbance in Massachusetts history. Property damage was estimated at more than $100,000.

Nathan M. Pusey, Harvard's president since 1953, had only recently announced that he would step down in another year. Almost three centuries earlier, in 1675, the opposition of the College's two dozen students had made life miserable for Harvard's third president, Leonard Hoar. For reasons that remain unclear, Hoar was so disliked that his students deserted in a body. The College closed down for the winter; Hoar resigned, after only three years in office, and died within a few months. The College was revived under president Urian Oakes; but not until the presidency of Increase Mather, a decade later, did it recover its forward momentum.

The eighteenth and nineteenth centuries saw rebellions aplenty. A frequent cause was the quality of food served in the College dining commons. After the Butter Rebellion of 1766, which began

with a mass walkout from the commons, half the College was suspended. Later came the Bread and Butter Rebellion of 1805, the
Cabbage Rebellion of 1807, and the Great Rebellion of 1814. The
last of these was quelled only when the faculty hired a caterer (a
"cook superior to any in the United States") to manage the com-
missary.

Harvard's disciplinary measures were the target of the next major uprising, the Great Rebellion of 1823. Protesting the expulsion
of one of its members, an unusually rowdy senior class gathered
under the Rebellion Tree near Harvard Hall and swore an oath to
leave College until the classmate was reinstated. With Commencement in the offing, the faculty responded by expelling 43 students
out of a class of 70. After this rebellion, the governing boards conducted a review of disciplinary and instructional methods and initiated a series of reforms. One was a rearrangement of vacation
schedules, on the theory that warm weather was conducive to rioting.

A memorable blowup occurred in the spring of 1834, when
the faculty tried to make an example of a handful of habitual trou-
blemakers. Their classmates protested by petitioning; when that
failed, an unpopular tutor's windows were broken, his furniture
was destroyed, and the College bell was rung in the middle of
the night. In late May, the entire sophomore class was dismissed
and ordered to leave Cambridge at once. President Josiah Quincy
then committed the grave error of invoking the Grand Jury of
Middlesex County to proceed against the offenders. This elicited
an explosive reaction. The "black flag of rebellion" was hung from
Holworthy Hall, classroom chairs and windows were smashed, and
Quincy was hung in effigy from the Rebellion Tree. A bomb went
off during chapel, and when the smoke cleared, "A Bone for Old
Quin to Pick" was seen written on the walls.

Quincy had violated a longstanding tradition, handed down
from the English universities, and it cost him whatever popularity
he might otherwise have enjoyed. As early as 1659, the President
and Fellows had resolved that "we judge it not convenient, neither
do we allow [that the Town Watch] should lay violent hands on

any of the students, being found within the precincts of the Coll. yard." No Harvard president would call public authorities into the Yard again until April 1969, when the reaction of outraged students would be as strong as it had been in 1834.

More enlightened administrative policies helped ward off further rebellions for generations, though rioting remained a more or less regular rite of spring. From the turn of the century to the 1950s, a shout of *Oh, Rinehart!* would be enough to draw restive students into the Yard for nocturnal high jinks. The rallying-cry originated on a June evening in 1900, when Ralph R. ("Railroad") Kent '00 stood beneath the Grays Hall window of his classmate John B. G. Rinehart and tried repeatedly to hail him. Rinehart wasn't in, but Walter Prichard Eaton '00 irascibly responded with his own "Oh, Rinehart!" Others in the Yard spontaneously took up the chant, and the night air filled with "Rineharts."

Harvard Square was the flash point for a large-scale riot in the spring of 1932. Persons unknown had stolen the 45-pound clapper of the Memorial Hall bell, and a rumor that it had been found in Matthews Hall drew hundreds of students to the Yard. A rumpus that lasted into the night erupted in the Square. Eggs were thrown and electric trolleys were rocked off their wires. Rioters set fire to the gates of the University Theatre and invaded Radcliffe dormitories. Using tear gas to restore order, police arrested nine students and one officer of the College.

The 1950s saw a series of Harvard Square riots in which students directed catcalls at passersby or shot at them with water pistols. Less playful was the Pogo Riot of May 1952. Cartoonist Walt Kelly, creator of the comic strip "Pogo," had failed to show up for a ballyhooed lecture, and a thousand frustrated students spilled into the Square. Fighting broke out when police attempted to disperse them, and 28 students were arrested. A number were beaten by Cambridge police officers, some of whom were later reprimanded for using excessive force.

The Diploma Riots of May 1961—protesting Harvard's adoption of a diploma with text in English rather than the traditional Latin—began more decorously, with a Latin oration delivered on the steps of Widener Library by a toga-clad, laurel-crowned senior. About 2,000 students then marched to the President's House, where Nathan Pusey, a classicist, responded in Latin to a largely uncomprehending throng. The marchers then trooped to the Square chanting "Latin Si, Pusey No!" A second night of disorder ended with arrests and some restrained use of tear gas by the Cambridge police.

Nothing comparable has occurred in the last three decades— probably the longest riot-free interval in Harvard history.

Related entries: Diplomas; Presidents; the Yard.

Regalia

Reading academic regalia requires an ability to deal with arcana. Harvard formerly had a small committee whose members did just that at its annual meetings: it was called the SAD Committee, the acronym standing for Seals, Arms, and Diplomas. (One of the co-authors of this book was once a member of both the SAD Committee and the "Happy Committee"—the Harvard Alumni Association's Committee on the Happy Observance of Commencement.)

The language of regalia is arcane indeed: academic gowns are ornamented with crow's-feet and fastened by frogs. The headpiece is a mortarboard. The hood has an appendage called a liripipe. The cut and hue of today's robes and headgear are derived from the outerwear of medieval monks, whose flowing gowns and roomy hoods helped warm them in the unheated abbeys of medieval Europe. In the earliest universities—Bologna and Salerno in Italy, Oxford and Cambridge in England—students and faculty wore such robes and hoods daily. In time the color and trim of a hood came to signify the degree that a scholar was pursuing.

Today the lining of a hood—its patterning and coloration—indicates the degree-granting institution and is supposedly regulated by an intercollegiate code devised in 1895. Harvard's academic dress is "non-code": the University had set its own standards for regalia in 1886 and did not wish to change. Harvard's doctoral hood lining is crimson; the gown too is crimson, with black velvet facings and sleeve bars. At first, only Ph.D. candidates from the Graduate School of Arts and Sciences wore crimson gowns and hoods, but doctoral candidates in all schools now do so.

Sleeve bars, crow's-feet, yokes, and other embellishments are semiotic signifiers. The color of the crow's-foot on a doctoral gown indicates the faculty granting the degree: Medicine (green), Design (brown), Public Health (salmon pink), Divinity (scarlet), Law (purple), Government (peacock blue), Education (light blue), Dentistry (lilac), Business Administration (medium gray), or Arts (white). The crow's-foot in a Ph.D. gown is dark blue. A hood's length indicates the wearer's place in the academic pecking order: a doctoral hood is four feet long, a master's three-and-a-half feet, a bachelor's three feet.

Masters of Harvard's residential houses wear on the left shoulder a two-foot-long tippet, edged with the house colors and bearing the house arms. All degree candidates wear the mortarboard, a skullcap sewed to a stiff square top ordinarily adorned by a black tassel. Marshals and officers of the graduating class, as well as graduate marshals, wear red tassels; Harvard's president wears a gold one. Scholars holding degrees from foreign institutions may sport brimmed hats or soft caps in a variety of colors and designs.

In the eighteenth century, Harvard upperclassmen were urged to don gowns "on all public occasions," but the practice never took hold. Today, academic attire is mandated only on a few public occasions, such as the installation of a new president, the occasional out-of-season conferral of an honorary degree, major University anniversaries, and certain rites of Commencement Week: the Phi Beta Kappa Literary Exercises, chapel services, and the graduation ceremony—when, in deference to ancient tradition, one wears monastic garb to symbolize one's attainment of maturity and *gravitas,* one's disdain for shifting tastes and passing fads. (Bear that in mind when the television camera zooms in on a row of black-robed degree candidates, with their garlanded mortarboards, face paint, cell phones, bouncing beach balls, and bottles of bubbly.)

Harvard regalia does *not* include certain elements that still have a place at other universities: no mace, no presidential medallion, no hooding of honorary degree recipients. The absence of these symbols and rituals has been ascribed to the influence of Harvard's Puritan past, with its stress on simplicity, purity, and the avoidance of finery and self-display. A likelier factor is the nineteenth-century Unitarianism that left Harvard with an aversion to ritualism and other "high-church" accoutrements. Indeed, today's Commencement may stand as a model of simplified ritual and bare-bones regalia.

Related entries: Commencement; Crimson; Degrees; Fashion; Honorary Degrees. *Related Website:* www.marshal.harvard.edu.

Research Centers and Institutes

After World War II, many faculty members at Harvard (and other American universities) began to associate more closely with scholars from other disciplines to study such large geographic areas as Russia, China and Japan, western Europe, and Latin America. Political scientists, historians, economists, and sociologists became increasingly aware of the limitations of single-discipline approaches to complex cultural problems. This led, over time, to a variety of research centers—or "institutes," or "projects"— throughout the University.

These multidisciplinary groupings emerged as exciting new venues of intellectual activity. In some cases, the scholarly focus gradually expanded beyond geographic areas to cover such thematic topics as international affairs, economic development, human rights, and literary and cultural studies. For the most part, these new groupings were successful in securing faculty commitment as well as outside funding from interested governmental agencies, foundations, corporate business, and individual donors.

Within the Faculty of Arts and Sciences and the nine graduate and professional schools, research centers, institutes, and projects have continued to proliferate. The total number has been estimated at more than 300. Some representative examples:

CENTERS

Asia Center

Astrophysics Center

Bagnoud Center for Health and Human Rights

Barker Center for the Humanities

Belfer Center for Science and International Affairs

Carpenter Center for the Visual Arts

Davis Center for Russian and Eurasian Studies

De Gunzburg Center for European Studies

Hauser Center for Nonprofit Organizations

Jewish Studies Center

Middle Eastern Studies Center

Risk Analysis Center

Textile and Apparel Research Center

Murray Research Center

Population and Development Studies Center

Rockefeller Center for Latin American Studies

Warren Center for Studies in American History

Weatherhead Center for International Affairs

INSTITUTES

Harvard-Yenching Institute

Institute for Advanced Theatre Training

Institute for Learning in Retirement

Institute for Theoretical Atomic and Molecular Physics

Institute of Politics at the Kennedy School

Korea Institute

Reischauer Institute of Japanese Studies

W. E. B. DuBois Institute for Afro-American Research

PROJECTS

Civil Rights Project at Harvard

Global Environmental Assessment Project

Pluralism Project

Cold War Studies

Schooling and Children

Project Zero

What distinguishes a center from an institute or project? Each category may have its exceptions, but certain defining lines are generally accepted.

Centers are larger and more permanently endowed units within a particular faculty or school. Their directors are appointed by a dean. Size is not necessarily a criterion. The relatively new Weatherhead Center for International Affairs, which is amply endowed, is a major presence in the Faculty of Arts and Sciences. It administers many faculty appointments and fellowship programs. Much smaller, but thriving nevertheless, is the Center for Textile and Apparel Research (also affiliated with Boston University and the University of Miami), which involves far fewer faculty members and programs.

Institutes, a somewhat more recent manifestation, tend to focus on specialized topics or student and staff activities. Examples would include the Kennedy School of Government's large and dynamic Institute of Politics, and the popular Institute for Learning in Retirement, a part of the Division of Continuing Education. Much smaller, and far more specialized, is the Faculty of Arts and Sciences' Institute for Theoretical Atomic and Molecular Physics.

Projects are smaller still; even more delimited in their activities; and, by and large, less well funded. Their directors are usually appointed by department heads or administrators. The School of Education has the largest number of research projects; one, called Project Zero, actually consists of many individual projects.

An even larger category of faculty and student research groupings has sprouted in recent years. These are *programs,* and they may number well over 400. Programs support highly specific academic pursuits, and they may come and go, depending on the ideas, enterprise, and fundraising skills of the faculty members who initiate and sponsor them. The program directors are often the sponsors themselves.

The trend toward research centers, institutes, and projects may have peaked. President Summers has expressed reservations about promoting their growth. His go-slow approach reflects a belief in the traditional role of departments as basic academic units and a concern that centers and institutes could compete with, and drain intellectual energy from, the departments.

Reunions

It's a beautiful sunny day in early June. Harvard Yard is filled with colors—sky-blue overhead, a carpet of brilliantly green grass underfoot; crimson banners hanging from trees; students, faculty members, and alumni attired in blazers and academic costumes of many hues. For the thousands of alumni returning to their alma mater for class reunions, a high point is meeting with classmates in the outdoor Tercentenary Theatre for the Thursday morning Commencement exercises and the annual meeting of the Harvard Alumni Association (HAA) in the afternoon.

But these are just two of many carefully planned events involving classmates returning to Harvard for reunions. The three- or four-day schedules typically include symposia with prominent classmates and faculty; class meetings and reports; exhibits of books and art works by class members; group photographs; picnics; Boston harbor cruises; cocktails and banquets; golf and tennis outings; evening dances with entertainment; and memorial services for departed members of the class. Much time is set aside for socializing and reminiscing, and special activities are organized for spouses and children of all ages. Over a period of perhaps 200 years (the dates of the first reunions are uncertain), these events have offered memorable opportunities to re-bond with old friends and with an institution intimately associated with early maturity. Attendance rates at major reunions today can be as high as 70 percent of the class.

The big ones are the twenty-fifth, thirty-fifth, and fiftieth. Meticulously planned as much as three years in advance by class committees and HAA staff members, they take place during a weeklong interval before and during Commencement. In various ways, those attending receive privileged treatment: the president and deans usually address them; they get preferential seating at most events; they march in special units in the alumni procession on Commencement afternoon; and they are apt to be showered with memorabilia. The price tag can amount to $500 or more per person, though in recent years the HAA has provided certain deductions and even "scholarships" for alumni who cannot afford the full bill.

Other reunions, such as the thirtieth, fortieth, and forty-fifth, may be held at different times of the year in order to prevent overloading Harvard facilities at Commencement time. These reunions are also carefully prepared gatherings with traditionally scripted schedules. Attendance is usually considerably lower than at the major reunions, but some especially close-knit classes may succeed in attracting a large draw. Wartime classes and, perhaps surprisingly, classes that graduated during the turbulent 1960s and 1970s have broken attendance records in non-major reunions.

One traditional practice at the annual meeting of the Alumni Association has been the public recognition of the oldest alumnus and alumna attending a class reunion. These are often centenarians who stand and receive the assembly's applause. A development of recent years has been the appearance of graduates attending a seventy-fifth reunion. In 1998, fifteen members of the class of 1923 participated actively, if sedately, in the first such reunion. All stayed at Boston's Ritz Hotel, courtesy of an affluent classmate. (A concerned reunion official had teasingly suggested Massachusetts General Hospital!)

The professional schools mount their own reunions in much the same way, using their own venues for events. The Business School schedules class reunions on various weekends throughout the year, and these get-togethers have often broken attendance records for percentage of participation. The Law School and Medical School also organize very successful reunions.

Reunions are not for everyone. A significant minority of Harvard graduates never attend reunions and perhaps never will. An HAA survey taken in the late 1980s showed that reasons for staying away included the financial cost, the travel involved, scarcity of time, anxieties about "not knowing anyone," and the fear that "ev-

eryone present will be more successful than I am." Another frequent response was, "I'm just not the reunion type." Yet the size of
reunion gatherings continues to grow year by year.

Of course, there is another important—and usually under-
stated—aspect of Harvard reunions. In a sense, it is part of a tacit
bargain between the University and its graduate sons and daugh-
ters. The argument goes this way. Harvard rejoices in the success
and fame of its graduates. It invites all of them to return periodically, to bond again with one another and with their institution,
and to find out what has happened in higher education since their
departure. As part of the bargain, Harvard hopes for and solicits
the financial support of returning alumni, especially at reunion
times, when emotions of recollection and gratitude may run higher
than usual. Harvard, of course, is not alone among American
universities and colleges in using reunions as occasions for fundraising.

Overt solicitations for financial support are mostly accomplished far in advance of the reunion, in quiet conversations between class officers and class members who have the wherewithal
to contribute substantially. A motivating factor in this endeavor is
competition among successive reunion classes. The results of reunion giving—dollar totals, along with acknowledgments of the
work of class solicitors—are publicly announced and acclaimed at
the HAA's afternoon exercises (to the dismay of some who find the
practice a bit crass, but to the satisfaction of others who believe the
hard work and generosity of class members should be recognized).

If there is one singular institution connected with higher education in America, it may be the existence of hyper-organized reunions. Most universities around the world, all heavily supported
by government funds, have, at best, only recently seen merit in inviting graduates back for periodic reunions. Eyeing needed private
support, some universities, like Oxford, Cambridge, and Heidel-
berg, have instituted rudimentary, but much more casual, get-
togethers for their former students. As universities in Europe, Asia,
and elsewhere recognize the multiple benefits as compared with
the moderate costs of sponsoring reunions for their graduates, the

time may arrive when holding regular alumni reunions will become standard operating practice for universities everywhere.

Related entries: Alumni; Commencement; Fundraising.

Rhodes Scholars

Since 1903, a trust created by Cecil Rhodes, the British colonialist and entrepreneur, has awarded scholarships to American college seniors for two or three years of study at Oxford University. Today's students can compete for an array of international grants inspired by the Rhodes program—Fulbrights, Marshalls, Trumans, Gateses, and many more. But a Rhodes Scholarship on one's résumé is a "dazzler" that outshines others.

Harvard's record in Rhodes competition is stellar. No other institution has had so many winners, both overall (the total now stands at more than 300) and in a single year (ten in 1988). From 1988 to 2003, Harvard garnered 80 Rhodeses, exceeding the combined total for Yale, Princeton, and Stanford, the second-, third-, and fourth-ranking institutions. Neil Rudenstine, Harvard's president from 1991 to 2001, was a Rhodes Scholar; so were at least 20 Harvard faculty members. Over the years, four of the Rhodes Trust's five American secretaries have held Harvard degrees. So the Harvard-Rhodes nexus is well established.

Rhodes Scholarships are awarded annually to 32 American students. Another 60 scholars are drawn from eighteen other constituencies around the world. With the exception of Germany, all are or were parts of the British Commonwealth. (In a codicil to his will, Cecil Rhodes earmarked five scholarships for German students, noting that "the object is that an understanding between the three great powers will render war impossible and educational relations make the strongest tie.") Several countries—such as Kenya, Malaysia, Pakistan, Singapore, Uganda, Zambia, and Zimbabwe—did not exist as such when Cecil Rhodes wrote his will. The recipient group has also changed in ways that Rhodes would not have foreseen, or have welcomed. More than one-third of today's Rhodes Scholars are nonwhite, and about half are women.

The first black Rhodes Scholar was Alain LeRoy Locke '07. Locke was shunned by many of his fellow American Rhodes Scholars, and no American black won a Rhodes again until 1963. Women weren't eligible for the scholarships until 1976, when an act of Parliament amended the terms of Rhodes's will. Harvard's Office of Career Planning and Off-Campus Learning had a prominent part in an American-based movement that led to the passage of the act.

The Rhodes Trust does not record racial or ethnic data, but since 1968, when Thomas S. Williamson Jr. '68 became the College's first African-American Rhodes Scholar of recent times, Harvard is thought to have had the most black winners. Since 1977, when seniors Laura Garwin, Alison Muscatine, and Denise Thal were among the first 13 American women to win Rhodes Scholarships, Harvard has also sponsored the most women scholars— more than 40 to date.

American Rhodes Scholars are chosen from an initial field of almost a thousand applicants, endorsed in a typical year by some 320 colleges and universities. In recent years, more and more state universities and smaller colleges have fielded candidates. One may apply either from the state in which one resides or from the state in which one attends college. State selection committees screen nominees, subjecting them to famously grueling interviews. Much weight is given to leadership potential and intellectual breadth (Cecil Rhodes inveighed against "mere bookworms"). Each state's finalists then appear before one of eight district committees, which select the 32 winners.

In a given year, Harvard may nominate as many as 40 or 50 candidates, who must survive an internal selection process that is generally believed to be even more rigorous than those of other institutions. House tutors help groom Rhodes hopefuls, coaching them in "dossier presentation" and interview techniques.

The announcement of each year's Rhodes Scholars, late in the fall semester, is always well publicized. Since the mid-1990s, Harvard has averaged about four per year. Lean years are a rarity, but they do occur. Only one candidate was selected in 1987, just two in 1999, and in 2000, for the first time in 71 years, no Harvard nominee made the final cut. With the encouragement of the Rhodes Trust, the College endorsed a somewhat larger number of candidates the following year, and had five winners—tops in the nation.

Harvard's dominance in Rhodes competition has, at least in part, been a byproduct of the College's longstanding effort to assemble a truly national student body. The recruitment and financial aid policies of the admissions office are designed to attract a flow of exceptional students from the hinterlands; the Rhodes program's home-state/college-state option gives some of those students an edge over candidates from more populous states, and often over other hinterlanders who attend college closer to home.

Harvard's Rhodes Scholars have attained distinction in a range of fields—though relatively few have made their marks in the sciences or held high governmental office. David Souter '61 is a justice of the U.S. Supreme Court. Bonnie St. John '86, who, as a handicapped skier, had won a silver medal in the 1984 Olympics, was named by President Clinton (also a Rhodes Scholar) as the National Economic Council's first Director of Human Capital Issues. Boisfeuillet Jones Jr. '68, J.D. '74, is publisher and chief executive officer of the *Washington Post;* James Fallows '70 is a well-known journalist and editor, as is Michael Kinsley '72, "Crossfire" panelist and editor of the virtual magazine *Slate.* Walter Isaacson '74 rose to editorial director of Time Inc. and chairman of CNN before assuming the presidency of the Aspen Institute. John Brademas '50, after 22 years as a congressman from Indiana, served as president of New York University. Robert Darnton '60, professor of history at Princeton, was a recipient of a MacArthur Foundation "genius grant."

The Rhodes Trust's American secretaries have included Harvard alumni Frank Aydelotte, M.A. '03; Courtney Smith '38, PH.D. '43; William J. Barber '46; and Elliot F. Gerson '74. All were Rhodes Scholars themselves.

Related entries: Admissions; Harvard College. *Related Website:* www.rhodesscholar.org.

ROTC

Harvard was the first institution to form a Reserve Officers Training Corps (ROTC) unit, but the University ended its connection with the program during the Vietnam War.

In the summer of 1916, with America's entry into World War I in the offing, President Woodrow Wilson signed the National Defense Act, which created the ROTC program. A "Harvard Regiment," organized five months earlier with a thousand student volunteers, became the nation's first ROTC unit. More than 1,200 trainees were commissioned over the next two years. When naval ROTC was established in 1926, Harvard was one of six schools initially chartered. In the years following World War II, ROTC scholarships supported three or four hundred of the College's 6,000-odd students. Graduate and professional school students also took ROTC training.

Institutional links to the military became a vexed issue during the Vietnam conflict. Protesting students demanded an end to a program that was seen as making Harvard complicit in an unjust war. In response to the student strike of April 1969, the Faculty of Arts and Sciences voted to terminate the University's participation in ROTC. The last trainees were commissioned in 1973. Yale, Columbia, Dartmouth, Stanford, and other institutions ended their ROTC programs at about the same time.

The University later made a contractual arrangement that allowed Harvard students to train with MIT's ROTC unit. When the status of gay men and women in the military became an issue in the early 1990s, a faculty vote halted payments to MIT. Since then, a group of concerned alumni has voluntarily footed the bill. More recently, President Lawrence Summers has expressed firm support for the concept of ROTC. After the events of September 11, 2001, he addressed a Veterans' Day letter to Harvard's cadets and midshipmen, "to let you and your colleagues know how strongly I value the commitment to national service embodied in your participation in the Reserve Officers Training Corps."

Shannon Hall—an unassuming building near the Divinity School, named for one of the 373 Harvard men who died in service in World War I—and nearby Vanserg Hall formerly served as the headquarters of Harvard ROTC units. They have since been converted to house classrooms, offices, and a day care center.

Related entries: Fire; Gay and Lesbian; Rebellions and Riots; Vanserg Hall.

S

Harvard's statuary giants include two life-sized rhinos who have
guarded the doors of the Biological Laboratories since 1930.
The beasts, known as Bessie and Victoria, took temporary
leave when renovations began in 2003.

Sanders Theatre

Sanders is Harvard's Carnegie Hall. It is also a lecture hall and an occasional stage for drama, dance, and academic ceremonials.

Forming the eastern end of Memorial Hall, Sanders Theatre is Harvard's largest formal auditorium, with a capacity of 1,165. Its nearest rivals are the Kennedy School of Government's John F. Kennedy Jr. Forum (originally the ARCO Forum) and the Business School's Burden Hall, both seating about 800. Chairs placed onstage at Sanders increase its capacity by a hundred seats.

Built with a bequest of $50,000 from Charles Sanders, class of 1802 and a former bursar of the College, the hall opened in 1876. The architects of Memorial Hall, Henry van Brunt and William Ware, were clearly influenced by Christopher Wren's Sheldonian Theatre at Oxford University. The stage is wide and open; pews for audience members are laid out in a semicircle at the ground and balcony levels. Sight lines are excellent in almost every part of the hall, and the proximity of the seats to the stage makes for a sense of intimacy. The pews, walls, and ceiling are largely of heavily shellacked ashwood, creating a warm and inviting ambience.

The hall's acoustics were much admired when Sanders was new. The Harvard physicist Wallace Sabine, a pioneer acoustician, borrowed seat cushions from the hall for experiments that yielded a formula for predicting reverberation times. As the acoustical consultant for Boston's future Symphony Hall, Sabine altered the building's interior design to improve its sound properties. His studies of sonic transmission laid the foundation for the science of architectural acoustics, and his name is perpetuated in that of an international unit of measurement for sound absorption: the sabin.

The acoustical virtues of Sanders Theatre are still appreciated today. An unamplified voice can be heard well throughout the hall, and orchestral timbres can resonate brilliantly in certain parts of it. But Sanders also has dead spots (some of them onstage), and though the floor seats may be the most intimate, that area doesn't offer the best sound. There's no suitable area where performers can wait offstage; drafts make tuning difficult; and rustling paper or coughing anywhere in the hall can be heard almost everywhere.

Once opened, Sanders immediately became Harvard's premier location for public events and performances. For years it was the site of the annual Commencement exercises—a tradition that lasted until 1922, when the ceremony was moved outdoors to accommodate the growing number of degree candidates and their families. In 1968 a deluge forced the Commencement exercises back into Sanders, but the problem of whom to admit (of those on hand, only one out of 20 could be seated) proved so vexing that all Commencements since then have been held *al fresco* in the Tercentenary Theatre, no matter how inclement the weather.

Reflecting its designers' assumption that the hall would be a place for rhetoric and debate, the theatre's exterior is ornamented with the sculpted heads of famous orators of the ages: Demosthenes, Cicero, St. Chrysostom, Bossuet, Chatham, Burke, and Webster. In the twentieth century, orators great, near-great, and not-so-great—world leaders, politicians, artists, poets, humorists, scientists, and movie stars—have addressed audiences from the Sanders stage. Among them have been Theodore Roosevelt, Franklin D. Roosevelt, Winston Churchill, Martin Luther King Jr., Chinese president Jiang Zemin, and Mikhail Gorbachev. Every Harvard president since Charles William Eliot has spoken from the Sanders podium.

Sanders has long been used for the College's largest lecture courses, as well as for the prestigious Charles Eliot Norton lectures, the annual Phi Beta Kappa Literary Exercises, and other academic events. Until the 1960s, the Boston Symphony Orchestra gave regular concerts at Sanders. The Boston Baroque, Boston Chamber Music Society, Boston Philharmonic, the Pro Arte Orchestra, and the Christmas Revels perform there, as do the Harvard-Radcliffe Orchestra, Bach Society Orchestra, Mozart Society Orchestra, Harvard Glee Club, Collegium Musicum, Radcliffe Choral Society, and other undergraduate musical groups. With so much term-time activity from September to June, Sanders is rarely dark.

Many concertgoers find themselves gazing curiously at the two outsize statues that flank the Sanders stage, or at the lengthy Latin inscription that fills up much of the high wall above it. The statues are of James Otis, Revolutionary lawyer and patriot, and Josiah Quincy, Harvard's fifteenth president. The inscription, composed by George Martin Lane, professor of Latin from 1851 to 1897, translates as follows:

> Here, in the woods and wilds, Englishmen, fugitives from home, in the year of our Lord 1636, the sixth after the settlement of the Colony, holding that the first thing to cultivate was wisdom, founded a College by public enactment and dedicated it to Christ and his Church. Upraised by the generosity of John Harvard, aided again and again by patrons of learning both here and abroad, entrusted finally to the charge of its Alumni, from small beginnings guided to a growth of greater powers by the judgment, foresight, and care of its Presidents, Fellows, Overseers, and Faculties, it has ever cultivated the liberal arts and public and private virtues, and cultivates them still.

Related entries: Architecture; Kennedy School of Government; Memorial Hall; Music; Statues and Monuments. *Related Website:* www.fas.harvard.edu/memhall/sanders.html.

Sardis

Though field work takes many Harvard scholars to remote parts of the world, few of the University's research programs are actually based outside the Cambridge-Boston area. One of the oldest, and certainly the most distant, of the outliers is the Archaeological Exploration of Sardis—a site in western Turkey not far from the Aegean Sea. Originally a Princeton project, the archaeological dig ran out of funding and was abandoned for a time. In 1958 an entrepreneurial Harvard faculty member, Professor George M. A. Hanfmann, saw value in continuing the excavations and put together a consortium of support at Harvard and Cornell.

To prospective donors, Hanfmann explained that the ancient city of Sardis had once been the capital of the prosperous, pre-Christian Lydian Empire. Much of the city's fame came from the famously rich King Croesus, who reigned in the sixth century B.C. This bit of background, conjuring up visions of buried gold, silver, and jewelry, helped restart the suspended excavations.

After years of laborious digging, however, any expectations of booty remained unrealized. Neither the palace nor the treasury of Croesus were found. Generations of looters had evidently carted off the remains of the monarch's immense fortune.

Even so, the project's archaeologists have unveiled treasures of great historical interest. These include royal burial mounds that date back to the archaic period; city walls of unusual construction; and gold-working installations of considerable technical sophistication. From later eras are a spectacular temple of Artemis; a luxurious complex of baths and gymnasium; and a remarkable synagogue with a row of adjoining shops.

A special feature of this "big dig" in Turkey has been its transition to a deeper and deeper dig as excavations went on. Layer upon layer of the remains of successive settlements have been uncovered, extending backward and downward through modern Turkish, Byzantine, Roman Hellenistic, classical Greek, Persian, Lydian, and archaic civilizations. More than 14,000 objects have been inventoried so far; many are on display in a museum in Manisa, Turkey. (By law, all artifacts discovered at Sardis and the surrounding area must remain in Turkey.)

Generations of specialists, both American and Turkish, have trained at the Sardis site. Many have gone on to careers as archaeologists, art historians, architects, conservators, numismatists, epigraphers (scholars who study writings on stones), object illustrators, photographers, and anthropologists. Professor Hanfmann retired in 1976, and the Sardis Expedition has since been directed by Professor Crawford H. Greenewalt '59 of the University of California at Berkeley.

Excavation takes place during the height of the summer, when daytime temperatures can range from the 90s to 115 degrees. The best times to visit are late April to early June or September to October, when temperatures are not quite so high. In May, wild-flowers are abundant and snow is still visible on the Tmolus mountain range behind Sardis.

Related entry: Harvard Elsewhere. *Related Website:* www.artmuseums .harvard.edu/sardis/publications.html.

Science Museums

Of the almost twenty museums maintained by the University, the majority are devoted to the sciences. They range from the Botanical Museum, with its much-visited Glass Flowers, to the Medical School's little-known Warren Museum, a repository of early medical instruments and bizarre anatomical parts.

• *Museum of Natural History.* This public museum actually consists of three separate institutions: the Botanical Museum, the Museum of Comparative Zoology, and the Mineralogical and Geological Museum. All are housed in the University Museum, an enormous U-shaped building two blocks north of Harvard Yard, constructed in stages between 1859 and 1915.

• *Botanical Museum.* Not much is on public view here; the chief attraction is the Ware Collection of Blaschka Glass Models of Plants, better known as the Glass Flowers. Research is this museum's main activity: its large plant collections, including fossils, are available for scholarly use, and the library of its herbarium has extensive collections in economic botany, botanical history, ethnobotany, orchidology, and forestry. Faculty and students associated with the museum have gathered specimens in Mexico, South America, Canada, Greenland, South Africa, Australia, Afghanistan, and elsewhere. Historically, this museum has been a leading center for work in paleobotany. It was founded in 1858 by Professor Asa Gray, a renowned botanist and early exponent of Darwinian theory; materials shipped from the Royal Botanical Gardens at Kew formed the basis of its collections.

• *Museum of Comparative Zoology.* The MCZ's troves of stuffed birds and animals, fossils, dinosaur skeletons, and preserved insects are vast: 80,000 mammals, 300,000 birds, half a million amphibians and reptiles, a million fish, a million marine and terrestrial invertebrates, 1.1 million fossils, 7 million insects, 10 million mollusks—all told, some 21 million specimens. Among the prize exhibits is the 42-foot skeleton of *Kronosaurus queenslandicus,* which swam the seas 120 million years ago, disappeared about the time of the dinosaurs, and may have been the largest marine reptile that ever lived. The skeleton of a narwhal measures 23 feet in length, including the five-foot tusks; an 800-pound, six-million-year-old turtle carapace is the largest in existence. There's also the 12-foot "Harvard Mastodon," dug up in New Jersey in 1844; a dinosaur egg believed to be 65 million years old; and a huge mountain gorilla from the Eastern Congo, whose chest measures five feet, two inches in circumference. Specimens of extinct or threatened bird species include the great auk, the passenger pigeon, the California condor, the whooping crane, the heath hen, the Labrador duck, and the ivory-billed woodpecker. Closely allied with the Department of Organismic and Evolutionary Biology, the MCZ has up-to-date laboratory facilities, and its Ernst Mayr Library shelves more than 274,000 volumes of monographs and journals, natural history art works, and archival materials.

The MCZ is sometimes called the Agassiz Museum after its nineteenth-century founder, Louis Agassiz, professor of zoology and geology at Harvard's Lawrence Scientific School. It was Agassiz who persuaded the state legislature to charter the museum in 1859. (Under the terms of the charter the MCZ has a separate board known, confusingly, as the Faculty of the Museum of Comparative Zoology.) Its building and endowments were funded largely by Agassiz's son, Alexander, who made a copper-mining fortune in Michigan's Upper Peninsula, and by Alexander's son George Russell Agassiz.

• *Mineralogical and Geological Museum.* A systematic mineral collection and displays of gemstones are the principal exhibits in the Mineralogical Museum's mineral gallery. Now part of the Department of Earth and Planetary Sciences, the museum was created in 1891 to display a collection begun in 1784 by Dr. Benjamin Waterhouse of the Medical School. Once a "mineralogical cabinet" in Harvard Hall, it now holds more than 150,000 specimens. The

Smith Collection, acquired in 1883, gave the museum international standing in the study of meteorites. Taken as a whole, the mineral gallery provides a comprehensive sampling of the earth's crust.

All of the Museum of Natural History's exhibits, including the Glass Flowers Gallery, are open daily from 9 A.M. to 5 P.M. Holders of Harvard I.D. cards and one guest are admitted free. The museums are open to the public without charge on Wednesdays from 3 to 5 P.M. (September through May) and on Sunday mornings.

• *Peabody Museum of Archaeology and Ethnology.* One of the oldest anthropological museums, the Peabody holds millions of archaeological objects. Its ethnological collections include articles brought back from the missions of Lewis and Clark, as well as the fossil, skeletal, mummified, or cremation remains of some 22,000 human beings. Its photographic collection lists a half million images. Located in a wing of the University Museum, the Peabody collaborates with the Museum of Natural History on educational programming. One admission fee admits visitors to both museums.

Four permanent exhibits are on view. On the ground floor is the imposing great hall of the North American Indian. On the third floor are "Encounters with the Americas," exploring the aftermath of Columbus's arrival in the New World, and "Distinguished Casts: Curating Lost Monuments at the Peabody Museum." Pacific Islands Hall, on the balcony level, displays objects from Melanesia, Micronesia, Polynesia, and other Pacific island groups.

The Peabody was established in 1866 as an independent institution allied with Harvard; its trustees transferred it to the University in 1897. The museum has always encouraged field work, though funding usually comes from outside sources. Recent expeditions have taken faculty-led teams to the American Southwest, Central America, Brazil, North Africa, Iran, and the South Pacific. The Peabody has an active repatriation office, created in response to Congress's enactment in 1990 of the North American Graves Protection Act. The act requires museums to determine the origin of Native American artifacts and skeletal remains and to restore them to their rightful owners.

• *Semitic Museum.* This museum's century-old building on Divinity Avenue, across the street from the Peabody Museum, displays archaeological materials from the Near East. Founded in 1889, the Semitic Museum moved into its present building in 1903. Initially housed there were the Department of Near Eastern Languages and Civilizations, a library, a repository for research collections, a public educational institute, and a center for archaeological exploration. In the early years of the twentieth century, archaeologists associated with the Semitic Museum made the first scientific excavations in the Holy Land and participated in digs in the Sinai, where the earliest alphabet was discovered. During World War II the museum's building served as a headquarters for naval training programs, and academic activities did not resume until the 1970s. Today it is once again home to the Department of Near Eastern Languages and Civilizations. Its collections of Near Eastern artifacts hold more than 40,000 items, including pottery, cylinder seals, sculpture, coins, and cuneiform tablets, many unearthed in museum-sponsored excavations in Israel, Jordan, Iraq, Egypt, Cyprus, and Tunisia. The collections exist primarily for teaching and research, but the museum mounts regular exhibitions and is open to the public from 10 A.M. to 4 P.M on weekdays and 1 to 4 P.M on Sundays.

• *University Herbaria.* The Gray and Farlow herbaria, a block north of the Semitic Museum, contain about five million dried plant and fungal specimens. The Gray Herbarium, named for the nineteenth-century Harvard botanist Asa Gray, has one of the world's leading collections of vascular plants (those with fluid-carrying vessels). The Farlow Herbarium specializes in nonvascular plants and fungi. Both are closely associated with the Botanical Museum, the Arnold Arboretum, and the Harvard Forest.

• *Other museums.* The Arboretum, in Boston's Jamaica Plain, is a living outdoor museum that nurtures some 15,000 plants and trees. At the Harvard Forest's Fisher Museum in Petersham, Massachusetts, 23 dioramas depict the history and ecology of central New England forests. The curious Warren Museum, with its 13,000 anatomical parts and models, early instruments, and medical memorabilia, is part of the Medical School's Countway Library.

Beyond the Greater Boston area are the terraced gardens and the Byzantine and Pre-Columbian art collections of Dumbarton Oaks, an estate in the Georgetown section of Washington, D.C. In Florence, Italy, are the gardens and art works of the Center for Italian Renaissance Studies at the Villa I Tatti. The latter can be seen only by special arrangement.

Related entries: Arnold Arboretum; Dumbarton Oaks; Harvard Hall; Glass Flowers; Harvard Elsewhere; Harvard Forest; Sardis; Scientific Instruments; Villa I Tatti; Warren Museum. *Related Websites:* www.harvard.edu/museums; www.hmnh.harvard.edu (Museum of Natural History); www.peabody.harvard.edu; www.fas.harvard.edu/~semitic; www.huh.harvard.edu (herbaria).

Scientific Instruments

Although Harvard has been buying and preserving scientific instruments for three centuries, a formal collection was established only at the end of World War II. As so often happens at Harvard, the inspiration for such a collection came from a farsighted alumnus—in this case, David P. Wheatland '22. He realized that many valuable instruments were in danger of being discarded as outmoded and useless devices; he also understood that these devices could be used for teaching and research about scientific discoveries.

Housed in a wing of the Science Center on Oxford Street, the Collection of Historical Scientific Instruments has grown in size to nearly 20,000 objects and documents. The scientific fields represented in the collection cover a broad range: astronomy, biology, chemistry, geology, horology (clocks and watches), meteorology, navigation, physics, experimental psychology, and surveying. Some particularly interesting examples include:

- An early machine for generating electricity, employing a headboard and footboard and thus known as "the flying bedstead."
- An early battery, or Leyden jar, holding "electrical fluid."
- Mark Twain's microscope.

- A perfusion pump, used to keep vital organs alive outside the body and designed by the pioneer aviator Charles Lindbergh.
- William James's homemade device for studying optical illusions (he reputedly used fabric from his wife's bathing suit).
- Cameras and color-vision apparatus used by inventor Edwin Land '30, founder of Polaroid Corporation and prime mover in the creation of the undergraduate Science Center and the Freshman Seminar program.
- Recently acquired artifacts from the former Harvard Cyclotron Laboratory, built in 1948 for high-energy physics research.

For anyone interested in the history of science, the collection offers intriguing examples of the way inventive scientists of the past attacked some of the major challenges of their eras.

Related entries: Extinct Harvard; Science Museums; Warren Museum.
Related Website: www.peabody.harvard.edu/museum_scientific.html.

Signet Society

The College's principal literary and artistic society is quartered in an 1820 Federal-style frame house at 46 Dunster Street. Above the odd mix of Doric columns and Ionic pilasters at the main entrance are the society's arms: a signet ring encircled by bees, beneath a hand holding a book inscribed *Veritas.* Carved below is a passage from Plato's *Phaedo.* Some heavy symbolism, but who notices? And on a good day, the Signet's daily lunch tables *can* be a buzzing beehive of ebullient talk about books read, lectures heard, films seen, plays attended, and art exhibitions visited. Ample time is also allotted for gossip about doings at Harvard and political developments in Cambridge, Washington, and other parts of the world. The talkers? Undergraduates, graduate students, faculty members, alumni, and invited guests from the realms of—or with an interest in—arts and letters.

The Signet was founded by Charles J. Bonaparte, class of 1871, to shore up literary traditions that appeared to be languishing at the Hasty Pudding Club. The society acquired its present quarters in 1902. A listing of past initiates would include such usual suspects as William James, Charles William Eliot, Charles Eliot Norton, Van Wyck Brooks, T. S. Eliot, Conrad Aiken, Robert Sherwood, Lincoln Kirstein, James Agee, David Rockefeller, Leonard Bernstein, Norman Mailer, John Ashbery, John Updike, and John Lithgow.

Annual Christmas and spring dinners feature star turns by well-known writers and musicians, and in the spring the society annually awards its Signet Medal to an admired author or performer.

Related entries: Hasty Pudding Show; Society of Fellows.

Society of Fellows

As a former honorary fellow once put it, "to be in the Society of Fellows is to be at the center of intelligence of the center of intelligence. It's the best club in the world." Created by President A. Lawrence Lowell in 1932, the society gives exceptional young scholars the opportunity to pursue study in any department of the University, free from formal requirements. For a junior fellow, there is just one firm obligation: to show up on Monday evenings for an elegant dinner at the society's Eliot House rooms.

Eight to ten junior fellows are generally elected each year. As with other prestigious fellowships, one does not apply but must be nominated, preferably by someone knowledgeable about the candidate's academic work. Each three-year fellowship provides a liberal stipend and unlimited access to courses, seminars, laboratories, libraries, and athletic facilities. Junior fellows are selected for their resourcefulness, initiative, and intellectual curiosity, and because their work holds exceptional promise.

The society elects scholars from all over the world. Fellowship holders typically range from physicists, mathematicians, and biologists to classicists, historians, literary scholars, and social scientists. Most of the thirteen senior fellows, all distinguished faculty members, are regulars at the Monday dinners. Guests are often invited. In addition to its Eliot House rooms, the society maintains a modest Greek Revival house at 78 Mount Auburn Street. Some of the junior fellows—mostly those in the humanities and social sciences, who do not require laboratory space—have small offices there.

Modeled on the Prize Fellows program of Trinity College, Cambridge, the Society of Fellows was formed by Lowell only months before he retired as president. Potential sources of funding proved elusive, but at length Lowell announced that an anonymous donor had pledged $1.5 million for the new venture. Not until after his death eleven years later was it learned that Lowell had given the money himself, and that he had bequeathed $800,000 as added endowment in memory of his wife, Anna Parker Lowell.

Notable writers, scientists, and academics who were once junior fellows include Arthur M. Schlesinger Jr., Richard Wilbur, E. O. Wilson, Noam Chomsky, and Henry Rosovsky. Members of the society can count more than seventeen Nobel Prizes among them.

Related entries: Alpha-Iota of Massachusetts; Nobel Laureates; Signet Society.

Soldiers Field

Harvard's playing fields, its massive football stadium, and most of its principal indoor athletics facilities are located at Soldiers Field, a 90-acre tract on the Allston-Boston side of the Charles River. Dedicated in 1890, the grounds memorialize six young Harvard men who died in the Civil War. The names of these "friends, comrades, kinsmen" of Major Henry Lee Higginson, class of 1855—the donor whose gift of undeveloped land helped create the playing fields—are engraved on a marble shaft near Harvard Stadium. In addition to football, baseball, and softball fields, the Soldiers Field complex includes:

- Beren Tennis Center, with 18 outdoor courts and spectator seating for 500, and the Palmer Dixon Tennis Courts, with three indoor courts and spectator seating for 350.
- Blodgett Pool, a 50-meter Olympic-size swimming and diving facility that seats 1,200.
- Bright Hockey Center, an ice rink seating 2,800.

- Dillon Field House, with dressing rooms, medical rooms, and a second-floor lounge.
- Gordon Indoor Track and Tennis Center, with a 220-yard banked polyurethane track enclosing five indoor tennis courts, and seating 1,200 for track meets.
- Jordan Field, an artificial-turf area for lacrosse and field hockey, with seating for 900.
- Lavietes Pavilion, with an intercollegiate basketball court, a seating capacity of 2,050, and an astroturf covering that allows indoor practice for intercollegiate field sports.
- McCurdy Track, a 400-meter outdoor track with field event areas.
- Murr Athletic Center, with sixteen international-size squash courts and six indoor tennis courts. The squash courts, with seating for 1,000, are named for John M. Barnaby II '32, a long-serving and highly successful varsity squash and tennis coach.

Murr Center also houses a strength and conditioning facility and offices for athletics department administrators. On the ground floor is the Lee Family Hall of Athletic History, with free-standing displays of equipment and artifacts and a mural-like timeline tracing some of the highlights of Harvard's long athletic tradition.

The Soldiers Field complex is dominated by century-old Harvard Stadium, built in 1903 and renovated in 1984. The nation's oldest football stadium, it is also the world's first massive ferroconcrete structure. Its design, combining elements of Roman stadia and Greek amphitheaters, was overseen by the New York architect Charles McKim, whose firm would later plan the nearby Business School campus; the construction plans were executed by faculty members from Harvard's engineering department. The structure was built in just four and a half months, at a cost of $310,000. Almost a third of that amount was donated by the class of 1879 as a twenty-fifth reunion gift. The stadium originally seated 22,000, but the additions of a colonnade in 1910 and of steel stands at the north end in 1929 raised its capacity to 57,750. The steel stands were removed in 1951; the stadium's seating capacity is now officially listed as 31,000.

The stadium has been the site of more than 600 Harvard football games. Professional football, high school football, track and field, soccer, rugby, lacrosse, field hockey, and even (in the early days) ice hockey have also been played there. It is used almost year-round by rowers, skiers, and other athletes who train by "running stadiums" up and down its concrete aisles. On occasion, the stadium has served as an amphitheater for large-scale theatrical productions, including the *Agamemnon* of Aeschylus (1906); Schiller's *Maid of Orleans* (1909); the *Iphigenia* and *Trojan Women* of Euripides and Wagner's *Siegfried* (1915); and the *Bacchae* of Euripides (1982). It also provided the setting for a Harvard 350th anniversary extravaganza in 1986, with narration by the television journalist Walter Cronkite, music by the Harvard University Band and the Boston Pops Orchestra, historical tableaux, stand-up comedy, and a final fusillade of fireworks.

Close to Soldiers Field are Ohiri Field, for men's and women's intercollegiate soccer; Business School tennis courts; Shad Gymnasium, open only to Business School students and faculty members; and two venerable boathouses, Newell (1900) and Weld (1907).

Related entries: Architecture; Athletics; Fundraising; Portrait Collection (Higginson); Songs and Marches; Statues and Monuments. *Related Website:* gocrimson.ocsn.com/facilities/rec_facilities.html.

Songs and Marches

The literature of published Harvard songs and instrumental pieces is vast and various. The nineteenth century saw an outpouring of Harvard marches, Harvard grand waltzes, a "Harvard Quick Step," and a "Crimson Schottische." But much of the canon dates from the golden age of Harvard song-and-march writing, which dawned in the 1890s and ended just after World War I. This era produced most of the great football songs that form the core of the Harvard University Band's repertoire—"Up the Street," "Our Director," "Ten Thousand Men of Harvard," and many others, as well as dozens of titles that are now forgotten.

There's much more to Harvard music than football songs, of course: anthems and hymns for ceremonial occasions, and a curious trove of what used to be called "variety" songs. Of the ceremonial songs, "Fair Harvard" is the best known. It is traditionally sung or played at academic exercises, at the alumni meeting on the afternoon of Commencement Day, after football games, and sometimes at memorial services. At the Commencement exercises, the entrance of Harvard's president is heralded by a fanfare composed by Walter Piston '24, then the Naumburg Professor of Music; the "Harvard Hymn" of an earlier faculty member, John Knowles Paine, ends the exercises. Though not composed for Harvard occasions, Gounod's "Domine salvum fac" ("Lord, make safe our president"); the uplifting "Alleluia" of Randall Thompson '20; William Tans'ur's "Give ear, my children, to my law"; and the centuries-old German student song "Gaudeamus Igitur" are other Commencement standards. Tans'ur's recasting of the Seventy-eighth Psalm, which dates from about 1755, has been sung at Harvard at least since 1806. The familiar "Auld Lang Syne" traditionally closes out the luncheon following Harvard's Phi Beta Kappa Literary Exercises.

Other compositions intended for ceremonial use are now unsung, in both senses of the word. High-minded examples include four anthems by M. A. DeWolfe Howe, class of 1887: "The Answer of the Stars," honoring Harvard's World War I soldiers and set to music by Frederick Converse, class of 1893; "Harvard, Sovereign Mother," originally set to one of Elgar's "Pomp and Circumstance" marches but refitted to music by Converse; "The Shores of Harvard," to music by Gustav Holst; and "Fathers and Sons," performed at one of the World War II Commencements and set to a theme from Saint-Saëns' C minor piano concerto. Somewhat lighter in tone, but just as forgotten, is "Old Harvard," written for the Glee Club in 1922 by David T. W. McCord '21 and set to the "Brabançonne," the national anthem of Belgium.

Under the heading of ephemera come such curiosities as Ethel Hill Nye's "My Love's a Harvard Boy"; C. Lawrence Smith Jr.'s "A Toast to Harvard"; and "Long May She Live, Our Harvard Fair!" and "Johnny Harvard" (authors unknown). The last enjoyed popularity in the earlier part of the twentieth century; it begins, "Oh, here's to Johnny Harvard! fill him up a full glass," and ends,

"Drink, drink, drink . . . drink, drink, drink, Yes, drink." In a series of letters to the *Alumni Bulletin* written after Prohibition was instituted in 1919, "Johnny Harvard" was indignantly attacked by Delcevare King, class of 1895, as subverting the law of the land.

Harvard's football songs are its musical strong suit. An early specimen of the genre is "Foot-Ball Song 1891," author or authors unknown. Hailing Harvard's 12–6 triumph over Yale in 1890, which ended a fourteen-year string of Eli victories, it concluded with a paean to captain Arthur Cumnock, class of 1891:

All honor to old Arthur Cumnock,
He has bravely subdued our fears,
The Championship is in Cambridge,
And, by Zeus, it shall stay there for years.

Harvard did not defeat Yale again until 1898. By then, however, the first of the great fight songs had been published and enthusiastically adopted by students, football crowds, and the Glee Club. "Up the Street," with music by Robert G. Morse, class of 1896, and words by W. L. W. Field, class of 1898, and "Our Director" (music by Jean M. Missud, words by F. E. Bigelow) were both copyrighted in 1895. "Veritas March" (words and music by John Densmore '04) came out in 1903, the year Harvard Stadium was built. The advent of the stadium was a stimulus to such young song writers as Densmore, Richmond Fletcher '08, and S. B. Steel and R. G. Williams '11. Fletcher wrote the music for "Soldiers Field" (1905), and words and music for "Gridiron King" (1906); Steel and Williams wrote "Harvardiana" (1909). John Reed '10 wrote the lyrics for "Score" (1909), with its neat final couplet, "It might be worse, boys, call up a hearse for / poor old Yale." The last of the classic marches, "Ten Thousand Men of Harvard" (1914), was the work of Alfred Putnam '18 and Murray Taylor '18. With the exception of "Our Director," all the great fight songs of the golden age were written by undergraduates. Putnam and Taylor were freshmen when their march was published.

No longer played, but reflective of their time, are such early songs and marches as "Glory for the Crimson," "Harvard's Best,"

"Harvard's Day," "Harvard Every Day," "Harvard Festival March,"
"Harvard Holds Sway," "Harvard's Song of Victory," "Harvard
Spirit," "Harvard's Victory," "The Harvard Yard," "Men of Harvard," "Onward to the Goal," "The Stadium," "The Sun of Victory," "The Union," and "Victory."

Such a plethora of songs and marches from the pre-World War I
era must have been daunting to composers of more recent times.
Only three later songs found secure places in Harvard's musical
canon. One is "Wintergreen," adapted from the opening chorus
of George and Ira Gershwin's 1931 hit *Of Thee I Sing* but inlaid
with snatches of "Soldiers Field" and "Our Director." A generation
later came Richmond Fletcher's nautically inspired "Yo-Ho," introduced by the Harvard Band in the 1950s. The third addition was
an early satirical song of the devilishly clever Thomas A. Lehrer
'47, written in 1945 and adopted by the band a decade later. "Fight
Fiercely, Harvard" was, as Lehrer put it, a genteel corrective to "un-
couth, even violent" fight songs:

Fight fiercely, Harvard! Fight, fight, fight!
Demonstrate to them our skill.
Albeit they possess the might,
Nonetheless *we* have the will.
How we will celebrate our victory:
We shall invite the whole team up for tea! (How jolly!)
Hurl that spheroid down the field, and fight, fight, fight!

Fight fiercely, Harvard! Fight, fight, fight!
Impress them with our prowess, do.
Oh, fellows, do not let the Crimson down;
Be of stout heart and true.
Come on, chaps, fight for Harvard's glorious name!
Won't it be peachy if we win the game? (Oh, goody!)
Let's try not to injure them, but fight, fight, fight!

Harvard's fight songs are preserved in a number of song books
issued since 1866, but the University Band, founded in 1919, plays
the most vital caretaking role. Famous for its huge bass drum,

its manic scrambles during halftime shows, and for its plangent sound, the Band is a fixture at Harvard football games, breaking into full-throated song from time to time. Its signature offering is a dog-Latin adaptation of "Ten Thousand Men of Harvard":

> Illegitimum non carborundum, domine salvum fac!
> Illegitimum non carborundum, domine salvum fac!
> Gaudeamus igitur! Veritas non sequitur!
> Illegitimum non carborundum, ipso facto!

The band also plays at hockey and basketball contests and at University, community, and charity events. Before the Commencement exercises, its crimson-jacketed players perform for almost an hour while audience members are seated. The band's medleys of Harvard songs and marches, arranged by Leroy Anderson '29—a onetime band trombonist whose arrangements are still staples of the Boston Pops Orchestra's repertoire—remain perennial favorites.

Harvard's contributions to the literature of collegiate music, incidentally, go beyond its own gates. The authorship of Yale's "Whiffenpoof Song" has been attributed to Guy Hamilton Scull, Harvard class of 1898. Almost every word of the chorus is lifted from Rudyard Kipling's "Gentlemen-Rankers," but if Scull had a hand in changing "gentlemen-rankers out on the spree" to "gentleman songsters off on a spree," it was all in a day's work for a Harvard man.

Related entries: "Fair Harvard"; Commencement; Music; Soldiers Field.
Related Website: hcs.harvard.edu/~hub/songs.

Statues and Monuments

John Harvard gets the lion's share of attention, but the Brunswick Lion is also worth a look—as are the Rhinos, the Dragon, the Onion, the Reclining Figure, and other examples of Harvard statuary.

Daniel Chester French's statue of an idealized John Harvard, cast in 1884, is one of three life-sized seated bronze figures in

or near Harvard Yard. The others depict the abolitionist senator
Charles Sumner and the poet, essayist, and philosopher Ralph
Waldo Emerson. Anne Whitney's statue of Sumner (class of 1830,
LL.B. 1835, LL.D. 1859) stands on a triangular island just north of
Harvard Square. When a commission was formed to honor Sumner after his death in 1874, Whitney anonymously submitted a
model for the statue, but was disqualified when commission members found that she was a woman. Having been a strong political
supporter of Sumner, Whitney did not give up. She finished the
statue in her eightieth year, and it was unveiled in 1902. Frank
Duveneck's statue of Emerson (class of 1821, LL.D. 1866) was completed at about the same time. It was installed on the ground floor
of the newly constructed Emerson Hall in 1906.

The Lion of Brunswick lords it over the outdoor courtyard of
Adolphus Busch Hall (formerly the Germanic Museum, now the
home of the de Gunzburg Center for European Studies). Given to
Harvard by the Duchy of Brunswick in 1913, the statue is a copy of
a bronze erected in 1166 at Duke Henry the Lion's castle. Above the
lion, atop the west end of what was originally the museum's Renaissance Hall, is a figure—half man, half horse—thought to represent Chiron, teacher of Achilles. The sculptor was Roger Noble
Burnham, class of 1899, a Harvard instructor in modeling at the
time Adolphus Busch Hall was constructed.

In Memorial Hall, on the other side of Kirkland Street, are four
heroically scaled standing figures, carved in marble in the mid-
nineteenth century. William Wetmore Story's Josiah Quincy and
Thomas Crawford's James Otis flank the Sanders Theatre stage.
Randolph Rogers's John Adams and Richard Saltonstall Greenough's Governor Winthrop stand at the east end of what is now the
Annenberg Hall dining room. The Quincy statue was acquired
through a subscription in 1878; the others were commissioned for a
Gothic chapel at Cambridge's Mount Auburn Cemetery. When
the chapel was remodeled, the statues were relegated to the cemetery office; there they remained until 1935, when Mount Auburn
gave them to Harvard. A fourth Mount Auburn statue, Justice
Story, stands in the Law School's Langdell Hall.

No Harvard statues are more massive in scale than the two life-sized bronze rhinoceroses—dubbed Victoria and Bessie—guarding the main entrance to the Biological Laboratories, north of the Yard. They were sculpted by Katharine Lane Weems, who also created the fine reliefs of birds, animals, and fish along the building's facades. Victoria and Bessie were hoisted off their platforms and put into temporary storage when laboratory renovations began in 2003.

More recent sculptures have tended toward the abstract. Richard Lippold's "World Tree," a 27-foot-high stainless steel pylon, is the centerpiece of the quadrangle of Harkness Commons and Graduate Center, adjoining the Law School. Installed in 1950, it was described by its maker as a "transparent sphere" symbolizing the inner tensions of its time. Irreverent Harkness residents called it "the jungle gym" or "the clothes rack," placed false birds on its branches, and planted ball bearings under it as a fertility rite.

At the sunken entrance to Harvard Yard's Nathan M. Pusey Library is the so-called "Onion" (1965), a wrought-iron stabile by Alexander Calder, AR.D. '66. Close by, in front of Lamont Library, is Henry Moore's "Four Piece Reclining Figure" (1972), a luminous bronze that stands six feet high. The Fogg Museum has four smaller works by Moore, one of the greatest of twentieth-century sculptors.

Another striking contemporary work is Dimitri Hadzi's 24-foot-high "Omphalos," erected in 1985 near the Harvard Square subway kiosk. Shaped to resemble a signpost, it is a reminder that the Square is a geographic and intellectual crossroads; Hadzi's title (Greek for navel) is a riff on Oliver Wendell Holmes's description of Boston as the hub of the universe.

The Chinese dragon stele in Harvard Yard, between Widener Library and Boylston Hall, is a monument of a different sort. The gift of alumni in China, it was presented during the 1936 Tercentenary celebration in recognition of Harvard's longstanding ties with China. Part dragon, symbol of power and happiness, and part tortoise, symbol of endurance and long life, the statue was carved during the Ch'ing dynasty (1796–1821) and sent by the emperor to a provincial governor as a mark of imperial favor. A long inscription in classic Chinese characters states that "during the past thirty years, nearly a thousand students from the Republic of China have attended Harvard University and have been privileged to receive instruction and guidance."

On the Allston side of the Charles River, a marble shaft memorializes six fallen Union soldiers for whom Soldiers Field is named. Other memorials include a number of tablets and a relief, affixed to a wall of Harvard Stadium, that shows the crouching figure of Percy Haughton, class of 1899, Harvard's all but unbeatable coach of football from 1908 to 1916. Across North Harvard Street, a plaque on an unhewn boulder records the naming of the varsity soccer and lacrosse field in memory of Christian L. Ohiri '64, a star soccer player who died of leukemia at 27.

Related entries: Adolphus Busch Hall; Cambridge/Boston; John Harvard—and His Statue; Memorial Church; Memorial Hall; Portrait Collection; Sanders Theatre; Soldiers Field.

T

The tower of Memorial Hall, consumed by flames in 1956, was
restored in 1999. The project cost was $4 million.

Theatre Collection

Largely through the efforts of Professor George Pierce Baker, who conducted a pioneer course in playwriting, the University Library established a theater collection in the early years of the twentieth century. Alumni and others donated material, and the holdings grew year by year. They came to include not just books and manuscripts but also playbills, posters, photos, portraits, clippings, tickets, contracts, letters, designs, model sets, figurines, medallions, audio recordings, and films and videotapes. The term "theater" was interpreted broadly: it took in all of the many forms of popular stage entertainment, including vaudeville and the music hall, minstrelsy, the circus, pantomime, puppetry, toy theater, and magic shows. At last count, the Theatre Collection contained more than five and a half million items. Among its major sections are:

- The Robert Gould Shaw collection on theater history.
- The Evert Jansen Wendell theater collection.
- The Howard D. Rothschild collection on the Ballets Russes of Serge Diaghilev.
- The George Brinton Beal circus collection.
- The Marian Hannah Winter collection on popular entertainment.

Collections of personal papers include those of Maude Adams, Robert Anderson '39, George Pierce Baker, class of 1887, George Balanchine, Samuel Beckett, Sarah Bernhardt, Edwin Booth, John Mason Brown '23, David Garrick, Eugene O'Neill, Neil Simon, Cornelia Otis Skinner, Wole Soyinka, LITT.D. '93, Tennessee Williams, LITT.D. '82, and Robert Wilson. The collection also includes the sketches and papers of many set designers, among them Max Reinhardt, Jo Mielziner, Robert Edmond Jones '10, Lee Simonson '09, and Donald Oenslager '23. Their drawings and models, along with theater posters, photographs, and manuscripts from many eras, are regularly displayed in showcases inside and outside the Theatre Collection, on the upper level of the Nathan M. Pusey Library.

Related entries: Arts; American Repertory Theatre; Extinct Harvard; Hasty Pudding Show; Libraries. *Related Website:* hcl.harvard.edu/houghton/ departments/htc/theatre.html.

Towers

The distinctive spires of Harvard's skyline—best seen from the parkway on the far side of the Charles River—help define and identify the University, setting it off from the surrounding cityscape. Except for the tower of Memorial Hall (1878, rebuilt in 1999) and the campanile of St. Paul's Church (1915), the other half-dozen spires rose between 1926 and 1932, when the University's physical plant was expanding at an unprecedented clip.

The 100-foot tower of the Business School's Baker Library—a focal point for the school's new campus on the south side of the Charles—was the first to rise. Planned by McKim, Mead & White, the campus had its groundbreaking in June 1925 and was virtually finished by October 1926. The spires of four new residential houses across the river, completed in 1930–31, appeared next. The dominating tower was and is that of Lowell House, 150 feet high and reminiscent of Philadelphia's Independence Hall. The tower affords a sweeping view of the river; hung in its belfry is a *zvon,* or Russian chime, of seventeen bells, the largest weighing 13 tons. In the tower's music room is a piano that had to be hoisted there with a crane. To the left of the Lowell House tower, as viewed from across the river, is the exquisite Georgian clock tower of Eliot House. At right is the gold-domed tower of Adams House, and beyond it the mitred spire of the Dunster House clock tower, modeled on Christopher Wren's Tom Tower at Christ Church, Oxford.

The bell tower of Memorial Church (1932) was the last steeple added to Harvard's skyline. Inspired by Charles Bulfinch's 1806 restoration of the tower of Boston's Old North Church, it rises 172 feet; the shaft of its gilded weathervane adds another 25 feet. At 197 feet, this tower is seven feet taller than that of Memorial Hall. The church's eight-foot weathervane—which is replated with about $3,000 worth of gold leaf every dozen years or so—is shaped like a medieval pennant. Atop it is a crown with two openings in the form of Greek crosses. Since the church and the houses were planned by the same firm, Coolidge, Shepley, Bulfinch, and Abbott, their towers are in close architectural harmony.

By no means as high, but not to be overlooked in the panorama of Harvard towers, is the Yard's only other spire: the graceful cupola of Harvard Hall (1766). For almost a century, until Memorial Hall was built, this was the College's loftiest spire. Another notable tower is the soaring campanile of St. Paul's Church near Adams House. Not a University building, but planned by a Harvard graduate, St. Paul's is the masterwork of a little-known architect, Edward T. P. Graham '00. Adept in the Italianate style, Graham was apparently influenced by the church of San Zeno Maggiore in Verona. After years of disrepair, the clocks and bells in the tower of St. Paul's were restored and again toll quarter-hours and the angelus. As a gloss on this Roman Catholic church's presence in a largely Protestant community, the bells bear an inscription from the Book of Isaiah: *Vox clamatis in deserto* (A voice crying in the wilderness).

A towering event in the annals of Harvard spires occurred in 1999, when a crane lowered a three-and-a-half-ton copper-clad roof deck and balustrade onto the rebuilt spire of Memorial Hall. The addition of slatework and copper dormers and finials topped off a $4 million restoration project. The splendid Victorian building had been left headless when its tower was destroyed by fire in 1956.

Related entries: Architecture; Bells; Fire; Gold Coast; Harvard Hall; Memorial Church; Memorial Hall.

Trademark Protection and Technology Transfer

The Harvard Brewing Company was founded in 1898; the moribund company and its Harvard Lager brand of beer were revived a century later, to the annoyance of Harvard University's Office for

Technology and Trademark Licensing. Another foamy enterprise, John Harvard's Brew House, is a chain of restaurants in five states and the District of Columbia. The Harvard bedframe has long been a popular item in furniture stores. Harvard brick is a masonry standard; Harvard style is a form of notation for citing references in scholarly books and journals. Harvard beets are described in Condénet's "Epicurious" Website as "a century-old dish . . . probably named for its color (a resemblance to Harvard crimson); it seems to have no other connection with the school." Cambridge grocery stores once sold Harvard oranges. A Japanese company markets a line of Harvard menswear. Obviously there's some magic in the Harvard name.

Part of the mission of the Office for Technology and Trademark Licensing (OTTL) is to guard against efforts to appropriate the University's name or insignia for unauthorized purposes. Basing its activities on the principle that Harvard University is "one of the most widely known and respected trademarks of any kind," OTTL's trademark program monitors and polices uses and misuses of "Harvard," "Harvard University," "Crimson," "H," the "Ve ri tas" shield, and other worldwide trademark registrations owned by the University.

Most unauthorized third-party uses are in the educational field, and the trademark program's range of operations is worldwide. Recent examples include the program's successful shutdown of a "Harvard International University" in Indonesia, a "Harvard Business College" in South Africa, and a "Harvard Language School" in China. Though the majority of the policing involves educational institutes, the program's staff is alert to other forms of commercialization. The threat of legal action is usually enough to persuade abusers to cease and desist. The office also controls the use of Harvard's name by licensing "traditional insignia items" (apparel, stationery, toys, and the like), thus allowing the University to realize a share of the economic value produced by the sale of such goods. Harvard receives royalties on those sales in addition to licensing fees. Income over and above the cost of the trademark program itself is transferred to a fund that supports undergraduate financial aid.

The financial manipulations of Viktor Kozeny '85 may have constituted the most spectacular violation of the trademark program's guidelines for the proper and ethical use of the Harvard name. In the 1990s, the young Czech émigré financier created a company called Harvard Industrial Holdings as part of an extravagant investment scheme. He amassed a fortune, but thousands of his countrymen—as well as some American institutions—lost money when Kozeny's "Harvard" investment funds fizzled. "The Pirate of Prague" retreated to his homes in Aspen, Colorado, and the Bahamas, where he was said to enjoy a sumptuous exile. Facing numerous lawsuits and fraud charges brought by Czech and American authorities, Kozeny was expected to be tried in absentia. In October 2003 he was charged by the district attorney of Manhattan with fifteen counts of first-degree grand larceny and two counts of first-degree criminal possession of stolen property; other charges were reportedly pending.

The OTTL also oversees technology transfer. The office helps patent Harvard-derived inventions, technologies, and materials, and licenses them to private industry for the development of such products as pharmaceutical drugs, medical devices, and synthetics for research use. OTTL promotes collaborative undertakings: its Website invites inquiries about corporate partnerships, noting that

> Harvard University currently has over 300 technologies available for licensing in areas ranging from drug discovery to optoelectronics. Harvard scientists report over 120 new inventions per year, and the University typically files over 60 new U.S. patent applications in the same period . . . In a typical fiscal year, Harvard licenses over 75 inventions and receives over $15 million in royalty income. Over 35 companies have started up around technologies licensed from Harvard.

The Website includes a listing of technologies that are available for licensing. In general, inventions and technical innovations created at Harvard become the intellectual property of the University. When a faculty member or other researcher makes a discovery that appears to be patentable, OTTL evaluates it to determine whether or not to seek a patent on Harvard's behalf. Licensing arrangements vary; the University sometimes takes equity in a company as part of a deal.

Licensing revenue constitutes an increasingly significant income stream for the University. In one recent year, royalties and fees from technology licensing alone came to $24.3 million. In the same year, OTTL had a budget of about $1.1 million, exclusive of legal expenses, which added another $4.2 million in overhead.

Related entry: Harvard Elsewhere. *Related Website:* www.techtransfer.harvard.edu.

Tuition

The cost of tuition is a variable and volatile subject. The dollar amount differs with each Harvard faculty, but any announcement of a tuition increase is apt to elicit criticism of the timing and steepness of the hike. At the undergraduate level, the four-year bill for a "paying guest"—admissions office parlance for a student who is sufficiently well fixed to pay full tuition—is close to whopping by most people's standards. A T-shirt selling in Cambridge bears the Harvard shield and the legend, "This shirt cost my parents and me $170,000." True, the majority of College and graduate and professional school students do receive generous financial aid. That said, a Harvard education remains indisputably pricy, and it gets pricier every year.

Until the 1950s, tuition increases were few and far between. The College tuition went from $104 a year to $150 just before Charles William Eliot's presidency began in 1869. Eliot fought off attempts to raise it again, arguing that any increase would shrink the proportion of public school students applying to Harvard. Tuition was still $150 when Eliot retired in 1909. His successor, A. Lawrence Lowell, saw the necessity of raising tuition to meet rising costs. When Lowell stepped down in 1933, the tab had reached $400. James B. Conant followed Lowell; when he left office in 1953, tuition had gone up to $600. Nathan M. Pusey, succeeding Conant, was the first president to endorse annual increases. By 1956, tuition had been bumped up to $1,000 a year. A decade later, Pusey cautiously predicted that the level could reach $4,000 by 1988. The actual level in that year was $12,015. Compounding means that annual increases add up. Since 1988, tuition has more than doubled, though median family income has risen less sharply (about 70 percent). College tuition for the academic year 2003–04 was $26,066; with fees and room and board charges added on, the full package came to $40,450.

Even so, one can argue that a Harvard education, though far from cheap, is still something of a bargain. Studies suggest that when the elements that go into the so-called maintenance overhead—faculty salaries, scholarships, libraries, scientific laboratories, residential housing, classroom technology, athletic and health care facilities—are factored in, students pay much less than the actual cost of the education they get. One might also add, as Thomas Mortenson did in the *Postsecondary Education Opportunity* newsletter, "About the only thing more expensive than going to college is not going to college."

Still, there are other issues. Why have tuition rates been allowed to rise so rapidly in recent years, compared with inflation and the indexed prices of other goods and services? Officials at Harvard and elsewhere emphasize that tuition increases are always coupled with increases in scholarship funds. Moreover, the rate of tuition hikes at Harvard and other institutions has slowed; instead of the 6 or 7 percent annual increases of previous decades, Harvard has averaged 4 or 5 percent in recent years.

But high tuition levels look like a permanent fixture. Some critics continue to call on Harvard to draw down greater amounts from its large endowment to stabilize or reduce tuition fees. Arguments have been marshaled on both sides, and the debate is ongoing.

Related entries: Admissions; Endowment.

U

Harvard goes underground: excavations for Widener Library took
place in the spring of 1913. Initial plans called for the storage
of about 300,000 books in subterranean shelf space.

UHS

For undergraduates, graduate students, faculty, staff, and retirees, medical services are at hand around the clock at the University Health Services (UHS). Occupying five floors within Holyoke Center, in the heart of Harvard Square, UHS also has clinical facilities at the schools of Business, Law, and Medicine.

UHS consolidates many medical services: urgent care clinics, primary care, pediatrics, laboratories, and a ten-bed hospital. More than a hundred physicians, psychologists, and dentists are on staff, along with an equal number of nurses, technicians, and health assistants. On a busy day, 500 or more patients may receive treatment. More than 30,000 members of the Harvard community (and from several other educational institutions in the area) are covered by Harvard's health services program.

A UHS doctor's day may range from the humdrum to the unusual. Routine checkups often occupy much of it. Given the average age of the patient population, gynecological, birth control, and pregnancy services are in demand. (UHS also supervises an undergraduate program of peer contraceptive counseling.) Specialized services include dentistry, dermatology, mental health, nutrition, opthalmology, orthopedics, physical therapy, and substance abuse counseling.

Extensive travel, and the international ties of many students and faculty, mean that UHS doctors often see patients with exotic diseases or infections contracted abroad. They also treat occasional outbreaks of mass food poisoning or contagious fevers in the houses. The mental health division of UHS is heavily used, especially at exam time. In addition to a full range of psychiatric services, the division offers an array of wellness and fitness programs—from training in the relaxation response to restorative yoga, and from Feldenkrais-Functional Integration to on-site massage therapy and Shiatsu.

Related entry: Life Raft. *Related Website:* www.huhs.harvard.edu.

Underground

There's more to Harvard than meets the eye. Much goes on underground. Most of the University's infrastructure—giant boilers, steam lines, intricate electrical and telephone relays, servomechanisms, and metering instruments—is below ground level. Without complex networks of steam and food tunnels, water mains, and sanitary and storm drainage systems, the daily life of the place would grind to a halt. And what would Harvard be like without the subway line that has linked it to Boston since 1912? As opportunities for aboveground expansion diminish, Harvard burrows downward to create spaces for library and museum collections, academic and administrative offices, classrooms, eating places, and parking. Parts of Harvard's underworld are open only to operating engineers and maintenance workers. Others are in constant use by the University community.

The biggest and busiest underground space isn't Harvard's. It's the cavernous Harvard Square subway station, greatly enlarged in the 1980s. The University's new North Precinct parking garage and a chilled-water plant in the Undergraduate Science Center are the next-largest subterranean spaces. At the other end of the scale would be any of the 300-odd electrical and utility manholes dotted around the environs of Harvard Yard and the more distant Business and Medical school campuses. Somewhere in between come the tunnels. The Cambridge-Allston steam tunnels—largest of a half-dozen separate systems—incorporate some five miles of underground passageways and pipe trenches.

The Harvard Square subway station was renovated as part of a $586 million construction project that extended the northern terminus of the Massachusetts Bay Transit Authority's Red Line from Cambridge through Somerville to Alewife Station. The old station was demolished and replaced by a vast lobby, more than three stories deep, with rounded walls, a large mezzanine area, and merchandising stalls. In addition to subway platforms, the station houses a terminal serving diesel buses and trackless trolleys; the busway boasts a notable stained-glass mural by the late Gyorgy

Kepes, founder and former director of MIT's Center for Advanced Visual Art. Disused platforms of the old subway station can be dimly discerned from Red Line trains running to or from Boston; a stretch of abandoned tunnel leads under Harvard and Brattle squares toward what once was an aboveground car yard. When that yard was relocated as part of the Red Line extension, Harvard acquired the twelve-acre property as a site for the Kennedy School of Government complex.

Back to the nether regions. The capacious North Precinct underground garage is a key piece in an ambitious development plan for the area north of the University Museum. To make way for much-needed science laboratories, administrators opted to expropriate almost 600 surface parking spaces and replace them below ground level. The new garage occupies land where the Cambridge Electron Accelerator, the Harvard Cyclotron, the High Energy Physics Laboratory, and the Palfrey House previously stood. The high-energy physics centers, long obsolete, were demolished; the Greek Revival Palfrey House, built in 1831, will now occupy a site not far from its original location. The North Precinct garage, with space for 730 cars, was designed to serve as a deck supporting new lab buildings.

In cubic volume, Harvard's chilled-water plant in the Science Center's sub-basement is about two-thirds the size of Boston's Symphony Hall. From two rooftop cooling towers, chilled water cascades down to the plant through pipes three feet in diameter; the facility serves the air-conditioning and process-cooling needs of some 70 University buildings in Cambridge. In the summer of 2003 ground was broken behind the Science Center for a 135,000-square-foot Laboratory for Interface Science and Engineering, with facilities for vibration-sensitive research in mesoscale and nanoscale science. Two-thirds of the new building will be underground.

The Radcliffe Quadrangle, the Law School, and the Business School each have tunnel systems for the movement of goods and services. The river houses are joined by a quarter-mile-long service tunnel originally created to deliver food from the central kitchen

on JFK Street. Subterranean Harvard's most picturesque prome-
nades, however, are the tunnels of the Cambridge Steam Distribution System. Largely constructed in the late 1920s, this labyrin-
thine network brings high-pressure steam to about 200 buildings
in Cambridge and Allston. As in President Lowell's day, much of
Harvard relies on steam for space heating and hot water; the larger
kitchens use it for cooking, and laboratories must have it on tap.
Starting from the Blackstone generating plant at Western Avenue
and Memorial Drive, the system's main tunnel leads to the houses
and to Harvard Yard, branching off to the Business School via the
Weeks Bridge. Created before the advent of remote monitoring devices, these tunnels had to allow headroom and working space for
crews inspecting the system's countless pipe joints, pressure gauges,
meters, and shutoff valves. Until 1968, when construction of the
Cambridge Street underpass blocked off the main tunnel as it left
the Yard, it was possible—with a bit of a crawl here and there—to
take a subterranean stroll from the Business School to the Law
School (and almost to the present site of the Northern Precinct
parking garage). A stroller, however, would have emerged mop-
ping his or her brow. Ambient temperature in the tunnels hovers
around 100 degrees, and peaks as high as 140 degrees have been recorded.

Chronic space squeezes have driven the conversion of many
Harvard Yard basements into office, classroom, and storage areas.
A generation ago, the University News Office occupied cramped
quarters in the basement of University Hall; until 1992, its photo
lab was in Weld Hall's basement. The architects of more recent
buildings have not overlooked the potential of below-grade space.
The Science Center's lower level houses computer labs and electrical and machine shops. Pusey Library, with its Map Collection,
Theatre Collection, exhibition areas, University Archives, and faculty offices, is almost wholly underground. Since that library's
completion in 1973, Widener, Pusey, and Lamont libraries have
been linked by underground tunnels.

Related entries: Architecture; Dining Services; Kennedy School of
Government; Maps; Memorial Hall.

University Professors

Most universities have ways of cosseting faculty superstars. Some give them high-flown titles like Distinguished Professor, or Eminent Scholar, and relieve them from teaching obligations and other duties. They thus become intellectual ornaments, occasionally seen from afar at the faculty club or walking to their offices.

Harvard hasn't taken that tack. Its superstars are called University Professors, and almost all of them teach. There are currently about 20 (excluding some with emeritus status), drawn from the schools of Arts and Sciences, Business, Medicine, Law, and Government. Not all University Professors are household names, even in academe, but each is top-of-the-line in his or her field.

A University Professorship brings collegial acclaim and in certain cases an increase in salary. It also permits its holder to work without disciplinary restrictions and "to roam freely about the entire University." In 1935, President James B. Conant used those words in announcing "a new type of professorship." In Conant's view, Harvard had been growing horizontally into "a federation of separate academic entities." As a corrective, he proposed a new and "vertical development," and the new professorships were a key element. Some incumbents might be recruited from outside the University—might even be talented independent scholars attached to no particular institution. These individuals would be encouraged to cross departmental boundaries, and indeed professional boundaries, to amplify their own scholarly careers.

Things have turned out somewhat differently. Instead of a small group of elite scholars in Arts and Sciences, there are University Professors in several schools. Though the first professorships were minimally endowed by University funds, all are now endowed by donors. For the most part, the goal of allowing scholars to work outside conventional disciplines has not been realized. Most University Professors, declining the chance to roam, have stayed within their original fields. "People don't change their projects because they get this title," says political scientist and University Professor Stanley Hoffmann.

Current members of this exclusive cadre include Dr. S. James

Adelstein, who heads the Medical School's Laboratory for Experimental Nuclear Medicine; President Emeritus Derek Bok; molecular biologist Walter Gilbert; humanities professors Stephen Greenblatt (English), Stephen Owen (Chinese literature), Helen Vendler (English), and Christoph Wolff (Music); political scientists Stanley Hoffmann, Samuel Huntington, and Sidney Verba (director of the University Library); mathematician Barry Mazur; economist Dale Jorgenson; Business School professors Robert Merton and Michael Porter; constitutional law professor Frank Michelman; philosopher Hilary Putnam; astronomer Irwin Shapiro; and social scientist William Julius Wilson.

The Villa I Tatti, on the outskirts of Florence, houses
Harvard's Center for Italian Renaissance Studies
and is set off by elegant formal gardens.

Vanserg Hall

If there's a waif among Harvard's 500-odd buildings, this is it. Vanserg Hall, a pink-painted wooden structure between the Biological Laboratories and the Divinity School, has lived on borrowed time for more than half a century. It was built in 1943 as a temporary facility for Radio Research Laboratory scientists working on radar countermeasures; Harvard bought it from the government in 1946. It has since housed a Veterans Administration guidance center, naval ROTC offices, an electronics lab, a dining room for graduate students, a piano-tuning operation, and the offices of various undergraduate organizations. It is currently used as a child care center, for classrooms, and for some of the offices of the Harvard-Yenching Institute, an independent foundation that supports higher education in the humanities and social sciences in East and Southeast Asia.

The building permit for this aging "temporary" structure must still be renewed every two years. Though devoid of interesting architectural features, it was designed by Coolidge, Shepley, Bulfinch & Abbott, the Boston firm that planned the residential houses, the Fogg Art Museum, the Memorial Church, the Biological Laboratories, and many other notable University buildings. And no, the name does not honor a Harvard benefactor called Vanserg. It's an acronym for the hall's postwar users: *V*eterans *A*dministration, *N*aval *S*cience, *E*lectronic *R*esearch, and *G*raduate School.

Related entries: Architecture; ROTC.

Villa I Tatti

A gentle hill in Tuscany, sentinel cypresses and olive groves, a sixteenth-century farmhouse much restored and enlarged, a great library and rooms full of art treasures: this is Harvard's Center for Italian Renaissance Studies at the Villa I Tatti, a short drive from Florence.

Preeminent as a lodestone for research on the Italian Renaissance, I Tatti was once home to the legendary Bernard Berenson, who presented it to Harvard half a century ago. A member of the class of 1887, expatriate, humanist, connoisseur, author, art adviser to the rich and famous, Berenson made himself a supreme authority on Italian Renaissance painting and sculpture, accruing a fortune by authenticating paintings and recommending purchases to people like P. A. Widener and Isabella Stewart Gardner. Berenson settled in Florence in 1900, and when I Tatti was put up for sale in 1907, he went into debt to buy it. He and his wife, Mary, proceeded to rebuild the house, gardens, and library into one of the great residences in Tuscany; later, in the 1930s, he began long and difficult discussions with Harvard about the possibility of conveying the villa as a gift to the University. How could any institution turn down such generosity? But Harvard was concerned that there would not be an adequate endowment to keep up the estate and was uncertain about its ability to maintain autonomy in Benito Mussolini's Italy.

In 1959, the year of Berenson's death, the Harvard Corporation finally accepted Villa I Tatti as one of its few foreign outposts. Under a series of able and aggressive directors, the center quickly fulfilled Berenson's hopes of making it a "retreat for ripe humanists." Today, I Tatti has a range of notable programs. About fifteen scholars from all over the world are in residence each year as fellows. It has been said that no major scholar of the Italian Renaissance has failed to spend time there: nearly 500 men and women have been fellows over the years. They have been joined by a stream of visiting professors, research associates, and independent scholars.

Then there are the libraries themselves. Best known is the Biblioteca Berenson, consolidating Berenson's own collections with large additions of old and new studies and at least 400 periodicals. The Morrill Music Library, which holds manuscripts, books, and recordings, is considered to be Italy's finest reference library for medieval and Renaissance music; the Fototeca is an extraordinary collection of more than 300,000 photographs, many one of a kind.

The villa is a regular setting for conferences on Renaissance topics. One of the most noted was an international gathering convened in 1992 to discuss the life and work of the fifteenth-century ruler, poet, and art patron Lorenzo de'Medici. A majority of the distinguished scholars presenting papers were former I Tatti fellows.

In 2001, the Center sponsored publication of the first volumes in the Villa I Tatti Renaissance Library. This ambitious project aims to make available the major literary, historical, philosophical, and scientific works of the Italian Renaissance—to put the "lost continent of Neo-Latin literature" back on the map, in the words of Professor James Hankins, who edits the series. Published by Harvard University Press, these attractive blue books—sporting Berenson's bee logo on their spines like a tasteful tattoo—present the original Latin texts with an English translation on facing pages, in the manner of the series' more established older cousin, the Loeb Classical Library.

As a recent director put it, the Villa I Tatti is a realization of "that Renaissance dream of the *locus amoenus*," an agreeable retreat where humanist scholars "retire into the peaceful hills to contemplate and discuss the really important things."

Related entries: Harvard Elsewhere; Harvard University Press; Research Centers and Institutes; ZephGreek. *Related Website:* www.itatti.it.

Virtual Harvard

Armed with a Web browser and video player, you can attend a Harvard course or a faculty forum, explore a singular library collection, take in an art exhibition, or rerun the football team's winning touchdown against Princeton. And you can do so from anywhere in the world, at any hour of the day or night. Like the speed of computer chips, the menu of cyber-programs may be destined to double every eighteen months, but these are some that you can download here and now.

• *Courses for credit.* The Extension School sponsors an expanding list of "distance education" courses: many are in computer science, but also included are such offerings as English Romantic Poetry, American Constitutional History, and Introduction to Metaphysics. These wave-of-the-future courses stream videos of lectures and related materials; enrolled students have the option of attending lectures in person or watching them online. Certain courses are available only online. Though enrollment in Harvard College courses is restricted to undergraduates, a steadily growing number—especially in the sciences—have their own instructional Websites.

• *Continuing education.* Most of the graduate and professional schools are actively developing online content and tools. The Business School's wholly owned Harvard Business School Interactive (HBSi) manages custom programs for executives. The Graduate School of Education's "Wide World" courses are tailored for professional teachers and educational administrators. Through online courses, lectures, and "computer-mediated seminars," the Law School's Berkman Center for Internet and Society explores such law-related Internet issues as governance, privacy, intellectual property, antitrust, content control, and electronic commerce. The Medical School's Harvard Medical International (HMI), in conjunction with Ireland's Royal College of Surgeons and Intuition Publishing, has developed an electronic curriculum designed to help surgical residents in Ireland prepare for basic examinations.

• *Collections and exhibits.* An array of Websites gives access to some of the vast holdings of Harvard's libraries and museums. "Daguerreotypes at Harvard," for example, retrieves some of the more than 3,500 plates preserved throughout the University. "Treasures at Risk" samples a few of the books, manuscripts, and scientific instruments too fragile to be put on public display. "Sargent at Harvard" and "Ben Shahn at Harvard" are searchable databases with images and textual information relating to two important American artists; "University Art Museums Collections Online" taps information about 76,000 art works that form more than half of the permanent holdings of the University Art Museums. "Lilacs at the Arnold Arboretum" has everything but the fragrance, including guidance on planting and caring for lilacs in New England gardens. In what may be an augury of the future, the Busch-Reisinger Museum has mounted an Internet-only exhibition—a mixed-media, interactive showing of art works from Germany's Bauhaus school, with digital links to other objects by

Bauhaus artists and craftsmen in the University Art Museums' database.

Harvard@Home, another online innovation, offers the whole nine yards: lectures and faculty forums, public addresses, conferences, Alumni College sessions, and highlights of colorful events punctuating each academic year: Harvard-Yale football, the Hasty Pudding Theatricals' Man and Woman of the Year awards, Commencement exercises. Introduced in 2001, Harvard@Home is a joint venture of the Alumni Association, Faculty of Arts and Sciences, and *Harvard Magazine,* in collaboration with faculty members and visiting lecturers. Its downloadable programs range from 45 minutes to three hours; examples include lectures or forums on "Islam and America," "State of the Global Environment," "Solving Cubic Equations," "Beethoven's Ninth Symphony," and "Virtual Continuity: What Will Be Expected of Libraries in the Next Millennium?" New programs are added on a monthly basis.

The Website "Digital Harvard: A Gateway to Online Educational Resources" (www.digital.harvard.edu) provides a sampling of current digital undertakings across the University.

Related entries: Alumni; Continuing Education; Harvard Magazine; Information Technology. *Related Websites:* athome.harvard.edu; www.artmuseums.harvard.edu; www.extension.harvard.edu/DistanceEd.

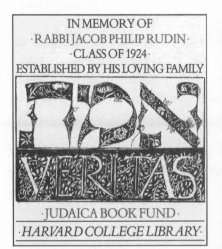

IN MEMORY OF
·RABBI JACOB PHILIP RUDIN·
·CLASS OF 1924·
ESTABLISHED BY HIS LOVING FAMILY

·JUDAICA BOOK FUND·
·HARVARD COLLEGE LIBRARY·

HARVARD COLLEGE LIBRARY

IN MEMORY OF
PERMELIA E. CHENEY HERSEY
1848   1926
THE GIFT OF HER SON
FRANK WILSON CHENEY HERSEY
CLASS OF 1899
FOR RECENT BOOKS IN BRITISH AND AMERICAN LITERATURE

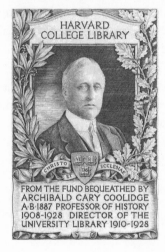

HARVARD
COLLEGE LIBRARY

FROM THE FUND BEQUEATHED BY
ARCHIBALD CARY COOLIDGE
A·B·1887 PROFESSOR OF HISTORY
1908-1928 DIRECTOR OF THE
UNIVERSITY LIBRARY 1910-1928

PATRICK GRANT II

IN MEMORY OF

CLASS OF 1908

HARVARD COLLEGE LIBRARY

THE GIFT OF HIS WIFE
MARIE·DISSTON·GRANT
1886 1927

W

Widener Library's great variety of bookplates testifies to
the generosity of many generations of bibliophiles.

Wadsworth House

After Massachusetts Hall, Wadsworth House is the second oldest Harvard building still standing. It's the Yard's only wooden structure, and the only one not enclosed by the Memorial Fence. The main part was completed in 1727, when the house became the residence of the College's newly elected president, Benjamin Wadsworth. Eight of Wadsworth's successors lived there until 1849, when president-elect Jared Sparks chose to continue to live in his own house on Quincy Street. A new President's House was built on lower Quincy Street in 1860.

Ralph Waldo Emerson, class of 1821, boarded in Wadsworth House as an undergraduate; as a new assistant professor of history, Henry Adams, class of 1858, lodged there fifty years later. The College preachers had offices there in the 1880s. Today the house provides office space for the University Marshal, the director of the University Library, and a few senior faculty members.

Gambrel-roofed, with five third-floor dormers, and painted in a distinctive mustard color, Wadsworth House is considered a representative gem of Early Georgian domestic styling. Once it stood serenely on the edge of the Yard, with a garden and courtyard in front of it and an apple orchard in the rear. When Massachusetts Avenue was widened in 1912, the house lost its front yard, wooden fencing, and eighteenth-century gateposts. Now it survives in the heart of Harvard Square, gracing a principal entrance to the Yard from Massachusetts Avenue and the Red Line subway stop. Whether or not they pause to savor it, pedestrians can get a fine view of the house's splendid façade from front and side.

Related entries: Architecture; Quincy Street; the Yard.

Warren Museum

The strangest of Harvard's collections is the Warren Anatomical Museum, named for a prominent nineteenth-century surgeon whose contributions to its holdings comprised about a thousand curious specimens, among them his own skeleton. The museum—

which once filled the top floors of the Medical School's Building A and was regarded as the "crown" of the school's quadrangle—contains an estimated 13,000 items. Most are in storage, but a portion of the collection is displayed at the Countway Library of Medicine in the Longwood Medical Area.

Dr. John Collins Warren (1778–1856) was the son of Dr. John Warren, one of the Medical School's founders. He began collecting unusual anatomical and pathological specimens as early as 1799; he later helped plan Harvard's first gymnasium and took part in the first ether-assisted operation, performed at Massachusetts General Hospital in 1846. Resigning his Medical School professorship in 1847, Dr. Warren conveyed most of his collection to the school, with a $5,000 endowment to help care for it. Among its holdings are

- The glass inhaler used by Dr. W. T. G. Morton in the famous ether operation.
- The microscope collection of Dr. Oliver Wendell Holmes.
- The elaborately tattooed skin of a Boston sailor.
- A bisected specimen of an infant, preserved in formalin.
- A stuffed specimen of a two-headed calf.
- The skull collection of Dr. Johann Kaspar Spurzheim, the co-founder of phrenology.
- A collection of Peruvian skulls.
- The "Crowbar Skull" of Phineas Gage.

Gage, a Vermont construction foreman, was working for the Rutland & Burlington Railroad in 1848 when a powder charge prematurely exploded, blasting an iron bar through his head. The thirteen-pound tamping iron tore directly through Gage's frontal lobes, but he remained conscious and survived until 1860. Though the accident produced a marked personality change—he became "fitful, irreverent, and grossly profane, showing little deference for his fellows"—it made Gage one of the great medical curiosities of his time. Five years after his death, his mother was persuaded to donate his skull (and the tamping iron) to the Warren Museum. The Crowbar Skull remains its most notable exhibit.

Many of the museum's organs and artifacts were apparently lost or stolen when the collection was dismantled and moved to the Countway Library in the 1970s. The samples displayed in the library's fifth-floor Warren Museum Exhibition Gallery are on view from nine to five on weekdays. The gallery is open to the public without charge.

Dr. Warren's skeleton reposes in a closet lined with cherrywood. Under the terms of the doctor's will, the closet is opened for private inspection once a year.

Related entries: Medical School; Science Museums. *Related Website:* www.countway.med.harvard.edu/warren.

WHRB

Harvard Radio began in 1940 as the closed-circuit Crimson Network (WHCN), formed by students interested in the technical challenge of radio and financed with funding from the *Harvard Crimson.* The staff and location were separate from the *Crimson,* but the books were evidently in the paper's possession. Three years later Harvard's pioneer broadcasters broke with the *Crimson* and achieved independence as WHRV (Harvard Radio Voice). In its earliest days, the station broadcast at 550 kilocycles AM through electrical wiring in the houses and the Yard. It became WHRB (for Broadcasting) in 1951, and in 1957 added open-channel FM; AM was eliminated in 1973. Today the station is heard in the Greater Boston listening area at 95.3 FM; on the Internet it streams from www.whrb.org. The station is student-run and staffed by undergraduates (with an occasional alumnus sitting in), working as announcers, commentators, reporters, programmers, and technicians.

Programming at WHRB is eclectic. The station's most notable tradition may be its musical orgies, airing a single composer, performer, band, or topic (songs of World War II, for example) for extended stretches during Harvard's winter and spring reading periods. Extensive surveys of the output of Bach (nine full days), Haydn, Mozart, Verdi, Shostakovich, Ligeti, Schnittke, and other composers famous and obscure are typical orgy fare, along with retrospectives on jazz (Coltrane, Parker, Davis), rock bands, songwriters, and singers. In term time there are regular programs of classical, jazz, blues, R&B, and underground rock music. "Hillbilly at Harvard" has been a Saturday-morning staple for a half-century; Sunday morning broadcasts of services at Memorial Church for more than 40 years. Sports events, concerts, public appearances by visiting celebrities, and the major ceremonies of Commencement Week get full coverage. From time to time the station carries interviews with faculty members who share their expertise on Chinese or Russian politics, the human genome project, missile defense systems, the search for extraterrestrial intelligence, or mechanisms for counting votes in national elections.

Since the late 1950s, WHRB has broadcast a full opera every week. When the Boston radio station WCRB abruptly terminated the weekly Saturday-afternoon broadcasts of the Metropolitan Opera in the late 1990s, WHRB came to the rescue of the large local constituency of opera lovers by adding the complete series of Met matinées.

Beholden to no corporation but itself, all-volunteer and thus able to limit the advertising it takes and the need to conform to commercial goals (constrained only by FCC regulations), WHRB treasures its independence and exhibits a resourceful determination to air high-level, enriching programs unmatched at most other spots on the dial.

Related entries: Harvard College; Harvard Crimson; Music; Wireless Club. *Related Website:* www.whrb.org.

Widener Library

The imperial presence of the Harry Elkins Widener Memorial Library dominates Harvard Yard: this mammoth building is truly the elephant in the University's living room. Given its symbolic value, that may be fitting. "As the heart and matter of a university," wrote the Harvard architectural historian Bainbridge Bunting, "a library should be imposing in mass and design." And Widener is.

The largest of the 90-plus units in the University Library system, Widener houses almost three and a half million volumes—primarily in the humanities and social sciences—on ten floors of stacks and some 65 miles of shelving. It stores another million and a half volumes at the Harvard Depository in suburban Southborough.

Erected in 1913–14, the library was given by Eleanor Elkins Widener, of Philadelphia, as a memorial to her son Harry, a member of the class of 1907. He and his father had gone down with the *Titanic*. An avid and knowledgeable bibliophile, Harry Widener left his book collection to his mother, with the request that it be conveyed to Harvard when it could be properly accommodated. Mrs. Widener considered adding a wing to the severely overtaxed Gore Hall library but decided to donate a new library instead. As a condition of her gift, she reserved the right to pick the architect. President A. Lawrence Lowell was in no position to argue: Harvard desperately needed a new library. Mrs. Widener selected Horace Trumbauer, a Philadelphian whose work was not universally liked by fellow architects. "Mrs. Widener does not give the University the money to build a new library, but has offered to build a library satisfactory in external appearance to *herself*," Lowell wrote to the Boston architect Charles Coolidge. "The exterior was her own choice, and she has decided architectural opinions." Never had a donor had such direct influence on Harvard's built environment.

The approximate size and plan of the building—a hollow square with two interior courtyards—had already been established by a committee of University architects. The grandiose building desired by Mrs. Widener and conceived by Trumbauer's firm was a further example of the austere, formalistic Imperial style displayed in the Law School's Langdell Hall and the Medical School's quadrangle. As Bunting has noted, its fabric was not out of key with its neighbors', though its scaling was unprecedented at Harvard:

> Widener is clearly Imperial and Classical rather than Georgian, but the use of brick is compatible with other buildings in the Yard and the white stone columns and trim relate to the ancient granite of University Hall. The marble-clad inte-

rior staircase with mural paintings by John Singer Sargent and the Widener Memorial Room are fitting preliminaries to the enormous reading room, which extends the entire breadth of the building and is the most ostentatious interior space at Harvard.

Unlike that of the library it replaced, Widener's entrance faces the Yard's central quadrangle. A wide flight of steps, topped by a row of twelve stone columns with Corinthian capitals, leads to the main floor. Hallmarks of the fifteenth-century printers Aldus, Caxton, Fust, Rembolt, and Schoeffer are carved over the center door. The interior plan, with its grand staircase leading to a large reading room, follows a pattern set by the Boston Public Library in 1895 and emulated by most American libraries until after World War II. A landing halfway up the staircase opens onto the elegant Widener Memorial Rooms, in the library's central rotunda. Preserved there is Harry Widener's 3,300-volume collection; it includes first folios of Shakespeare and a Gutenberg Bible, added by the Widener family in 1944.

The library is said to have been the last major self-supporting masonry building, with no outer framework of structural steel, to be built in America. (Its marble-floored stacks do have steel supports.) Below the main floor are four stack levels. As a result of last-minute economies, the lowest, C and D, were still skeletons when the library opened (C even lacked a floor). After World War II, the bottom level would be linked by tunnels to the Houghton, Lamont, and Pusey libraries. "Any changes, additions, or alterations" to the rest of the building were prohibited by the terms of Mrs. Widener's gift. When a walkway was built between Widener and Houghton, the architects sought to stay within the letter of the law by connecting it to a Widener window instead of cutting a door. (The walkway is scheduled for removal in the spring of 2004.)

Mrs. Widener laid the building's cornerstone in June 1913; the library was dedicated on Commencement Day two years later. Horace Trumbauer was among that year's honorary degree recipients.

The initial cost of the building has been estimated at more than $4 million. When it opened, Widener was viewed as a highly advanced research facility, with abundant natural light, a ventilation system that drew fresh air through the building, steam heat in the winter, and windows that could be opened in the summer. It later became clear that light, air, and temperature fluctuations were not conducive to the preservation of books and manuscripts. A five-year, $90-million renovation program, begun in 1999, has provided new climate-control and lighting equipment; new electrical, fire-suppression, and security systems; refurbished stacks and public areas; and two new reading rooms in what had previously been courtyard space.

At the outset, only faculty members and advanced graduate students could have access to Widener's stacks. That policy was altered to accommodate the curriculum of the College and a changing pattern of library usage. Undergraduates, who now make up half of Widener's regular clientele, can enter the stacks by swiping their identification cards through a card-reader. Leaving the building takes slightly longer. In 1930 it was announced that "books, book-bags, briefcases, and the like" would henceforth be subject to inspection. Users were required to exit through a turnstile, an innovation that was subsequently taken up by most academic libraries. Any criticisms of the new policy were apparently muted by the arrest in 1931 of a ring of professional thieves who had stolen books from Widener and other libraries. That same year, 2,054 books filched from Widener were found at the suburban home of a former high school principal who had master's degrees from the Graduate School of Arts and Sciences and the School of Education.

Widener continued to present a tempting target for book thieves. In 1977, somewhere between 3,000 and 5,000 boxed-up books from Harvard, Boston, and various English libraries were discovered in the office of a graduate student in history who was about to take off for a teaching position in California. In 1991, a former nonresident tutor at Eliot House disappeared, leaving behind him almost 300 cartons of books purloined from Widener, Curry College, and the Boston Public Library.

Widener is in every sense an international library. Its research materials—books, journals, microforms, films, pamphlets, posters, audio recordings, electronic resources, ephemera—are written in more than a hundred languages and have been gleaned from almost every country in the world. Especially noted are the collections of Africana, Americana, European local history, Judaica, Latin American studies, Middle Eastern studies, and Slavic studies, as well as collections for the study of Asia, the British Commonwealth, France, Germany, Italy, Scandinavia, and Greek and Latin antiquity. These research materials include major holdings in linguistics, ancient and modern languages, folklore, economics, history of science and technology, philosophy, psychology, and sociology. The library's staff engages with scholars and fellow librarians from all over the world.

Related entries: Architecture; Harvard Elsewhere; Houghton Library; Lamont Library; Libraries; Underground. *Related Website:* hcl.harvard.edu/widener.

Wireless Club

Not to be confused with radio station WHRB, the Harvard Wireless Club was founded in 1909 and is America's oldest amateur radio club. Its call letters/numbers are W1AF, and it maintains three operating positions, one on VHF and two on HF. The club has an active membership of mostly male undergraduates, graduate students from all schools, alumni, faculty, and staff.

Amateur radio is not "CB" or commercial radio: it is a network of federally licensed operators who use their equipment to talk with other "hams" (sometimes called "rag-chewing") worldwide, and to conduct various radio experiments. In emergency situations, amateur operators often provide alternate means of communication.

Related entry: WHRB.

ΠΡΟΒΟΥΛΟΣ

ἆρ᾽ ἐξέλαμψε τῶν γυναικῶν ἡ τρυφὴ
χὠ τυμπανισμὸς χοἰ πυκνοὶ Σαβάζιοι,
ὅ τ᾽ Ἀδωνιασμὸς οὗτος οὑπὶ τῶν τεγῶν,
390 οὗ ᾽γώ ποτ᾽ ὢν ἤκουον ἐν τἠκκλησίᾳ;
ἔλεγεν ὁ μὴ ὥρασι μὲν Δημόστρατος
πλεῖν εἰς Σικελίαν, ἡ γυνὴ δ᾽ ὀρχουμένη
"αἰαῖ Ἄδωνιν" φησίν. ὁ δὲ Δημόστρατος
ἔλεγεν ὁπλίτας καταλέγειν Ζακυνθίων,
395 ἡ δ᾽ ὑποπεπωκυῖ᾽ ἡ γυνὴ ᾽πὶ τοῦ τέγους
"κόπτεσθ᾽ Ἄδωνιν" φησίν. ὁ δ᾽ ἐβιάζετο,
ὁ θεοῖσιν ἐχθρὸς καὶ μιαρὸς Χολοζύγης.
τοιαῦτ᾽ ἀπ᾽ αὐτῶν ἐστιν ἀκολαστάσματα.

ΚΟΡΥΦΑΙΟΣ

τί δῆτ᾽ ἄν, εἰ πύθοιο καὶ τὴν τῶνδ᾽ ὕβριν;
400 αἲ τἄλλα θ᾽ ὑβρίκασι κἀκ τῶν καλπίδων
ἔλουσαν ἡμᾶς, ὥστε θαἰμάτίδια
σείειν πάρεστιν ὥσπερ ἐνεουρηκότας.

ZephGreek, a custom-designed electronic typeface used by
Harvard University Press for its Loeb Classical Library series,
was inspired by original drawings for
a typeface called Porson Greek.

X Cage

Harvard librarians of earlier eras would put explicitly sexual or pornographic works under lock and key in an "X Cage." The practice was based partly on a concern for the morals of unsuspecting browsers and partly on the obvious need to safeguard holdings that might otherwise be mutilated or removed by prurient bookworms, professional thieves, or agents of the Watch and Ward Society. (Now notorious for literary censorship that made "banned in Boston" a byword, the Watch and Ward Society was formed in 1878 by a group of civic leaders, among them the Reverend Phillips Brooks, class of 1855; Endicott Peabody, first headmaster of Groton School; and the Reverend William Lawrence, class of 1871, later Episcopal bishop of Massachusetts and fellow of the Harvard Corporation.)

With the passage of time, the criteria for X-caging became less stringent. An 1888 edition of John Cleland's eighteenth-century *Memoirs of Fanny Hill,* a famously salacious genre piece, is in Widener Library's X Cage, but an unexpurgated 1985 edition, titled *Fanny Hill: Memoirs of a Woman of Pleasure,* is on open shelving, along with a 1988 concordance to the work. *My Secret Life* (author anonymous), privately published in Amsterdam in 1880, was X-caged, as was a Paris edition of Frank Harris's *My Life and Loves.* But 1960s editions of Henry Miller's *Rosy Crucifixion* trilogy (*Nexus, Plexus,* and *Sexus*), and his *Tropic of Capricorn* and *Tropic of Cancer*—all of them once embargoed from importation into the United States—are on the ALA (American Literature) shelves. Widener Library's X-caged materials are now stored at the Harvard Depository in Southborough. They can be recalled to Widener but do not circulate out of the building.

Since a picture is worth a thousand words, the X Cage of the Fogg Art Museum's Fine Arts Library holds the zestiest listings. In it are such scholarly works as *The Grotesque in Photography* (New York, 1977); *Scopophilia: The Love of Looking* (New York, 1985); and *Fully Exposed: The Male Nude in Photography* (London, 1990). So much for Fanny Hill and her priapic English squires.

X-cage holdings may be accessed by qualified researchers.

Related entries: Libraries; Widener Library; Z Closet.

The Yard

"Harvard Yard" denotes a historic, fenced-in, four-acre preserve, crisscrossed by paths, that contains some thirty academic and residential buildings and forms the geographic and spiritual center of the University. The Old Yard, bordering Harvard Square, is where the College was born. The New Yard, east of University Hall, attained its present configuration only in the twentieth century.

Terminology matters here. The lot originally chosen as the site for the future college's earliest buildings was on Cow-yard Row. The *Harvard University Handbook* (1936) notes that

> At Harvard the word *Yard* has withstood the fashion which, introduced at Princeton in 1774, transformed in the succeeding century practically every College Yard and College Green in America into a classic Campus . . . The term *Yard* has changed in meaning as the location of the principal College buildings has shifted. For a time, in the middle of the nineteenth century, it even gave way to the more general designation "College Grounds," but during President Eliot's regime the word *Yard* again came into use.

To refer to the Yard as "the campus" today is to mark oneself as an outsider.

From the outset, the Yard has maintained a functional balance between residential, academic, and religious buildings. Its oldest surviving structure, Massachusetts Hall (1721), is a kind of paradigm of the Yard itself: it is shared by freshmen, who room on the two top floors, and the president and five vice presidents of Harvard, who have offices on the first and second floors. Massachusetts is one of the Yard's thirteen freshman residence halls. University Hall, more or less in the middle of the Yard, is the administrative headquarters of the Faculty of Arts and Sciences; Lehman Hall, Wadsworth House, and Loeb House are also used for administrative purposes. Harvard Hall, Boylston Hall, Sever Hall, Robinson Hall, and Emerson Hall are classroom buildings. The Yard's two largest structures, Memorial Church and Widener Library, form the north and south sides of a quadrangle in the New Yard that is known as the Tercentenary Theatre; Commencement exercises and other ceremonial occasions take place there. In the southeast corner of the Yard, connected to Widener by underground passages, are three other libraries: Lamont, Pusey, and Houghton.

With its stately elms, well-tended grass, evocative quadrangles, and storied buildings, the Yard exerts an alluring aesthetic appeal. Much of the credit goes to John Thornton Kirkland, Harvard's president from 1810 to 1828. Before his time, the Yard had evolved randomly and disreputably. Kirkland found it "an unkempt sheep-commons"—almost devoid of trees, without regular pathways, and blighted by the presence of the College brewhouse, a woodyard, a pigpen, and several privies. The new president cleared them away, planted grass and trees, and laid out the paths used today.

His successors did less well at keeping up the Yard's residence halls. Gaslight was installed in the post-Civil War years, but even after the turn of the century many of the older buildings still had no central heating and no plumbing above the basement. Such deficiencies spurred an exodus to the private residence halls built on and around Mount Auburn Street in the 1890s. For a time the Gold Coast replaced the Yard as the center of undergraduate life, and social stratification increased. When A. Lawrence Lowell became president in 1909, everything changed. New freshman residence halls rose on the banks of the Charles; to increase class solidarity, seniors were encouraged to room in the Yard. By then all of its dormitories had been fitted with bathrooms and showers, and some had electric lighting. The last great change came with the creation of the house system in 1930. Upperclassmen took over the former freshman halls and new halls constructed close to the river, and the Yard dorms were set aside for the first-year class. So it remains: Harvard freshmen are "Yardlings."

The Yard has had fences of various sorts since 1639, when the first Harvard building was raised and the College steward recorded a payment for "Fencing the yard with pale 6 feet and 1/2 high." In the first year of the Revolutionary War, Continental Army soldiers billeted at Harvard used the College fence for firewood, and it took more than a decade to put up a new one. The monumental brick-and-ironwork Memorial Fence that now encloses the Yard was designed by McKim, Mead & White and was largely erected between 1901 and 1914. The construction cost was met by various College classes whose dates are worked into the iron ornamentation. The fence incorporates nine major gates and seventeen minor ones, donated by classes, clubs, or individuals. The most elaborate, Johnston Gate (1890), was the New York architect Charles McKim's first Harvard commission. It opens onto Harvard Square and is the principal entrance to the Yard.

Related entries: Architecture; Commencement; First Year; Fountains; Gates; Gold Coast; Guardhouse; Harvard College; Harvard Hall; Houghton Library; Houses; Lamont Library; Memorial Church; Quincy Street; Statues and Monuments; Underground; Wadsworth House; Widener Library.

Z Closet

Unlike the books and portfolios in the X Cages of Harvard libraries, the holdings locked in the Houghton Library's Z Closet are not X-rated. Nor can they be neatly shelved. The Z Closet contains artifacts that complement the library's rare books, manuscripts, and other papers: Charles Dickens's screw-tipped walking stick, with which the novelist may have warded off vagrants on his famously long walks through the shadowy streets of London or on Hampstead Heath; a straw boater sported by T. S. Eliot '10; locks of hair snipped from the heads of Nathaniel Hawthorne and William Wordsworth; handcuffs owned by the escape artist Harry Houdini.

Augmenting its cache of Emily Dickinson's papers, the library has an entire roomful of Dickinsonia. Preserved there are the poet's writing table, her piano, a device she used to seal letters, family portraits, a sampler she cross-stitched as a child, and her tiny pinky ring.

Related entries: Houghton Library; Libraries; X Cage.

ZephGreek

At his death in 1933, James Loeb, class of 1888, bequeathed a thriving publishing venture, the Loeb Classical Library, to Harvard.

This series of handy Greek (green) and Latin (red) texts, with facing translations, soon became the gold standard throughout the English-speaking world. In recent times, the Library, published by Harvard University Press, has undergone a vigorous program of revision, updating, and addition. This includes the reintroduction of the original vocabulary for such raucous authors as Aristophanes and Martial, whose salty language had been bowdlerized in earlier translations. Today, this extensive library—approximately 500 volumes of ancient texts—can be ordered almost anywhere in the world with the click of a mouse.

But the Loeb's translations were not all that required a facelift. In 1995 the Press introduced a new electronic typeface, specially designed to improve the appearance and readability of the Loeb volumes and also to honor Zeph Stewart, Andrew W. Mellon Professor of the Humanities Emeritus, and a trustee of the Loeb Classical Library Foundation since 1973. Technologies 'N Typography, one of the Press's vendors, tracked down the original drawings of Porson Greek—the classic typeface that had been used for Loebs since the beginning of the series—to help them create the handsome electronic font that graces the Greek Loebs today. Along the way, they also invented ZephText, an English (and Latin) typeface that complements ZephGreek in the way that Caledonia had complemented Porson almost a century earlier.

Related entries: Harvard University Press; Lectures; Villa I Tatti. *Related Website:* www.hup.harvard.edu.

Appendix

Like most institutions, Harvard has its own acronyms and slang for administrative units, academic programs, buildings, and organizations. Other terms, like *detur,* are peculiar to Harvard and very ancient. Some examples:

Ad Board. The Administrative Board (see DISCIPLINE).

Afro-Am. The department of Afro-American Studies.

ART. The American Repertory Theatre, a professional troupe based at Loeb Drama Center; pronounced A-R-T.

B School. The Business School.

Bandie. A Harvard Band member.

Big Wigg. The larger part of Wigglesworth Hall, a freshman residence hall. Its tenants are *Bigwigs.*

Billy Jim. William James Hall, high-rise home of behavioral sciences.

BFA. Board of Freshman Advisors.

Blocking group. A self-selected bloc of *Yardlings* applying for adjoining suites in a residential house (see HOUSES).

The Bricks or *The Projects.* Canaday Hall, the most recently built (1973) of the *Yard's* residence halls.

The But. Hurlbut Hall, a freshman residence hall and former apartment building just outside the *Yard.*

The castle. The Lampoon building (see LAMPOON).

The Chuck. The Charles River.

Clav. Claverly Hall.

Cliffie. Until the demise of Radcliffe College, a female undergraduate. Now obsolete (see RADCLIFFE).

Clubbie. A member of one of the eight remaining *final clubs.*

Comp (also: *comping*). To try out (compete) for selective undergraduate organizations like the *Crimson.*

Concentration. What other colleges call a major.

Confi Guide. The *Confidential Guide* to undergraduate courses published annually by the *Crimson.*

Coop. The Harvard Cooperative Society, a Harvard Square fixture since 1882. *Coop* rhymes with hoop; to say *Co-op* would brand you as an outsider.

Core. A required slate of courses composing about a quarter of the undergraduate program (see CORE CURRICULUM).

The Crime. An old and somewhat pejorative nickname for the *Harvard Crimson* (see HARVARD CRIMSON).

Crimeds. Editors of "Harvard's only breakfast-table daily."

Crimson Cash. A credit-card system for students, negotiable for food, photocopies, and other sundries.

CS. Computer Science.

Deanlet. A lower-level academic administrator; what earlier generations would have called a baby dean.

Deturs. Prize books awarded for superior academic performance during freshman year. The term is derived from the Latin *detur,* "it is given."

Div Ave. Divinity Avenue.

Div School. The Divinity School.

Ec. Economics.

ECHO. Eating Concerns Hotline and Outreach; pronounced "echo."

Ed School. The Graduate School of Education.

Entry, or *Entryway.* A *Yard* residential unit housing 20 to 46 first-year students.

ETOB. An acronym for "Every Tub on its Own Bottom," an old metaphor for the diffused power existing at many levels of a decentralized administrative hierarchy; pronounced E-T-O-B (see ETOB).

Expos. The Expository Writing Program, a first-year requirement.

FAS. The Faculty of Arts and Sciences, comprised of Harvard College; the Graduate School of Arts and Sciences; and the Division of Continuing Education; pronounced F-A-S.

Final club. One of the eight exclusive clubs that are relicts of WASP ascendancy at Harvard. So called because aspiring *clubbies* once had to join a "waiting" club before being considered for a more selective "final" club. Electees to top-tier clubs were not permitted to join another *final club.*

The Fishbowl. A common space in Currier House; also, the computer lab in the Maxwell Dworkin building (see INFORMATION TECHNOLOGY).

FDO. Freshman Dean's Office.

FOP, FAP, and *FUP.* Freshman Outdoor Program, Freshman Arts Program, and Freshman Urban Program, administered by the *FDO;* sometimes pronounced "fop," "fap," and "fup."

The Game. The Harvard-Yale football game.

Gleek. Glee Club member.

Gov Docs. The Government Documents and Microtext Division of the Harvard College Library, housed in Lamont Library.

The Greenhouse. A food shop in the Science Center; also, a Harvard Square restaurant.

Grays. Sweat gear, imprinted "Property of Harvard Athletic Department," favored by certain athletes for classroom wear; also, a freshman residence hall.

Grill Rat. A patron of fast-food places in the houses.

GSAS. Graduate School of Arts and Sciences.

GSD. Graduate School of Design.

Gunner. A student who tries to dominate class discussions.

HAND. House and Neighborhood Development Program, a student-run community outreach organization administered by Phillips Brooks House; pronounced "hand."

HASCS. Faculty of Arts and Sciences Computer Services; manages microcomputer labs in the Science Center, undergraduate residence halls, and computer kiosks, as well as student email and Internet access.

HBS. The Business School.

Head of the Charles. An October regatta that attracts world-class rowers and thousands of spectators. ("Head" refers to the Charles River racing marker that is furthest upstream.)

HEMP. The Dudley Co-op, an off-campus residence (from "Center for High-Energy Metaphysics"); pronounced "hemp."

HGSE. See *Ed School.*

HCL. Harvard College Library and its eleven component libraries.

HD. The Harvard Depository in Southborough, Massachusetts, where the libraries' overflow books are warehoused (see HARVARD ELSEWHERE).

HIID. Institute for International Development.

HIO. The International Office.

HLS. The Law School.

HMC. Harvard Management Company.

HMS. The Medical School.

HoCo. A House Committee.

HOLLIS. The Harvard OnLine Library Information System, a Web-based search engine with listings for more than nine million holdings in the *HCL* system. Its name, like that of Hollis Hall—a freshman dormitory built in 1763—honors an early Harvard benefactor, the eighteenth-century London merchant Thomas Hollis.

HUGHP. Harvard University Group Health Program, a health-care plan administered through UHS; prounced "hugh-P."

HUL. Harvard University Library and its 90-plus component libraries; pronounced H-U-L or "hull."

HUPD. The Harvard University Police Department, respected for humane community policing and solicitude for student safety and welfare; prounounced "hup-dee."

The Hutch or *the Bunny Hutch.* Leverett House.

HSA. Harvard Student Agencies, largest and most successful of collegiate student-run corporations.

IAB. The Indoor Athletic Building, now Malkin Athletic Center (the *MAC*).

Indy. *The Harvard Independent,* a weekly.

IOP. The Kennedy School of Government's Institute of Politics.

ITT. The Albert H. Gordon Indoor Track and Tennis Center.

JCR. The junior common room in a residential house.

Jock. Anyone pursuing an interest with fervor *(gov jock, ec jock, theater jock)*; not limited to athletes.

The Jungle. Currier House dining hall. (Has vegetation in the center.)

K House. Kirkland House.

The Kong. The Hong Kong, a perennially popular restaurant.

Kroks. The Harvard Krokodiloes, oldest of the College's a capella singing groups.

KSG (or *K School*). The John F. Kennedy School of Government.

LASPAU. Latin American Studies Program at American Universities, a nonprofit organization affiliated with Harvard and governed by an independent, inter-American board of trustees; pronounced "las-paw."

Let's Go. A series of travel guides compiled by peripatetic undergraduates and published by *HSA.*

Lifer. An administrator who went to Harvard or Radcliffe and has spent a career at Harvard; sometimes applied to highly involved alumni.

LoHo. Lowell House.

MAC. What was formerly the *IAB.*

MAC Quad. An area of scrubby grass bounded by the *MAC, K House,* and Eliot and Winthrop Houses.

Mass Ave. Massachusetts Avenue, the principal thoroughfare linking Harvard with Boston and with suburban neighborhoods to the west. It runs through Harvard Square.

Mass Hall. Massachusetts Hall, Harvard's oldest building. The term also refers to the office of the president, located in Massachusetts Hall since 1939. The recipient of a telephone call from *Mass Hall* can assume that it comes from the president, the provost, a vice president, or one of their delegates. Such calls are generally answered with alacrity.

Master (or *Co-Master*). A faculty member (or spouse) in charge of one of the thirteen undergraduate Houses.

Mem Hall. Memorial Hall.

Mem Chu. Memorial Church.

Nerd Cage. Computer terminal room in the Science Center.

'Noch's. Pinocchio's, a pizza house.

MCZ. Museum of Comparative Zoology.

OCS. Office of Career Services.

One-L, Two-L, Three-L. Law School designations for first-, second-, and third-year students.

The Pack. Pennypacker Hall, a freshman residence.

Orgo. Organic chemistry.

The Pain. Au Bon Pain, a Harvard Square snackery not far from *the Pit.*

PBH. Phillips Brooks House.

PfoHo. Pforzheimer House; formerly *NoHo* (North House).

Phool. A *Harvard Lampoon* initiate (see LAMPOON).

The Pit. The sunken perimeter of the Harvard Square subway entrance; a lounging and smoking place for idle teenagers from nearby suburbs.

'Poonie or *'Poonster.* A *Harvard Lampoon* member (see LAMPOON).

Primal Scream Night. A pre-exam-period ritual. On the stroke of midnight male undergraduates in the buff race around the Yard and into Harvard Square. Still unclothed, some may also engage in the ritual of checking out a book from Lamont Library. Female staff members have the option of staying home on Primal Scream Night. The archetypal PSN occurs at the start of the winter exam period, but the Summer School has also adopted the custom.

The Pro. Harvard Provision Company, a liquor store of long standing.

Pudding Pot. A replica presented by *Pudding Show* promoters to the Hasty Pudding Theatricals' Man and Woman of the Year.

Pudding Show. A mildly raunchy musical presented in March of each year at the Hasty Pudding Theater. The Hasty Pudding Club / Institute of 1770 (aka "the Pudding") is not a *final club.*

Punched. Invited to attend a *final club* "punch," an occasion for the appraisal of prospective *clubbies.* Fall is the prime *punching* season.

Quadded. To be assigned to one of the three residential houses surrounding what was formerly the Radcliffe Quadrangle, a fifteen-minute walk from Harvard Square. Most *quadded* students are soon reconciled to their fate: in senior class surveys, Quad houses consistently rank at or near the top (see HOUSES).

QRAC. The Radcliffe Quadrangle Recreational Athletic Complex, a gym built in 1973 as a facility for *quadded* undergraduates; pronounced "Q-RAC."

QRR. The *Core*'s quantitative reasoning requirement.

The Qube. Quincy House library.

Reading Period. A ten-day interval provided for study before final exams. Not always used for the purpose for which it was intended.

River Rat. A river house resident.

SCR. The senior common room in a residential house. Usually restricted to faculty members and tutors.

Schneider. A Harvard Band functionary who arranges parties.

Section 12. Where the most fervent Bright Hockey Center fans sit.

Seventeen Quincy Street. The former President's House, now the headquarters of the Governing Boards and renamed Loeb House. An occasional site of festive gatherings.

Shopping Period. A week at the start of each term in which students may audit (or "shop") as many course offerings as they wish.

Spags. Spaghetti Club, a bar and dance club on Winthrop Street.

SPH. School of Public Health.

The T. Massachusetts Bay Transportation Authority; more parochially, its Red Line branch linking Harvard Square with Boston and points on the Blue, Green, and Orange Lines.

Table. To put up a table at the entrance to a dining hall or a registration area in order to promote a forthcoming event, sell tickets, recruit members, or gather signatures. Requires approval by the Dean of the College.

TAP. Tuition Assistance Plan. It allows University employees who work at least seventeen and a half hours a week to enroll in academic courses for a $40 fee. Eligibility has been extended to a number of part-time union workers; pronounced "tap."

Tercentenary Theatre. The quadrangle bounded by Widener Library, University Hall, Memorial Church, and Sever Hall. Locus of Harvard's three-hundredth-anniversary celebration in 1936, it is now the site of the annual Commencement exercises.

TF. Teaching Fellow.

Troll. Anyone using the lowest level of a library (particularly, Cabot Science Library).

Turkey shoot. A spring meeting in which *Crimson* staffers choose, sometimes contentiously, their next editor-in-chief and top board members.

UC. Undergraduate Council. Budding politicos vie for seats in fall elections.

UHS. University Health Services.

U-mail. University mail system.

UT. The University Theater (now a cineplex) on Church Street.

Vermont. Where *quadded* house residents once sardonically located themselves, as opposed to "New York" (the river houses).

VES. Visual and Environmental Studies.

Whispering Arch. A groove in an outside arch of Sever Hall; supposedly, words whispered on one side can be clearly heard on the other.

Whrbie. A staffer at station WHRB; pronounced "wherbie."

Wigglet. The smaller part of Wigglesworth Hall (see *Big Wigg*).

Wonky. Defined in the *New Dictionary of American Slang* (HarperCollins, 1986) as "wonky adj *esp Harvard students* Tedious and serious, esp anxious and overstudious in an academic situation: *'Jenny Cavilleri,'* answered Ray. *'Wonky music type.'*—Erich Segal." The associated term *wonk,* originated in the 1950s by *Lampoon* members, has passed into general use and now connotes a respectable level of expertise and absorption, as in "policy wonk."

World Domination Room. Private dining room in Quincy House with large world map on one wall.

The X. Loeb Experimental Theatre; also, *the Ex.*

The Yard. Since the earliest days, when Harvard was sited on Cow-yard Row, its center of gravity has been "the Yard" (see THE YARD).

Yardling. A freshman denizen of the Yard (see FIRST YEAR).

Acknowledgments

The authors are greatly indebted to Barbara Meloni, a staff member at the Harvard University Archives, for her enterprising and diligent research; she has been vital to the *A to Z* project since its inception. Susan Wallace Boehmer, senior editor for manuscript development at Harvard University Press, has played multiple roles: straw boss, crying towel, textual paramedic, and more. Without her unwavering encouragement, unimpeachable editorial instincts, and unerring blue pencil, the project would surely have foundered.

Harvard University Press has published other A to Z books. That Harvard itself might be ripe for such treatment was first seen by Aida Donald, then assistant director and editor-in-chief of the Press. When she pitched the idea to the University marshal, Richard Hunt, he agreed to take it on—provided that he could bring in Robert Shenton, the former secretary of the University's governing boards and another longtime Harvard administrator, as co-author. That required some wheedling, but Shenton finally assented and soon warmed to his work.

That work ended in February 2000, when Bob Shenton died in a fall while vacationing with his wife, Betsy, at Vieques, Puerto Rico. His sudden death was a severe setback to the *A to Z* project, but Hunt then found another seasoned Harvard-watcher to help see it through. John Bethell—former editor of *Harvard Magazine,* and the author of *Harvard Observed: An Illustrated History of the University in the Twentieth Century*—stepped in, editing Shenton's drafts, researching and writing many additional entries, and preparing digital text files for the prepress stage of the publishing process.

All writers who delve into Harvard's past must feel thankful for the existence of Samuel Eliot Morison's *Three Centuries of Harvard* (Cambridge: Harvard University Press, 1936). Since institutional practices and events of the past frame a fair number of entries in *Harvard A to Z,* Professor Morison's venerable and invaluable book has been well-thumbed. So have *Harvard Observed* (Cambridge: Harvard University Press, 1998) and *Harvard: An Architectural History,* by Bainbridge Bunting, completed and edited by Margaret Henderson Floyd (Cambridge: The Belknap Press of Harvard University Press, 1985). "Harvard Fiction: Some Critical and Bibliographical Notes," by Hamilton Vaughan Bail (Worcester, Massachusetts: Proceedings of the American Antiquarian Society, 1959), proved a useful guide to some of the earlier novels cited in the "Fictional Harvard" entry.

We are also abidingly grateful to Andrea Goldstein, Robin McElheny, and Brian Sullivan, of the Harvard University Archives, for their steadfast assistance. Many other friends and associates also helped our project along by providing factual information and advice. Our grateful thanks to all, and to the family members who have borne the brunt of our sometimes graceless efforts to hunt down an elusive statistic or to construct declarative sentences worthy of the institution that this book seeks to describe.

Illustration Credits

Harvard Planning + Allston Initiative: map

J. F. Coakley, *Veritas Imprimata: The Typography of the Harvard Arms* (Oxford: Jericho Press, 1995): A

Harvard University Archives: B, E, F, G, I-J-K, L, O, P, Q, U, W

Kris Snibbe/Harvard News Office: C, M

Stephanie Mitchell/Harvard News Office: D

Harvard Theatre Collection: H

Harvard News Office: N

Gluyas Williams/New Yorker/Cartoonbank: R

Jon Chase/Harvard News Office: S, T

Harvard University Center for Italian Renaissance Studies: V

Harvard University Press: X-Y-Z

Index

Architecture, 19–24, 164, 323, 351; Adolphus Busch Hall, 6–8; Brattle Theatre, 44; bridges and towers, 61, 337–338; Carpenter Center, 54–55; drawings, 214; Dumbarton Oaks, 98; Gold Coast, 164–166; Gore Hall, 247; Guardhouse, 177–178; Harvard Brick, 152; Harvard Hall, 188–189, 190; Harvard Square, 51; Harvard Square subway station, 345; Harvard Union, 197, 198; Hillel, 202; Holden Chapel, 203; Houghton Library, 215; houses and clubs, 19, 133–134, 216–217; Lamont Library, 236; landmark buildings, 115–117; Medical School, 251, 254; Memorial Church, 254–255; Memorial Hall, 256–257, 257–258, 259; Quincy Street, 291; Radcliffe Institute for Advanced Study, 339; redbrick, 6, 19, 22, 23, 31, 121, 188, 215, 217, 236, 291; restoration projects, 23–24; Sanders Theatre, 314, 315; scale of buildings, 53; underground, 347; Wadsworth House, 357; Widener Memorial Library, 254, 360–362. *See also* Architectural styles; *Harvard: An Architectural History* (Bunting)
Archives, 25–26, 78, 177, 357; Harvard Film, 55–56, 130–131
Arms, 26–27, 203, 300, 323; on diplomas, 86–87
Arnold Arboretum, 27–30, 184, 321
Artemas Ward Homestead, 184
Art museums, 30–33; Memorial Hall (stained glass), 258. *See also* Busch-Reisinger; Fogg Art Museum; Sackler Art Museum
Arts, 33–35, 301; libraries, 245; portrait collection, 275–277. *See also* Art museums; Drama and theater; Music; Signet Society
Arts Medal, 34
Athletics, 35–40, 138, 144, 183, 329–330, 331; crimson uniforms, 35, 37, 38, 40, 54, 78, 183; in fiction, 127; Head of the Charles Regatta, 58; house sports teams, 217–218; Ivy League, 35, 38,

225–226; at Radcliffe College, 295; at Soldiers Field, 325–327; varsity squads, 138; women in, 38–39, 225
Auden, W. H., 15
Austin, Dorothy, 156

Baccalaureate, senior-class, 92
Ballmer, Steven, 96, 222
Barker Center for the Humanities, 197, 277, 291
Batts, Deborah, 156–157
Begley, Louis, 180
Behrman, S. N., 114
Belknap, Waldron Phoenix, 199
Bells, 42–44, 298, 299; Harvard Hall, 188; Lowell House tower, 133, 337; Memorial Church, 254; Memorial Hall, 136, 258; rung at Commencement, 67; St. Paul's Church, 338
Benchley, Robert, 237, 238
Berenson, Bernard, 351–352
Berle, Adolf A. Jr., 284
Bernstein, Leonard, 243, 262, 324
Bibring, Grete, 146
Biddies, 115
Biological Laboratories, 333
Bloody Monday, 111–112
Bloom, Harold, 243
Bly, Robert, 180
Board of Overseers, 166, 167, 168, 169, 182, 280; honorary degree selection and, 211
Bogart, Humphrey, 45, 210
Bok, Derek, 275, 279, 280, 281, 349; on academic consulting, 69; arts and, 18, 33; community relations and, 53; curricular reform and, 75–76; as dean of Law School, 240; Faculty Club and, 119; Harvard Foundation and, 187, 188; the Kennedy School of Government and, 232, 233; portrait of, 275, 276; on the presidency, 282; residence at Elmwood, 103, 104
Bond, William H., 214
Books and novels connected to Harvard, 125–130, 141–142, 189; Faulkner, 61–62; Law School depictions, 241;